Lecture Notes in Computer Science

Edited by G. Goos and J. Hartmanis

209

Advances in Cryptology

Proceedings of EUROCRYPT 84
A Workshop on the Theory and Application
of Cryptographic Techniques
Paris, France, April 9–11, 1984

Edited by T. Beth, N. Cot and I. Ingemarsson

Springer-Verlag
Berlin Heidelberg New York Tokyo

Editors

Thomas Beth
Department of Statistics and Computer Science
Royal Holloway College, University of London
Egham, Surrey TW20 0EX, United Kingdom

Norbert Cot
U.E.R. Mathématiques, Logique Formelle, Informatique, Université Paris-5
Sorbonne, 75005 Paris, France

Ingemar Ingemarsson
Department of Electrical Engineering, Linköping University
S-58183 Linköping, Sweden

Workshop Organizers

N. Cot, General Chairman
I. Ingemarsson, Program Chairman
H. Groscot, Secretary
S. Akl, Program
H. Beker, Program
T. Beth, Program
D. Chaum, Program
D. Davies, Program
D. Denning, Program
W. Diffie, Program
J. Gordon, Program

S. Harari, Program
J. Lebidois, Program
G. Longo, Program
J. Massey, Program
M. Mignotte, Program
A. Odlyzko, Program
J.J. Quisquater, Program
R. Rivest, Program
C. Schnorr, Program
G. Simmons, Program
M. Martin, Registration

The Workshop was sponsored by
International Association of Cryptographic Research
U.E.R. Mathématiques, Logique Formelle, Informatique
(Université René Descartes, Sorbonne)

CR Subject Classifications (1985): E.3

ISBN 3-540-16076-0 Springer-Verlag Berlin Heidelberg New York Tokyo
ISBN 0-387-16076-0 Springer-Verlag New York Heidelberg Berlin Tokyo

Printing and binding: Beltz Offsetdruck, Hemsbach/Bergstr.
2145/3140-543210

PREFACE

This book contains the proceedings of EUROCRYPT 84, held in Paris in 1984, April 9-11, at the University of Paris, Sorbonne.

EUROCRYPT is now an annual international European meeting in cryptology, intended primarily for the international community of researchers in this area. EUROCRYPT 84 was following previous meetings held at Burg Feuerstein in 1982 and at Udine in 1983. In fact EUROCRYPT 84 was the first such meeting being organized under IACR (International Association of Cryptology Research). Other sponsors were the well-known French association on cybernetics research called AFCET, the LITP (Laboratoire d'Informatique théorique et de Programmation), which is a laboratory of computer science associated with CNRS, and the department of mathematics and computer science at the University René Descartes, Sorbonne.

EUROCRYPT 84 was very successfull, with about 180 participants from a great variety of foreign countries and close to 50 papers addressing all aspects of cryptology, applied as well as theoretical. It also had a special feature, i.e. a special session on smart cards particularly welcome at the time, since France was then carrying on an ambitious program on smart cards.

EUROCRYPT 84 was a great experience. We like to thank all the sponsors and all the authors for their submission of papers.

Paris, December 1984.

Norbert COT

CONTENTS

SECTION V : APPLICATIONS

SECTION VI: SMART CARDS

SECTION I

GENERAL THEORY, CLASSICAL METHODS

CRYPTOLOGY

AND COMPLEXITY THEORIES

G. RUGGIU

THOMSON-CSF
Laboratoire Central de Recherches
Domaine de Corbeville

BP 10 91401 ORSAY FRANCE

ABSTRACT

Complexity Theories have recently been proposed as a basis for evaluation of crypto
machine performance. They are compared to Shannon's model. They shed a new highlight
on randomness notion. But it is stressed that the statistical point of view remains
the more secure.

CRYPTOLOGY AND COMPLEXITY THEORIES

Complexity theories have recently been proposed as a basis for evaluation of the cryptographic system performance. We will present in this short survey, the different approaches used to connect these two notions.

The complexity theories are rather new and their motivation is the analysis of algorithm efficiency. Their main characteristic is that they are very general theories that deal with very general algorithms; their most concrete result give some information about asymptotical behaviour of algorithms.

The central problem of cryptology is the evaluation of security of secrecy system, that is to say how a system is immune against a cryptanalysis. When this cryptanalysis is possible such an evaluation must measure how much time and informations are required to get the solution.

1. The model of Shannon

The first mathematical treatment of this problem was achieved by Shannon[1] in the forties. His theory allowed to formalize the problem properly. As a consequence he could give some guidelines for designing secrecy systems.

The Shannon approach is based on a probabilistic model, the core of the theory is the evaluation of the probabilities of clear-texts. There are two main parameters :
- the a priori probability of clear-texts: $P(m)$
- the conditional probability $P(m/c)$ of the clear-text m when the cryptogram c is intercepted.

The main concept defined by Shannon is the "perfect secret": a crypto system is a perfect secret when $P(m) = P(m/c)$, $\forall m,c$. So the knowledge of a cryptogram gives no information about the clear-text: cryptanalysis of such system is impossible.

But perfect secrecy has limitations: it requires a number of keys as least as great as the number of clear messages. This means that the keys must be as long as the messages. So, it is obvious that these systems are impracticable except in particular situations because keys must be exchanged over a secure channel.

In practice, most systems have finite keys. How to characterize the security of these systems ? Shannon showed that for these systems, there exists a minimum length of the messages, called "unicity distance", for which the cryptanalysis has a unique solution. This distance exists because of the redundancy of the language which the clear texts belong to.

In that case the solution can be found by trying all the different keys: the key which gives a likelihood clear-text is the good one. If the number of trials is too large, this exhaustive search must be considered as impossible: cryptanalyst is hoped not to have enough time to find the solution.

But how to be sure that all these trials are necessary? The complexity theory of algorithms is an attempt to answer this question.

2. The complexity of algorithms

This theory tries to give a measure of the difficulty to solve a problem[2] .Generally, an algorithm which solves a problem defines a computation which requires two types of ressources: time (or number of steps of computation) and space (or memory to store informations used by the computation). These define complexity measures. The complexity is a function of the length of inputs of the computation.

Let us recall the main results of complexity theories. In a universal computational model (for example the Turing machines), a hierarchy of functions is defined, according to the time complexity, that is to say, the number $f(n)$ of computation steps. Complexity classes are defined in accordance with the increasing rate of n, the input length.

For example we have the following classes :

- linear : $f(n) = 0(n)$
- polynomial : $f(n) = 0(n^a)$
- exponential : $f(n) = 0(2^n)$
- etc ...

The notation $0(\alpha)$ means that the asymptotical value is proportional to α.

It is generally considered that a problem the complexity of which is at least exponential is intractable, in the sense that there is no practical algorithm to solve it. On the other hand polynomial time complexity is often identified with practical computability. (There is no clear cut off for the degree of polynomial time bounds). So it is important to distinguish polynomial time algorithms from exponential ones.

A new notion is needed: polynomial time reducibility. A problem A is polynomial time reducible to B if there is a total computable function f, computed in time bounded by a polynomial in length of input x, such that :

$$A(x) = B (f(x)), \forall x.$$

A has been polynomially reduced to B. Another notion is the relative completeness: let B a problem in a collection C of problems. If every A in C is polynomially reducible to B, B is said C-hard, and if B belongs to C, it is said C-complete. So, in a sense, C-complete problems are the hardest or the most difficult in C.

3. The NP-completeness

To search intermediate classes between the polynomial and exponential ones, nondeterministic algorithms have been considered. In these algorithms several instructions may be applicable at any point in the computation. Anyone of these instructions may be chosen.

So non-deterministic algorithms define as much computations as possible choices, and at least, one of them leads to the solution. So if the machine "guesses" the solution it chooses the good computation, if the machine cannot guess the solution, it has to try all the possible computations which, generally, are in exponential number.

The class of algorithms solvable by a polynomial time algorithm is called P; the class NP consists of the problems solvable by a non-deterministic algorithm in polynomial time (the machine is supposed to guess the solution).

It is very important to know the relationship between P and NP. This problem is one of the most important in the theory of computation.

To day, the situation is not very clear. It is generally agreed that P is properly contained in NP. If it is so, NP should be a good intermediate between P and difficult problems. An other class is very interesting: CO-NP. It consists of problems whose complementary problems are in NP (it is supposed that these problems are of type "yes-no" and complementary problems are "no-yes". it is not known if NP = CO-NP. Under the hypothesis CO-NP ≠ NP, the NP-complete problems are not in the intersection of NP and CO-NP. So they are more difficult that those in NP ∩ CO-NP. For example, the composite numbers problem belongs to NP ∩ CO-NP. But if any NP-complete problem is in the intersection of NP and CO-NP, then NP = CO-NP.

G. Brassard[3] showed that if some one-way function f exists, then P is properly contained in the intersection of N and NP, and if f^{-1} is NP-hard, then NP = CO-NP A function is one-way if it is easy to compute (f ∉ P) and f^{-1} is difficult (f^{-1} ∉ P).

Now it is obvious that encryption and decryption operations are in P, since they generally are in linear time[4]. But the decipherment is a non-deterministical cryptanalysis since the good key is guessed.

Now we arrive at the main question: Is the cryptanalytic problem NP-complete ? If it is so, there would be evidence that it is intractable.

From a very general point of view the cryptanalytic problem amounts to solve a boolean equation, whose the unknown are the bits of the key. This problem is NP-complete.

Surely, the cryptanalysis of a specific cryptomachine is not NP-complete, because it is a particular boolean equation. But there is no reason to find a specific algorithm for this machine. This would mean that the cryptomachine would have some particularities usable by a specific algorithm. So the first guideline for designing a cryptosystem is the absence of any logical particularity.

However it must be stressed that complexity theory must be applied to cryptanalysis very cautiously:

- the computational theory deals with worst cases and a highly complex function may be easy to compute almost always.

- in cryptography an exact solution is not needed, and some NP-complete problems are known to have good approximate solution to compute.

- the crytanalysis may have enough auxiliary information so that he is able to solve the problem even if it is NP-complete[5].

4. The complexity of sequences
Let us examine another point of view. Instead of analyzing the machine itself, what can be said about the output sequence produced by the machine ?

The lack of any logical particularity of the machine must find expression in the structure of the output which must look like a random sequence.

According to Kolmogorov[6] and Chaitin[7] the complexity I of a sequence S is the length of the shortest program P such that a computer C which accepts P as input, produces S as output. It can be shown that this complexity is independant of C.

This complexity measure has some important properties :

- the complexity of a sequence S is at most of the length of S, because it is always possible to describe S by exhibiting it; such a program is of the length of S.

- the complexity of most of the sequences of length k is about k. For example for n large enough, 99,8% of all sequences of length n, have a greater complexity than n-10.

Now we can define an algorithmically random sequence. It will be noted: A - random .

Roughly a sequence is A - random if its complexity is of about its length. More precisely, a sequence S of length n is t-A-random if its complexity is greater than n - t.

But there is no algorithm to decide if a sequence is A-random. However when n is large enough the probability that a sequence of length n is A-random is close to one. So if a sequence is defined by tossing a coin, the probability that it is A-random is close to one.

The main interest of this theory is to establish connexions between complexity and randomness. As a consequence, it justifies that if the output of a crypto-machine is A-random, then the machine has not logical particularity and the cryptanalysis is probably hard.

By chance, A-randomness is consistent with probabilistic definition: if a sequence is A-random then, it is statistically random. But the converse is not true: some sequences that are statiscally random are not A-random[8]. This means that statistical tests, although they cannot decide if a sequence is A-random, are a good approxima-te algorithm to decide randomness: if a sequence is not statistically random, then it is not A-random.

5. The apparent complexity

But in fact, the sequence S produced by a cryptomachine is known to have low com-plexity, of the order of the length of the key K: for each clear-text m, we have the equation :

$$S = f_m (K).$$

As it is enough to consider clear-text m of length of unicity distance the complexi-ty of S is the one of K. But for every m, f_m^{-1} must be difficult (every f_m is one-way) so that it is infeasible to solve in K this equation. To find K is equivalent to find a program which genrates S. This leads to a new notion: the apparent comple-xity I_A, which aims at measuring the diffiulty to complete f_m^{-1}. Different measures of I_A have already been proposed[9],[10] and are deduced from the structure of the sequence itself. We can now define apparent-randomness: a sequence is apparent ran-domn   if its apparent complexity is maximum (generally of the order of its length).

Let us observe that generally if S is A-random, it is apparent-random. Let us suppose that $I_A(S)$ is defined by the shortest program P_S such that on the computer C, the output of P_S is K :

$$C (P_S) = K \quad <=> \quad S = f_m (K)$$

If S is not apparent-random, the length $\ell(P_S)$ of P_S must be very short compared to the one of S.

$$\ell(P_S) \ll \ell(S)$$

The computer C can compute S from a program for f_m and K :

$$S = C (f_m, K).$$

Let X(S) the complexity of S.
   Then $X(S) = \ell(f_m) + \ell(K) \simeq \ell(K)$ for K is large enough. So: $\ell(K) \simeq \ell(S)$. But

S = $C(f_m, C(P_S))$; so: $X(S) \simeq \ell(P_S) \ll \ell(S)$ that is impossible if S is A-random.

So the complexity notion can be approximate by algorithm, statistics, and apparent complexity. The corresponding notions of randomness are related in the following way :

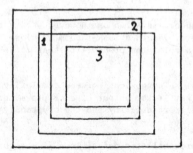

1: Apparent-random sequences

2: Statistical random sequences

3: A-random sequences.

The only effective algorithm is the statistical tests, and the problem is to define adequate statistical tests for randomness; and this question is far from being clear to day.

6. Conclusion

To conclude the application of complexity theories to evaluation of crypto machines leave much to be desired. Every theory has its pitfalls and shortcomings. Much remains to be done to achieve this goal.

However every theory provides complementary point of view on the subject. But to day, none of them gives any useful tools to evaluate the security of crypto machines, and tell now, statistical tests remain the most trustful evaluation.

References

[1] C. SHANNON - Communication Theory of Secrecy Systems B.S.T.J. Vol. 28, October, 1949, p. 656.

[2] M. MACHTEY, P. YOUNG - An introduction to the general Theory of algorithms - North-Holland, 1978.

[3] G. BRASSARD - A note on the complexity of cryptography - I E E E Trans. on I.T., Vol. IT-25,n° 2, March 1979, p. 232.

[4] W. DIFFIE, M. HELLEMAN - New directions in cryptography, I E E E Trans. on I.T., Vol. IT-22, n° 6, November 1976, p. 644.

[5] A. LEMPEL - Cryptology in transition, Computing Surveys, Vol. 11, n° 4, December 1979, p. 285 (Example, p. 300).

[6] A. KOLMOGOROV - Three approaches to the quantitative definition of information. Problemy Peredaci Informacii 1, 4-7, 1965.

[7] G. CHAITIN - Algorithmic Information Theory - IBM J. Res. Dev. Vol. 21, July 1977, p. 350.

8   T. FINE - Theories of Probability. Academic Press, 1973 (Chapter V).

9   A. LEMPEL, J. ZIV - On the complexity of sequences - I E E E Trans. on I.T.,
Vol. IT-22, n° 1, January 1976, p. 75.

10 E. FISHER - Measuring Cryptograhic performance with production Processes.
Cryptologia, Vol. 5, n° 3, July 1981, p. 158.

ON CRYPTOSYSTEMS BASED ON POLYNOMIALS
AND FINITE FIELDS

R. Lidl (University of Tasmania, Australia)

ABSTRACT

In many single-key, symmetric or conventional cryptosystems the elements of a finite field can be regarded as the characters of a plaintext and ciphertext alphabet. Some properties of polynomials or polynomial functions on finite fields can be used for constructing cryptosystems. This note demonstrates by way of examples that great care has to be taken in choosing polynomials for enciphering and deciphering. Often complex looking polynomial functions induce very simple permutations of the elements of a finite field and therefore are not suitable for the construction of cryptosystems. Also an indication is given of some further areas of research in algebraic cryptography.

1. BINOMIALS

There are several examples of cryptosystems that involve polynomials and finite fields; see e.g. [1], [4], [6], [8]. We have to confine our choice of polynomials to a relatively small class of polynomials because of two reasons: the polynomial $f(x)$ should induce a permutation of the elements of a finite field F_q; that is $f: F_q \to F_q$, $a \to f(a)$ should be a permutation. Polynomials $f(x)$ with this property are called *permutation polynomials*. Second, the inverse of f should be easy to compute for deciphering purposes by the authorized receiver. These two requirements of f considerably narrow the choice of polynomials.

Monomials x^k have been studied repeatedly as to their suitability for cryptography. In public-key (asymmetric) cryptosystems the RSA scheme uses the corresponding polynomial functions as enciphering and deciphering functions modulo an integer n. Some conventional exponentiation ciphers use the difficulty of calculating discrete logarithms for finite fields.

We consider *binomials* for conventional cryptosystems and show that their usefulness is very limited. Let

$$(1) \qquad f(x) = ax^k + bx$$

where k > 2 is fixed independently of a prime power q. Niederreiter and Robinson [13] showed that no binomial of this form is a permutation polynomial of F_q for sufficiently large q. In detail:

THEOREM ([13], p.209). _Let k > 2. Then:_

(i) _if k is not a prime power, then for all finite fields_ F_q
 with $q \geq (k^2-4k+6)^2$ _there is no permutation polynomial of_
 F_q _of the form (1) over_ F_q _with ab ≠ 0,_

(ii) _if k is a power of the prime p, then for all finite fields_
 F_q _with_ $q \geq (k^2-4k+6)^2$ _and characteristic not equal to p_
 there is no permutation polynomial of F_q _of the form (1)_
 over F_q _with ab ≠ 0._

This result can be generalized to polynomials of the form $ax^k + bx^j \in F_q[x]$, ab ≠ 0, $1 \leq j < k$, see [13, p.211]. Again, for sufficiently large q none of these binomials is a permutation polynomial of F_q.

Since the above results hold for k being independent of q, let us consider the situation where k is of the form (q+1)/2, q odd. Then the family of polynomial functions in $F_q[x]$ of the form

(2) $$f(x) = ax^{(q+1)/2} + bx$$

is closed under composition. It is easily verified that for two polynomials $f_i(x) = a_i x^{(q+1)/2} + b_i x$, i = 1,2, we have

$$(f_1 \circ f_2)(x) = f_1(f_2(x)) \equiv (a_1 c + b_1 a_2)x^{(q+1)/2} + (a_1 d + b_1 b_2)x \pmod{(x^q - x)},$$

where $c + d = (a_2 + b_2)^{(q+1)/2}$ and $c - d = (b_2 - a_2)^{(q+1)/2}$. Thus it is possible to easily find the inverse g(x) of a given polynomial f(x) of the form (2) from $f(x) \circ g(x) = x$, $g(x) \circ f(x) = x$. In [13] it is shown that a polynomial $f(x) = x^{(q+1)/2} + bx \in F_q[x]$ is a permutation polynomial of F_q if and only if $b^2 - 1$ is a nonzero square in F_q. So it appears that polynomials of the form (2) may be suitable candidates for enciphering functions in a cryptosystem. We note, however, that the mappings of F_q into itself which are induced by permutation polynomials (2) are very simple, since $f(s) = (a+b)s$ for a square $s \in F_q$ and $f(t) = (b-a)t$ for a non-square $t \in F_q$. Therefore the mapping f is linear on the squares or non-squares of F_q.

It may be fruitful to study binomials on the integers mod n and use them in RSA type cryptosystems instead of monomials x^k.

2. CHEBYSHEV POLYNOMIALS OF THE SECOND KIND

Several generalizations of the RSA cryptosystem have been suggested based on different enciphering functions; see [1], [9] and [12]. In some of these papers Chebyshev polynomials of the first kind (or Dickson polynomials, as they are called in an algebraic/number theoretic context) and their multivariate generalization play a central role. Here we consider Chebyshev polynomials of the second kind as to their suitability for constructing cryptosystems over F_q. The *Chebyshev polynomial* $f_k(x)$ *of the second kind* is defined by

$$f_k(x) = \sum_{i=0}^{\lfloor k/2 \rfloor} \binom{k-i}{i}(-1)^i \, x^{k-2i} \quad .$$

We note that $f_k(x)$ is a polynomial of degree k with integer coefficients. Alternative ways of defining the polynomials $f_k(x)$ are by recursive equations

$$f_{k+2}(x) - x f_{k+1}(x) + f_k(x) = 0 \quad \text{with } f_0(x) = 1, \ f_1(x) = x \ ;$$

or by the functional equation

$$f_k(x) = (u^{k+1} - u^{-(k+1)})/(u-u^{-1})$$

where $x = u + u^{-1}$ and $u \neq \pm 1$,

$$f_k(2) = k + 1 \text{ and } f_k(-2) = (-1)^k(k+1).$$

The following result gives sufficient conditions to ensure that $f_k(x)$ induces a permutation of F_q. Let $q = p^e$, p an odd prime.

THEOREM (Matthews [11]). *The polynomial $f_k(x)$ is a permutation polynomial of F_q if k satisfies the congruences*

(3) $k + 1 \equiv \pm 2 \pmod{p}$, $k + 1 \equiv \pm 2 \pmod{\frac{1}{2}(q-1)}$, $k + 1 \equiv \pm 2 \pmod{\frac{1}{2}(q+1)}$.

Proofidea.   Let S be the subset of F_{q^2} consisting of all solutions of equations of the form $x^2 - ax + 1 = 0$, $a \in F_q$. Then $= \{u \in F_{q^2} | u^{q-1} = 1 \text{ or } u^{q+1} = 1\}$. The integer k must be odd, since either $\frac{1}{2}(q-1)$ or $\frac{1}{2}(q+1)$ is even. Thus $f_k(-x) = f_k(x)$. Let $u \in F_{q^2}$ and $u^2 - xu + 1 = 0$. If $u^{q-1} = 1$, then $u^{\frac{1}{2}(q-1)} = \pm 1$. Now, if $u^{\frac{1}{2}(q-1)} = 1$, then $u^{k+1} = u^2$ or $u^{k+1} = u^{-2}$, since $k + 1 \equiv \pm 2 \pmod{\frac{1}{2}(q-1)}$. Therefore $f_k(x) = (u^2-u^{-2})/(u-u^{-1}) = u + u^{-1} = x$, or $f_k(x) = -(u+u^{-1}) = -x$. The remaining cases $u^{\frac{1}{2}(q-1)} = -1$, $u^{q+1} = 1$ and $u = \pm 1$ are treated similarly. □

It follows that f_k is its own inverse:

$$(f_k \circ f_k)(x) = f_k(f_k(x)) = x, \text{ whenever k satisfies (3)}.$$

Here the composite $f_k(f_k(x))$ is reduced modulo $x^q - x$. This would be a suitable property for a symmetric cryptosystem with secret key k. The above proof, however, shows that the mapping of F_q into itself induced by a permutation polynomial $f_k(x)$ is not very complex at all, since $f_k(-a) = -f_k(a)$ and $f_k(a) = a$ or $-a$ for each $a \in F_q$. So the complicated enciphering function f_k induces a simple permutation of F_q.

3. COMMUTING POLYNOMIAL VECTORS

In order to implement digital signatures it is useful if the enciphering function E and the deciphering function D commute with respect to substitution; that is $E \circ D = D \circ E$. If E_i and D_i are the enciphering function and deciphering function, respectively, of person i then these functions are easy to handle if we require

$$E_i \circ E_j = E_j \circ E_i, \ E_i \circ D_j = D_j \circ E_i, \ D_i \circ D_j = D_j \circ D_i.$$

This leads to studying *commuting* or *permutable polynomials*. In [9] all possible classes of commuting polynomials in one variable were determined according to their suitability in RSA-type cryptosystems. Because of the following result, the classical Chebyshev polynomials $T_n(x)$ of the first kind are of special interest. Bertram showed (see e.g. Rivlin [15, p.161]) that over an integral domain R of characteristic zero, if $n \geq 2$ and the polynomial $f(x)$ of degree $k \geq 1$ commutes under substitution with $T_n(x)$, then $f(x) = T_k(x)$ if n is even and $f(x) = \pm T_k(x)$ if n is odd. (A similar result holds if char R = p). A two-dimensional generalization of this theorem was derived in [9]. We say that two polynomial vectors (f_1,f_2) and (g_1,g_2) in $R[x,y]^2$ commute if

$$(f_1(g_1,g_2), \ f_2(g_1,g_2)) = (g_1(f_1,f_2), \ g_2(f_1,f_2)).$$

In short

$$(f_1,f_2) \circ (g_1,g_2) = (g_1,g_2) \circ (f_1,f_2).$$

In [8], [9] or [10] a two-dimensional generalization of the Chebyshev polynomials $T_n(x)$ is presented in terms of a polynomial vector $(g_k(x,y), \ \bar{g}_k(x,y))$ or $(g_k,\bar{g}_k)$ for short. Let R be an integral domain of a characteristic that does not divide $n \geq 2$. Then the following generalizes Bertram's result:

*THEOREM ([7]). If f ∈ (R[x,y])² is of degree k ≥ 1, then f commutes
with (gₙ,ḡₙ) if and only if f is of the form*

$$f = (\alpha g_k, \alpha^2 \overline{g}_k) \quad or \quad f = (\alpha \overline{g}_k, \alpha^2 g_k).$$

where α = 1 if n ≢ 1 (mod 3) or α³ = 1 if n ≡ 1 (mod 3).

In the one-variable case all classes of commuting polynomials (so-called
permutable chains) have been determined (see e.g. Lausch and Nöbauer [5] and [9]).
The corresponding classification in the case of polynomial vectors in two
variables is still an open problem. The Theorem above is a first result in
this direction. Commuting polynomial vectors can be used for digital
signatures analogous to the one-dimensional situation described in [9].

4. FURTHER PROBLEM AREAS

Brawley, Carlitz and Levine [2] have determined the polynomials
$f(x) \in F_q[x]$ which permute the set $F_q^{n \times n}$ of n×n matrices with entries
in F_q under substitution, that is $f : F_q^{n \times n} \to F_q^{n \times n}$, $A \longrightarrow f(A)$ is a permutation
of matrices.

*THEOREM ([2]). The polynomial f(x) ∈ Fq[x] is a permutation polynomial
of Fq^{n×n} if and only if*

(i)   f(x) is a permutation of Fqʳ, 1 ≤ r ≤ n; and

(ii)   f'(x) does not vanish on any of the fields Fq,...,Fq⌊n/2⌋.

Such permutation polynomials could be used for enciphering plaintext
messages which are arranged in matrix form. A first step would be to
determine specific polynomials f(x) which are suitable as enciphering
functions of such cryptosystems.

A different problem area is concerned with the study of iterative
roots of functions over finite fields. The *iterates* of a function
$g : F_q \to F_q$ are defined inductively by $g^0(x) = x$ and $g^n(x) = g(g^{n-1}(x))$, $n > 0$.
If f is another function on F_q, with the property $g^n = f$, $n \geq 2$, then g is
called an *iterative root of order n* of f or an nth iterative root of f.
In [3] the existence of iterative roots of f are investigated for special
types of functions, such as linear functions, power function x^k and
Chebyshev polynomials of the first kind. Apart from theoretical existence

theorems (developed in [3]) it could be potentially useful in cryptography to explicitly determine iterative roots of given functions.   Our interest in this topic arose from the question: "When is $f(f(z)) = az^2 + bz + c$ for all complex numbers z ?"   Rice, Schweizer and Sklar [14] showed that the answer is: never.

References

1. Brändström H.: A public-key cryptosystem based upon equations over a finite field.   Cryptologia 7 (1983) 347-358.

2. Brawley, J.V., L. Carlitz and J. Levine: Scalar polynomial functions on the n×n matrices over a finite field. Linear Alg. Appl.10 (1975) 199-217.

3. Dunn, K.B. and R. Lidl: Iterative roots of functions over finite fields. Math. Nachrichten (to appear).

4. Ecker, A.: Über die mathematischen Grundlagen einiger Chiffrierverfahren. Computing 29 (1982) 277-287.

5. Lausch, H. and W. Nöbauer: Algebra of Polynomials. North Holland, Amsterdam 1973.

6. Levine, J. and J.V. Brawley: Some cryptographic applications of permutation polynomials.   Cryptologia 1 (1977) 76-92.

7. Lidl, R. and G.L. Mullen: Commuting polynomial vectors over an integral domain (to appear).

8. Lidl, R. and W.B. Müller: A note on polynomials and functions in algebraic cryptography.   Proceedings 11th Australian Conference of Combinatorial Mathematics.   Ars Combinatoria (to appear).

9. Lidl, R. and W.B. Müller: Permutation polynomials in RSA-cryptosystems. Proceedings CRYPTO '83 Santa Barbara. Plenum Publ. (to appear).

10. Lidl, R. and H. Niederreiter: Finite Fields. Encyclopedia of Mathematics and its Applications vol.20. Addison-Wesley, Reading, Massachusetts 1983.

11. Matthews, R.: Permutation polynomials in one and several variables. Ph.D. thesis, University of Tasmania, 1983.

12. Müller, W.B. and W. Nöbauer: Some remarks on public-key cryptosystems. Studia Sci. Math. Hungar. 16 (1981) 71-76.

13. Niederreiter, H. and K.H. Robinson: Complete mappings of finite fields. J. Austral. Math. Soc. (Series A) 33 (1982) 197-212.

14. Rice, R.E., B. Schweizer and A. Sklar: When is $f(f(z)) = az^2+bz+c$ for all complex z? Amer. Math. Monthly 87 (1980) 252-263.

15. Rivlin, T.J.: The Chebyshev Polynomials. J. Wiley & Sons, New York, 1974.

Department of Mathematics,
University of Tasmania,
Hobart, Tasmania, 7001,
Australia.

ALGEBRAICAL STRUCTURES OF CRYPTOGRAPHIC TRANSFORMATIONS

Józef P. Pieprzyk
Institute of Telecommunication
Technical Academy of Bydgoszcz
Bydgoszcz, POLAND

In the paper, application of idempotent elements to construction of cryptographic systems has been presented. The public key cryptosystem based on idempotent elements and the cryptographic transformation that preserves elementary arithmetic operations have been described.

1. Introduction

Various methods are being applied to design cryptographic systems. There is, however, a cryptosystem class which can be defined by means of peculiar algebraical structures. They are injected in a vector space which is spanned over idempotent elements of an algebraical ring.

The purpose of the work is presentation of mathematical tools which may be adapted to project a wide class of cryptosystems. Let Z_N be a ring with addition and multiplication modulo N where $N=p_1 \ldots p_n$ and p_i is prime for $i=1,\ldots,n$. Now, let us take into account an integer $x \in Z_N$ Then, we can determine the sequence of integers in the form

$$(x_1,\ldots,x_n) \tag{1}$$

while $x_i = x \pmod{p_i}$ for $i=1,\ldots,n$ and $p_i \neq p_j$ for $i \neq j$. On the other hand, we define the integer

$$LCM(x_1,\ldots,x_n)=LCM\left(x_1 \pmod{p_1},\ldots,x_n \pmod{p_n}\right) = [\![x_1; \ldots ;x_n]\!] \tag{2}$$

where LCM stands for the least common multiple. The vector $[\![x_1;\ldots;x_n]\!]$ belongs to the ring $\overset{n}{\underset{i=1}{\oplus}} Z_{p_i}$ in which addition and multiplication are given as follows:

$$[\![x_1;\ldots;x_n]\!] + [\![y_1;\ldots;y_n]\!] = [\![x_1+y_1 \pmod{p_1};\ldots;x_n+y_n \pmod{p_n}]\!]$$
$$[\![x_1;\ldots;x_n]\!] [\![y_1;\ldots;y_n]\!] = [\![x_1 y_1 \pmod{p_1};\ldots;x_n y_n \pmod{p_n}]\!]$$

As is known [2], the rings Z_N and $\overset{n}{\underset{i=1}{\oplus}} Z_{p_i}$ are isomorphic, so

$$Z_N \approx \overset{n}{\underset{i=1}{\oplus}} Z_{p_i}$$

Example 1:

Let us take into account the ring Z_{30} and $p_1=2$, $p_2=3$, $p_3=5$. If $x=17$, then

$$x=[\![17 \pmod 2;17 \pmod 3;17 \pmod 5]\!] = [\![1;2;2]\!] \in Z_{30}$$

The original value of x can be calculated according to the following expression:

$$LCM\left(1,3,5,7,9,11,13,15,17,\ldots ;2,5,8,11,14,17,\ldots ;2,7,12,17,\ldots \right) =17$$

For the elements $x=17$ and $y=22$, we can find

$$x+y = 17+22 = 9 \pmod{30}=[\![1;2;2]\!] + [\![0;1;2]\!] = [\![1;0;4]\!]$$
$$xy = 17\cdot22 = 14 \pmod{30}=[\![1;2;2]\!] [\![0;1;2]\!]=[\![0;2;4]\!]$$

From all elements of the ring $\overset{n}{\underset{i=1}{\oplus}} Z_{p_i}$, we choose

$$e_1=[\![1;0;0; \ldots ;0;0]\!]$$
$$e_2=[\![0;1;0; \ldots ;0;0]\!]$$
$$\vdots$$
$$e_n=[\![0;0;0; \ldots ;0;1]\!] \tag{3}$$

Vectors e_i (i=1,...,n) are also called basic idempotent elements. They have the following properties:

PR1. $\bigvee\limits_{i=1,...,n} e_i^2 = e_i$

PR2. $e_1+...+e_n = 1 \pmod{N}$

PR3. $\bigvee\limits_{\substack{i,j \\ i \neq j}} e_i e_j = 0 \pmod{N}$

PR4. $x = [\![x_1;...;x_n]\!] = \sum\limits_{i=1}^{n} x\,e_i = \sum\limits_{i=1}^{n} x_i e_i \pmod{N}$

PR5. A sum of arbitrarily chosen basic idempotent elements is an idempotent one.

Example 2:

There are three basic idempotent elements in the ring Z_{30}, namely

$e_1 = [\![1;0;0]\!] = 15$

$e_2 = [\![0;1;0]\!] = 10$

$e_3 = [\![0;0;1]\!] = 6$

2. Algebraical structure of public key cryptosystems

In this point, we present two public key cryptosystems, namely the Rivest-Shamir-Adleman cryptosystem (RSA system) and the cryptosystem based on the knapsack problem (Merkle-Hellman cryptosystem). Both cryptosystems are being designed by means of suitable algebraic rings.

Authors of the RSA system [5] proposed the cryptographic functions in the form

$$c = E_k(m) = m^k \pmod{N} \qquad (4)$$
$$m = D_{k'}(c) = c^{k'} \pmod{N} \qquad (5)$$

where m,c,k,k' represent a message, a cryptogram, a public key, and a secret key, respectively, and $N=p_1...p_n$ (p_i are different primes for i=1,...,n) determines the ring in which cryptographic transformations are being carried out. In order to find the original message at the receiver's side, the following congruence must be fulfilled:

$$D_k(c) = D_{k'} \cdot (E_k(m)) = c^{k'} = m^{kk'} = m \pmod{N} \qquad (6)$$

As a result, we get the congruence in the shape

$$m^{kk'-1} = 1 \pmod{N} \qquad (7)$$

Transforming (7), we obtain

$$[\![m_1;...;m_n]\!]^{kk'-1} = [\![1;...;1]\!] \qquad (8)$$

Thus, we have the sequence of congruences given by

$$m_i^{kk'-1} = 1 \pmod{p_i} \text{ for } i=1,...,n \qquad (9)$$

As is known [2], the sequence of congruences has a solution when
$$\bigvee_{i=1,\ldots,n} (kk'-1)\,|\,(p_i-1) \tag{10}$$
So the integer $(kk'-1)$ must fulfill the equation
$$kk'-1 = LCM(p_1-1,\ldots,p_n-1) = \lambda(N) \tag{11}$$
Since, in the RSA system, the integer k is chosen randomly from all the elements of set Z_N, the integer k' is calculated at the receiver's side according to the following congruence
$$kk' = 1\,(\mathrm{mod}\ \lambda(N)) \tag{12}$$

Now, let us take into account an unauthorized user (UU) who observes both a cryptogram and a public key, and additionally knows the the cryptographic transformations and the value of integer N. When he wants to obtain the message from the cryptogram, he may employ two approaches. The first one relies on the factorization of N into primes as the UU can find $\lambda(N)$ and finally decipher the cryptogram. If the UU additionally knows that $n \geqslant 3$, then he may use the Pollard method [4] to carry out the factorization of N. This method requires $O(p^{\frac{1}{2}})$ elementary processing operations where p is the smallest among all the primes p_i, $i=1,\ldots,n$. Hence, in the RSA system, one chooses the integer N in the form $N=p_1 p_2$ where p_1 and p_2 are of the same order since the Pollard method turns out to be not efficient for N of the order of a decimal integer composed of 200 digits. Thus, $\lambda(N)$ may be written as
$$\lambda(N) = LCM(p_1-1, p_2-1) \tag{13}$$
At last, let us notice that difficulties in breaking the cipher for the RSA system result from the fact that the ring $\bigoplus_{i=1}^{n} Z_{p_i}$ cannot be determined easily by the UU when he knows only the ring Z_N.

We are now going to describe a cryptographic system that is based on idempotent elements. This cryptosystem similarly to the Merkle-Hellman system [1] (MH system) is used to encipher binary messages. Let us assume that the initial condition of that system has been defined by the choice of n primes $p_1,\ldots,p_n$ and let $N=p_1\ldots p_n$. Thus, in the ring Z_N, there exist n basic idempotent elements of the form
$$e_1 = [\![1;0;\ldots;0]\!] \quad \ldots \quad e_n = [\![0;0;\ldots;1]\!]$$
Similarly as in the MH system, we convert elements e_i according to the congruence
$$k_i = e_i a\,(\mathrm{mod}\ q)\ ;\ i=1,\ldots,n \tag{14}$$
where $q > \sum_{i=1}^{n} e_i$ (q is a prime), integer a is randomly chosen from the set Z_q, and the sequence $k=(k_1,\ldots,k_n)$ represents the public key. At the transmitter, there is generated a cryptogram for a message m=

$(m_1,\ldots,m_n)$. It is generated according to the expression

$$c = \left| \sum_{j=1}^{u} m_{i_j} k_{i_j} - \sum_{j=u+1}^{n} m_{i_j} k_{i_j} \right| \tag{15}$$

where the subset $\{m_{i_j} ;\ j=1,\ldots,u\}$ is create arbitrarily by the sender.
At the receiver's side, the cryptogram is processed as follows:

$$c' = c\, a^{-1} \pmod{q} \tag{16}$$

Substituting (15) into (16), we get

$$c' = \left| \sum_{j=1}^{u} m_{i_j} e_{i_j} - \sum_{j=u+1}^{n} m_{i_j} e_{i_j} \right| \pmod{q} \tag{17}$$

Since under the sign of absolute value, we may have both the positive
and negative values, we get two integers c' and c'' obeying the
congruence (17), where

$$c'' = q - c' \tag{18}$$

Using c' and c'', we find two sequences

$$c' \to (c_1',\ldots,c_n') \quad \text{where } c_i' = c' \pmod{p_i} ;\ i=1,\ldots,n$$
$$c'' \to (c_1'',\ldots,c_n'') \quad \text{where } c_i'' = c'' \pmod{p_i} ;\ i=1,\ldots,n$$

One of the sequences given above is the message we are looking for. As
it has been proved in [3], one can find such a transformation (14) that
one of these sequences will already be rejected at the beginning of
deciphering process.

It is noteworthy that the cipher considered is based, similarly to
the MH system, on the knapsack problem. Hence, it has advantages and
drawbacks similar to that system. Nevertheless, compared to the MH
system, the cryptosystem based on idempotent elements has two additional
advantages, namely it:
- decreases the redundancy of cryptograms,
- makes the knapsack problem much more difficult to solve.
We should also point to the flexibility of the considered system as it
allows to encipher messages represented not only by binary sequences.

Giving our attention to algebraic properties, we may state that
constructions of two rings Z_N and $\bigoplus_{i=1}^{n} Z_{p_i}$ are kept secret since their
disclosure may allow to discover the clear message. In order to protect
the rings, we have injected idempotent elements into the field Z_q.

Of course, the cryptosystem with idempotent elements can be treated
as modification of the MH cryptosystem. Nevertheless, considering these
cryptosystems, we may notice what influence over quality of a cryptosystem has determination of its algebraic structure. In the MH system,
a vector of integers $(d_1,\ldots,d_n)$ (where $\sum_{i=1}^{j-1} d_i < d_j$ for $j=2,\ldots,n$)
creates the initial condition (the vector space) of the cryptosystem.

But this simple vector space stands in the way of flexible creation of cryptograms. Situation is quite different when we deal with the cryptosystem based on idempotent elements.

3. Algebraic structure of cryptographic transformations which preserve arithmetic operations

In many situations, processing tasks may be performed using only two elementary arithmetic operations (addition and multiplication). Also input messages (integers) are required not to be accessible to the UU while they are being not only transmitted over the channel but processed in the computer system as well (see Fig.1). So the cryptographic transformation which preserves the arithmetic operations (also called cryptomorphism) has to fulfill the following conditions:

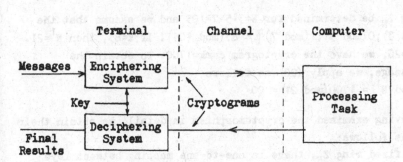

Fig.1. Application of cryptomorphisms

C1. $\bigvee\limits_{m',m''\in M} f(m'+m'',k) = f(m',k) + f(m'',k)$

C2. $\bigvee\limits_{m',m''\in M} f(m'm'',k) = f(m',k) \cdot f(m'',k)$

C3. $\bigvee\limits_{d\in Z^+} \bigvee\limits_{m\in M} f(dm,k) = d\, f(m,k)$

for a fixed key $k\in K$, where M,K and Z^+ are sets of messeges, keys, and positive integers, respectively, and f is a cryptomorphism. The simplest form of such a cryptomorphism takes the shape

$$c = f(m,k) = mk \qquad (19)$$

while $m\in M$, $k\in K$, $c\in C$ (C is the set of cryptograms), and $M,K,C\subset Z_N$ ($N=p_1\ldots p_n$; p_i are primes for $i=1,\ldots,n$ and $p_i\neq p_j$ for $i\neq j$). Moreover, the key set is exclusively composed of idempotent elements of the ring Z_N .

Example 3:

For the ring Z_{12}, the set of keys contains three elements, namely $K=\{1,4,9\}$.

A key is an idempotent element of Z_N so there are two integers N^0 and N^1 which fulfill the following congruences:

$$k = 0 \pmod{N^0} \tag{20}$$
$$k = 1 \pmod{N^1} \tag{21}$$

whereas $N=N^0 N^1$. As a result, we have that the cryptographic function of deciphering system is determined by the formula

$$m = f^{-1}(c,k) = c \pmod{N^1} \tag{22}$$

where $m \in M$, $c \in C$, $k \in K$, and k assigns one and only one value of N^1 while N is fixed. Furthermore, in order to find the correct message, it has to fulfill inequality in the form

$$0 \leqslant m \leqslant N^1 - 1 \tag{23}$$

Example 4:

Let the ring Z_N be determined for $N=3\cdot5\cdot7=105$ and we assume that the key $k=[\![1\,(\text{mod }3)\,;0\,(\text{mod }5)\,;1\,(\text{mod }7)]\!] = 85\,(\text{mod }105)$. If $k=85$, then $N^1=21$. Thus, for $m=20$, we have the cryptogram $c=mk=1700$. To obtain the original message, we apply (22) as follows

$$m = c \pmod{N^1} = 1700 \pmod{21} = 20$$

After having examined the cryptomorphism in detail, we obtain their properties as follows:

P1. For fixed ring Z_N, there is one-to-one mapping between keys (idempotent elements) and pairs (N^0, N^1), where $N=N^0 N^1$.

P2. The enciphering and deciphering transformations are defined according to the following formulae:
$$f(m,k) = mk$$
$$f^{-1}(c,k) = c \pmod{N^1}$$

P3. For any message $m \in Z_{N^1}$, there are m different cryptograms in the shape
$$c = m' + f(m'',k)$$
where $m'+m'' = m$ and $m'=0,\ldots,m-1$

P4. If an integer m has its inverse m^{-1} $\left(m, m^{-1} \in Z_{N^1}\right)$, then cryptograms of m and m^{-1} satisfy the following congruence:
$$f(m,k)\, f(m^{-1},k) = 1 \pmod{N^1}$$

Taking into account the properties, we can formulate four restrictions which have to be imposed to ensure a correctness of computations. These are:

R1. All message which are necessary to execute a program should satisfy the inequality

$$0 \leqslant m \leqslant N^1 - 1 \; ; \; m \in M \tag{24}$$

R2. A final result which would be obtained without using a cryptographic protection also has to fulfill (24).

R3. The execution of a processing task must be possible using only four basic arithmetic operations and all intermediate results have to have the form of either integers or fractions.

R4. Cryptograms of a numerator and a denominator should be determined when both the message and the anticipated final result are fractions.

Example 5:

Suppose that the expression $a = \dfrac{4+m}{2m^2 - 4}$ should be calculated for $m=3$. Of course, if we perform the calculations for clear message $m=3$, we shall get $a=0,5$. Let us assume that $N=3 \cdot 5 \cdot 7$ and key $k = \text{LCM} \left(1 \,(\text{mod } 3), 1\,(\text{mod } 5), 0\,(\text{mod } 7) \right) = 91$. In order to simplify our computations, instead of the cryptogram $c=mk=273$, we accept the cryptogram $c=m'+m''k = 2+91=93$ for $m'+m''=3$ and $m'=2$. Thus, we have

$$f(a,k) = \frac{4+f(m,k)}{2\,f^2(m,k) - 4} = \frac{4+93}{2 \cdot 8649 - 4} = \frac{97}{17294} = \frac{f(a',k)}{f(a'',k)}$$

For cryptogram $f(a',k)$, we obtain the clear form of the numerator

$$a' = f^{-1}(97,k) = 97\,(\text{mod } 15) = 7$$

However, for $f(a'',k)$, we get

$$a'' = f^{-1}(17294,k) = 17294\,(\text{mod } 15) = 14$$

Whence, we have the final result $a=0,5$. As any fraction can be presented in different ways, special precautions should be undertaken in case of fraction calculations. In order to illustrate difficulties, we take the expression

$$f(a,k) = \frac{97}{17294} = \frac{194}{34588}$$

After having deciphered cryptograms of the numerator and the denominator we get the wrong final result.

4. Conclusions

Cryptographic transformations in public key cryptosystems depend on determination of suitable algebraic structures. In the RSA system, such a structure is defined by means of only two basic idempotent elements. Next, in the cryptosystem with idempotent elements, the algebraic structure of a ring is based on many basic idempotent elements. Moreover, the more idempotent elements are applied the higher quality of the system (opposite to the RSA system).

Also, we have presented how an algebraic structure can be applied for construction of cryptomorphisms. Only the simplest case has been considered and the cryptographic transformation relies on multiplying a message by a cryptographic key which is an idempotent element. It is possible to notice that cryptomorphisms can be defined by the aid of a matrix of idempotent elements.

5. References

[1] Merkle R., Hellman M.E., Hiding Information and Receits in Trapdoor Knapsack, IEEE Trans. Inf. Theory, IT-24, September 1978, pp. 525-530
[2] Narkiewicz W., The Numbers Theory, PWN, Warsaw, 1977
[3] Pieprzyk J.P., Rutkowski D.A., Application of Public Key Cryptosystems to Data Security, Rozprawy Elektrotechniczne to be published
[4] Pollard J.M., A Monte Carlo Method for Factorization, BIT 15, 1975, pp.331-334
[5] Rivest R.L., Shamir A., Adleman L., A Method for Obtaining Digital Signatures and Public Key Cryptosystems, Communications of the ACM, Vol.21, February 1978, pp.120-126

NON LINEAR NON COMMUTATIVE FUNCTIONS FOR DATA INTEGRITY

S. HARARI

Université de Toulon et du Var

Château Saint Michel

83130 - LA GARDE

1- INTRODUCTION :

Several authors have recently proposed digital signature schemes [I],
[2],... In an environment where identification is not possible, and the
transmission safe the use of these schemes certify that the data origi-
nated from the legitimate person. However in an environment where identification can be ensured by other means and where transmission is done in an unsafe medium, the use of these same schemes ensure data integrity : any modification of the data during transmission shows up when
one checks the corresponding signature.

The systematic use of signature functions for data integrity has two
important shortcomings :
I) The redundancy introduced by the signature schemes is about as long
as the data to be protected.
2) The average number of computing steps per protected digit is very
large.

In this paper we introduce some functions allowing the use of data integrity witnesses which introduces minimal redundancy (50 digits for
about 10.000 digits of data). The average number of operations per protected digit is kept small.
We study the cryptographic strength of these functions and show that it
increases with the length of the data being protected.

II -- SEAL FUNCTIONS

Let τ be the set of texts made of strings of h decimal digits : $\tau = R^{h}$
where R is the ring of decimal digits. Let $\mathfrak{J}$ be the set of strings of p

decimal digits : $\mathcal{Y} = R^p$. A seal function $\mathbf{S}$ is a function :

$$s : \mathcal{C} \longrightarrow \mathcal{Y}$$

A seal of a text T is then s(T)

The seal function is used or storing in the following way :

Prior to the transmission of the data on an unsafe medium, a seal is computed. It is then processed with the data.

When retrieving the data from an unsafe medium; a seal is recomputed from the data and compared with the one that is retrieved from the unsafe medium. If the two seals coïncide the data is considered free from alterations.

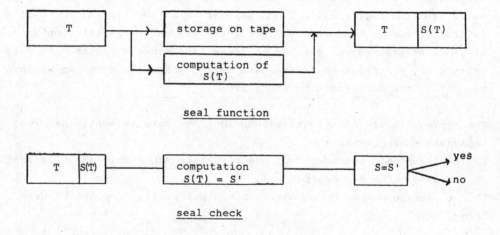

seal function

seal check

III - CONSTRAINTS ON THE SEAL FUNCTION

a) length of the seal

The seal being a decimal quantity, a length p of more then 20 decimal digits is enough to ensure that random attacks on the seal have a low probability of succeeding. If n is any integer between 10.000 and 100.000, then one is sure that in any application the data flow is not interrupted too often for seal computation or recomputation.

b) attacks on the seal and unforgeability

The data that is to be protected by the seal is highly structured. The structure and content is known to an opponent. The aim of an opponent to the system is to modify the data, and if necessary (and possible) the seal, in such a way that the modified seal is legitimately associated to the modified data.

Let $n = 10.000$ and $p = 20$

Let $s = R^{10.000} \longrightarrow R^{20}$ be a seal function.
For a given seal S, the cardinality of S^{-1} (S), that is the set of texts having a given seal is of the order of R^{9980}.
Any structure in that set, will help an opponent in finding many of its elements.
Any structure relating $S^{-1}(S)$ and $S^{-1}(S')$ for two different seal S and S' will also help an opponent in finding many of its elements.
This leads us to the following conditions.

i) The mapping

$s : R^n \longrightarrow R^p$ is a random variable, uniformely distributed on R^p for each probability distribution on R^n.

ii) For any given text $(t_1,...,t_n)$. Let $I = \left\{1,...,n\right\}$
The mapping :

$$I \times R \longrightarrow R^p$$
$$(i,r) \longrightarrow s (t_1,...,t_{i-1}, t_i+r, t_{i+1},...,t_r) - s (t_1,...,t_n)$$

Should be a uniformely distributed random variable, for each probability distribution on I x R.

iii) Let S_n be the permutation group of $I = \left\{1,...,n\right\}$, and 6 an element of S_n, for any given text $(t_1,..., t_n)$ the mapping

$$S_n \longrightarrow R^p$$
$$6 \longrightarrow s (t_{6(1)},...,t_{6(n)}) - s (t_1,...,t_n)$$

should be a uniformely distributed random variable for each probability distribution on S_n.

c) computational complexity of seal function
A seal function is primarily intended to be used in software. Therefore

a seal function should have a low computational complexity per protected digit. Most of the well known cryptographic algorithms have
a high computational complexity ciphered digit of data and therefore
perform poorly in software. Using a cryptographic algorithm in a feedback mode, meets the unforgeability requirements, but leads to a very
slow seal computation.

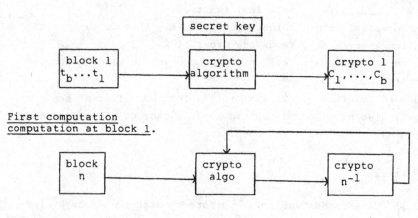

First computation
computation at block 1.

computation at block n.

IV - SOME EXAMPLES OF SEAL FUNCTIONS

a) the sum function
Let b be any integer between 1 and n :

$$\text{For a text } (t_1,\ldots,t_n)$$

Let $T_1 = t_1 t_2 \ldots t_b$, $T_2 = t_{b+1} \ldots t_{2b}, \ldots, t_n = t_{(n-1)b+1} \ldots t_{nb}$

Define the seal of the text $t_1 \ldots t_n$ as

$$S(t_1 \ldots t_n) = \sum_i T_i$$

This seal depends on every digit of the text, but does not satisfy
neither requirement i) nor ii). Any permutation of the digits of the
text corresponding to the permutation of blocks on the T_i's lead to
the same seal.

the same seal.

b) the sum of cryptos

Let C be a cryptographic function, assigning to each set of b integers of text, a cryptogram of length d

$$C : \mathfrak{T} \longrightarrow \mathfrak{T}$$
$$C : R^b \longrightarrow R^d$$

$$(t_1, \ldots, t_b) \longrightarrow (c_1, \ldots, c_d) = c\ (t_1, \ldots, t_b)$$

let $\quad C_1 = c_1 \ldots c_d \qquad = c(t_1, \ldots, t_b)$

$\quad\quad C_2 = c_{d+1} \ldots c_{2d} \qquad = c(t_{b+1}, \ldots, t_{2b})$

$$\ldots$$

$\quad\quad C_n = c_{(n-1)d+1}, \ c_{nd} = c(t_{(n-1)b+1} \ t_{nb})$

$$\ldots$$

and let $\quad S(t_1, \ldots, t_n) \qquad = \sum_i c_i$

This seal function satisfies requirement i) but not ii). Any permutation of the digits of the text corresponding to the permutation of blocks being ciphered lead to the same seal.

c) the concatenation of signatures

Let r,q be two large primes, kept secret and m = q.r
Let 1 be the length of m; and $T_1 = t_1 t_2 \ldots t_1$, $T_2 = t_{1+1} \ldots t_{21}, \ldots,$
$T_n = t_{(n-1)1+1}, \ldots t_{n1}, \ldots$

The legitimate owner of the text knowing the factorisation of m, can easily compute square roots in Z_m.

Let $s_1 = \sqrt{T_1} \bmod m$, $s_2 = \sqrt{T_2} \bmod m, \ldots,$ $s_n = \sqrt{T_n} \bmod m$,

Define $s(t_1, \ldots, t_n)$ as $(s_1, \ldots, s_n)$

This seal function meets most of the requirements on unforgeability. Its shortcoming is the computational effort as well as the length of the seal which is as long as the text itself; and a permutation of two portions of the text as well as their corresponding signature, lead to a new legitimate altered seal.

d) <u>a new seal function (1)</u>

Let $A = (a_{ij})$ be square matrix in order n, whose entries are random integers, chosen by the originator of the text and kept secret.

Let $T = (t_1,\ldots,t_n)$ be a text

$$s(T) = T^t A T = \sum_{i<j} a_{ij} \cdot t_i \cdot t_j$$

is the seal of T

This seal involves only arithmetic operations for its computation. The total number of operations to compute a seal is seen to be $O(n^2)$ multiplications and $O(n^2)$ additions. It is easily checked that the unforgeability requirements are met.

A potential forger of seals has to know the matrix a_{ij} in order to create a legitimate seal for a given text.

Let us suppose that the forger holds

u texts $(t_1^{(1)},\ldots,t_n^{(1)}),\ldots,(t_1^{(u)},\ldots,t_n^{(u)})$ and their corresponding

seals $s_1, s_2,\ldots,s_u$.

To obtain the matrix (a_{ij}) he has to solve the following system

$$\sum_{i,j} a_{ij}\, t_i^{(1)} t_j^{(1)} = s_1$$

$$\sum_{i,j} a_{ij}\, t_i^{(u)} t_j^{(u)} = s_u$$

In this system the t_i, t_j, and $s^{(u)}$ are knowm.

Two methods are indicated to make this system unsolvable.

- Change the matrix (a_{ij}) often enough so that a potential forger cannot obtain enough information from existing seals in order to solve the system.

- Choose n large enough, so that the best known algorithms for solving dense linear systems fail to do so in a short amount of time. The seal system is strengthened by increasing the length of the text being protected.

e) a new seal function (2)

Let $A = (a_1,\ldots,a_{n'})$ be a sequence of random integers of length n', chosen the originator of the text and kept secret

Define $\quad S(T) = A^t\, T\, A = \sum_{i<j} a_i\, a_j\, t_{ij}$

This seal function involves only arithmetic operations to compute a seal, and the total number of operations is then $2n'^2$ additions and $2n'^2$ multiplications. It meets the unforgeability requirements.

A potentail forger has to know the sequence A in order to create a legitimate seal for a given text.

Let us suppose he knows u texts $(t_1^{(1)},\ldots,t_n^{(1)}),\ldots,(t_1^{(u)},\ldots,t_n^{(u)})$ and their corresponding seals $s_1,\ldots,s_u$.

He therefore has to solve a system, which is quadratic in the unknow a_i's.

$$\sum_{i,j} a_i\, a_j\, t_j^{(1)} = s_1$$

$$\sum_{i,j} a_i\, a_j\, t_j^{(u)} = s_u$$

The complexity of finding the a_i's is equivalent to factoring this polinominal.

The complexity of this problem is $O (n^3 + \log n \; n^2)$ in a modular version of the problem.

ooo OOOO ooo OOO ooo

REFERENCES :

[1] Ong schnorr Shamir. An efficient signature schemes based on quadratic equations. 16th Symposium on the theory of comp. 1984, Washington.

[2] Rabin M.O. Probabilistic algorithms in finite fields. Siam J on Computing 9 (1980) 273-280.

[3] S. HARARI. Functions in transmission and storage.
    NATO-ASI. The impact of Processing techniques on communications.
    Château de Bonas 11-12 july 1983.

[4] Knuth - The art of computer programming seminumerical algorithms
    Vol.2 Sec. Ed. 1980, Addison Wesley.

Wire-Tap Channel II

L. H. Ozarow
A. D. Wyner

AT&T Bell Laboratories
Murray Hill, New Jersey 07974

ABSTRACT

Consider the following situation. K data bits are to be encoded into $N > K$ bits and transmitted over a noiseless channel. An intruder can observe a subset of his choice of size $\mu < N$. The encoder is to be designed to maximize the intruder's uncertainty about the data given his N intercepted channel bits, subject to the condition that the intended receiver can recover the K data bits perfectly from the N channel bits. The optimal tradeoffs between the parameters K, N, μ and the intruder's uncertainty H (H is the "conditional entropy" of the data given the μ intercepted channel bits) were found. In particular, it was shown that for $\mu = N - K$, a system exists with $H \approx K - 1$. Thus, for example, when $N = 2K$ and $\mu = K$, it is possible to encode the K data bits into $2K$ channel bits, so that by looking at any K channel bits, the intruder obtains essentially no information about the data.

Wire-Tap Channel II

L. H. Ozarow
A. D. Wyner

AT&T Bell Laboratories
Murray Hill, New Jersey 07974

1. Introduction

In this paper we study a communication system in which an unauthorized intruder is able to intercept a subset of the transmitted symbols, and it is desired to maximize the intruder's uncertainty about the data without the use of an encryption key (either "public" or "private").

Specifically, the encoder associates with the K-bit binary data sequence S^K an N-bit binary "transmitted" sequence X^N, where $N > K$. It is required that a decoder can correctly obtain S^K with high probability by examining X^N. The intruder can examine a subset of his choice of size μ of the N positions in X^N, and the system designer's task is to make the intruder's equivocation (uncertainty) about the data as large as possible. The encoder is allowed to introduce randomness into the transformation $S^K \rightarrow X^N$, but we make the assumption that the decoder and the intruder must share any information about the encoding and the randomness. This assumption precludes the use of "key" cryptography, where the decoder has the exclusive posession of certain information.

As an example, suppose that $K = 1$, $N = 2$, $\mu = 1$. Let the data bit be S, and let ξ be a uniform binary random variable which is independent of S. Let $X^2 = (\xi, \xi \oplus S)$, where "$\oplus$" denotes modulo 2 addition. If the intruder looks at either coordinate of X^2 he gains no information about S, so that the system has perfect secrecy. The decoder, however, can obtain S by adding (modulo two) the two components of X^2.

Our problem is to replicate this type of performance with large K, N, μ. In fact we assume that $K \approx RN$, $\mu \approx \alpha N$, where R, α are held fixed and N becomes large. Roughly speaking, we show that perfect secrecy is attainable provided that μ is not too large, specifically $\mu \leq N - K$ or $\alpha \leq 1 - R$. In Section 2 we give a precise statement and discussion of our problem and results, leaving the proofs for Sections 3-5.

This problem is similar to the wire-tap channel problem studied in Reference 1. A special case of the problem studied there allows an intruder to examine a subset of the encoder symbols which is chosen at random by nature. In the present problem, the system designer must make his system secure against a more powerful intruder who can select which subset to examine.

2. Formal Statement of the Problem and Results

In this section we give a precise statement of our problem and state the results.

First a word about notation. Let U be an arbitrary finite set. Denote its cardinality by $|U|$. Consider U^N, the set of N-vectors with components in U. The members of U^N will be written as

$$\mathbf{u}^N = (u_1, u_2, ..., u_N) \, ,$$

where subscripted letters denote components and boldface superscripted letters denote vectors. A similar convention applies to random vectors which are denoted by upper-case letters. When the dimension of a vector is clear from the context, we omit the superscript. Finally, for random variables X, Y, Z etc., the notation $H(X)$, $H(X|Y)$, $I(X;Y)$, etc. denotes the standard information theoretic quantities as defined, for example, in Gallager [2].

We now turn to the description of the communication system.

(i) The *source* output is a sequence $\{S_k\}_1^\infty$, where the S_k are independent, identically distributed binary random variables.

(ii) The *encoder* with parameters (K, N) is a channel with input alphabet $\{0, 1\}^K$ and output alphabet $\{0, 1\}^N$ and transition probability $q_E(\mathbf{x}^N | \mathbf{s}^K)$. Let S^K and X^N be the input and output respectively of the encoder.

(iii) The *decoder* is a mapping

$$f_D: \{0, 1\}^N \rightarrow \{0, 1\}^K \, .$$

Let $\hat{S} = (\hat{S}_1, \hat{S}_2, ... \hat{S}_K) = f_D(X^N)$. The *error-rate* is

$$P_e = \frac{1}{K} \sum_{k=1}^N Pr\{S_k \neq \hat{S}_k\} \, .$$

(iv) An intruder with parameter $\mu \leq N$ picks a subset $S \subseteq \{1, 2,..., N\}$, such that $|S| = \mu$, and

is allowed to observe X_n, $n \in S$. Let $Z^N = (Z_1,..., Z_N)$, defined by

$$Z_n = \begin{cases} X_n, & n \in S, \\ ?, & n \notin S, \end{cases}$$

denote the intruder's information. The system designer seeks to maximize the equivocation

$$\Delta \triangleq \min_{S: |S| = \mu} H(S^K | Z^N).$$

Thus, the designer is assured that no matter what subset S the intruder chooses, the intruder's remaining uncertainty about the source vector is at least Δ. When $\Delta = K$, the intruder obtains no information about the source, and the system has attained perfect secrecy.

In this paper we study the tradeoffs between K, N, Δ, and P_e. As we shall see, it will be useful to consider the normalized qualities K/N, μ/N, Δ/K. Thus K/N is the "rate" of the encoder = the number of data bits per encoded bit, μ/N is the fraction of the encoded bits which the intruder is able to observe, and Δ/K is the normalized entropy.

Let us remark that the intruder which observes Z^N can reconstruct the data sequence S^K with a per bit error probability of say P_e'. It follows from Fano's inequality that $h(P_e') \geq \Delta/K$, where $h(\cdot)$ is the binary entropy function defined below Eq. (2.2). Thus $\Delta/K \approx 1$ implies that $P_e' \approx 1/2$ which is essentially perfect secrecy.

We will say that the triple (R, α, δ) is *achievable* if for all $\epsilon > 0$ and all integers $N_0 > 0$, there exists an encoder/decoder with parameters $N \geq N_0$, $K \geq (R - \epsilon)N$, $\mu \geq (\alpha - \epsilon)N$, $\Delta \geq (\delta - \epsilon)N$, and $P_e \leq \epsilon$. We will show in the sequel that (R, α, δ) is achievable for $0 \leq R, \alpha, \delta \leq 1$, and

$$\delta \leq \begin{cases} 1, & 0 \leq \alpha \leq 1 - R, \\ \dfrac{(1-\alpha)}{R}, & 1 - R \leq \alpha \leq 1. \end{cases} \tag{2.1}$$

A graph of the achievable (α, δ) pairs for fixed R is given in Figure 1.

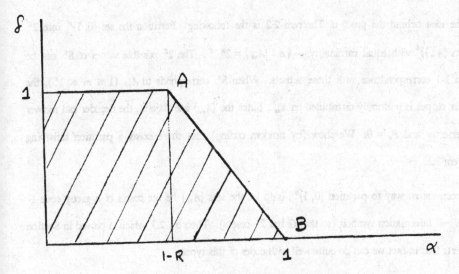

Figure 1. Achievable (α, δ) for fixed R.

The following theorem, a proof of which is given in Section 3, is a "converse" result which gives a necessary condition on achievable (K, N, Δ, P_e).

Theorem 2.1: If (K, N, Δ, P_e) is achievable, then

$$\Delta \le \begin{cases} K, & 0 \le \mu \le N-K, \\ N-\mu+Kh(P_e), & N-K \le \mu \le N. \end{cases} \tag{2.2}$$

where $h(\lambda) = -\lambda \log \lambda - (1-\lambda) \log (1-\lambda)$ is the binary entropy function.

Now if (R, α, δ) is achievable, for arbitrary $\epsilon > 0$, there must be an encoder/decoder with parameters $N, K \ge (R-\epsilon)N, \mu \ge (\alpha-\epsilon)N, \Delta \ge (\delta-\epsilon)N, P_e \le \epsilon$. Applying Theorem 2.1 to this code yields

$$\delta \le \begin{cases} 1, \\ \dfrac{(1-\alpha)}{R} + O(\epsilon) + h(\epsilon), & 1-R \le \alpha + O(\epsilon) \le 1, \end{cases}$$

which is (2.1) as $\epsilon \to 0$. Thus conditions (2.1) are necessary for a triple to be achievable. Theorem 2.2, which is also proved in Section 3, implies that (R, α, δ) is achievable if (2.1) is satisfied.

Theorem 2.2: Let $1-R < \alpha < 1$. Then, for all $\epsilon > 0, N_0 \ge 1$, there exists an $N \ge N_0$ and an encoder/decoder with parameters $K = RN, \mu = \alpha N, \Delta/K \ge [(1-\alpha)/R] - \epsilon$, and $P_e = 0$.

38

The idea behind the proof of Theorem 2.2 is the following. Partition the set $\{0, 1\}^N$ into 2^K subsets $\{A_m\}_1^{2^K}$ with equal cardinality — i.e. $|A_m| = 2^{N-K}$. The 2^K possible values of S^K can be put in 1-1 correspondence with these subsets. When S^K corresponds to A_m $(1 \le m \le 2^K)$, the encoder output is uniformly distributed on A_m. Since the $\{A_m\}$ are disjoint, the decoder can recover S^K perfectly and $P_e = 0$. We show (by random coding) that there exists a partition satisfying Theorem 2.2.

A convenient way to partition $\{0, 1\}^N$, is to let the sets $\{A_m\}$ be the cosets of a group code G with $N-K$ information symbols (so that G has 2^K cosets). Theorem 2.3, which is proved in Section 4, asserts that in fact we can do quite well with codes of this type.

Theorem 2.3: If the triple (R, α, δ) satisfies (2.1), then it is achievable using an encoder/decoder derived from a group code.

The following simple lemma allows us to establish the achievability of all triples on the straight line of Figure 1 connecting points A and B by proving only the achievability of point A.

Lemma 2.4: Suppose that we are given an encoder/decoder f_E, f_D with parameters N, K, P_e. Suppose there are two intruders which have parameters $\mu = \mu_1, \mu_2$ and $\Delta = \Delta_1, \Delta_2$, respectively. Then, if $\mu_2 \ge \mu_1$

$$\Delta_2 \ge \Delta_1 - (\mu_2 - \mu_1) . \tag{2.3}$$

Remark: Inequality (2.3) can be rewritten as

$$(\Delta_2/K) \ge (\Delta_1/K) - \left(\frac{\mu_2/N - \mu_1/N}{K/N}\right),$$

from which we conclude that (R, α_1, δ_1) achievable implies that (R, α_2, δ_2) is achievable where $\alpha_2 \ge \alpha_1$, and

$$\delta_2 = \delta_1 - \left(\frac{\alpha_2 - \alpha_1}{R}\right).$$

In particular, if $\alpha_1 = 1-R$, $\delta_1 = 1$, then

$$\delta_2 = (1-\alpha_2)/R .$$

Proof of Lemma 2.4: Let $S_1 \subseteq S_2 \subseteq \{1, 2, ..., N\}$, where $|S_1| = \mu_1$, $|S_2| = \mu_2$. Let Z_i^N correspond to S_i $(i = 1, 2)$, i.e. $Z_i = (Z_{i_1}, ..., Z_{iN})$ and

$$Z_{ij} = \begin{cases} X_j, & j \in S_i, \\ ?, & j \notin S_i . \end{cases}$$

Then

$$H(S^K |Z_2) - H(S^K |Z_1) = H(S^K |Z_2, Z_1) - H(S^K |Z_1)$$

$$= -I(S^K; Z_2 |Z_1) \geq -H(Z_2 |Z_1) \geq -(\mu_2 - \mu_1) ,$$

where the first equality follows from $S_1 \subseteq S_2$. Thus

$$H(S^K |Z_2) \geq H(S^K |Z_1) - (\mu_2 - \mu_1)$$

$$\geq \Delta_1 - (\mu_2 - \mu_1) .$$

(2.4)

from the definition of Δ. Minimizing (2.4) over all S_2, with $|S_2| = \mu_2$ yields (2.5) and the lemma.

Finally, we state a theorem which is a rather surprising strengthening of Theorem 2.2. Its proof is given in the full version of this paper. [3]

Theorem 2.5. For arbitrary K, N $(1 \leq K \leq N)$, and $\mu = N - K$, there exists an encoder-decoder with $P_e = 0$ and

$$\Delta \geq K - 1 - \frac{2.23}{\sqrt[4]{N}} .$$

3. Proof of Theorems 2.1 and 2.2

Assume that S^K, X^N, Z^N, $\hat{S}$ correspond to a source/encoder/decoder as defined in Section 2, with parameters K, N, Δ, P_e. Then, making repeated use of the identity $H(U, V) = H(U) + H(V |U)$, we obtain

$$\Delta = H(S^K | Z^N) = H(S, Z) - H(Z)$$

$$= H(S, X, Z) - H(X|S, Z) - H(Z)$$

$$= H(S|X, Z) + H(X, Z) - H(X|S, Z) - H(Z)$$

$$= H(S|X, Z) + H(X|Z) - H(X|S, Z) . \qquad (3.1)$$

Now

$$H(S|X, Z) = H(S|X, Z, \hat{S}) \le H(S|\hat{S})$$

$$\le Kh(P_e) ,$$

where the last inequality follows from Fano's inequality (see [2]). Also, since $H(X|Z)$ is the entropy of those $N - \mu$ coordinates of X not specified by Z, we have $H(X|Z) \le N - \mu$. Finally, noting that $H(X|S, Z) \ge 0$, we have from (3.1)

$$\Delta \le N - \mu + Kh(P_e) ,$$

which is Theorem 2.1.

We now give a proof of Theorem 2.2 which proceeds along the lines suggested in Section 2. Let K, N be given, and let $\{A_m\}$, $1 \le m \le 2^K$, be a partition of $\{0, 1\}^N$ into subsets $A_m \subseteq \{0, 1\}^N$ such that $|A_m| = 2^{N-K}$. As in Section 2, the partition defines a code: to encode message m $(1 \le m \le 2^K)$, we let X^N be a randomly chosen vector in A_m. Since the A_m are disjoint, $P_e = 0$ and $H(S|X, Z) = 0$. Further, since the 2^K messages are equally likely and $|A_m| = 2^{N-K}$, X is uniformly distributed on $\{0, 1\}^N$, so that its coordinates are independent identically distributed uniform binary random variables. Thus $H(X^N | Z^N) = N - \mu$. We conclude from (3.1) that for this encoder

$$\Delta = N - \mu - H(X^N | S^K, Z^N) . \qquad (3.2)$$

Now let $z \in \{0, 1, ?\}^N$ be a possible value for the intruder's information, and let $x \in \{0, 1\}^N$. We say that z is "consistent" with x, if z can be obtained from x by changing a subset of the coordinates of x to $?$'s. Next, let $L \ge 1$ be an integer to be chosen later. We say that a partition $\{A_m\}$ is "good" if for all m $(1 \le m \le 2^K)$ and all $z \in \{0, 1, ?\}^N$ with exactly $N - \mu$ $?$'s,

$$\text{card }\{x \in A_m : z \text{ is consistent with } x\} < L .$$

If our encoder corresponds to a "good" partition for some L, then

$$H(X^N | S^K, Z^N) < \log L ,$$

and (3.2) yields

$$\Delta \geq N - \mu - \log L . \tag{3.3}$$

At the conclusion of this section we will prove the following proposition about the existence of "good" partitions. This will lead us directly to Theorem 2.2.

Lemma 3.1: Let K, N, μ be such that

$$N - \mu - K < 0 . \tag{3.4}$$

Then, there exists a "good" partition (with parameters K, N, μ) provided

$$L > \frac{2N + K + 2 \log e}{K + \mu - N} . \tag{3.5}$$

Now let R, α, ϵ, N_0 be given as in the hypothesis of Theorem 2.2. Then, using $2 \log e \leq 3$, we write for $N \geq 1$,

$$\frac{N + K + 2 \log e}{K + \mu - N} \leq \frac{1 + R + 3}{\alpha - (1 - R)} \triangleq B < \infty .$$

Thus there exists a "good" partition with $L \leq B + 1$, and we conclude from (3.3) that there exists a code with $\Delta/K \geq (1 - \alpha)/R - \dfrac{\log(B + 1)}{RN}$. If we choose $N \geq N_0, \, \epsilon R / \log(B + 1)$, the existence of this code establishes Theorem 2.2. It remains to prove Lemma 3.1.

Proof of Lemma 3.1: Let $\{A_m\}, 1 \leq m \leq 2^K$, be a partition of $\{0, 1\}^N$, where $|A_m| = 2^{N-K}$. Let $\Psi(A_1, ..., A_{2^K}) = 0$ or 1 according as $\{A_m\}$ is "good" or not. We write

$$\Psi(A_1, ..., A_{2^K}) \leq \sum_{m=1}^{2^K} \sum_z \phi(A_m, z) , \tag{3.6}$$

where the inner sum is taken over all $z \in \{0, 1, ?\}^N$ with exactly $N - \mu$ '?'s, and $\phi(A_m, z) = 1$ if

$$\text{card } \{x \in A_m : z \text{ is consistent with } x\} \geq L ,$$

and $\phi(A_m, z) = 0$ otherwise.

We now choose the partition at random with uniform distribution on the set of partitions of $\{0, 1\}^N$ into 2^K classes of equal size. The expectation $E \Psi$, satisfies

$$E \Psi \leq \sum_m \sum_z E \Phi(A_m, z) . \tag{3.7}$$

The expectation in the right member of (3.7) is taken, as indicated, with z held fixed. Let us define the following quantities.

$$Q(z) = \{x \subseteq \{0, 1\}^N : x \text{ is consistent with } z\} ,$$
$$n_1 = |Q(z)| = 2^{N - \mu} , \tag{3.8}$$
$$n = |\{0, 1\}^N| = 2^N ,$$
$$r = |A_m| = 2^{N - K} .$$

We now compute $E \Phi(A_m, z)$. The r members of A_m are chosen at random from $\{0, 1\}^N$ (without replacement). The probability that exactly ℓ members of A_m belong to $Q(z)$ is

$$\frac{\binom{n_1}{\ell}\binom{n - n_1}{r - \ell}}{\binom{n}{r}} \triangleq \pi_\ell .$$

To see this, observe that there are $\binom{n}{r}$ ways of choosing the set A_m. The ℓ members of A_m which belong to $Q(z)$ can be chosen in $\binom{n_1}{\ell}$ ways, and the remaining $(r - \ell)$ members of A_m can be chosen from the complement of $Q(z)$ in $\binom{n - n_1}{r - \ell}$ ways.

Now

$$\pi_\ell = \frac{\binom{n_1}{\ell}\binom{n - n_1}{r - \ell}}{\binom{n}{r}} \leq \frac{\binom{n_1}{\ell}\binom{n}{r - \ell}}{\binom{n}{r}} .$$

Also, using $\binom{n_1}{\ell} \leq n_1^\ell / \ell!$, and

$$\frac{\binom{n}{r-\ell}}{\binom{n}{r}} = \frac{n!}{(n-r+\ell)!(r-\ell)!} \cdot \frac{r!(n-r)!}{n!}$$

$$= \frac{r(r-1)(r-2)...(r-\ell+1)}{(n+\ell-r)(n+\ell-r-1)...(n-r+1)} \le \frac{r^\ell}{(n-r)^\ell} = \frac{(r/n)^\ell}{(1-r/n)^\ell},$$

we have

$$\pi_\ell \le \frac{(n_1 r/n)^\ell}{\ell!(1-r/n)^\ell},$$

Thus

$$E\Phi(A_m, z) = \sum_{\ell-L}^{2^{N-K}} \pi_\ell \le \sum_{\ell-L}^\infty \frac{(n_1 r/n)^\ell}{\ell!(1-r/n)^\ell}.$$

Using (3.8), we have $(n_1 r/n) = 2^{N-\mu-K}$, $(1-r/n) \ge 1/2$, so that

$$E\Phi(A_m, z) \le \sum_{\ell-L}^\infty 2^{(N-\mu-K)\ell} \frac{2^\ell}{\ell!}$$

$$\le 2^{(N-\mu-K)L} \sum_{\ell-0}^\infty \frac{2^\ell}{\ell!} = 2^{(N-\mu-K)L} e^2.$$

Substituting into (3.7) we have

$$E\Psi \le \sum_m \sum_z 2^{(N-\mu-K)L+2\log e}$$

$$\le 2^{(N-\mu-K)L+2\log e+K+2N}.$$

If L satisfies (3.5), then $E\Psi < 1$. Since Ψ is integer valued, there must exist a particular partition, say $\{A_m^*\}$ such that $\Psi(A_1^*,...,A_{2^K}^*) = 0$. This is our "good" partition.

4. Group Codes and Theorem 2.3

In Sections 2 and 3, we discussed how to construct encoder/decoders based on a partition $\{A_m\}$ of $\{0,1\}^N$. In this section we consider the special case where the partition $\{A_m\}$ is defined by a group code and its cosets.

Let H be a $K \times N$ parity-check matrix, which we assume has rank K. Let the partition $\{A_m\}$, $1 \leq m \leq 2^K$, be the code defined by H and its cosets. Thus $|A_m| = 2^{N-K}$, for $1 \leq m \leq 2^K$. To encode message $\mathbf{s} = (s_1,..., s_K)$, the encoder makes a random selection of one of the 2^{N-K} members of the A_m corresponding to $\mathbf{s}$. This is equivalent to letting $\mathbf{X}^N$ be a random choice from the 2^{N-K} solutions of

$$H\mathbf{X}^t = \mathbf{s}^t , \tag{4.1}$$

where $\dagger$ denotes matrix transpose. Note that, since $\mathbf{S}$ is uniformly distributed on $\{0, 1\}^K$, $\mathbf{X}^N$ is uniformly distributed on $\{0, 1\}^N$, and its coordinates $X_1, X_2,..., X_N$ are i.i.d. uniform binary random variables.

The decoder observes $\mathbf{X}^N$ and computes $H\mathbf{X}^t$, which is the message. Thus $P_e = 0$. We now show how to compute Δ in terms of certain distance-like properties of the parity check matrix.

Definition: Let $C_1, C_2,..., C_N$ be the columns of H (C_n is a K-vector). Let $S \subseteq \{1, 2,..., N\}$ and define $D(S)$ to be the dimension of the subspace spanned by $\{C_n\}, n \in S$. For a given $K \times N$ parity check matrix H, define for $0 \leq \mu \leq N$,

$$D^*(\mu) = \min_{|S|=N-\mu} D(S) . \tag{4.2}$$

We now state

Lemma 4.1: Let $D^*(\mu)$ correspond to the $K \times N$ parity-check matrix H. Let w, w' be the minimum weight of the code and dual code, respectively defined by H. Then (1) for $N-w+1 \leq \mu \leq N, D^*(\mu) = N-\mu$; (2) for $0 \leq \mu \leq w'-1, D^*(\mu) = K$.

Proof: Assertion (1) follows immediately on observing that all sets of $w-1$ columns of H are linearly independent. Thus $D(S) = |S|$, for $|S| \leq w-1$. If $N-w+1 \leq \mu \leq N$, then $N-\mu \leq w-1$, so that

$$D^*(\mu) = \min_{|S|=N-\mu} D(S) = N-\mu ,$$

which is assertion (1).

Now assertion (2) states that all submatrices $\hat{H} = (C_{i_1} C_{i_2}..., C_{i_q})$ of H have rank K when $q \geq N - w' + 1$. To establish this assertion assume that rank $\hat{H} < K$. Then there exists a set of linear row manipulations which transform $\hat{H}$ into a matrix with a row of 0's. These identical row manipulations will transform H into a matrix for which a row as weight $\leq N - q$. Since the dual code is the row space of H, $N - q \geq w'$ or $q \leq N - w'$, establishing assertion (2).

We now give

Lemma 4.2: When an encoder/decoder is constructed to correspond to the parity check matrix H, then

$$\Delta = D^{*}(\mu) . \tag{4.3}$$

Proof: Let S, X, Z correspond to an encoder/decoder with parameters K, N, Δ $(P_e = 0)$, derived as discussed above, from a parity-check matrix $H = (C_1,..., C_N)$. Since $P_e = 0$, and X^N is uniformly distributed on $\{0, 1\}^N$, Eq. (3.2) applies. Thus Lemma 4.2 will be established when we show that

$$H(X^N | S^K, Z^N) = N - \mu - D^{*}(\mu) . \tag{4.4}$$

Now suppose that $S^K = s$ and $Z^N = z$. Without loss of generality, assume that the last μ coordinates of z are copies of the corresponding coordinates of X. Thus, given $S^K = s, Z^N = z$, the remaining unknown coordinates of X are precisely the solutions for $x_1,..., x_{N-\mu}$ of

$$\sum_{n=1}^{N-\mu} C_n x_n = s' + \sum_{n=N-\mu+1}^{N} C_n x_n \triangleq \alpha . \tag{4.5}$$

Since the number of solutions is $N - \mu - \text{rank} (C_1,..., C_{N-\mu})$, and given $S = s, Z = z$ all these solutions are equally likely, (4.4) follows. Hence the lemma.

Before continuing with the proof of Theorem 2.3, we digress to apply Lemma 4.2 in an example. Let $K = 4, N = 8$, and construct an encoder/decoder using the self-dual Hamming code with block length 8 and 4 information and 4 check digits. Then $w = w' = 4$, so that

$$\Delta = D^*(\mu) = \begin{cases} 4 = K, & 0 \le \mu \le 3, \\ 3, & \mu = 4, \\ N - \mu, & 5 \le \mu \le 8. \end{cases}$$

Thus the encoder/decoder is optimal for all μ except $\mu = 4$, when Δ is but one bit less than ideal.

We will establish Theorem 2.3 via a random code argument. Towards this end, we establish the following lemmas.

Lemma 4.3: Let $1 \le m \le n$ and let the $m \times n$ matrix A over $GF(2)$ be chosen at random with uniform distribution on the set of 2^{mn} binary $m \times n$ matrices. Then, for $1 \le L \le m$,

$$Pr\{\text{rank } A < m - L\} \le 2^{-(L+1)(n-m)+n}$$

Proof: Let us choose the n columns of A sequentially and independently. Let $d(j)$ be the dimension of the linear space spanned by the first j columns. Suppose that $d(j) = k \le m$. With probability 2^{k-m}, $d(j+1) = k$; and with probability $(1-2^{k-m})$, $d(j+1) = k+1$. This sequential choice of the columns is modelled by the Markov chain of Figure 2.

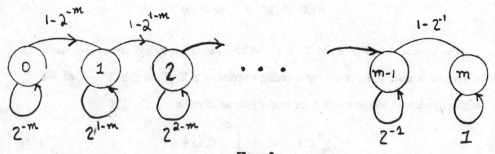

Figure 2

Begin at state 0. With each choice of a column, advance one state if and only if this choice increases the dimension of the space spanned by the columns chosen so far. The rank of the matrix A is $d(n)$, and is equal to the state at which we find ourselves after all n columns are chosen. Let $\Gamma(k)$ denote the set of paths π which start at state 0 and terminate at state k ($0 \le k \le m$). Then

$$Pr\ \{\text{rank }A < m-L\} = \sum_{k=0}^{m-L-1}\ \sum_{\pi \in \Gamma(k)} Pr\ \{\pi\}\ . \tag{4.6}$$

Now let the path $\pi \in \Gamma(k)$. This path contains exactly $n-k$ self-loops, each of which has probability $\leq 2^{-m+k}$. Thus, for $\pi \in \Gamma(k)$,

$$Pr\ \{\pi\} \leq 2^{(-m+k)(n-k)}\ .$$

Also since $|\Gamma(k)| = \binom{n}{k}$, eq. (4.6) yields

$$Pr\ \{\text{rank }A < m-L\} \leq \sum_{k=0}^{m-L-1} \binom{n}{k} 2^{-(m-k)(n-k)}\ .$$

Since the exponent is non-decreasing in k $(k \leq m \leq n)$, we have

$$Pr\ \{\text{rank }A < m-L\} \leq \sum_{k=0}^{m-L-1} \binom{n}{k} 2^{-(L+1)(n-m+L+1)}$$

$$\leq 2^n 2^{-(L+1)(n-m)}\ ,$$

which is Lemma 4.3.

Lemma 4.4: Let $1 \leq m \leq n$, and let the $m \times n$ matrix A over $GF(2)$ be chosen at random with uniform distribution on the set of 2^{mn} binary $m \times n$ matrices. Then

$$Pr\{\text{rank }A = m\} = \prod_{j=0}^{m-1} (1 - 2^{j-n})$$

$$\geq \exp\left\{\frac{-m\,2^{m-1-n}}{1-2^{m-1-n}}\right\} \geq (1 - \frac{m\,2^{m-1-n}}{1-2^{m-1-n}})\ .$$

Proof: Choose the rows of A sequentially. As in the proof of Lemma 4.3, the probability that the dimension of the space spanned by the first j rows is equal to j is

$$(1-2^{-n})(1-2^{-n+1})...(1-2^{-n+j-1})\ .$$

The rest of the lemma follows from $\ln(1-u) \geq -u/(1-u)$ and $e^{-u} \geq 1-u$.

We now turn to Theorem 2.3. Let $R > 0$ be given and held fixed. We will show that $\delta = 1$, $\alpha = 1-R$ is achievable, and the remainder of the theorem will follow from Theorem 2.4. Let $\epsilon > 0$

be arbitrary. We will show that there exists an encoder/decoder with parameters N, $K = RN$, $\mu = (1-R-\epsilon)N$, $\Delta \geq K-L$, provided that

$$L \geq 3/\epsilon. \tag{4.7}$$

We proceed as follows. Let H be a $K \times N$ parity-check matrix, and let L satisfy (4.7). Let $D^*(\mu)$ correspond to H, and define

$$\Psi(H) = \begin{cases} 1, & D^*(\mu) < K-L \text{ or } \text{rank}(H) < K, \\ 0, & \text{otherwise}. \end{cases} \tag{4.8}$$

We must show that there exists an H with $\Phi(H) = 0$. We can write

$$\Psi(H) \leq \sum_{\substack{S \subseteq \{1,...,N\} \\ |S| = \mu}} \Phi(H,S) + \Phi_0(H), \tag{4.9a}$$

where

$$\Phi_0(H) = \begin{cases} 1, & \text{rank}(H) < K, \\ 0, & \text{otherwise}. \end{cases} \tag{4.9b}$$

and

$$\Phi(H,S) = \begin{cases} 1, & D(S) < K-L, \\ 0, & \text{otherwise}. \end{cases} \tag{4.9c}$$

If we choose $H = (C_1,..., C_N)$ at random with uniform distribution on the set of $2^{K \cdot N}$ binary $K \times N$ matrices, (4.9) yields

$$E\Psi(H) \leq \sum_{|S|=\mu} E\Phi(H,S) + E\Phi_0(H). \tag{4.10}$$

Let S, with $|S| = \mu$, be arbitrary, and let $A = (C_{i_1}C_{i_2}..C_{i_{N-\mu}})$, where $S = \{i_1,..., i_{N-\mu}\}$. Then $\Phi(H,S) = 1$ if and only if $\text{rank} A < K-L$, and $E\Phi(H,S) = Pr\{\text{rank} A < K-L\}$. We can apply Lemma 4.3 with $n = N-\mu$, $m = K$, to obtain

$$E\Phi(H,S) \leq 2^{-(L+1)(N-\mu-K)+(N-\mu)}. \tag{4.11}$$

Similarly we can apply Lemma 4.4 with $A = H$, $n = N$, $m = K$, to obtain

$$E\,\Phi_0(H) \le \frac{K2^{K-N-1}}{1-2^{K-N-1}} \le \frac{K2^{K-N}}{1-2^{K-N}} . \tag{4.12}$$

Since there are no more than 2^N subsets S, (4.10)-(4.12) yields (using $N-\mu-K = \epsilon N$, $K = RN$)

$$E\,\Psi(H) \le 2^{-(L+1)(N-\mu-K)+(N-\mu)+N} + \frac{K2^{K-N}}{1-2^{K-N}}$$

$$\le 2^{-L\epsilon N+2N} + \frac{RN2^{-(1-R)N}}{1-2^{-(1-R)N}} . \tag{4.13}$$

Since L satisfies (4.7), the first term in the right member of (4.13) $< 1/2$. Furthermore, for N sufficiently large, the second term in (4.13) is also $< 1/2$. Thus

$$E\,\Psi(H) < 1 .$$

Since $\Psi(\cdot)$ is an integer valued function, there must exist a $K \times N$ matrix H_0 such that $\Psi(H_0) = 0$; so that rank $H_0 = K$ and for the corresponding encoder/decoder, $\Delta = D^*(\mu) \ge K-L$, which is what we set out to prove. Thus we have shown that for arbitrary $R > 0$, the triples (R, α, δ) where $\alpha \le 1-R$, $\delta \le 1$, are achievable, completing the proof of Theorem 2.4.

REFERENCES

[1] Wyner, A. D., "The Wire-Tap Channel," *BSTJ*, **54**, pp. 1355-1387, October 1975.

[2] Gallager, R. G., *Information Theory and Reliable Communication*, Wiley, New York, 1968.

[3] Ozarow, L. H., and A. D. Wyner, "Wire-Tap Channel II", to appear in AT&T Bell Laboratories Technical Journal.

EQUIVOCATIONS FOR HOMOPHONIC CIPHERS

Andrea Sgarro

Istituto di Matematica

Università di Trieste

34100 Trieste (Italy)

Abstract. Substitution ciphers can be quite weak when the probability
distribution of the message letters is distinctly non-uniform. A time-
honoured solution to remove this weakness is to "split" each high-pro
bability letter into a number of "homophones" and use a substitution
cipher for the resulting extended alphabet. Here the performance of a
homophonic cipher is studied from a Shannon-theoretic point of view.
The key and message equivocations (conditional entropies given the in
tercepted cryptogram) are computed both for finite-length messages and
"very long" messages. The results obtained are strictly related to
those found by Blom and Dunham for substitution ciphers. The key space
of a homophonic cipher is specified carefully, so as to avoid misunder
standings which appear to have occurred on this subject.

Work done within the research program of GNIM-CNR.

1. <u>Introduction</u>.

Simple substitution ciphers (s.s.c.'s) are probably the oldest type of ciphers put to work, and yet they are still in good health in the form of (individually weak) components of (hopefully good) complex cipher system (e.g. the Data Encryption Standard). The key of a s.s.c. is a permutation of the message-letter alphabet $A=\{a_1,a_2,\ldots,a_s\}$, $s\geq 2$; once a key is chosen each single letter output by the message source is replaced by its substitute. S.s.c.'s have been studied rather deeply in the last decade; cf. /1, 2, 3/; in the first two papers the strength of a cipher is assessed by evaluating the equivocations ("uncertainties") on side of the spy who has intercepted a cryptogram (key equivocation or message equivocation, according whether the spy is interested in finding out the correct key or the correct message); in /3/ the error probabilities are evaluated when the spy uses the best statistical pro cedure to recover the correct key or message from the intercepted cryp togram. Further work on s.s.c.'s is done in /4/, which contains a discus sion on the role of the "Shannon-theoretic approach" to cryptography and, more generally, on the relevance of purely statistical cryptogra phic models.

A s.s.c. is very weak when the probability distribution (p.d.) P ruling the message source, which we assume to be memoryless and station ary, is distinctly non-uniform; ($P=\{p_1,p_2,\ldots,p_s\}$, $p_i>0$, $\sum p_i=1$; un specified summations are meant over all values of the index). A time-honoured solution to remove this weakness is to make use of a cryptogram-letter alphabet C of size t larger than s, the size of the message-let ter alphabet; for example, the letters of C might be the ordered couples of message letters. Then any large probability p_i can be broken down by associating to the corresponding letter a_i many possible cryptogram substitutes, t_i, say: each time a_i occurs in the message one of these is chosen at random and actually substituted for a_i. The resulting ci pher is called a <u>homophonic cipher</u> (or, rather, a simple, that is single-letter, homophonic cipher; a more formal description is given below). Homophonic ciphers, which are a generalization of s.s.c.'s (refound for $t_i=1$, $1\leq i\leq s$, that is, essentially, when $A=C$) have been recently studied in /5/. In this paper we take the equivocation approach to assess the strength of homophonic ciphers, thereby generalizing the work done in /1/ and /2/ for s.s.c.'s.

A mathematical tool which we shall use is the notion of an <u>exact type</u>. Consider A^n, the set of the s^n sequences of length n built over A; an exact type (of order n over A) is a subset of A^n made up of a sequence together with all its permutations. Of course, if $(n_1, n_2, \ldots, n_s)$ is the composition of any of these sequences, n_i being the number of occurrences of letter a_i, $(n_i \geq 0, \sum n_i = n)$, the size of the corresponding exact type is the multinomial coefficient $n!/n_1!n_2! \ldots n_s!$. Statisticians will recognize here an obvious link with the notion of sufficient statistic; we simply stress that the sequences of an exact type have all the same probability. A powerful technique based on asymptotically tight bounds for the size and the probability of exact types has been made popular in the circle of information theorists by the fundamental textbook /6/. This technique is applied in /3/ to the error probability approach to s.s.c.'s and in/7/ to the equivocation approach to the same ciphers.

Before going to mathematical developments, we have to give a more formal description of a homophonic cipher. Two alphabets, A and $C = \{c_1, c_2, \ldots, c_t\}$, $t \geq s$, are given, C being the cryptogram-letter alphabet; also s integers are given which sum to t: $t_1, t_2, \ldots, t_s$, $t_i \geq 1$, $\sum t_i = t$. A key is specified by giving s disjoint subsets of C of size $t_1, t_2, \ldots$ and t_s, respectively. Each time letter a_i is output by the message source, one of the t_i letters of the i-th subset is chosen with (conditional) probability $1/t_i$ and is substituted for letter a_i. The knowledge of the key is enough to reconstruct the correct message from any of the possible corresponding cryptograms. Before transmission begins, a key is chosen at random and independently of the message output by the source; the key is communicated to the legitimate receiver via a secure special channel; ("at random" means that the key is a uniform random variable, or r.v., over the set of all possible keys). The cryptogram is derived from the message and sent over the normal unsafe channel, where it is intercepted by the spy.

We find it convenient to give a more careful description of the key of a homophonic cipher. Such a key can be represented by a sequence in

A^t with composition $(t_1, t_2, \ldots, t_s)$ (alphabet letter a_i occurs t_i times, $\sum t_i = t$). The meaning of this representation is that if a_i is the j-th component of the sequence, then c_j is a possible substitute for a_i under the given key. We shall actually identify each possible key with the corresponding sequence in A^t, so that for us the set of keys will be an exact type in A^t. Clearly the number of all keys for a homo phonic cipher $(A, C; t_1, t_2, \ldots, t_s)$ is the multinomial coefficient $t!/t_1! t_2! \ldots t_s!$

As shown in /5/, a homophonic cipher induces a s.s.c. in a quite natural way. A presentation follows which suits our purposes. Take an extended alphabet $U = \{u_1, u_2, \ldots, u_t\}$ with the same size t as the crypto gram alphabet C; although it would not be restrictive to take $U = C$ we keep them separate for the sake of notational clarity. The elements of U will be denoted at places by symbols like a_{ij}, $1 \leq i \leq s$, $1 \leq j \leq t_i$; in other words in U each message letter a_i is duplicated t_i times: the letters a_{ij} are called the homophones of letter a_i. No ambiguity should result from the fact that the letters of U have two names, e.g. u_1 is also called a_{ij} for some i and some j. A dummy memoryless and stationary source with alphabet U, called the extended source, is now built in the following way: each time the message source outputs a letter a_i, $1 \leq i \leq s$, the extended source outputs a letter a_{ij}, $1 \leq j \leq t_i$, with (conditional) uniform probability; then the (absolute) probability of letter a_{ij} is p_i/t_i. We call P* the p.d. made up of these probabilities; P* rules the statistical behaviour of the extended source. Note also that the output of the message source is a deterministic function of the simultaneous output of the extended source.

Take now the s.s.c. (U, C), whose t! keys can be represented (cf. above) as sequences in U^t where each letter occurs exactly once. To any key for (U, C) we can associate a key for $(A, C; t_1, t_2, \ldots, t_s)$ replacing each a_{ij} in the U^t sequence by a_i. A homophonic cipher can be put to work in the following way, which is readily shown to be equivalent to the original description. A key is chosen for the s.s.c. (U, C). The message source is set going together with the extended source syncronized with it. The key is applied to the extended message to give the cryptogram. From this key a "short" key can be obtained as above to be communicated

to the legitimate receiver. The "short" key applied to the cryptogram
does not allow the legitimate receiver to recover the extended message,
but it does allow him to recover the original message over A, which is
what he needs to know. The key for the s.s.c. (U, C) is a uniform r.v.
$K*$ with $t!$ values, while the "short" key for the homophonic cipher is
a uniform r.v. K with $t!/t_1!t_2!...t_s!$ values. We shall also write
$K*=(K, J)$, where J is again a uniform r.v., this time with $t_1!t_2!...t_s!$
values, which identifies $K*$ once K is known; note that K and J are
independent, as it appears from the values of the respective probabili
ties. K, J and $K*$ will be referred to as the <u>actual key</u>, the <u>supplemen</u>
<u>tary key</u> and the <u>extended key</u>. We stress the distinction between K and
$K*$: it is the former which is the "true" key of the homophonic cipher,
while $K*$ contains the "redundant information" J; cf. the discussion
at the end of section 4.

Let the r.v.'s M_n, U_n and C_n denote the first n letters output by
the message source, the extended source and the cryptogram source,
respectively. Some relations for relevant entropies are already im
plicit from the foregoing: $H(M_n|U_n)=0$, $H(M_n|K,C_n)=0$, $H(M_n|K)=H(M_n|K*)=$
$=H(M_n)$, $H(K,J)=H(K)+H(J)$, etc. In the following section we shall assess
the performance of a homophonic cipher by evaluating its equivocations.

2. The equivocations.

The equivocations of interest are: $H(K|C_n)$, the key equivocation,
$H(K|M_n,C_n)$, the key appearance equivocation, interesting in the case
of "chosen plain-text attacks", and, most important of the three,
$H(M_n|C_n)$, the message equivocation. Since (U, C) is a s.s.c. we already
know a lot about its own equivocations, $H(K*|C_n)$, $H(K*|U_n,C_n)$ and
$H(U_n|C_n)$; cf. /1,2,7/. Only the first will be needed. Its value is

$$(1) \qquad H(K*|C_n) = \log A + \sum_r P*^n(T_r) \log \frac{\sum_Q Q^n(\underline{u}_r)}{P*^n(\underline{u}_r)}$$

where $A=A(P,t_1,t_2,...,t_s)=d_1!d_2!...d_h!$, h being the number of distinct
probabilities appearing in $P*$, the first d_1 times, the second d_2 times,

etc.; $d_1+d_2+\ldots+d_h=t$; the r-summation is extended over all exact types T_r in U^n; $\underline{u}_r$ is any sequence in T_r; the Q-summation is extended over all p.d.'s Q which are obtained by permuting the components of P*, including P* itself: these p.d.'s are only $t!/A$ owing to ties in the components of P*; of course Q^n is the memoryless extension of Q over U^n. The term log A is a constant; it is certainly non-zero for a strict̲ ly homophonic cipher (one for which $t \geq s+1$). The second term goes to zero and it is exactly zero when P* is uniform and A achieves its maximum value log t! (cf. also section 3).

Some simple identities are helpful. For example: $H(K^*|C_n)=H(K,J|C_n)=$ $=H(K|C_n)+H(J|K,C_n)$; as $H(K^*|C_n)$ is known, it will be enough to compute $H(J|K,C_n)$ and then use:

(2) $\qquad H(K|C_n) = H(K^*|C_n) - H(J|K,C_n)$

Further: $H(K,M_n|C_n)=H(K|C_n)+H(M_n|K,C_n)=H(K|C_n)$ because M_n is a deter̲ ministic function of key and cryptogram; and also $H(K,M_n|C_n)=H(M_n|C_n)+$ $+H(K|M_n,C_n)$. By comparision (cf. /2/):

(3) $\qquad H(M_n|C_n) = H(K|C_n) - H(K|M_n,C_n)$

Now we deal directly with $H(J|K,C_n)$ and $H(K|M_n,C_n)$

Theorem 1.

$$H(J|K,C_n) = H(J) = \sum \log t_i!$$

Proof. Assume (k,j) and (k,i) are two extended keys for the s.s.c. (U, C) with the same actual key k. With respect to each other these keys only scramble equiprobable homophones relative to the same message-alphabet letter. Therefore, for any cryptogram $\underline{c}$, $\text{Prob}\{C_n=\underline{c}|K^*=(k,j)\}=$ $\text{Prob}\{C_n=\underline{c}|K^*=(k,i)\}$. This means that C_n and J are conditionally indepen̲ dent given K, and therefore $H(J|K,C_n)=H(J|K)$. But we already know that J and K are independent, so $H(J|K)=H(J)$. To complete the theorem, recall that J is a uniform r.v. with $t_1!t_2!\ldots t_s!$ values. QED

In theorem 2 the r-summation is extended over all exact types T_r in U^n and $h_i=h_i(T_r)$ is the number of distinct letters a_{ij} which do not occur in the sequences of T_r, $1 \leq i \leq s$, $0 \leq h_i \leq t_i$, $\sum h_i \leq t-1$.

Theorem 2.

$$H(K|M_n,C_n) = \sum_r P*^n(T_r) \left[\log(\sum h_i)! - \sum \log h_i!\right]$$

The non-zero terms in the summation are those for which at least two h_i's are positive, that is, at least two unequivalent homophones are missing.

Proof. Assume that a couple message-cryptogram, $\underline{m}$, $\underline{c}$, is given of positive joint probability. Let us try to reconstruct the key, which is
a sequence in A^t: e.g., if a_i and c_i are letters in the same position
in the given couple, a_i is the j-th component of the key. However, gaps
might be left because letter a_i might not occur, or it might occur in
correspondence to less than t_i distinct cryptogram letters. If h_i denotes
the number of times letter a_i is missing in the partially reconstructed
key, the number of possible keys left is $(\sum h_i)!/h_1!h_2!...h_s!$. Because
of symmetry each such key has the same conditional probability, and so

$$H(K|M_n=\underline{m},\ C_n=\underline{c}) = \log(\textstyle\sum h_i)! - \sum \log h_i!$$

Note that the integers h_i can be computed directly from the extended sequence $\underline{u}$ output by the extended source, h_i being simply the number of
distinct letters a_{ij} which do not occur in $\underline{u}$. Note also that the set
of $\underline{u}$-sequences with given integers h_i is a union of exact types. Therefore, grouping together $\underline{u}$-sequences in the same type:

$$H(K|M_n,C_n) = \sum_r P^{*n}(T_r)\left[\log(\textstyle\sum h_i)! - \sum \log h_i!\right]$$

Clearly the quantity inside square brackets is zero only when at most
one h_i is positive. This proves the last statement in the theorem. QED

Note that the key-appearance equivocation is zero only for $t=2$,
and then the homophonic cipher is also a s.s.c. $(s=t=2)$.

Now (1), (2) and (3), together with the two theorems, give the
exact values of the equivocations $H(K|C_n)$, $H(K|M_n,C_n)$ and $H(M_n|C_n)$.

3.Asymptotic results.

It will be shown now that the key-appearance equivocation
$H(K|M_n,C_n)$ becomes negligible with increasing message length n.
Therefore for large n's both $H(K|C_n)$ and $H(M_n|C_n)$ are approximately
equal to the constant term

$$\log A - \sum \log t_i!$$

("unremovable uncertainty"); cf. also the observations below formula
(1). Note that the factors d_j which appear in the definition of A (cf.
again (1)) are made up summing one or more t_i's bacause equivalent

homophones have all the same probability. So, as it should be, the unremovable uncertainty is non-negative. It is zero when only equiva lent homophones are equiprobable (the numbers d_j and the numbers t_i are the same up to their order).

Now we investigate the behaviour of $H(K|M_n,C_n)$ as a function of n. To extend the validity of theorem 3 below to the case t=2, when $H(K|M_n,C_n)$ is zero, we adopt the (natural) convention that a term of the form $\exp\{n[-\infty+\varepsilon_n]\}$, $\lim_n \varepsilon_n=0$, means zero. We set
$$D=D(P,t_1,t_2,\ldots,t_s)=\min_{1\le i<f\le s}(p_i/t_i+p_f/t_f)\le 1 \quad \text{(D=1 if and only if s=t=2).}$$
Theorem 3.
$$H(K|M_n,C_n) = \exp\{n[\log(1-D)+\varepsilon_n]\}, \quad \lim_n \varepsilon_n=0$$
Proof. Take t≥3. We start with the obvious bounds:
$$\log 2 \sum_r P*^n(T_r) \le H(K|M_n,C_n) \le \log(t-1)! \sum_r P*^n(T_r)$$
the summations being restricted to types which correspond to non-zero terms in the summation of theorem 2. Denote by $M(i,j;f,g)$ the set of U^n-sequences such that a_{ij} and a_{fg} are missing in them; $1\le i<f\le s$, $1\le j\le t_i$, $1\le g\le t_j$; $M(i,j;f,g)$ is a union of exact types. One has:
$$\sum_r P*^n(T_r) = P*^n(\bigcup_r T_r) = P*^n(\bigcup M(i,j;f,g));$$
the sets in the latter union, which is not disjoint, are no more than $\binom{s}{2}[(t-1)!]^2$. One has also:
$$P*^n(M(i,1;f,1)) = P*^n(M(i,j;f,g)) = (1-p_{i1}^*-p_{f1}^*)^n = (1-p_i/t_i-p_f/t_f)^n$$
Assume that D is achieved, say, for i=1, f=2. Then:
$$P*^n(M(1,1;2,1) = (1-D)^n \ge P*^n(M(i,j;f,g))$$
and the bounds for $H(K|M_n,C_n)$ can be relaxed to:
$$\log 2 (1-D)^n \le H(K|M_n,C_n) \le \binom{s}{2}[(t-1)!]^2 \log(t-1)!(1-D)^n$$
This ends the proof. QED

Observe that the proof of the theorem implicitly gives asymptotically tight bounds for ε_n which are independent of P (t≥3):
$$n^{-1}\log\log 2 \le \varepsilon_n \le n^{-1}\log\{\binom{s}{2}[(t-1)!]^2 \log(t-1)!\}$$

The parameter D which appears in theorem 3 does not coincide with the corresponding parameter obtained by Dunham /2/ for the key appear ance equivocation $H(K*|U_n,C_n)$ of the s.s.c. (U, C). He proved that $H(K*|U_n,C_n)=\exp\{n[\log(1-\hat{D})+\hat{\varepsilon}_n]\}$, $\lim_n \hat{\varepsilon}_n=0$, where $\hat{D}$ is the sum of the two smallest components of P*; since these components may be relative to equivalent homophones, one has $\hat{D}\le D$.

The asymptotic behaviour of $H(K^*|C_n)$ is well-known (cf. /1,7/), and so we have all we need. We shall write down explicitly the asymptotic formula for $H(M_n|C_n)$, the most complex (and in a way the most relevant) of the three equivocations:

$$H(M_n|C_n) = H(K|C_n) - H(K|M_n,C_n) = \log A - \sum \log t_i !$$
$$+ \exp\{n[\log(1-B)+\delta_n]\} - \exp\{n[\log(1-D)+\varepsilon_n]\}, \lim_n \delta_n = \lim_n \varepsilon_n = 0$$

$B=B(P,t_1,t_2,\ldots,t_s)$ is defined as $\min(\sqrt{p_i/t_i}-\sqrt{p_j/t_j})^2$, the minimum being taken over all distinct P^*-probabilities, $1 \le i, j \le s$, $p_i/t_i \ne p_j/t_j$; B is set equal to 1 for P^* uniform , so that the corresponding exponential term becomes zero. Of course, if $B<D$, one can write the message equivocation as:

$$H(M_n|C_n) = \log A - \sum \log t_i ! + \exp\{n[\log(1-B)+\delta_n']\}, \lim_n \delta_n'=0,$$

while, if $B>D$, one has instead:

$$H(M_n|C_n) = \log A - \sum \log t_i ! - \exp\{n[\log(1-D)+\varepsilon_n']\}, \lim_n \varepsilon_n'=0.$$

4. Final remarks.

At the beginning of section 3 it has already been pointed out that, for large message lengths n, both the key and the message equivocation are approximately equal to the "unremovable uncertainty" $\log A-\sum \log t_i! \ge 0$. The condition for the unremovable uncertainty to be zero is that only equivalent homophones are equiprobable. An advantageous situation is found instead when P^* is uniform (all the homophones are equiprobable); then the homophonic cipher is said to be matched (cf. /5/) and the unremovable uncertainty equals $\log t!-\sum \log (tp_i)!$, tp_i integers. In principle, when the components of P, the p.d. of the message source, are rational, one can always achieve P^* uniform for a sufficiently large cryptogram-alphabet size t; however, alphabet extension runs counter to complexity requirements (it also leads to the growth of the term $\sum \log t_i!$). Once a threshold $T>s$ is given, always assuming that the cipher will be used for a long time, one should judiciously choose the parameters $t,t_1,t_2,\ldots,t_s$, $s \le t \le T$, in order to achieve a large unremovable uncertainty. Were it not so, the performances of the homophonic cipher might even be worse than those of the s.s.c. (A, A) for the same message source, for example when equal probabilities p_i and p_j are split to give distinct probabilities p_i/t_i and p_j/t_j, so that letters a_i and a_j become statistically distinguishable only in the case of the homophonic cipher.

Assume a cipher system (K,M_n,C_n) is given. We call two keys k and h <u>indistinguishable</u> when $T_k^{-1}(\underline{c})=T_h^{-1}(\underline{c})$ for all cryptograms $\underline{c}$, of any length $(T_k^{-1}(\cdot)$ denotes the cryptogram-to-message transformation determined by key k; note that in the case of a homophonic cipher the message-to-cryptogram transformation $T_k(\cdot)$ is not deterministically defined). The spy (and also the authorized receiver, for that) is interested only in the equivalence class of indistinguishable keys to which k belongs, rather than in k itself. Sometimes the extended key, K*, has been misinterpreted as the "true" key of a (strictly) homophonic cipher. If one neglects the fact that distinct extended keys with the same actual key are indistinguishable, one is lead to give over-optimistic evaluations of the cipher's performances. In particular, the negative term $-\sum \log t_i!$, which appears both in key and message equivocation, is ignored. Our description of the various types of "keys" in terms of suitable exact types makes it transparent why the "true" key of a homophonic cipher is precisely the actual key, K. Distinct actual keys are always distinguishable.

References.

/1/ R.J. Blom, "Bounds on key equivocation for simple substitution ciphers",IEEE Trans. Inform. Theory, vol. IT-25, pp. 8-18,Jan 1979.
/2/ J.G. Dunham, "Bounds on message equivocation for simple substitution ciphers", IEEE Trans. Inform. Theory, vol. IT-26, pp. 522-527, Sept. 1980
/3/ A. Sgarro, " Error probabilities for simple substitution ciphers", IEEE Trans. Inform. Theory, vol. IT-29, pp. 190-198, March 1983
/4/ A. Sgarro, "Exponential-type parameters and substitution ciphers"; a preliminary version called "Remarks on substitution ciphers" has been presented at the 1983 IEEE ISIT held at St. Jovite (Quebec)

/5/ J.G. Dunham, "Substitution and transposition ciphers", submitted

/6/ I. Csiszar and J. Körner, Information theory: Coding theorems for discrete memoryless systems. New York: Academic, 1981

/7/ A. Sgarro, "Simple substitution ciphers", in Secure digital communications, ed. by G. Longo. CISM Courses and Lectures No. 279, Springer-Verlag, Wien-New York, pp. 61-77, 1983

PROPAGATION CHARACTERISTICS OF THE DES

Marc Davio[1,3], Yvo Desmedt[2] and Jean-Jacques Quisquater[1]

[1] Philips Research Laboratory,
Avenue Van Becelaere, 2,
B-1170 Brussels, Belgium;

[2] Katholieke Universiteit Leuven,
Laboratorium ESAT,
Kardinaal Mercierlaan, 94,
B-3030 Heverlee, Belgium;

[3] Université Catholique de Louvain,
Batiment Maxwell,
Place du Levant, 3,
B-1348 Louvain-la-Neuve, Belgium.

Abstract. New general properties in the S–boxes were found. Techniques and theorems are presented which allow to evaluate the non-substitution effect in f and the key clustering in DES. Examples are given. Its importance related to the security of DES is discussed.

1. Introduction

The Data Encryption Standard, in short DES, is NBS' cryptographic standard for the protection of commercial computer data (FIPS, 1977). Since 1981, it is also an ANSI standard. In the meantime, it is called DEA by ANSI (ANSI, 1980), and it is yet in use in many industrial applications. Recently it has been proposed to become an ISO (International Standard Organisation) standard under the name of DEA1 (ISO, 1983).

There exist several reasons to explore the internal structure and the functional properties in the DES.

1. It can help to understand the DES. Remark that the design criteria of the DES are still classified (Bernhard, 1982).

2. A better understanding of DES can have two consequences: on the one hand, the detection of weaknesses can speed up a cryptanalysis attack. The detection of inherent strengths will on the other hand simplify the task of defining new standards when they will be needed.

3. The structure can be used in order to simplify or to speed up hardware and software implementations.

To achieve the proposed goals, we first overview (Section 2) the technical description of the DES as it appeared in the NBS publication. The reader, who knows the NBS description of the DES, can skip Section 2. As the full description of all functions in the DES is very long, we refer to the literature (FIPS, 1977; Konheim, 1981; Meyer & Matyas, 1982; Morris & al., 1977) for these functions.

In Section 3 general properties in the S-boxes and in the key scheduling will be combined.

We analyze several functions in order to combine their properties. As a consequence this can be used to find different cleartexts for which the function f in DES gives the same output. These results can also be used to analyze the key clustering in DES. It means to verify if there exists different keys which gave for most cleartext the same ciphertext.

2. NBS description of the DES

The DES algorithm, as described by NBS (FIPS, 1977), consists of three fundamental parts: *enciphering computation, calculation of $f(R, K)$* and *key schedule calculation.* They are are briefly described below.

First observe that several boxes are used in the DES algorithm. It would be a too long explanation to give the details of all these boxes; it can be found in the NBS description. The kind of boxes (e.g. permutation) will be mentioned.

Remark that the input numbering starts from 0 for some boxes and from 1 for the other ones.

In the *enciphering computation*, the input is first permuted by a fixed permutation IP from 64 bits into 64 bits. The result is split up into the 32 left bits and the 32 right bits, respectively, this is L and R. Then a bitwise modulo 2 sum of the left part L and of $f(R, K)$ is carried out. After this transformation, the left and right 32 bit blocks are interchanged. Observe that the encryption operation continues iteratively for 16 steps or rounds. In the last round, no interchange of the last obtained left and right parts is performed; the output is obtained by applying the inverse of the initial permutation IP to the result of the 16-th round.

In the *calculation of* $f(R, K)$ the 32 right bits are first expanded to 48 bits in the box E, by taking some input bits twice, others only once. Then a bitwise modulo 2 sum of the expanded right bits and of 48 key bits is performed. These 48 key bits are obtained in the *key schedule calculation*, which will be explained later on. The results of the modulo 2 sum go to the eight S-boxes; each of these boxes has six inputs and four outputs. The S-boxes are nonlinear functions. The output bits of the S-boxes are permuted in the box P.

Let us finally describe the *key schedule calculation*. The key consists of 64 bits, of which 56 bits only are used. The other 8 bits are not used in the algorithm. The selection of the 56 bits is performed in box PC_1, together with a permutation. The result is split into two 28 bit words C and D. To obtain the 48 key bits for each iteration, the words C and D are first left shifted once or twice. A selection and a permutation PC_2 are then applied to the result. The output of PC_2 is the 48 bit key word which is used in $f(R, K)$. An additional table tells the user how many shifts must be performed to obtain the next 48 key bits of the key for the following round. DES can be used in four modes (FIPS, 1980; Konheim, 1981).

3. Propagation characteristics

We first analyze the new properties, which we observed in the expansion phase, the S-boxes and the key scheduling. We combine our results with older ones (Davio & al., 1983) in order to discuss the non-substitution property in f and the key clustering in DES. Let us first discuss the importance of the fact that f is not a substitution and of the key clustering.

3.1. The importance of the propagation characteristics

If f is not a substitution the cardinality of the image play an important role in the evaluation of the security of DES. Indeed if the image of f contains only one element, the DES is completely linear. More generally, if the cardinality of the image of f is small DES may be insecure.

If there exist a key clustering in DES, it may be that for a large amount of cleartexts the effect of modifying the key on a special way do not affect the ciphertext. If this is true for DES it simplifies enormously an exhaustive attack.

3.2. The expansion phase

The expansion phase plays a very important role in this section.

3.3. The S-boxes

3.3.1. An introduction

We observed several new properties in the S-boxes. Most of our new properties are valid for all S-boxes and are consequently called "general properties". In the following sections some of these properties are used in order to analyze in which measure f is not a substitution and to analyze the key clustering. We did not apply all general properties in the following sections; perhaps in the future one will be able to explain why the S-boxes have these properties or to use them in some deeper analysis of DES.

Two kinds of properties are discussed. In the first kind we fix some input bits of the S-boxes (1,2, ... , or 5 of the 6 possible bits). We are interested in what changes are propagated at the output and how? E.g. for the output one can wonder if the 4 output bits are always be distinct if we change the non-fixed input bits, or if for some inputs the output is not affected. Secondly we discuss how the output changes if we complement some input bits of the S-boxes.

We number the inputs of one S-box by $abcdef$. We number the S-boxes from 1 to 8 and denote them as S_i. Remark that representations of the S-boxes, other than in the NBS norm, may be useful (Davio & al., 1983).

3.3.2. Properties of the S-boxes if some input bits are fixed

The inputs a, b, e, f of the S-boxes play a special role in DES. Indeed one half of the message input bits in each round influences two S-boxes. These bits will go to the mentioned input bits. These bits will play an important role in the analysis of the non-substitution property of the function f in DES. The next properties draw special attention to the mentioned input bits. The following properties can however easily be generalized. One can easily verify them using a computer program.

We number the properties by a double numbering technique, such that it is easy to refer to them.

1. The observed properties hold for all S-boxes. We analyze if the output

of an S-box can or cannot change if one modifies the inputs of an S-box in the following way:

(a) fix the inputs e and f

(b) one is allowed to change c and d to an arbitrary value c' and d'

(c) one changes the inputs a and b as described in the properties

1.1. $\neg(\forall c, d, c', d', e, f : S_i(0, 0, c, d, e, f) \neq S_i(1, 0, c', d', e, f))$

1.2. $\neg(\forall c, d, c', d', e, f : S_i(0, 1, c, d, e, f) \neq S_i(1, 1, c', d', e, f))$

1.3. $\forall c, d, c', d', e, f : S_i(0, 1, c, d, e, f) \neq S_i(1, 0, c', d', e, f)$

1.4. $\forall c, d, c', d', e, f : S_i(0, 0, c, d, e, f) \neq S_i(1, 1, c', d', e, f)$

Remark: One can wonder why e.g. $S_i(0, 0, c, d, e, f)$ was not compared with $S_i(0, 1, c', d', e, f)$. This property is already known, indeed it is known (Konheim, 1981) that each row (see NBS notation) of each S-box is a permutation. In other words $S_i(a, b, c, d, e, f) \neq S_i(a, b', c', d', e', f)$ independent of $b, c, d, e, b', c', d', e'$. The properties described here are in fact a generalization of it.

2. The observed properties hold for all S-boxes, except property 2.4. We analyze if the output of an S-box can or cannot change if one modifies the inputs of an S-box in the following way:

(a) fix the inputs a and b

(b) one is allowed to change c and d to an arbitrary value c' and d'

(c) one changes the inputs e and f as described in the properties

2.1. $\neg(\forall a, b, c, d, c', d' : S_i(a, b, c, d, 0, 0) \neq S_i(a, b, c', d', 0, 1))$

2.2. $\neg(\forall a, b, c, d, c', d' : S_i(a, b, c, d, 1, 0) \neq S_i(a, b, c', d', 1, 1))$

2.3. $\neg(\forall a, b, c, d, c', d' : S_i(a, b, c, d, 0, 1) \neq S_i(a, b, c', d', 1, 0))$

2.4. If $i \neq 4$ then:
$\neg(\forall a, b, c, d, c', d' : S_i(a, b, c, d, 0, 0) \neq S_i(a, b, c', d', 1, 1))$
If $i = 4$ then:
$\forall a, b, c, d, c', d' : S_i(a, b, c, d, 0, 0) \neq S_i(a, b, c', d', 1, 1)$

Remark: The properties 1.3 and 1.4 change if one also allows that the input e changes to the input e'. Then it will be possible to find identical outputs for special inputs. A similar remark is true for property 2.4 ($i = 4$) if one allows that the input b changes.

3.3.3. Complementation properties of the S-boxes

A well known (Hellman & al., 1976) property for the S-boxes is that if one complements one input of an S-box at least two output bits will change. We analyze the effect of complementing two input bits, while leaving the other ones unchanged. It is evident that one can easily generalize our properties for the case that 3 or more bits are complemented. The first aim was to observe whether it is possible to maintain a constant output if only two bits are complemented. First observe that in order to maintain a fixed output one has to complement bit a or f, otherwise we conflict with the permutation property of the "rows" in the S-boxes. For special $abcdef$ inputs the output of an S-box remains unchanged if one complements two of the input bits.

It is remarkable that only if ab is complemented we have that the output for all S-boxes changes. This is however very easy to prove starting from our properties 1.3 and 1.4 of the previous section. In a similar way one can use properties 2.3 and 2.4 to prove the above conclusion for complementing ef.

3.4. The key scheduling

In our analysis of the key clustering we used in detail the key scheduling in DES. The ideas of Neutjens on the key scheduling in DES were very useful in this context (Neutjens, 1983). We now overview them and explain them systematically. We number the 56 key bits from 1 to 64 as in the NBS description (FIPS, 1977).

First of all remark that after PC_1 one can split up the key scheduling in DES completely in two parts. PC_2 does not affect this decomposition (Davio & al., 1983). As a consequence of this decomposition, one can separate for one round in DES the selection of the key bits which will influence the first 4 S-boxes and the last 4 S-boxes. Let us now construct the equivalent scheme. All used notations, e.g. the registers C and D, originate from the NBS representation of DES.

We represent the register content of C by $(c_1, c_2, ..., c_{28})$ and that of D by $(d_1, d_2, ..., d_{28})$. Mostly in the key scheduling the registers C and D are shifted *twice* to obtain the K_i of the ith round, e.g. $(c_1, c_2, c_3, ..., c_{28})$ is transformed into $(c_3, c_4, c_5, ..., c_2)$. This can now be reformulated for the C register as *one* shift on the following *two* registers $(c_1, c_3, c_5, ..., c_{27})$ and $(c_2, c_4, c_6, ..., c_{28})$. We call them respectively the odd and the even registers. One can then realize the key scheduling with 4 registers instead of two, which shift only once when in the NBS the registers shift two times. This reorganization affects the PC_2.

One has now still to discuss what happens if only one shift is performed on C and D as in the iterations $1, 2, 9$ and 16 using our equivalent representation. The first shift in the first iteration can be realized together with PC_1. In the other situations we interchange the content of the odd and the even registers, by performing first a shift on the old content of the odd register and no shift on that of the even register. We then change also the name of each register: odd becomes even, even becomes odd. Indeed $(c_1, c_3, c_5, ..., c_{27})$, $(c_2, c_4, c_6, ..., c_{28})$ is then changed into $(c_2, c_4, c_6, ..., c_{28})$, $(c_3, c_5, c_7, ..., c_1)$. One can verify that previous operations are identical to one shift in the NBS notation.

The register D can be treated in a similar way. Remark that it is more difficult to perform one shift in the NBS representation. However we are able to see better which bits of the key affect a particular S-box.

Let us now apply all the described properties.

3.5. The function f is not one-to-one for fixed K

Let us remember here that f consists of the expansion box E, of the EXOR-ing with the key bits, of the S-boxes and of the permutation P. It has sometimes been wondered whether the f function is by itself a substitution. The answer to that question is negative (Davio & al., 1983; Konheim, 1981). A more systematic discussion is given in this section.

We will now use the properties described in section 3.3.2. to demonstrate how they can be used in the analysis of the non-substitution of f. Evidently we assume that the key K is fixed. We analyze which bits of the message part R (see NBS notation) one must change in order to maintain the same output of f. We will progressively increase the number of changed bits. First we only change the inputs (or message part of the input) of one, two and then three S-boxes and generalize afterwards. We will mostly use the new as well as the well known (Hellman & al., 1976; Konheim, 1981) general properties of the S-boxes, together with the structure of E (Davio & al., 1983).

Theorem 1 : If for fixed key, one only changes the input of one S-box the output of f will change.
Proof : In order not to affect the inputs of the other S-boxes one can only change the inputs c and d. However if a and f are not changed an S-box forms a substitution.
◇

Theorem 2 : If for fixed key, one changes only the input of two neighbourhood S-boxes the output of f will change.
Proof : Let us call the two affected S-boxes, S_i and S_{i+1} and let us define S_9 as being S_1 (this again shows that it can be more interesting to start the numbering from 0, see (Davio & al., 1983)). In order not to affect the input of S_{i-1} the inputs a and b of S_i may not change and similarly for the inputs e and f of S_{i+1} in order not to affect the inputs of S_{i+2}. In order not to conflict with the permutation properties of the "rows" of the S-boxes and using the previous remark, at least f in S_i must be complemented in order to maintain a fixed output. A similar remark is true for the input a of S_{i+1}. As consequence of the

expansion box E a complementation of the input e (respectively f) of S_i is equal to a complementation of the input of a (respectively b) of S_{i+1}. *So in order to produce a same output we have at least to complement a and b in S_{i+1}.* Remark that the inputs c and d in S_{i+1} do not influence the proof. In other words even if one additionally changes the inputs c and d in S_{i+1} or do not, the output of S_{i+1} will change, by virtue of property 1.3 and 1.4 of the S-boxes.

◇

Theorem 3 : If for fixed key, one changes only the input of three neighbourhood S-boxes the output of f will for some inputs remain identical, only if one complements at least the inputs a, b and e of the middle of the three S-boxes, the input c or d of the last S-box and if one does not complement the input f of the middle of the three S-boxes.

Proof : We call the three S-boxes S_{i-1}, S_i and S_{i+1}, S_0 is equal to S_8 and S_9 equals S_1. The proof is for a large part similar to that of theorem 2. Let us first give the similar part of the proof.

We must fix the inputs a and b of S_{i-1}, and e and f of S_{i+1}. The input f of S_{i-1} must be complemented and similarly for the input a of S_{i+1}. This last condition is equivalent to saying that the inputs b and e of S_i must be complemented. Now we apply the consequences of theorem 2 to continue our proof.

If a and b are both complemented in S_{i+1}, the output will change (see proof of theorem 2 or properties 1.3 and 1.4 of the S-boxes). Using previous observations the input b in S_{i+1} may not be complemented, or equivalently f in S_i. At this moment we already know that for S_i b and e must be complemented and f may not. Because each row in the S-boxes is a permutation and because f may not be complemented in S_i, a must be complemented in S_i. Remark that in fact one must still complement bit c or d in S_{i+1}. Indeed if only one input bit in an S-box is complemented, the output changes.

◇

We have now proven the theorem. It is now very easy to generate in a systematic way several examples for which the function f remains constant even if some bits are complemented.

3.6. The key clustering

We analyze the clustering from the point of view that DES contains j rounds, where j is between 1 and 16. The input for these j rounds is fixed, while we complement or change some bits of the key. So if we speak now about an input of an S-box, this input is related to a modification of the key.

We first prove some general theorems for the key clustering, and afterwards we give some examples.

3.6.1. A general approach

First of all for a fixed input the permutation IP has no influence on the key clustering. We can start the analysis from L_s and R_s. This means that if we are interested in a complete DES analysis $s = 0$ and $j = 16$. Let us now apply DES with the key K and K' and call the subkeys K_1 till K_{16} and K'_1 till K'_{16}. The key K will produce some L and R register content, while K' produces L' and R'. The effect of the first of the j rounds is that in the case we use the key K we have $L_{s+1} = R_s$ and $R_{s+1} = L_s \oplus f(R_s, K_{s+1})$. Applying the key K' we obtain $L'_{s+1} = R_s$ and $R'_{s+1} = L_s \oplus f(R_s, K'_{s+1})$. After t rounds we obtain using key K the register contents $L_{s+t} = R_{s+t-1}$ and $R_{s+t} = L_{s+t-1} \oplus f(R_{s+t-1}, K_{s+t})$. Using the key K' we have: $L'_{s+t} = R'_{s+t-1}$ and $R'_{s+t} = L'_{s+t-1} \oplus f(R'_{s+t-1}, K'_{s+t})$. Remark that in general by changing the key the contents of the registers L and R change too. Let us now call $H_{s+t} = f(R_{s+t-1}, K_{s+t}) \oplus f(R'_{s+t-1}, K'_{s+t})$. It is now easy to see using (Davio & al., 1983) that the global effect of a change in the key has no final effect on the ciphertext if the two following conditions are satisfied together.

1. $H_{s+1} \oplus H_{s+3} \oplus H_{s+5} \oplus ... \oplus H_t = 0$, where $t = s + j$ if j is odd, else $t = s + j - 1$.

2. $H_{s+2} \oplus H_{s+4} \oplus H_{s+6} \oplus ... \oplus H_u = 0$, where $u = s + j$ if j is even, else $u = s + j - 1$.

Using previous conditions it is now easy to analyze the conditions necessary for key clustering if one analyzes only 1, 2, 3 or 4 rounds. The analyze of more rounds seems to be more difficult if one want to have a complete analysis.

3.6.2. An analysis of the key clustering in a DES with 1 or 2,3 or 4 rounds

In the case 1 round is considered we must have $H_{s+1} = 0$. This means $f(R_s, K_{s+1}) = f(R_s, K'_{s+1})$. Using previous knowledge on the S-boxes this means that the input of an S-box is not changed or that at least two bits change. It is very easy to generate several examples for this case. Using the fact that E is an expansion of 32 bits to 48 bits and its structure (Davio & al., 1983) and because PC_2 selects only 48 bits out of the 56 bits of the key we have the following result. *For each (cleartext,ciphertext) pair in a one round DES there exist exactly 2^{24} keys which generate the same (cleartext,ciphertext) pair starting from a fixed cleartext.* If a similar remark remains true for the complete DES algorithm (16 rounds), DES is very easy to break using a simplified exhaustive attack. Let us therefore start to analyze more rounds.

In the case 2 rounds are considered we must have $H_{s+1} = 0$ and $H_{s+2} = 0$. This means $f(R_s, K_{s+1}) = f(R_s, K'_{s+1})$, as in previous case, and additionally $f(R_{s+1}, K_{s+1}) = f(R_{s+1}, K'_{s+1})$, because from the first equality we have $R'_{s+1} =$

R_{s+1}. Remark that the S-boxes must satisfy similar conditions as in the case only one round was considered. However to satisfy it for the two rounds together we must take the key scheduling in DES into consideration. We now give a simple example of it.

Example 1. If one complements the bits 3 and 44 (in the NBS notation) of any 64 bit key, then there exists 6.2^{59} pairs of (cleartext, ciphertext) which remain identical during round 1 and 2 in DES. In other words, 1/5 of all pairs (cleartext, ciphertext) are not affected by the complementation of 2 bits of the key, during round 1 and 2.

Let us now explain what happens and how one can calculate the (cleartext,ciphertext) pairs. The bits 3 and 44 go both after the key scheduling in the first round to S_3 and become there the inputs a and e. We can verify that for 6 out of 32 (or 12 out of 64) possible inputs a complementation of a and e in S_3 does not change the output. This means that the possible inputs for which the above property is true are restricted from 2^{64} to 6.2^{59}. The cardinality of the set of cleartext for which the explained clustering is satisfied is independent of the used key. However the set of cleartext for which the above clusering changes if other keys are considered. This is a consequence of the structure in the function f. Now we must still analyze which restrictions the second round imposes on the possible cleartext. The analysis in this example is straightforward because the key bits 3 and 44 are not selected in the second round, so no extra condition is necessary.

One may observe that we were lucky in the construction of the previous example. First the non-selection of the key bits in the second iteration seems to be lucky. Secondly example 1 is only valid for rounds 1 and 2 in DES. In the following example the reader can observe that similar examples can be given for all rounds and that the non-selection of some key bits is not necessary.

Example 2. This example is true for most consecutive rounds. As a consequence of the ideas of Neutjens on the key scheduling (see section 3.4), two consecutive rounds can mostly be analyzed systematically (Neutjens, 1983). This is true if one uses two shifts in the key scheduling, as represented by the NBS, to move to the next round. This means the rounds 2-3, 3-4, 4-5, 5-6, 6-7, 7-8, 9-10, 10-11, 11-12, 12-13, 13-14 and 14-15. In order not to affect the generality we will use a more general descriptions of the property. If one complements the two bits of the key which will "arrive" in S-box 4 at locations a and e during the first of the two above rounds, then for every key there exists 36.2^{54} (or about 1/29 of all possible) pairs (cleartext, ciphertext) which remain identical during two consecutive rounds mentioned earlier. This can be analyzed using the ideas of Neutjens on the key scheduling (Neutjens, 1983) and using our properties of the S-boxes.

Let us now consider three consecutive rounds. First more restrictions on the cleartext are then imposed in order not to affect the ciphertext if one modify the key. This is a consequence of the key scheduling. However the output of the function f in the first and last (of the three) rounds must no longer be constant (see section 3.6.1). This relaxes the imposed restrictions. Let us give a short example to illustrate it. Remark the authors have yet generalized this example, but this is out of the scope of this paper.

Example 3 The three consecutive rounds may be 2-3-4, 3-4-5, 4-5-6, 5-6-7, 6-7-8, 9-10-11, 10-11-12, 11-12-13, 12-13-14 and 13-14-15. Hereto one complements (e.g.) three bits of the key. In our example the key bits must "arrive" at location a and d in S-box 8 in the first round (of the three consecutive) and at location d in S-box 4. We impose the extra condition that bit 15 of the output of f (after the box P) must be complemented in the first and last round as consequence of the modification of the key. We can then analyze that for 50% of the keys and for 1 on 1024 cleartext, the ciphertext is not modified. For the other 50% of the keys this happens for 1 on 4096 cleartexts.

4. Conclusions and perspectives

A cryptographic system can only be considered secure if a small modification in the cleartext and/or in the key strongly affect on a non-linear way the ciphertext. We described techniques for analyzing this constraint for DES. We found that if DES had only a few rounds it would be a bad system. Our analysis demonstrated at the same time that the known probalistic test done on DES are insufficient to conclude that the scheme is secure. Were it possible to work out on a 16-round DES the techniques presented here one could possibly prove the so often alleged existence of a key clustering in DES.

References
[1] ANSI X3.92-1981, "Data Encryption Algorithm,", American National Standards Institute, New York (December 31, 1980).

[2] R. Bernhard, "Breaching system security," *Spectrum*, vol. 19, pp. 24-31 (1982).

[3] M. Davio, Y. Desmedt, M. Fosseprez, R. Govaerts, J. Hulsbosch, P. Neutjens, P. Piret, J.-J. Quisquater, J. Vandewalle & P. Wouters, "Analytical characteristics of the DES," pp. 171-202, in *Advance in cryptology: Proceedings of Crypto 83*, ed. D. L. Chaum, Plenum Press, New York (1984).

[4] FIPS publication 46, "Data Encryption Standard," Federal Information Processing Standard, National Bureau of Standards, U.S. Department of Commerce, Washington, D.C. (January 1977).

[5] FIPS publication 81, "DES modes of operation," Federal Information Processing Standard, National Bureau of Standards, U.S. Department of Commerce, Washington, D.C. (1980).

[6] M. E. Hellman, R. Merkle, R. Schroeppel, L. Washington, W. Diffie, S. Pohlig & P. Schweitzer, "Results of an initial attempt to cryptanalyze the NBS data encryption standard," SEL 76-042, Stanford University (1976).

[7] ISO/DP 8227 (Draft proposal), "Data encipherment, specification of algorithm DEA1," (1983).

[8] A. G. Konheim, *Cryptography: A primer*, J. Wiley, New York (1981).

[9] C. H. Meyer & S. M. Matyas, *Cryptography: A new dimension in computer data security*, J. Wiley, New York (1982).

[10] R. Morris, N. J. A. Sloane & A. D Wyner, "Assessment of the NBS proposed Data Encryption Standard," *Cryptologia*, vol. 1, pp. 301-306 (1977).

[11] P. Neutjens, "Diepere inzichten en eenvoudige hardware voor DES cryptografisch algoritme aan de hand van equivalente strukturen," Final work, Katholieke Universiteit Leuven, Belgium (1983).

LINEAR CIPHERS AND RANDOM SEQUENCE GENERATORS
WITH MULTIPLE CLOCKS

James L. Massey and Rainer A. Rueppel
Insitute of Telecommunications
Swiss Federal Institute of Technology
8092 Zurich, Switzerland

Abstract

A construction is given for perfect linear ciphers that uses two digits
of key per plaintext digit, which appears to be the minimum possible.
The construction utilizes two shift-registers that are clocked at different speeds, and suggests a new type of random sequence generator in
which two linear feedback shift-registers are clocked at different
speeds and their contents combined at the lower clock rate. The effects
of variable speed are analyzed, and the linear complexity of the sequences produced by such generators is determined.

1. Introduction

We begin this paper by considering how much key is required in a perfect linear cipher. We show in Section 2 that two digits of key per
plaintext digit suffice, and we conjecture that this much key is also
necessary. The perfect linear cipher constructed in Section 2 utilizes
two shift-registers that are clocked at different speed, a "trick" that
we have borrowed from convolutional coding lore.

The perfect linear ciphers of Section 2 suggest a promising structure
for random sequence generation, which we propose in Section 3, that
utilizes two linear feedback shift-registers (LFSR's) clocked at different speeds. In Section 4, we investigate analytically the effects of
such variable speed in LFSR's. These results are then used in Section 5
to determine the linear complexity of the sequences produced by the previously suggested random sequence generator. We close the paper with
some additional observations and suggestions for generalizations.

2. Perfect Linear Ciphers and Convolutional Codes

Suppose that one wishes to use a ciphering system of the additive type
in which the ciphertext digit y_j is determined by the plaintext digit
x_j in the manner (reminiscent of a stream cipher) that

$$y_j = x_j + z_j \qquad\qquad j = 0,1,2,\ldots \qquad\qquad (1)$$

where the digit z_j is determined in some prescribed manner by the key K
and the previous plaintext digits. [All digits and operations are assumed to be in F_q, the finite field of q elements, unless specified
otherwise.] Suppose further that, for whatever reason, one demands that
the enciphering be linear in the plaintext with memory M so that

$$z_j = \sum_{i=1}^{M} c_i(j,K)x_{j-i} \qquad\qquad j = 0,1,2,\ldots \qquad\qquad (2)$$

where the coefficients $c_j(j,K)$ depend both on the time instant j and
the key K. (We suppose that the initial conditions x_{-1}, x_{-2},...., x_{-M}
required in (2) are dummy plaintext digits that may be chosen as convenient.) Suppose finally we demand that the enciphering be perfect in
the sense that, for some appropriate probability measure over the keys,

one has, for every choice of β in F_q and every $j \geqslant 0$,

$$Pr(z_j = \beta \,|\, z_{j-1}, \ldots, z_0, x_{j-1}, \ldots, x_0, \ldots, x_{-M}) = \frac{1}{q}. \qquad (3)$$

In other words, we require that, for each allowable plaintext sequence, the <u>additive sequence</u> $z_0, z_1, z_2, \ldots$ be a completely random q-ary sequence.

From (2), it follows that

$$Pr(z_j = 0 \,|\, x_{j-1} = \ldots = x_{j-M} = 0) = 1 \qquad (4)$$

so that perfect secrecy as specified by (3) is impossible without some plaintext restriction. From (4), we see that the <u>least plaintext restriction</u> compatible with perfect secrecy in such a linear cipher is

$$[x_{j-1}, x_{j-2}, \ldots, x_{j-M}] \neq [0, 0, \ldots, 0], \qquad j = 0, 1, 2, \ldots \qquad (5)$$

which we hereafter assume to be the only restriction on the plaintext. [For q = 2 and M = 1, we see that (5) implies x_j = 1, all j, so that no interesting system is possible; for all M > 1, however, the plaintext restriction admits interesting systems.]

We first make the quite trivial observation that perfect linear ciphers exist for every M and every F_q. One can simply choose the coefficients $c_i(j,K)$ independently at random from a uniform distribution over F_q; the plaintext restriction (5) guarantees that one of the independent "key digits" will then appear with a non-zero multiplier on the right in (2) so that (3) will be satisfied. This perfect linear ciphering system, however, requires M digits of key for each digit of plaintext. This large key requirement appears quite unsatisfactory (particularly for large M as would be desirable to ease the restriction specified by (5)) when one reflects that a perfect one-time system (which is an additive cipher in which the additive sequence is itself the random key) requires only one digit of key for each digit of plaintext. The <u>question</u> we now pose is: What is the least amount of key (measured in digits of key per plaintext digit) required for a perfect linear cipher as specified by (1), (2) and (3) with the plaintext restriction (5) ? We now show that two digits of key per plaintext digit is always sufficient, and we conjecture that this much key is also necessary for all $M \geqslant 2$.

To prove our claim, we consider the specific linear cipher system shown in Fig. 1 consisting of a random key generator (whose outputs are independently chosen from a uniform distribution over F_q) that drives a shift-register that is clocked at a rate d times faster than the shift-register driven by the plaintext source.

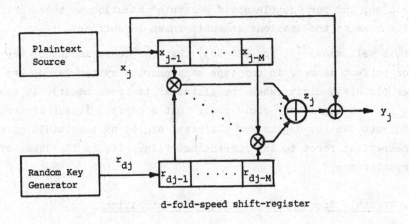

d-fold-speed shift-register

Fig. 1: A perfect linear cipher system, conjectured to use a minimum of random key digits when d = 2.

To show that (3) holds for the system of Fig. 1 under the restriction (5), consider at time j the <u>leftmost</u> <u>non-zero</u> digit in the upper shift-register, say x_{j-i}. From Fig. 1, we see that its multiplying coefficient $c_i(j,K)$ is just the random digit r_{dj-i}. But, provided that d > 1 so that the lower shift-register is shifting faster to the right than is the upper one, it follows because r_{dj-i} has just come abreast of x_{j-i} at time j that this same random digit at earlier time instants could have multiplied only digits that are to the <u>left</u> of x_{j-i} in the upper shift-register. But, as all these latter digits must be zeroes, it follows that the earlier generated digits $z_{j-1}, z_{j-2}, \ldots$ are all independent of r_{dj-i}; hence the fact that $x_{j-i} \, r_{dj-i}$ with $x_{j-i} \neq 0$ is a component of z_j implies that (3) is satisfied, as was to be shown. The linear cipher

of Fig. 1 requires d digits of key per plaintext digit, and we have
shown it to be perfect for all d $\geqslant$ 2. The least key, of course, is used
when d = 2.

In fact, we have borrowed our answer to the linear cipher problem posed
above from our earlier solution [1, pp.19-21] to a problem in error-
correcting codes. The problem there was to find the smallest ensemble
of time-varying codes such that the codewords enjoy pairwise independence -- this coding problem is formally identical to the linear cipher
problem, and our "double speed ensemble" solution to this coding problem remains the smallest ensemble known to suffice.

It is well known [2, pp. 680-683] that the least amount of key required
for perfect secrecy in any type of ciphering system is one key digit
per plaintext digit (when the plaintext is irredundant). It would thus
be interesting if one could prove that a perfect linear cipher requires
at least two key digits per plaintext digit, as this would give some
theoretical force to the rubric that "linearity is the curse of the
cryptographer".

3. Variable Speed in Random Sequence Generation

A perfect secrecy system of the additive type is of course an ideal
random number generator, i.e., its additive sequence $z_0, z_1, z_2, \ldots$ is a
sequence of digits drawn independently at random from a uniform distribution over F_q. This suggests that the basic structure of Fig. 1 may
be of use in random sequence generation. For this purpose, it is natural
to replace the plaintext source of Fig. 1 by an M-stage linear feedback
shift-register (LFSR) started in some non-zero state, as this automatically enforces the "plaintext restriction" (5) as well as introduces
some element of pseudo-randomness. It is a natural next step to replace
the random key generator of Fig. 1 by a second LFSR of length L(L $\geqslant$ M),
also started in some non-zero state but clocked at a speed d times that
of the first LFSR to produce the pseudo-random sequence which further
"randomizes" the "plaintext" to produce the desired "random" sequence
$z_0, z_1, z_2, \ldots$ The resulting random sequence generator is shown in Fig. 2
Such a device might be used as a random number generator or as a key
stream generator in a conventional stream cipher.

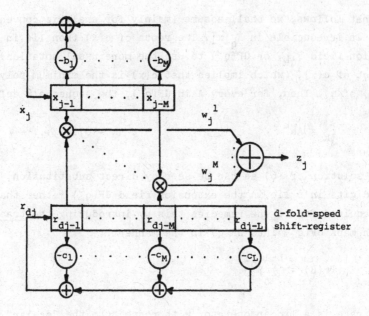

Fig. 2: A random sequence generator employing multiple speed
shift-registers.

In the following sections, we analyze the effect of the speed factor d
on the sequence produced by the generator of Fig. 2. Our interest is in
the new phenomena that result when the speed factor is treated as an
additional variable in shift-register sequence generation.

4. The Effects of Variable Speed

The sequence $\underset{\sim}{r} = r_0, r_1, r_2, \ldots$ of digits from F_q produced by the lower
LFSR in Fig. 2 satisfies the homogeneous linear recursion

$$r_k + c_1 r_{k-1} + \ldots + c_L r_{k-L} = 0 \qquad k = 0,1,2,\ldots \qquad (6)$$

(where k denotes the time instants of the high speed clock for this
LFSR) whose characteristic polynomial is

$$c(x) = x^L + c_1 x^{L-1} + \ldots + c_L. \qquad (7)$$

In what follows, we shall assume (mainly for analytic convenience) that $c(x)$ is irreducible in $F_q[x]$. The roots of $c(x)$ then lie in the extension field F_{q^L}, or $GF(q^L)$ to use the more usual notation. Let α be a root of $c(x)$, (which implies that $c(x)$ is the minimum polynomial over $GF(q)$ of α). Then, for every A in $GF(q^L)$, the sequence $\hat{\underset{\sim}{r}}$ defined by

$$\hat{r}_k = A\alpha^k \qquad\qquad k = 0,1,2,\ldots \qquad\qquad (8)$$

is a solution of (6) as can be seen by direct substitution; however, the digits in $\hat{\underset{\sim}{r}}$ lie in the extension field $GF(q^L)$ rather than in $GF(q)$ as required for $\underset{\sim}{r}$. One remedies this by introducing the trace operator which maps $GF(q^L)$ into $GF(q)$ in the manner

$$Tr(\beta) = \sum_{i=0}^{L-1} \beta^{q^i}. \qquad\qquad\qquad (9)$$

The trace is a linear operator with respect to the "scalar" field $GF(q)$, i.e., for a_1 and a_2 in $GF(q)$ and for β_1 and β_2 in $GF(q^L)$,

$$Tr(a_1\beta_1 + a_2\beta_2) = a_1\ Tr(\beta_1) + a_2\ Tr(\beta_2). \qquad\qquad (10)$$

It now follows from (10) that the $GF(q)$ sequence $\underset{\sim}{r}$ with

$$r_k = Tr(A\alpha^k) \qquad\qquad k = 0,1,2,\ldots \qquad\qquad (11)$$

is a solution of (6) for every A in $GF(q^L)$. In fact, since each choice of A gives a different sequence $\underset{\sim}{r}$, (11) gives all the $GF(q)$ solutions of (6), as there are exactly q^L such solutions corresponding to the q^L choices of the initial conditions $r_{-1}, r_{-2},\ldots,r_{-L}$ in (6). It is convenient to associate A with the corresponding initial state $[r_{-1}, r_{-2},\ldots, r_{-L}]$ of the lower LFSR in Fig. 2.

Now consider the sequence

$$\underset{\sim}{r}[d] = r_0, r_d, r_{2d}, \ldots \qquad\qquad\qquad (12)$$

that appears at the input tap of the lower LFSR at the (slower) clock

times j of the surrounding logic. We see from (12) that $r[d]$ is just
the d-th decimation of the sequence r and moreover that

$$(r[d])_j = r_{dj} = \text{Tr}(A\alpha^{dj}). \tag{13}$$

It is illuminating to write (13) as

$$(r[d])_j = \text{Tr}(A\beta^j) \tag{14a}$$

where $\qquad \beta = \alpha^d.$ $\hspace{5cm}$ (14b)

The period T of the original LFSR is the smallest positive integer t
such that $c(x)$ divides x^t-1; equivalently, T is the multiplicative order
of α in $GF(q^L)$ and thus $\alpha, \alpha^2, .., \alpha^{T-1}, \alpha^T = 1$ are the T distinct roots
of x^T-1. By proper choice of d ($1 \leqslant d \leqslant T$), it follows from (14b) that
β can be selected as any root of x^T-1 and hence as a root of any monic
irreducible polynomial that divides x^T-1. The multiplicative order of β
in $GF(q^L)$ will be $T/\gcd(d,T)$. The following proposition, which is a mild
generalization of known results for the decimation of maximal-length
sequences, is now an immediate consequence of (14a).

Proposition 1: If the sequence r produced by an L-stage LFSR of period T,
whose characteristic polynomial is the minimum polynomial over $GF(q)$ of
the element α, is observed at intervals of d clock cycles, then this
observed sequence $r[d]$ is a sequence producible by the LFSR of period
$T/\gcd(d,T)$, whose characteristic polynomial is the minimum polynomial
over $GF(q)$ of $\beta = \alpha^d$. Moreover, every sequence producible by the latter
LFSR is equal to $r[d]$ for some choice of the initial state of the former
LFSR.

The practical import of Proposition 1 is that multiple-clocking provides
a means by which a single LFSR with fixed feedback connections can be
used to generate sequences that appear to be produced by LFSR's with
different feedback connections. We shall call the LFSR, whose charac-
teristic polynomial is the minimum polynomial over $GF(q)$ of $\beta = \alpha^d$, the
LFSR simulated by the LFSR, whose characteristic polynomial is the minimum polynomial over $GF(q)$ of α, when the latter LFSR is shifted at d
times the observation rate.

Now consider the sequence $r^i[d]$ observed in the i-th stage of the lower LFSR of Fig. 2 at the slower clock times j of the surrounding logic. Then

$$(r^i[d])_j = r_{dj-i} = Tr(A\alpha^{dj-i})$$

$$= Tr(A\alpha^{-i}\beta^j) \qquad (15)$$

where β is given by (14b). (Note that $r[d] = r^0[d]$.) From (15), we see that this sequence is again a sequence producible by the LFSR simulated by the faster-shifting LFSR. We now consider the relationship between the sequences observed in adjacent stages of the faster-shifting LFSR.

If $s = s_0, s_1, s_2, \ldots$ is any periodic sequence, we shall call the sequence $\theta^n s = s_n, s_{n+1}, s_{n+2}, \ldots$ the n-th phase of the sequence s. If s can be described as

$$s_j = Tr(C\gamma^j) \qquad\qquad j = 0,1,2,\ldots$$

then it follows that

$$(\theta^n s)_j = Tr(C\gamma^n\gamma^j) \qquad\qquad j = 0,1,2,\ldots \qquad (16)$$

so that the phase shift n can be read off by comparing the multipliers of γ^j in the trace descriptions.

In general, the sequences $r^i[d]$, for $i = 1,2,\ldots,L$, will not be phase shifts of one another; rather, they will be "cyclically distinct" sequences producible by the simulated LFSR. However, when gcd(d,T) = 1 so that the simulated and simulating LFSR's have the same period, the sequences $r^i[d]$ will be phase shifts of one another. To see this, we note that gcd(d,T) = 1 means that d has a multiplicative inverse e modulo T, i.e., there exists an integer e $(1 \leqslant e < T)$ such that

$$de = QT + 1$$

and hence

$$\beta^e = \alpha^{de} = \alpha^{QT+1} = \alpha. \qquad (17)$$

In this case, we can write (15) as

$$(r^i[d])_j = Tr(A\beta^{-ie}\beta^j) \qquad (18)$$

The following proposition now follows from (18) and (16).

Proposition 2: When $\gcd(d,T) = 1$, then the sequence $\underset{\sim}{r}^i[d]$ observed every d clock cycles in the i-th stage of an LFSR of length L and period T with an irreducible characteristic polynomial over GF(q) and non-zero initial loading is the e-th phase of the sequence $\underset{\sim}{r}^{i+1}[d]$ observed every d clock cycles in the (i+1)-st stage, where e ($1 \leqslant e < T$) is the multiplicative inverse of d modulo T.

The practical import of Proposition 2 is that <u>simulating an LFSR by multiple-clocking of another LFSR gives simultaneous access to widely separated phases of the sequence produced by the simulated LFSR</u>, <u>rather than only to consecutive phases</u> as when this sequece is produced by the actual LFSR being simulated.

Proposition 3: The sequences $\underset{\sim}{r}^i[d]$, (i = 1,2,..,L), described in Proposition 2 are linearly independent over GF(q).

To prove this propsition, it suffices to show that the initial constants $A\beta^{-ie}$ (i = 1,2,..,L) in the trace descriptions of the L sequences are linearly independent over GF(q). If not, there would exist a_i (i = 1, 2,..,L) in GF(q) not all zero such that $a_1\beta^{-e} + a_2\beta^{-2e} + \ldots + a_L\beta^{-Le} = 0$, and hence β^e would be the root of a non-zero polynomial over GF(q) with degree less than L. But this is impossible since $\beta^e = \alpha$ has a minimum polynomial of degree L.

The practical import of Proposition 3 is that any sequence producible by the simulated LFSR can be obtained by a linear combination of the contents of the faster-shifting LFSR taken at the slower observation times. But this is not too surprising since any such sequence could also be produced by linear combinations of the contents of the actual LFSR being simulated. It does show, however, that no flexibility is lost when the LFSR is simulated by a faster LFSR observed under a slower clock, rather than directly implemented.

5. Linear Complexity of the Random Sequence Generator

The <u>linear complexity</u> $\Lambda(\underset{\sim}{z})$ of a periodic sequence $\underset{\sim}{z}$ is the degree L of the characteristic polynomial of smallest degree among those LFSR's that produce the sequence $\underset{\sim}{z}$, i.e., the length of the shortest LFSR that produces $\underset{\sim}{z}$. Linear complexity is widely used in cryptographic analysis despite its limitations as a "true complexity" measure for sequences. We now compute the linear complexity of the sequence z produced by the generator of Fig. 2 when the two component LFSR's have irreducible characteristic polynomials and relatively prime lengths L and M.

As we shall be dealing with extensions $GF(q^n)$ of $GF(q)$ for different n, we shall denote the trace operator from $GF(q^n)$ to $GF(q)$ by T_n so that, for γ in $GF(q^n)$,

$$T_n(\gamma) = \sum_{i=0}^{n-1} \gamma^{q^i}. \tag{19}$$

We shall make key use of the following identity, which is of some independent interest.

Lemma 1: If γ and δ are in $GF(q^L)$ and $GF(q^M)$, respectively, where $gcd(L,M) = 1$, then

$$T_L(\gamma)T_M(\delta) = T_{LM}(\gamma\delta). \tag{20}$$

Note that $GF(q^L)$ and $GF(q^M)$ are both subfields of $GF(q^{LM})$ so that the product in (20) of $\gamma\delta$ is well-defined in $GF(q^{LM})$. To prove (20), we first note from (19) that

$$T_{LM}(\gamma\delta) = \sum_{i=0}^{LM-1} \gamma^{q^i} \delta^{q^i}. \tag{21}$$

Next, we observe that, because $\gamma \epsilon\ GF(q^L)$ and $\delta \epsilon\ GF(q^M)$,

$$\gamma^{q^i} = \gamma^{q^{i \bmod L}} \tag{22a}$$

and

$$\delta^{q^i} = \delta^{q^{i \bmod M}} \tag{22b}$$

where "i mod n" denotes the remainder when i is divided by n. Because $gcd(L,M) = 1$, the Chinese remainder theorem implies that (i mod L, i mod M) takes on each pair (j,k) with $0 \leqslant j < L$ and $0 \leqslant k < M$ exactly once as i ranges from 0 to LM-1. Thus (21) and (22) imply

$$T_{LM}(\gamma\delta) = \sum_{j=0}^{L-1} \sum_{k=0}^{M-1} \gamma^{q^j} \delta^{q^k}$$

$$= \sum_{j=0}^{L-1} \gamma^{q^j} \sum_{k=0}^{M-1} \delta^{q^k}$$

which we recognize now from (19) to be the desired identity (20).

The following result is proved in [3] and is a simple consequence of the fact that the degree of the minimum polynomial over GF(q) of γ is the least positive integer t such that $\gamma^{q^t} = \gamma$.

Lemma 2: If the minimum polynomials of β and γ over GF(q) have degrees L and M, respectively, and gcd(L,M) = 1, then the minimum polynomial of βγ over GF(q) has degree LM.

Now suppose that the characteristic polynomials c(x) and b(x) of the two LFSR's of Fig. 2 are irreducible, that α is a root of c(x) and γ is a root of b(x), that $\beta = \alpha^d$ has the same multiplicative order in $GF(q^L)$ as α, and that the degrees L and M satisfy gcd(L,M) = 1. Then the i-th input sequence $\underset{\sim}{w}^i$ to the adder forming $\underset{\sim}{z}$ in Fig. 2 is given according to (18) by

$$(\underset{\sim}{w}^i)_j = T_L(A\beta^{-ie}\beta^j)T_M(B\gamma^{-i}\gamma^j), \tag{23}$$

where A and B are non-zero elements of $GF(q^L)$ and $GF(q^M)$ if, as we now assume, the initial states of the LFSR's are both non-zero. Using (20), we obtain

$$(\underset{\sim}{w}^i)_j = T_{LM}(AB\beta^{-ie}\gamma^{-i}(\beta\gamma)^j). \tag{24}$$

It now follows from Lemma 2 and (11) that $\underset{\sim}{w}^i$ is a non-zero sequence produced by an LFSR with an irreducible characteristic polynomial of degree LM, and hence that the linear complexity of $\underset{\sim}{w}^i$ is

$$\Lambda(\underset{\sim}{w}^i) = LM. \tag{25}$$

In fact, we see from (24) that each sequence $\underset{\sim}{w}^i$ is produced by this same LFSR of length LM and hence so also is their sum

$$\underset{\sim}{z} = \sum_{i=1}^{M} \underset{\sim}{w}^i. \tag{26}$$

To show that

$$\Lambda(\underset{\sim}{z}) = LM, \tag{27}$$

it remains only to show that $\underset{\sim}{z}$ is not the all-zero sequence $\underset{\sim}{0}$. Now (10), (24) and (26) show that $\underset{\sim}{z} = \underset{\sim}{0}$ only if

$$\sum_{i=1}^{M} (\beta^e \gamma)^i = \sum_{i=1}^{M} (\alpha\gamma)^i = 0,$$

where we have made use of (17), which would require $\alpha\gamma$ to be the root of the polynomial $x^{M-1} + x^{M-2} + \ldots + x+1$ over $GF(q)$. But this cannot be the case since Lemma 2 shows that the minimum polynomial of $\alpha\gamma$ over $GF(q)$ has degree LM. We have thus proved our desired result, namely:

Proposition 4: When the two LFSR's in Fig. 2 have relatively prime lengths, irreducible connection polynomials and non-zero initial states, and when the speed factor d is relatively prime to the period T of the faster-shifting LFSR, then the output sequence z will have linear complexity LM as will also each of the input sequences to the adder that forms z in Fig. 2.

6. Remarks

One could of course utilize the sequence z produced by the generator of Fig. 2 as the sequence "x" in another such "Fig. 2 generator", where the second LFSR would now be shifted at another speed factor d'. If this second LFSR has length N and gcd(LM,N) = 1, we see from Proposition 4 that we could obtain output sequences of linear complexity LMN. This process could be iterated as many times as desired.

One could also modify the Fig. 2 generator by also shifting the upper LFSR at another speed factor d'. The analysis of such generators is an obvious modification of that presented in this paper.

Finally, the reader may wonder why, in light of Proposition 4, one does not save hardware by using one of the w^i sequences as the generator output since its linear complexity equals that of z. The answer is that the sequence w^i may have a gross imbalance of 0's to 1's (when q = 2) and/or other short term "non-random" features. The intuitive argument of Section 3 that suggested the structure of the Fig. 2 generator also suggests that the short term statistics of z will be much more "random" than those of w^i. It appears feasible to carry out an analysis to verify this suspicion, but such an analysis is beyond our aim in this paper, which was to show the many interesting features that mulitple clocks can introduce in sequence generators. When such sequences generators are used for cryptographic purposes, the various speed factors can be put

under control of the secret key. Thus, such multiple-clocking gives
an added "dimension" to secure sequence generator design.

References

[1] J.L. Massey, "Error Bounds for Tree Codes, Trellis Codes, and
    Convolutional Codes with Encoding and Decoding Procedures", pp.1-57
    in Coding and Complexity (Ed. G.Longo), CISM Courses and Lectures
    No. 216, Springer-Verlag, Vienna and New York, 1975.

[2] C.E. Shannon, "Communication Theory of Secrecy Systems", Bell System
    Tech. J., vol. 28, pp.656-715, October 1949.

[3] E.L. Key, "An Analysis of the Structure and Complexity of Nonlinear
    Binary Sequence Generators", IEEE Trans. Info. Th., vol. IT-22,
    pp.732-736, Nov. 1976.

THE STOP-AND-GO-GENERATOR

T.Beth
F.C. Piper

1. Introduction

The usual method for generating binary sequences of acceptable properties with respect to period-complexity and statistics is based on a
deterministic finite boolean automaton

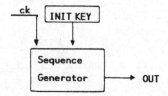

which after having been initialized by the key on every clock impulse
at time t outputs a bit u_t , $t \in \mathbb{N}_o$.

The cryptographic value of such a sequence generator depends obviously
on the complexity of this machine. Several concepts for its design
are known.

The best-understood-though not too desirable - finite state machine is
a linear feed back shift register (cf. Selmer, Golomb, Jennings).

In most practical applications socalled non-linear feedback machines are
being used while their complexity, the socalled *linear equivalent* is
described via the shortest linear recursion generating the same output sequence. Another concept of measuring complexity has recently been
proposed by Micali et al..

The art of designing finite boolean automata of high complexity has
naturally become one of the central topics of modern cryptography -
expecially in the light of readily accessible VLSI-implementations.
Examples of these have been described by Beker/Piper, Jennings, Beth.

A rather new concept of this kind seems to originate from the idea of a variable clock

While the usual concept is based on a clock with timing diagram

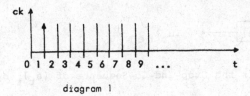

diagram 1

a variable clock has a timing diagram like

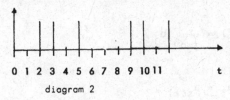

diagram 2

which could be produced from a usual clock (e.g. in diagram 1) AND-gated with a 0-1-sequence (as in diagram 3)

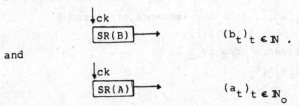

diagram 3

In a research project which has been initiated through a grant by the British Science and Engineering Research Council awarded to the two authors in the year 1983, the theory and realisations of these socalled *Stop-and-Go-Generators* are being investigated.

2. The Stop-and-Go-Generator

The general Stop-and-Go-Generator is built from two feedback shift registers (FSR)

$$\downarrow ck$$
$$\boxed{SR(B)} \longrightarrow \qquad (b_t)_{t \in \mathbb{N}} \ .$$

and

$$\downarrow ck$$
$$\boxed{SR(A)} \longrightarrow \qquad (a_t)_{t \in \mathbb{N}_o}$$

where the outputs of SR(B) are driving the clock of SR(B)

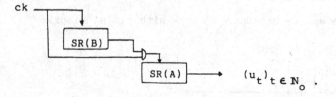

$(u_t)_{t \in \mathbb{N}_o}$.

The output-sequence $(u_t)_t$ is the Stop-and-Go-Sequence of $(a_t)_t$ by $(b_t)_t$.

2.1 Observation

With $s(t) = wgt(b_o, \dots, b_t) = \sum\limits_{j=o}^{t} b_j$

the bits are given by

$$u_t = a_{s(t)} \; .$$

From this observation we immediately conclude the following

2.2 Proposition

Let Π_1 resp. Π_2 be the period of the sequence $(a_t)_t$ resp. $(b_t)_t$.

$$w = wgt(b_1, \dots, b_{\Pi_2})$$

be the number of 1's in the full period of b_t .

If $(w, \Pi_1) = 1$ then the period of $(u_t)_t$ is

$$\Pi = \Pi_1 \cdot \Pi_2$$

The condition of Prop. 2.2 is necessary as the following example shows.

2.3 Example

Let $\underline{a} = (a_o, a_1, a_2, a_o, a_1, a_2, \dots)$ be any sequence of period 3 .
Let $\underline{b}$ the sequence with period (10101).
Then the Stop-and-Go-Sequence of $\underline{a}$ by $\underline{b}$ is

$$\underline{u} = (a_o a_o a_1 a_1 a_2 a_o a_o a_1 a_1 a_2 \dots)$$

of period 5 *and not 15 as we may expect.*
After determing the period we have to determine the linear equivalent.
As we know from coding theory weight function <u>wgt</u> is non-trivial analyti-
cally, we try another approach to describe the sequence u_t .

2.4 Example:

Obviously the following Boolean equations hold

$$u_o = a_o \qquad \text{(by definition)}$$
$$u_1 = b_1 a_1 + (1-b_1)a_o$$
$$u_2 = b_2 b_1 a_2 + (b_1(1-b_2) + b_2(1-b_1))a_1$$
$$+ (1-b_1)(1-b_2)a_o$$

In general we have

2.5 Lemma

For $n \in \mathbb{N}_o$ $u_n \in \text{BoolPol}[b_1, \ldots, b_n; a_o, \ldots, a_n]$

is a Boolean Polynomial in

$b_1, \ldots, b_n$ and $a_o, \ldots, a_n$ with degree $\delta_{\underline{b}}(u_n) = n$

wrt. $b_1, \ldots, b_n$.

From this we derive

2.6 Lemma

Let R_n denote the ring of Boolean polynomials

$$R_n = \text{BoolPol}[a_o, \ldots, a_n] \; .$$

Suppose the linear equivalent of $(b_t)_t$ is $L(B)$. Then u_n is the R-
linear combination of *all* $2^{L(B)} - 1$ monomials in $b_o, \ldots, b_{L-1}$.

With some special assumptions from this we can for instance derive the

2.7 Theorem

If $(a_t)_t$ and $(b_t)_t$ are binary sequences which belong to linearly disjoint field extensions then $(u_t)_t$ has the linear equivalent

$$L(U) = (2^{L(B)}-1)\ L(A)$$

Of course the situation assumed in the theorem is the "nicest" general
case. Other special cases are studied by Vogel, who considers the case of
equal field extensions (cf. Vogel) and by Gollmann, who investigates cascaded shift registers of *equal prime* period.

3. Concluding remarks

Under the correct assumptions cascading of primitive shift registers
leads to interesting results. But from Gollmann's work it is clear that
general results on cascaded arbitrary shift registers cannot be expected.

In order to guarantee a good statistical behaviour of the Stop-and-Go-
Sequence it is suggested that the output sequence u_t is finally XOR-ga-
ted with another PN-sequence.

The statistical behaviour of $(u_t)_t$ itself - though theoretically quite
good in special cases - is so that a cryptoanalytic attack would be promising in spite of the extremely high linear equivalent of the sequence.

4. References

Beker/Piper: Cipher Systems, Northwood 1982

Beth: Stream Ciphers, in: Secure Digital Communications, G. Longo ed.,
    Springer 1983

Gollmann: Doctoral Dissertation, University of Linz, Austria 1983

Golomb: Shift register sequences, Holden-Day 1967

Jennings: Multiplexed Sequences, in: Cryptography, T.Beth ed.,
    Springer LNCS 149, 1983

Selmer: Linear Recurrence Relations over Finite Fields, manuscript.
    Dept. of Math., University of Bergen, Norway 1960

Vogel: On the linear complexity of cascaded sequences, preprint,
    SEL Pforzheim, CP/ERMF, Germany 1984

PSEUDO RANDOM PROPERTIES OF
CASCADE CONNECTIONS OF CLOCK CONTROLLED SHIFT REGISTERS

Dieter Gollmann

Institut für Systemwissenschaften
Johannes Kepler Universität Linz , Austria

Abstract. Shift registers are frequently used in generators of pseudo random
sequences (see [1]). We will examine how cascade connections of clock controlled
shift registers perform when used as generators of pseudo random sequences.
We will derive results for the period, for the linear recursion and for the
pseudo-randomness of their output sequences.

1.Introduction.

Cascade connections of clock controlled shift registers are a generalization of
the idea of a "clock controlled automaton". Clock controlled automata were examined
by P.Nyffeler [4]. A clock controlled shift register switches to its next state
when input "one" is sent to its clock and remains unchanged when input "zero" is
applied. We connect these clock controlled shift registers to a cascade connection
as follows. The input to the cascade connection is sent to the clock of the first
register. The input to the clock of the i-th register, $i \geq 2$, is the sum (modulo 2)
of the input to the clock of the (i-1)-th register and the output of the (i-1)-th
register. Likewise the output of the cascade connection is the sum of the input
to the clock of the last register and of the output of the last register (see
also [2]).

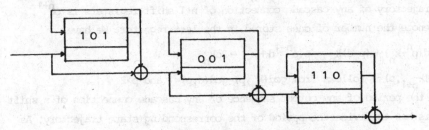

Fig.1. A cascade connection of clock controlled shift registers.

All shift registers in the cascade connection shall be of the same length p, p>2 prime. Furthermore we exclude shift registers with the initial states "all zero" or "all one". We will examine output sequences generated by the input sequence 111... .

2.Results.

2.1. Periods of the output sequences.

Regard a cascade connection of n clock controlled shift registers of length p. Obviously any state trajectory - and therefore any output sequence - of this cascade connection has at most period p^n. We are able to prove

Theorem 1: Any output sequence of any cascade connection of n clock controlled shift registers of length p, p>2 prime, has period p^n.

Proof: Let k_i denote the number of ones in the output sequence of a cascade connection of i shift registers during the period p^i.
First we prove that any state trajectory of any cascade connection of n shift registers has period p^n.
This is obviously true for n=1 as the initial state of the shift register is non-trivial. With the same argument we get $\gcd(k_1,p)=1$.
Now assume that any state trajectory of any cascade connection of n shift registers has period p^n and that $\gcd(k_n,p)=1$.
The period of a state trajectory of a cascade connection of n+1 shift registers has to be a multiple of p^n and the number of ones sent to the last register during this period has to be a multiple of p. So we have $m \cdot k_n = n \cdot p$ for some natural numbers m,n. From $\gcd(k_n,p)=1$ we get m=p, the period of any state trajectory of any cascade connection of n+1 shift registers is p^{n+1}.
Let d denote the number of ones stored in the last register. We have

$$k_{n+1} = d(p^n - k_n) + (p-d)k_n = p(p^{n-1}d + k_n) - 2dk_n$$

and $\gcd(k_{n+1},p)=1$ follows from $\gcd(k_n,p)=\gcd(d,p)=1$ and p>2.
Finally the period of any output sequence of any cascade connection of n shift registers has to divide the period of the corresponding state trajectory. As $\gcd(k_n,p)=1$ this period has to be p^n.

q.e.d.

2.2. Linear recursion.

We introduce some further notations.

Let $(q_{i,1},\ldots,q_{i,p})$ denote the initial state of the i-th register of some cascade connection of clock controlled shift registers.

Let $f_{i,k_{j-1}}$ denote the characteristical polynomial of the sequence $q_{i,1+mk_{i-1}}$, $1 \leq m \leq p$, where the indices $1+mk_{i-1}$ are computed modulo p.

Then the property "p^2 does not divide $2^{p-1}-1$" is sufficient to prove that the characteristical polynomial f of the output sequence generated by the given initial state can be computed by

Theorem 2: $\quad f(x) = (1-x) \prod\limits_{i=1}^{n} f_{i,k_{i-1}}(x^{(p^{i-1})})$.

For the proof of this theorem see [3].

It is important to note that the linear recursion depends on the initial states of the shift registers in the cascade connection.

"p^2 does not divide $2^{p-1}-1$" is no severe restriction as p=1093 is the first prime number to violate this condition.

Theorem 2 generalizes P.Nyffeler's result for the linear recursion of clock controlled automata [4].

For prime numbers p with $C_p(x) = \sum\limits_{i=0}^{p-1} x^i$ irreducible over GF(2) we can deduce

Theorem 3: $\quad f(x) = 1 - x^{(p^n)}$.

2.3. Pseudo-randomness.

Consider a sequence $R := ((R_i,q_i))_{i \in \mathbb{N}}$ of registers R_i with initial states q_i. The $2^k \times 2^k$-matrices $T(k;l) := (t(k;l)_{ij})$ give the relative frequencies of the transformations of the sequences of length k caused by the cascade connection of the registers $R_{(l-1)k+1},\ldots,R_{lk}$.

Lemma 1: For any natural number k any cascade connection of k shift registers can transform any input sequence $x_1..x_k$ to any given output sequence $y_1..y_k$.

Corollary: $\forall k,l \in \mathbb{N}, \forall i,j=1,\ldots,2^k$ $(t(k;l)_{ij} \geq \frac{1}{p^k})$.

Proof of Lemma 1: This lemma is true for k=1 as the initial states of all
shift registers are non-trivial.

We now assume that the lemma holds for some given number k.

Consider an arbitrary input sequence $x_0..x_k$, an arbitrary output sequence
$y_0..y_k$ and an arbitrary cascade connection of k+1 shift registers.

y_0=0: We set register k+1 to the initial state 1..0 (the zero is at the
output of the register). This initial state transforms some sequence
$y_1'..y_k'$ to $y_1..y_k$.

Let q be the state of the first k registers that transforms $x_1..x_k$
to $y_1'..y_k'$. Furthermore there exists a state $\delta^{-1}(q,x_0)$ that is transformed by x_0 to q.

If input x_0 and initial state $\delta^{-1}(q,x_0)$ yield output zero the initial
state of the last register shall be 1..0, otherwise ..01 .

Now $x_0..x_k$ is transformed to $y_0..y_k$.

y_0=1: We start with the last register in the initial state 0..1 and proceed
as above.

If input x_0 and initial state $\delta^{-1}(q,x_0)$ yield output zero the initial
state of the last register shall be 0..1, otherwise ..10 .

The corollary follows from the fact that p^k is the period of any state trajectory of any cascade connection of k shift registers of length p.

q.e.d.

T(k;l) is a primitive stochastic matrix for all $k,l \in \mathbb{N}$. We can make use of
the following lemma.

Lemma 2: Let T be a stochastic matrix of dimension n×n with $\lambda := \min_{i,j} p_{ij} > 0$.
Let d be a n-vector with $d \neq 0$, $\sum_{i=1}^{n} d_i = 0$. We define

$$d^* := Td , \quad \Delta_0 := \sum_{i=1}^{n} |d_i| , \quad \Delta_1 := \sum_{i=1}^{n} |d_i^*| .$$

We get: $\Delta_1 \leq (1-n\lambda)\Delta_0$.

The proof of Lemma 2 is similiar to the proof of Lemma 4.1. in [5].

Theorem 4: With Lemma 1 and Lemma 2 we get for the matrices $T(k;1)$

$$\left\| \prod_{1=1}^{n} T(k;1)\Delta \right\| \le (1 - (\tfrac{2}{p})^k)^n \|\Delta\| \quad \text{for all } n \in \mathbb{N}.$$

Δ gives the difference between the initial distribution of the input sequences of length k and the vector $(2^{-k},..,2^{-k})^t$ (i.e. equal distribution of the sequences of length k).

Let $rf_n(y_1..y_k)$ denote the relative frequency of the sequence $y_1..y_k$ in the output sequence of some cascade connection of n shift registers during the period p^n. From Theorem 4 we get

$$\lim_{n \to \infty} rf_n(y_1..y_k) = 2^{-k}.$$

We extend this result to the information entropy

$$H_k(n) := \sum_{(y_1..y_k)=(0..0)}^{(1..1)} rf_n(y_1..y_k) \cdot ld(rf_n(y_1..y_k)) :$$

$$\lim_{n \to \infty} H_k(n) = k.$$

When we increase the length of a cascade connection the relative frequencies of the word of length k converge towards equal distribution for any number k, the entropy converges towards its maximum.

Remark. The sequence of matrices $(T(k;1))_{1 \in \mathbb{N}}$ constitutes an inhomogenous Markov chain where the matrices $T(k;1)$ can be taken only from a finite set. Markov chains of this kind have been studied by J.Wolfowitz already in 1963 (see [6]).

The rate of convergence $(1 - (\tfrac{2}{p})^k)$ given in Theorem 4 cannot be improved for k=1. If a shift register of length p contains only a single one we get

$$T(1;1) = \frac{1}{p}\begin{pmatrix} p-1 & 1 \\ 1 & p-1 \end{pmatrix} \quad \text{and} \quad T(1;1)\begin{pmatrix} d \\ -d \end{pmatrix} = \frac{p-2}{p}\begin{pmatrix} d \\ -d \end{pmatrix}.$$

3. Conclusion.

We build a cascade connection from clock controlled shift registers of equal
length p, p>2 prime, where no shift register is in a trivial initial state.
Any output sequence of such a cascade connection has period p^n (i.e. maximal
period), the linear recursion of any output sequence can be computed directly
from the initial states of the shift registers (except for the case "p^2 divides
$2^{p-1}-1$"). For suitable prime numbers p we have linear recursion of length p^n
independent of the initial states.
The sequences of length k occur in the output sequence of a cascade connection
with relative frequencies converging towards equal distribution when we increase the length of the cascade connection. This holds for all numbers k.

Literature:

[1] H.Beker, F.Piper, Cipher Systems, Northwood, London, 1982

[2] D.Gollmann, On the identification of certain non-linear networks of
         automata, in: Cybernetics and Systems Research, ed.R.Trappl,
         North Holland, 1982

[3] D.Gollmann, Kaskadenschaltungen taktgesteuerter Schieberegister als
         Pseudozufallszahlengeneratoren, Dissertation, Universität Linz, 1983

[4] P.Nyffeler, Binäre Automaten und ihre linearen Rekursionen, Dissertation,
         Universität Bern, 1975

[5] E.Seneta, Non-negative Matrices, George Allen&Unwin Ltd, London, 1973

[6] J.Wolfowitz, Products of indecomposable, aperiodic, stochastic matrices,
         PAMS, 14, 733-737, 1963

On the linear complexity of cascaded sequences

Rainer Vogel
Standard Elektrik Lorenz AG
Abt. CP/ERMF 2
Ostendstraße 3
7530 Pforzheim
RFA

In the papers [1][2] Kjeldsen derived very interesting properties of cascade coupled sequence generators. For applications in ciphering we are interested to know the linear complexity of such sequences. In the following we first consider the examples 1 and 2.

Example 1

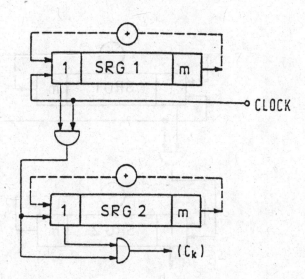

This sequence-generator works as follows:
Shiftregister 1 (SRG 1) is shifted with every clock. If the output of this register is 1 shiftregister 2 (SRG 2) is shifted and the generated bit of SR 2 is used for c_k.

If shiftregister 1 generates a 0 shiftregister 2 will not be shifted and the output of the generator is 0.

If we denote the sequence from shiftregister 1 with (a_k), the sequence from shiftregister 2 with (b_k), the sequence (c_k) at the output can be computed in the following way

$$c_k = a_k \cdot b_{G(k)} \qquad k \epsilon N$$

with $\qquad G(o) = 0$

$$G(k) = \sum_{i<k} a_i \qquad k \epsilon N$$

(The last sum denotes a usual addition)

Example 2

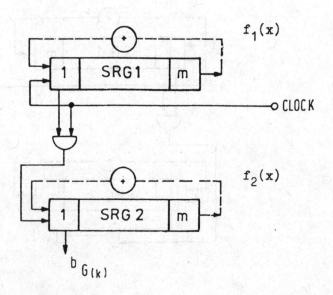

If we are only interested to generate the sequence $b_{G(k)}$, we use the generator of example 2. This structure works in the following manner: Generates shiftregister 1 an 1 the register SRG 2 is shifted and the output of SRG 2 is used for the output of the generator. Otherwise SRG 2 is not shifted and the previous generated bit of SRG 2 is used as output bit.

Later we give further examples. To get some answers about the linear complexity, we begin with example 2. For if we have derived the minimal polynom $g(x)$ of the sequence $(b_{G(k)})$, we can use known theorems (eg. Zierler[3]). Therefore we get for the minimal polynom $h(x)$ of the sequence (c_k)

$$h(x) \mid f_1 \vee g.$$

$f_1 \vee g$ is the polynom with the zeros $\alpha \cdot \beta$, α zero of $f_1(x)$, β zero of $g(x)$.

$f_1 \vee g$ is also denoted Hadamard product of f_1 and g.

But first we still remember some properties of the sequences generated by the generator of example 1. More general formulations and proofs are in the papers [1], [2].

1. If the number of 1's computed over the period of (a_k) is relatively prime to the period p_2 of the sequence (b_k) then for the minimal period p of (c_k) holds the equation

$$p = p_1 \cdot p_2.$$

This conditions are always satisfied if the feedback polynoms of the shiftregister are primitive polynoms with the degree m. In this case we have then

$$p = (2^m - 1).$$

2. The asumptions of the previous number are satisfied. Let w_i (p_i) i = 1,2 the weight of (a_k) resp. (b_k) computed over the period p_1 resp. p_2, then for the frequency w of the 1's in (c_k) it holds

$$w = \prod_{i=1}^{2} \frac{w_i (p_i)}{p_i}$$

If (a_k) and (b_k) are PN-sequences with the period 2^m-1, we have

$$w = \prod_{i=1}^{2} \frac{2^{m-1}}{2^m-1} \approx \frac{1}{4} .$$

General asumption for the rest of the paper: All feedbacks are primitive polynoms.

These last two results can be generalized on cascades with more than two stages. Further in the papers [1][2] are results on the autocorrelation properties of such sequences.

Computation of the linear complexity of the sequence ($b_{G(k)}$).

All following proofs are based on a theorem, which we found in a very old book on algebra of Dickson [2]. (1900) In a slightly reformulation it says:

Theorem

$f_1(x)$, $f_2(x)$, ... $f_N(x)$ be the set of all irreducible polynoms of degree m and exponent e

$$e = (2^m - 1)/d .$$

$\lambda \epsilon N$ be a number with the properties

(i) (λ, d) = 1

(ii) All prime divisors of λ are prime divisors of 2^m-1,

then holds

a) $\lambda \cdot m$ is the least number with the property $\lambda \cdot e | 2^{\lambda \cdot m}- 1$.

b) The polynoms $f_1(x^\lambda), \dots f_N(x^\lambda)$ are irreducible of degree $m \cdot \lambda$ and exponent $\lambda \cdot e$ and the set $f_1(x^\lambda), \dots f_N(x^\lambda)$ consists of all polynoms with these properties.

Proof [4, page 22]

In the special case

$$e = \lambda = 2^{m-1}$$

$$d = 1 \qquad\qquad \text{we get}$$

a) $m \cdot (2^m - 1) = \min \{ k : (2^m - 1)^2 | 2^k - 1 \}$

b) The set $f_1(x^{2^m - 1}), \dots f_N(x^{2^m - 1})$

is the set of all polynoms of degree $m \cdot (2^m - 1)$ with the exponent $(2^m - 1)^2$.

With the help of this theorem we examine the sequence $(b_{G(k)})$ and prove

$f_2(x^{2^m - 1})$ is the minimal polynom of $(b_{G(k)})$.

Proof

$(a_k) \longleftarrow f_1(x)$ } primitive polynoms
$(b_k) \longleftarrow f_2(x)$ } of degree m

With $p := 2^m - 1$ the sum $G(k)$ has the properties

$$G(k + n \cdot p) = G(k) + n \cdot G(p)$$

$$G(p) = 2^{m-1}$$

Using the operator $f(E^p)$ corresponding to the polynom $f(x^p)$, we get (E is the shift operator)

$$f_2(E^p) \, b_{G(k)} = \sum_{i=o}^{m} c_i \cdot b_{G(k+i \cdot p)}$$

$$= \sum_{i=o}^{m} c_i \cdot b_{G(k)+i \cdot G(p)}$$

$$= \sum_{i=o}^{m} c_i \cdot b_{G(k)+i \cdot 2^{m-1}}$$

$$(k':=G(k)) \quad = \sum_{i=o}^{m} c_i \cdot b_{k'+i \cdot 2^{m-1}}$$

$$= f_2(E^{2^{m-1}}) \, b_{k'}$$

$$= (f_2(E))^{2^{m-1}} \, b_{k'} = 0$$

With the theorem we now get

1. $f_2(x^{2^{m-1}})$ is the minimal polynom of the sequence $(b_{G(k)})$, because the polynom is irreducible.

   Thus the linear complexity of $(b_{G(k)})$ is $m \cdot (2^m - 1)$.

2. The sequence $(b_{G(k)})$ has the minimum period $(2^m - 1)^2$, because the exponent of $f_2 (x^{2^m-1})$ is $(2^m - 1)^2$.

Remarks

1. With two cascaded shiftregisters of length 61 the linear complexity of $(b_{G(k)})$ has the value

   $K = 1.4 \cdot 10^{20}$.

2. If the cascade consists of n registers of length m, we get
   linear complexity $\geq m \cdot (2^m - 1)^{n-1}$ Period $= (2^m - 1)$

3. It is possible to replace shiftregister 1 through a nonlinear shift-register which generates a de Bruijn sequence. In this case it is still possible to give a lower bound for the linear complexity.

Lower bound for the linear complexity in Example 1

From previous considerations we see: The minimal polynom $h(x)$ of the sequence $(c_k) = (a_k \cdot b_{G(k)})$ is a divisor of the polynom $f_1(x) \vee f_2 (x^{2^{m-1}})$.

But what about the degree of $h(x)$? The period $(2^m - 1)^2$ of the sequence (c_k) is an odd number. The irreducible components of $h(x)$ have the power $= 1$. If we write the sequence (c_k) with the zeros of $h(x)$ there must be zeros of order $(2^m - 1)^2$. The degree of each irreducible component with such a zero is equal $m(2^m - 1)$. For the degree of $h(x)$ we get therefore the lower bound $\deg h(x) \geq m \cdot (2^m - 1)$.

It is only possible to get lower bounds, but this is sufficient for the applications.

Example 3

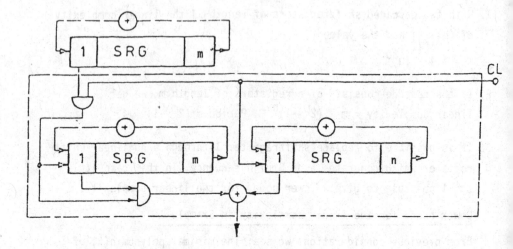

The sequences of example 1 have bad pseudo-noise properties, because
the frequency of 1's at the output is only 1/4. To remove this defect
we add (mod 2) another linear shiftregister sequence to the sequence
(c_k). If we assume $(m,n) = 1$ the following Lemma shows that the resulting
sequence has better pseudo-noise properties.

Lemma $[1]$

The periods of the sequences (a_k) und (b_k) are relatively prime. Each
m-tuple of weight w occurs with the frequency $f^w (1-f)^{m-w}$ in (a_k) and
with the frequency $g^w (1-g)^w$ in (b_k). Then each m-tuple of the weight
w in the sequence $(a_k + b_k)$ occurs with frequency

$$h^w (1-h)^{m-w} \qquad \text{with}$$

$$h = f + g - 2 f \cdot g.$$

If the sequence of SRG 3 is a PN-sequence of period $(2^n -1)$ $(m,n) = 1$ in the output sequence each m-tuple of weight w has thus the frequency $(\frac{1}{2})^m$.

For the linear complexity K of the output we have $K > m \cdot (2^m -1)$.

Example 4

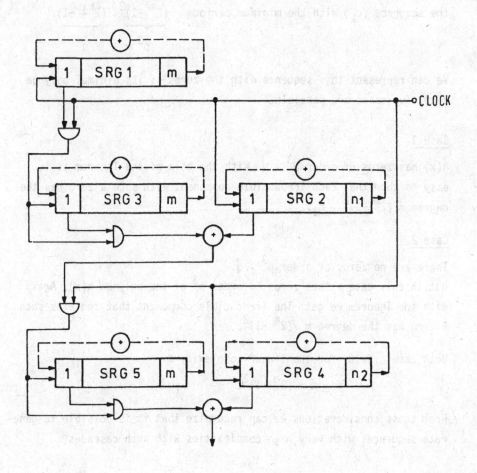

This example shows how a repetition of the method of example 1 leads
to sequences of very high complexity. If we assume that all feedback
polynoms are primitive polynoms, it is possible to proof that in each
stage the number of 1's is relatively prime to $2^m - 1$. The output sequence of this structure has the least period $(2^m - 1)^3 \cdot (2^{n_1} - 1) \cdot$
$(2^{n_2} - 1)$ if all the starting vektors of all registers are not equal 0.

As an example for the estimation of the linear complexity we examine
the sequence (c_k) with the minimum period $\underbrace{(2^m - 1)^3}_{p^3} \cdot \underbrace{(2^{n_1} - 1)}_{q}$.

We can represent this sequence with the zeros of its minimal polynom
$h(x)$. Two cases are possible.

Case 1

$h(x)$ has zeros of order $p^3 \cdot q$. With the help of the Theorem it is
easy to show that each irreducible component with such a zero has the
degree $m(2^m - 1)^2 \cdot n_1$.

Case 2

There are no zeros of order $p^3 \cdot q$.
But in this case exists zeros of order p^3 of the polynom $h(x)$. Again
with the Theorem we get: The irreducible component that contains such
a zero has the degree $m \cdot (2^m - 1)^2$.

Both cases yields for the linear complexity K

$$K \geq m \cdot (2^m - 1)^2.$$

From these considerations we can recognize that it is possible to generate sequences with very high complexities with such cascades.

References

1   Kjeldsen, Andresen
     Some Randomness Properties
     of Cascaded Sequences
     IEEE TRANS INF. Th. Vol IT 26
     No. 2, 227 ff (1980)

2   Johnsen, Kjeldsen
     Loop-free Compositions of Certain
     Finite Automata
     INF. AND CONTROL 22, 303 - 319
     (1973)

3   Zierler, Mills
     Products of linear recurring seq.
     J. Algebra 27, 1, 147 - 151 (1973)

4   Dickson
     Linear groups with an exposition
     of Galois field theory
     Springer 1900 (Dover Publ. 1958)

SECTION II

PUBLIC-KEY   SYSTEMS

RSA-bits are 0.5 + ε secure

C.P. Schnorr and W. Alexi
Fachbereich Mathematik
Universität Frankfurt

February 1984

Abstract   We prove by some novel sampling techniques that
the least significant bits of RSA-messages are $0.5 + \varepsilon$ - secure.
Any oracle which correctly predicts the k-th least significant
message bit for at least a $0.5 + \varepsilon$ - fraction of all messages
can be used to decipher all RSA ciphertexts in random polynomial time (more precisely in time $(\log n)^{O(\varepsilon^{-2}+k)}$) .

1. Introduction

The most interesting feature of modern cryptography is the
interaction of arguments from complexity theory, information
theory and number theory. As a result of this interaction
the cryptographic security of simple pseudo random number
generators has been based on reasonable number theoretic
assumptions, see M. Blum, S. Micali (1982) and A. Yao (1982).
The bit security of the RSA-scheme plays an important role in
this context. If the problem of deciphering the RSA-ciphertexts can be reduced to the problem of getting partial information on single cleartext bits then an interesting situation
arises. Either it is easy to decipher RSA-ciphertexts completely (in worst case without knowing the private key) or
it is infeasible to get even partial information on single
RSA-cleartext bits and in this latter case the RSA-encryption
provides a simple cryptographically secure pseudo random
number generator.

The bit security of the RSA-scheme was first studied by Goldwasser,
Micali, Tong (1982). They showed that obtaining the least
significant bit of an RSA-message is as hard as obtaining
the entire message. Formally they proved that any oracle
which queried on an RSA-ciphertext outputs the least significant bit of the corresponding message, can be used to
decrypt RSA efficiently. Ben-Or, Chor and Shamir (1983)
proved that the two least significant RSA bits are $3/4+\varepsilon$-
secure, i.e. any oracle for these bits which is correct for
an $3/4+\varepsilon$-fraction of the ciphertexts can be used to decrypt
RSA efficiently. They also showed that certain other bits are
$15/16+\varepsilon$-secure. The problem remained whether RSA-bits are
$1/2+\varepsilon$-secure. This would imply that RSA-bits yield a cryptographically secure pseudo random number generator. With some
novel sampling techniques U.V. and V.V. Vazirani (1983)
proved that the least significant RSA bits are $0.732+\varepsilon$
secure.

In this paper we finally prove that the least significant
RSA-bits are 0.5+ε-secure. More formally any oracle which
correctly predicts the k-th least significant RSA-bit for
at least a 0.5+ε-fraction of all messages can be used to
decipher all RSA ciphertexts in time $(\log n)^{O(\varepsilon^{-2}+k)}$.

2. The binary gcd-method for deciphering the RSA-scheme

For an integer $n \geq 1$ let $\mathbb{Z}_n^* = \{x \bmod n \mid x \in \mathbb{Z}, \gcd(x,n) = 1\}$ be the multiplicative group of integers modulo n which are relatively prime to n. The elements of $\mathbb{Z}_n^*$ will be represented by the integers x with $0 < x < n$, $\gcd(x,n) = 1$. Let $l_i(x)$ be the i-th least significant bit of x, i.e. $x = \sum_{i \geq 1} l_i(x) 2^{i-1}$ with $0 < x < n$. Call $x \in \mathbb{Z}_n^*$ even if $l_1(x) = 0$. Note that 2x may be odd; this happens iff $n/2 < x < n$ with n odd. Throughout the paper n will be odd. Let $E : x \longrightarrow x^e$ be an RSA encryption function and let $\mathcal{O}$ be an oracle which given $E(a)$ determines $l_1(a)$ the least significant bit of a.

Theorem 1 [Ben-Or, Chor, Shamir] There is a random polynomial time algorithm which queries the oracle $\mathcal{O}$ at most $O(\log_2 n)$ times and with probability $\geq 1/2$ deciphers $E(x)$.

The deciphering algorithm computes $b \in \mathbb{Z}_n^*$ such that $E(xb) = 1 \bmod n$ and $x := b^{-1} \bmod n$. A particular version of the binary gcd-algorithm computes b from randomly chosen elements b_1, b_2 with xb_1, $xb_2 < n/2$. The oracle is used for testing "$xb_1 < xb_2$?" and "xb_i even?". In fact
$$xb_1 < xb_2 \leftrightarrow \mathcal{O}E(2x(b_1-b_2)) = 0 \; ; \quad xb_i \text{ even} \leftrightarrow \mathcal{O}E(xb_i) = 0 \; .$$

An important observation is that oracle queries on large elements $2x(b_1-b_2)$ can be avoided. In section 3 we show that oracle queries on small elements can be answered correctly even if the oracle has error probability $0.5-\varepsilon$.

Algorithm 1 (the new deciphering algorithm)

1. pick random elements $b_1, b_2 \in \mathbb{Z}_n^*$ with $b_i x$ odd and
   $b_i x < 2^{-k} n$ for $i = 1, 2$; $c_1 := c_2 := 2^{-k}$;

2. $i := \begin{cases} 1 & \text{if } c_1 \geq c_2 \\ 2 & \text{if } c_2 > c_1 \end{cases}$;

   $b_i := (b_1 + b_2)/2 \bmod n$; $c_i := (c_1 + c_2)/2$;

3. if $xb_i = 1 \bmod n$ then $[x := b_i^{-1} \bmod n, \text{stop}]$;

   if $xb_1 = xb_2$ then stop (failure);

   if xb_i is odd then goto 2;

4. while xb_i even do $[b_i := b_i/2 \bmod n, c_i := c_i/2]$;
   goto 2;

The values c_i do not increase. An easy induction shows that
$xb_i \leq c_i n$ throughout the computation. Since c_1, c_2 cannot
become smaller than $1/n$, the oracle is queried at most $4 \log_2 n$
times in step 4. Since each pass of step 2 halves the
difference $(b_1 - b_2)$ there are at most $\log_2 n$ consecutive passes
of step 2. This proves

Lemma 2 In the new deciphering algorithm all oracle queries
are on elements $bx < 2^{-k} n$. The oracle is queried at most
$4 \log_2^2 n$ times.

3. The 0.5+ε-security of the least significant RSA-bit

Now consider the case that the oracle $\mathcal{O}$ makes errors.
Let $\mathcal{O}_\varepsilon$ be an oracle which has an $1/2+\varepsilon$-advantage in predicting the least significant bit, i.e.

$$\#\{x \in \mathbb{Z}_n^* : \mathcal{O}_\varepsilon[E(x)] = l_1(x)\} / \# \mathbb{Z}_n^* \geq 1/2 + \varepsilon .$$

We will exploit the relation (let $\oplus$ be the exclusive or)

$$l_1(a+b) = l_1(a) \oplus l_1(b) , \qquad \text{for } a,b \in \mathbb{Z}_n^*$$

which holds provided that $a+b$ does not overlap n .

Suppose we like to decipher $E(x)$ and

we already know some b with $xb < \varepsilon n/2$. Then we need to

know $l_1(xb)$. We show that knowledge of $l_1(xr)$ for a random

element $r \in \mathbb{Z}_n^*$ helps determing $l_1(xb)$:

Fact 3 Let $r \in \mathbb{Z}_n^*$ be a random element. Then for all $bx \in$
$\mathbb{Z}_n^*$ with $bx < \varepsilon n/2$

$$\text{prob}[\mathcal{O}_\varepsilon[E((r+b)x)] \oplus l_1(rx) = l_1(bx)] \geq (1+\varepsilon)/2 .$$

Proof "$\mathcal{O}_\varepsilon[E((b+r)x)] \oplus l_1(rx) = l_1(bx)$" holds if
$\mathcal{O}_\varepsilon[E((b+r)x)] = l_1((b+r)x)$ and if $bx + rx$ does not overlap n . Since $bx < \varepsilon n/2$, overlap over n occurs with
probability $\leq \varepsilon/2$. Moreover
$$\text{prob}[\mathcal{O}_\varepsilon[E((b+r)x)] = l_1((b+r)x)] \geq 1/2 + \varepsilon$$

Q.E.D.

By a <u>majority decision</u> we can determine $l_1(bx)$ for $bx < \varepsilon n$ with

arbitrary high security provided that we know $l_1(r_i x)$ for

sufficiently many independent elements $r_i \in \mathbb{Z}_n^*$:

Lemma 4 Let $r_1, \ldots, r_t \in \mathbb{Z}_n^*$, t odd, be independent random

elements. Then for all $x, b \in \mathbb{Z}_n^*$ with $xb < \epsilon n/2$, $\epsilon \le 1/4$

the event $"1_1(xb) \ne \lceil \frac{1}{t} \Sigma_{i=1}^t \mathcal{O}_\epsilon [E(x(b+r_i))] \oplus 1_1(xr_i) \rfloor"$

has probability $\le 2 \exp(-t \epsilon^2/3)$ ($\lceil \alpha \rfloor$ denotes the nearest

integer to α).

Proof We use the following version of the law of large

numbers, see e.g. Renyi VII, §4, theorem 1:

Let $X_1, \ldots, X_t$ be independent random variables with mean

value m and variance d , $|X_i - m| \le K$. Then

$$\mathrm{prob}\left[\left| \frac{1}{t} \Sigma_{i=1}^t X_i - m \right| \ge \mu d / \sqrt{t} \right] \le 2 \exp \left[\frac{-\mu^2}{2(1 + \frac{\mu K}{2d\sqrt{t}})^2} \right]$$

for all $\mu \le d\sqrt{t}/K$.

We apply the theorem to

$$X_i = \mathcal{O}_\epsilon [E(x(b+r_i))] \oplus 1_1(xr_i) \oplus 1_1(xb)$$

Clearly $X_i = 1$ iff $\mathcal{O}_\epsilon [E(x(b+r_i))] \oplus 1_1(xr_i) \ne 1_1(xb)$.

We know from Fact 3 that $m \le (1-\epsilon)/2$. $\epsilon \le 1/4$ implies

$K = 5/8$, $2 \le 1/d \le (2\frac{5}{8} \cdot \frac{3}{8})^{-1} \le 2.14$.

If $"1_1(xb) \ne \lceil \frac{1}{t} \Sigma_{i=1}^t \mathcal{O}_\epsilon [E(x(b + r_i))] \oplus 1_1(xr_i) \rfloor"$ then

$\left| \frac{1}{t} \Sigma_{i=1}^t X_i - m \right| \ge \epsilon/2$.

By the law of large numbers with $\mu = \sqrt{t} \, \epsilon/(2d)$ the latter

event has probability $\le$

$$2 \exp \left[\frac{-t \epsilon^2 / (4d^2)}{2(1 + \frac{\epsilon K}{(2d)^2})^2} \right] \le 2 \exp [-t \epsilon^2/3] .$$

Q.E.D.

<u>Corollary 5</u> Let $bx \in \mathbb{Z}_n^*$, $bx < \varepsilon n/2$, $\varepsilon \leq 1/4$ and let
$r_1, \ldots, r_t \in \mathbb{Z}_n^*$ be independent random elements,
$t \geq 3\varepsilon^{-2} \log(2s)$. Then $\text{prob}[l_1(bx) \neq \lceil \frac{1}{t} \Sigma_{i=1}^t O_\varepsilon [E((r_i+b)x)] \oplus$
$\oplus l_1(rx) \rfloor \leq 1/s$.

<u>Proof</u> By Lemma 4 the event in question has probability
$\leq 2 \exp[-t \varepsilon^2/3]$. Thus it is sufficient to choose $t \geq 3\varepsilon^{-2} \log$
$t \geq 3\varepsilon^{-2} \log(2s)$.

                                                                Q.E.D.

A key observation is that once we have guessed $l_1(r_ix)$ for
sufficiently many random elements $r_i \in \mathbb{Z}_n^*$ then we can
determine with sufficiently high security $l_1(bx)$ <u>for any</u>
$bx < \varepsilon n/2$.

<u>Theorem 6</u> There is a random $(\log n)^{O(\varepsilon^{-2})}$ -time algorithm
using oracle O_ε that inverts the encryption function $E(x)$.

<u>Proof</u> In order to decipher $E(x)$ do the following.
1. pick random elements $r_1, \ldots, r_t \in \mathbb{Z}_n^*$, (t will be determined
   below).
2. guess $b_1, b_2 \in \mathbb{Z}_n^*$ with $b_ix \leq \varepsilon n/2$ for $i = 1,2$.
3. guess $l_1(r_ix)$ for $i = 1, \ldots, t$.
4. simulate the binary gcd deciphering method but stop after
   at most $4 \log_2^2 n$ oracle queries. For each oracle query
   compute $l_1(xb) := \lceil \frac{1}{t} \Sigma_{i=1}^t O_\varepsilon [E((r_i+b)x)] \oplus l_1(r_ix) \rfloor$.

The algorithm succeeds if all the query answers are correct

and if the binary gcd method succeeds with initial values b_1, b_2. By Lemma 2 the oracle is queried at most $4 \log_2^2 n$ times. By Corollary 5 for $t := \lceil 3 \varepsilon^{-2} \log(2s) \rceil$ each query answer has error probability $\leq 1/s$. Choose $s := 8 \log_2^2 n$, then with probability $\geq 1/2$ all query answers are correct. It is important for our argument that $r_1, \ldots, r_t$ are independent of all intermediate elements bx occuring in the binary gcd method with initial values b_1, b_2. Guessing b_1, b_2 and $l_1(r_i x)$ for $i = 1, \ldots, t$ can be done within $2^t \varepsilon^{-2} = (\log n)^{O(\varepsilon^{-1})}$ trials. Therefore $E(x)$ can be deciphered in $(\log n)^{O(\varepsilon^{-2})}$ steps.

$$\text{Q.E.D.}$$

4. The security of other RSA-bits

Consider $l_i(x)$ the i-th least significant bit of $x \in \mathbb{Z}_n^*$,
i.e. $x = \Sigma_{i \geq 1} l_i(x) 2^{i-1}$ for x with $0 < x < n$. We note
that for small elements $a \in \mathbb{Z}_n^*$ we can express $l_1(a)$ by
$l_k(2^{k-1}a)$. In fact

(*) $\qquad l_1(a) = l_k(2^{k-1}a)$ for all $a < 2^{-k+1}n$.

Let $\mathcal{O}_{L,k}$ be any oracle which for given $E(a)$ determines
$l_k(a)$. By (*) we can implement the binary gcd deciphering
method using $\mathcal{O}_{L,k}$ provided we guess two initial values b_i
with $b_i x < 2^{-k}n$. This proves

__Theorem 6__ For every k there is a random $(2^k \log n)^{O(1)}$-time
algorithm using the oracle $\mathcal{O}_{L,k}$ which inverts the encryption
function $E(x)$.

Now suppose that $\mathcal{O}_{L,k}$ makes errors. Let $\mathcal{O}_{\varepsilon,k}$ be any oracle
that has ε-advantage in predicting the k-th least significant
bit $l_k(x)$ of x, more formally:

$\qquad \#\{x \in \mathbb{Z}_n^* : \mathcal{O}_{\varepsilon,k}[E(x)] = l_k(x)\}/\#\mathbb{Z}_n^* \geq 1/2 + \varepsilon$.

We implement the binary gcd deciphering method with oracle
$\mathcal{O}_{\varepsilon,k}$ as follows:

1. pick random elements $r_1, \ldots, r_t \in \mathbb{Z}_n^*$, $t = \lceil 3(4 + \log \log n)\varepsilon^{-2} \rceil$.
2. guess $l_k(r_i x)$ for $i = 1, \ldots, t$.
3. guess elements b_1, b_2 such that $x b_i \leq \varepsilon 2^{-k} n$ for $i = 1, 2$.
4. simulate the binary gcd deciphering method as follows. For
   each query on $xb < \varepsilon 2^{-k}n$ put

$$l_1(xb) := \lceil \frac{1}{t} \Sigma_{i=1}^{t} \mathcal{O}_{\varepsilon,k} [E(x(2^{k-1}b + r_i))] \oplus l_k(xr_i) \rfloor$$

and stop after at most $4 \log_2 n$ queries.

We have $l_1(xb)_{\bullet} = l_k(x2^{k-1}b) = l_k(x(2^{k-1}b+r_i)) \oplus l_k(xr_i)$

provided that $x2^{k-1}b + xr_i$ does not overlap n. Since

$bx < \varepsilon 2^{-k} n$ overlap over n occurs with probability $\leq \varepsilon/2$.

Therefore

$$l_1(xb) = \mathcal{O}_{\varepsilon,k}[E(x(2^{k-1}b + r_i))] \oplus l_k(xr_i)$$

occurs with probability $\geq (1 + \varepsilon)/2$. By the law of large

numbers each oracle query has error probability

$\leq 2 \exp[-t \varepsilon^2/3] \leq 1/(27 \log n)$ for $\varepsilon \leq 1/4$. Hence with

probability $\geq 1/2$ all query answers are correct.

The algorithm succeeds if all query answers are correct and

if $\gcd(xb_1, xb_2) = 1$. Guessing such elements b_1, b_2 with

$xb_i \leq \varepsilon 2^{-k} n$ and guessing $l_k(xr_i)$ for $i = 1, \ldots, t$ can be done by

$\varepsilon^{-2} 2^{2k} 2^t = (\log n)^{O(\varepsilon^{-2})} 2^{2k}$ trials. This proves

Theorem 7 For every k there is a random $(\log n)^{O(\varepsilon^{-2}+k)}$-time

algorithm using oracle $\mathcal{O}_{\varepsilon,k}$ which inverts the encryption

function $E(x)$.

5. Efficient deciphering with random oracles

The previous time bound $(\log n)^{O(\varepsilon^{-2}+k)}$ can be considerably improved if the oracle $\sigma_{\varepsilon,k}$ has no particular structure. We will prove that almost all oracles $\sigma_{\varepsilon,k}$ can be used to invert the encryption function $E(x)$ in random time $[\varepsilon^{-1} \log n \, 2^k]^{O(1)}$.

For fixed k we define a probability distribution on the set of all 0-1 valued oracles σ . Oracle σ has probability weight $(0.5 + \varepsilon)^s (0.5 - \varepsilon)^{\varphi(n)-s}$ with $s = \#\{y \in \mathbb{Z}_n^* \mid \sigma[E(y)] = 1_k(y)\}$, $\varphi(n) = \#\mathbb{Z}_n^*$. Let $\sigma R_{\varepsilon,k}$ be a random oracle with respect to this distribution, i.e. $\sigma R_{\varepsilon,k}[E(y)]$, for $y \in \mathbb{Z}_n^*$, are 0,1-valued, independent random elements with $\mathrm{prob}[\sigma R_{\varepsilon,k}[E(y)] = 1_k(y)] = 0.5 + \varepsilon$. We implement the binary gcd deciphering method with oracle $\sigma R_{\varepsilon,k}$ as follows.

1. for $t := \lceil 3(4 + \log \log n)\varepsilon^{-2} \rceil$ guess a random element r with $rx < n/(2t)$ and $rx = 0 \bmod 2^k$.
2. guess elements b_1, b_2 such that $b_i x \le 2^{-k}n$ for $i = 1,2$.
3. simulate the binary gcd deciphering method; for each query on $xb < 2^{-k}n$ put
   $$1_1(xb) := \lceil \tfrac{1}{t} \Sigma_{i=1}^{t} \, \sigma R_{\varepsilon,k}[E(x(2^{k-1}b + ir))] \rceil \rfloor$$
   and stop after at most $4 \log_2 n$ queries.

If $rx < n/(2t)$ and $rx = 0 \bmod 2^k$ then $1_k(irx) = 0$ and $irx = 0 \bmod 2^k$ for $i \le t$. If $xb < 2^{-k}n$ then $1_k(xb) = 1_1(x2^{k-1}b)$.

Hence for all $xb < 2^{-k}n$:

$prob[\mathcal{O}R_{\varepsilon,k}[E(x(2^{k-1}b + ir))] = l_1(xb)] = 0.5 + \varepsilon$.

By the law of large numbers each query answer has error
probability $\leq 2\exp(-\varepsilon^2 t/3) \leq 1/(27\log n)$ (This means that
the fraction of oracles $\mathcal{O}$ which in step 3 give a wrong
value $l_1(xb)$ for a particular query, is at most $2\exp(-\varepsilon^2 t/3)$;
this fraction is exponentially small for large t). With
probability $\geq 1/2$ all $4\log_2 n$ query answers with $\mathcal{O}R_{\varepsilon,k}$ are
correct. Hence the algorithm using oracle $\mathcal{O}R_{\varepsilon,k}$ succeeds
with probability $\geq 1/2$ if b_1,b_2,r have been guessed as
specified.

Guessing r and b_1, b_2 can be done (with probability $\geq 1/2$)
with $2^k 2t\, 2^{2k} = O(2^{3k}\varepsilon^{-2}\log\log n)$ trials. Thus $E(x)$ can
be deciphered (with probability $\geq 1/2$) in $O(2^{3k}\varepsilon^{-2}(\log n)^4)$
bit operations. $((\log n)^3$ bounds the number of bit operations
for evaluating $E(y))$. Thus we have proved

Theorem 8 For every k there is a random $[\varepsilon^{-1}\log n\, 2^k]^{O(1)}$-time
algorithm using oracle $\mathcal{O}R_{\varepsilon,k}$ which inverts the encryption
function $E(x)$.

It clearly follows that the time bound of theorem 8 holds for
all but a negligible fraction of oracles $\sigma_{\varepsilon,k}$ which have
an ε-advantage in predicting l_k . It is an open problem
whether the time bound $[\varepsilon^{-1}\log n\, 2^k]^{O(1)}$ can be obtained
for all oracles $\sigma_{\varepsilon,k}$.

References:

M. Ben-Or, B. Chor, A. Shamir, On the Cryptographic Security
of Single RSA Bits, Proc. STOC 1983, 421-430

L. Blum, M. Blum, M. Snub, A Simple Secure Pseudo-Random
Number Generator. Crypto 1982

M. Blum & S. Micali, How to Generate Cryptographically Strong
Sequences of Pseudo-Random Bits, Proc. FOCS 1982, 112-117.

S. Goldwasser, S. Micali, P. Tong, Why and How to Establish a
Private Code on a Public Network, Proc. FOCS 1982, 134-144.

M. Rabin, Digital Signatures and Public Key Functions as
Intractable as Factorization, MIT/LCS/TR-212, Technical
Report, MIT, 1979.

A. Renyi, Wahrscheinlichkeitsrechnung
VEB Deutscher Verlag der Wissenschaften Berlin 1966.

R. Rivest, A. Shamir & L. Adelman, A Method of Obtaining Digital
Signatures and Public Key Cryptosystems, CACM, February 1978.

A. Shamir, On the generation of Cryptographically Strong Pseudo-
Random Sequences, 1981 ICALP.

A. Yao, Theory and Applications of Trapdoor Functions, proc.
FOCS 1982, 80-91

U. V. and V. V. Vazirani, RSA bits are $.732 + \varepsilon$ secure.
TR U. Berkeley and Harvard University 1983.

On the Number of Close-and-Equal Pairs of Bits in a String
(with Implications on the Security of RSA's L.S.B)
(Extended Abstract)

Oded Goldreich
Laboratory for Computer Science
MIT,room NE43-836,Cambridge,MA 02139

Abstract

We consider the following problem: Let s be a n-bit string with m ones and $n - m$ zeros. Denote by $CE_t(s)$ the number of pairs, of equal bits which are within distance t apart, in the string s. What is the minimum value of $CE_t(\cdot)$, when the minimum is taken over all n-bit strings which consists of m ones and $n - m$ zeros?

We prove a (reasonably) tight lower bound for this combinatorial problem.

Implications, on the cryptographic security of the least significant bit of a message encrypted by the RSA scheme, follow. E.g. under the assumption that the RSA is unbreakable; there exist no probabilistic polynomial-time algorithm which guesses the least significant bit of a message (correctly) with probability at least **0.725** , when given the encryption of the message using the RSA. This is the best result known concerning the security of RSA's least significant bit.

Keywords: Cryptography, Combinatorial Analysis, the RSA Scheme, Bit Security, Combinatorial Bounds, Bit-String Properties, Public Key Cryptosystems.

Supported by a Weizmann Postdoctoral Fellowship

1. Introduction

This paper combines a combinatorial study with the application of its results to the analysis of a cryptological question. (The combinatorial problem is fully defined and solved in Sec. 2.)

1.1. Cryptological Background

The importance of the notion of "partial information" to cryptographic research has gained wide recognition through the pioneering works of Blum and Micali [BM] and Goldwasser and Micali [GM]. In this paper we consider a much more specific question: the cryptographical security of the least significant bit of a message encrypted by the RSA scheme (hereafter referred to as RSA's l.s.b) .

The RSA encryption scheme was presented by Rivest, Shamir and Adleman [RSA]. It is the best known implementation of the notion of a Public Key Cryptosystem, which was suggested by Diffie and Hellman [DH]. Encryption using the RSA is done by raizing the message to a known exponent, e, and reducing the result modulo a known composite number, N, the factorization[1] of which is kept secret. The inverse of e in the multiplicative group $Z^*_{\varphi(N)}$ is used for decryption and is kept secret. It is widely believed that the RSA is hard to break. This means that an adversary who does not know the secret $(e^{-1} \bmod \varphi(N))$ will not be able to compute the message from its encryption (i.e. to invert the encryption function).

However, even under this unbreakability assumption; it might be the case that the RSA leaks some "valuable" partial information. I.e. it might be that given the ciphertext, one can compute some function of half of the bits of the plaintext. Proving that, under the unbreakability assumption, this is infeasible will make the RSA much more attractive. This seems to be a high tool. Research attempts are meanwhile focused at the feasibility of guessing correctly the least significant bit of the plaintext (i.e. RSA's l.s.b.)[2].

By saying that *RSA's l.s.b is p-secure* we mean that guessing it correctly with probability at least p is as hard as inverting the RSA. Consider an **oracle** that when given the encryption (using the RSA) of a message guesses the least significant bit of the message correctly with probability p. Such an oracle will be called a *p-oracle for RSA's l.s.b* . Clearly, the existence of a polynomial time algorithm that inverts the RSA using a p-oracle for RSA's l.s.b implies that RSA's l.s.b is p-secure.

It is believed that RSA's l.s.b is $(\frac{1}{2} + \epsilon)$-secure , for arbitrary small constant ϵ. Proving this statement might be a major breakthrough on the way to proving that any "valuable" partial information about the message encrypted by the RSA is as hard to get as inverting the RSA. Progress towards this goal has been slow but consistant, in the recent years.

---

[1] To be exact, N is the produce of two large primes, p and q. $\varphi(\cdot)$ is the Euler's totient function, thus $\varphi(pq) = (p-1)(q-1)$.

[2] Nevertheless, results have been achieved also w.r.t. other kinds of partial information. For details consult [BCS] and [VV2].

The first step was taken by Goldwasser Micali and Tong [GMT] who proved that RSA's l.s.b is $(1 - \frac{1}{|N|})$-secure, where $|N|$ is the size of the RSA's modulus.

Ben-Or, Chor and Shamir greatly improved this result by proving that RSA's l.s.b is $(\frac{3}{4} + \epsilon)$-secure, where ϵ is fixed and arbitrary small. Their paper [BCS] contains an algorithm which inverts the RSA function. Their algorithm uses a $(\frac{3}{4} + \epsilon)$-oracle for RSA's l.s.b (in order) to determine the parities of certain multiples of the original message. For further details consult [BCS] or [VV2].

Vazirani and Vazirani [VV1] have presented a very sophisticated modification of the algorithmic procedure used by Ben-Or, Chor and Shamir. The theme of their modification is a much better use of the oracle answers. They showed that their modification is guaranteed to succeed when given access to a 0.741-oracle for RSA's l.s.b. Recently, they have improved their analysis by showing that their modification is guaranteed to succeed even if it uses a 0.732-oracle.

Using the combinatorial results obtained in this paper, we show that the Vazirani and Vazirani algorithm is guaranteed to succeed when it uses a 0.725-oracle for RSA's l.s.b. Other observations w.r.t the Vazirani and Vazirani algorithm as well as w.r.t other inverting algorithms are also implied.

1.2. Our Results

The following problem occured to us when trying to improve Ben-Or, Chor and Shamir's result [BCS]:

Let s be a n-bit string with m ones and $n - m$ zeros. Two bits in the string s are said to be t-close if they are within distance t apart. Denote by $CE_t(s)$ the number of pairs of equal t-close bits in the string s . What is the minimum value of $CE_t(\cdot)$, over all n-bit strings which consists of m ones and $n - m$ zeros?

In Sec.2 we prove a (reasonably) tight lower bound on this combinatorial problem. With respect to proving the "amount" of security of the least significant bit of the RSA, this is a double-edged-sword:

(1) It provides a powerful tool for analyzing certain algorithms for inverting the RSA using an $(\frac{1}{2} + \delta)$-oracle for RSA's l.s.b .

For example the algorithm proposed by Vazirani and Vazirani [VV1] is shown to work when it uses any 0.725-oracle for RSA's l.s.b (i.e. $\delta = 0.225$). This establishes the best result known conserning the security of RSA's l.s.b .

(2) It points out the weakness of various proof techniques for determining the cryptographic security of RSA's l.s.b .

For example the Vazirani and Vazirani algorithm [VV1] may fail to invert if it uses a $\frac{2}{3}$-oracle for RSA's l.s.b .

These implications will be discussed in Sec. 3 . We believe that the combinatorial result has also other implications.

2. The Combinatorial Results

In this section we give a formal definition of the combinatorial problem, discussed in the introduction, and prove a (reasonably) tight lower bound on it.

2.1. Definitions

Let $s = (s_0, s_1, s_2, .., s_{|s|-1})$ be a binary string of length $|s|$. We denote by $sh_i(s)$ the string which result from s by the application of i left cyclic shifts. I.e:

$$sh_i(s) = (s_i, s_{i+1}, s_{i+2}, .., s_{i+|s|-1}),$$

where indices are considered modulo $|s|$.

Define the *i-overlap* of a string, s, to be the number of positions which agree in s and $sh_i(s)$. The i-overlap of s will be denoted by $over_i(s)$, i.e.

$$over_i(s) = Hamming(s \equiv sh_i(s)),$$

where $\equiv$ denotes the bit by bit equal operation and $Hamming(s)$ denotes the number of ones in s. Note that $over_i(s) = |\{j: 0 \le j < |s| \land s_j = s_{j+i}\}|$.

Denote by AverOver(s,t) the average over the i-overlaps of s for $i \in \{1, 2, .., t\}$. I.e.

$$AverOver(s,t) = \frac{1}{t} \sum_{i=1}^{t} over_i(s)$$

We remind the reader that $CE_t(s)$ was used to denote the number of pairs, of equal bits which are within distance t apart, in the string s. I.e.

$$CE_t(s) = |\{(i,j): 0 \le i < j < n \land s_i = s_j \land j - i \le t\}|,$$

where $n = |s|$.

Clearly, $CE_t(s) = \sum_{i=1}^{t}|\{j: 0 \le j < n \land s_j = s_{j+i}\}|$. Thus,

$$CE_t(s) = t \cdot AverOver(s,t).$$

When evaluating $CE_t(s)$ consider "lines" which connect equal t-close bits in s (i.e. positions that contain equal values and are less than t bits apart in the string s). These lines are hereafter called *overlines*. Note that $CE_t(s)$ is nothing but the number of overlines in the string s.

Let n and m be integers such that $0.5n \le m < n$. Let $\delta = \frac{m-0.5n}{n}$. We denote by S_n^δ the set of n-bit binary strings with $m=(0.5+\delta)n$ ones (and $n-m$ zeros).

Denote by Aver(n,δ,t) the minimum value of AverOver($\cdot,t$) divided by n, when minimized over all strings in S_n^δ. I.e.

$$Aver(n,\delta,t) = min_{s \in S_n^\delta} \{ \frac{1}{n} \cdot AverOver(s,t) \}.$$

It is straightforward to see that for every $s \in S_n^\delta$, AverOver(s,n)$=(0.5 + 2\delta^2)n$.

In this section we study Aver(n,δ,t) for arbitrary t, $t<n$. We obtain non-trivial results, as the surprising fact that Aver($n,0,t$) converges to $\sqrt{2} - 1 \approx 0.414$, when $\frac{n}{t}$ and t are large enough.

2.2. Propositions

We will assume throughout this section that $t \leq \frac{1}{2}(n-2)$. We will analyze $\mathrm{Aver}(n,\delta,t)$ as follows: first we will show that the minimum of $CE_t(\cdot)$ is achieved by strings which belong to a restricted subset of S_n^δ; and next we will minimize $CE_t(\cdot)$ over this subset. This will establish a lower bound on $\mathrm{Aver}(n,\delta,t)$. The upper bound will be implied by the proof of the lower bound, since this proof specifies a string $s \in S_n^\delta$ for which $CE_t(s) \approx nt \cdot \mathrm{Aver}(n,\delta,t)$.

2.2.1. Reduction into a restricted subset

In this subsection we will show that when analysing $\mathrm{Aver}(n,\delta,t)$ it is enough to consider strings in S_n^δ which have the following property:

> The string contains no "short 3-alternations substring". A *short 3-alternations substring* is a substring of the form $\sigma \tau^+ \sigma^+ \tau$ and length less than $t+2$, where $\sigma \neq \tau \in \{0,1\}$. (Here, and throughout this paper, σ^+ denotes a non-empty string of σ's.)

Proposition 1: $over_i(s) = over_i(sh_j(s))$

Prop. 1 follows directly from the definitions which consider strings as if they were cycles. From this point on, we also take the liberty of doing so.

The proofs of the following propositions are omitted; they can be found in the full version of this paper ([G84]).

Proposition 2: Let $\sigma_j \in \{0,1\}$, for $1 \leq j \leq 2t$. Let α be a binary string. Let $n_{\tau_1 \tau_2} = CE_t(\sigma_1 \sigma_2 \cdots \sigma_t \tau_1 \tau_2 \sigma_{t+1} \sigma_{t+2} \cdots \sigma_{2t} \alpha)$. Then $n_{10} - n_{01} = 2(\sigma_1 - \sigma_{2t})$.

Note that *switching* τ_1 and τ_2 in the string $\sigma_1 \sigma_2 \cdots \sigma_t \tau_1 \tau_2 \sigma_{t+1} \sigma_{t+2} \cdots \sigma_{2t} \alpha$ results in the string $\sigma_1 \sigma_2 \cdots \sigma_t \tau_2 \tau_1 \sigma_{t+1} \sigma_{t+2} \cdots \sigma_{2t} \alpha$. The latter string has more overlines (than the former one) only if $\sigma_1 = \tau_2 \neq \tau_1 = \sigma_{2n}$. Note that the latter string has less overlines if $\sigma_1 = \tau_1 \neq \tau_2 = \sigma_{2n}$.

Proposition 3: Let α be a binary string and let x, y, z, u be integers such that $x + y \geq t$ but $y + z < t$. Then:

(i) $CE_t(\sigma \tau^x \sigma^y \tau^{z-1} \sigma \tau \alpha) \leq CE_t(\sigma \tau^x \sigma^y \tau^z \sigma \alpha)$.

(ii) $CE_t(\sigma \tau^x \sigma^y \tau^{z-1} \sigma \tau \sigma^{u-1} \tau^{t-u} \sigma \alpha) < CE_t(\sigma \tau^x \sigma^y \tau^z \sigma^u \tau^{t-u} \sigma \alpha)$.

(iii) $CE_t(\sigma \tau^x \sigma^y \sigma \tau^z \alpha) \leq CE_t(\sigma \tau^x \sigma^y \tau^z \sigma \alpha)$.

Proposition 4: Let $s \in S_n^\delta$ be a binary string such that $CE_t(s) = n \cdot t \cdot \mathrm{Aver}(n,\delta,t)$. (I.e. s is a string with minimum number of overlines among all strings in S_n^δ.) Then there exist a string, $s' \in S_n^\delta$, such that :

(i) The string s' contains a substring of the form 10^+1^+0 the length of which is at least $t+2$.[3]

(ii) $CE_t(s') < CE_t(s) + t^2$.

---

[3] We remind the reader that σ^+ denotes a non-empty string of σs.

Proposition 5: Let $s' \in S_n^\delta$ be a string, with minimum number of overlines, which satisfies Prop. 4 . Then with no loss of generality, the string s' contains no substring of the form 10^+1^+0 the length of which is less than $t + 2$. Furthermore, the string s' contains at most one substring of the form 01^+0^+1 the length of which is less than $t + 2$.

We remind the reader that $CE_t(s') < nt\text{Aver}(n,\delta,t)+t^2$ and that $s' \in S_n^\delta$.

Proposition 6: Let $s' \in S_n^\delta$ be a string as in Prop. 5. Then there exist a string $s'' \in S_n^\delta$ such that:

(i) The string s'' contains no substring of the form 10^+1^+0 the length of which is less than $t + 2$.

(ii) The string s'' contains no substring of the form 01^+0^+1 the length of which is less than $t + 2$.

(iii) $CE_t(s'') < CE_t(s') + t^2$.

We remind the reader that our objective is to given a good lower bound on $\text{Aver}(n,\delta,t)=\min_{s \in S_n^\delta} \frac{1}{nt} CE_t(s)$. Note that we have restricted our attention to strings that donot have short 3-alternations substrings; i.e. substrings of the form 01^+0^+1 or 10^+1^+0 which have length less than $t + 2$. This is sufficient since there exist such a string, namely s'', that has approximately the minimun number of overlines. I.e. $CE_t(s'') < nt\text{Aver}(n,\delta,t)+2t^2$. Formally we define R_n^δ to be the set of strings which belong to S_n^δ and do not have short 3-alternating substrings. $\text{Aver}_R(n,\delta,t)$ will denote $\min_{r \in R_n^\delta} \frac{1}{nt} CE_t(r)$. Clearly,

Proposition 7: $\text{Aver}(n,\delta,t) \leq \text{Aver}_R(n,\delta,t) < \text{Aver}(n,\delta,t)+\frac{2t}{n}$.

Let us define even a more restricted subset of S_n^δ: The set MR_n^δ is the subset of strings which belong to R_n^δ and do not have *long homogenous substrings*; i.e. substring of the form σ^{t+1}, where $\sigma \in \{0,1\}$. Also, $\text{Aver}_{MR}(n,\delta,t)$ will denote $\min_{r \in MR_n^\delta} \frac{1}{nt} CE_t(r)$. Let us first give a tight lower bound on $\text{Aver}_{MR}(n,\delta,t)$ and only later prove that this bound is approximately also a bound for $\text{Aver}_R(n,\delta,t)$.

2.2.2. Lower bound for $\text{Aver}_{MR}(n,\delta,t)$

Recall that each of the strings in $MR_n^\delta \subseteq S_n^\delta$ has the following properties:

(i) The string contains no short 3-alternating substrings.

(ii) The string contains no long homogenous substrings.

We will relay on the above properties of the strings in MR_n^δ in order to bound $\text{Aver}_{MR}(n,\delta,t)$. Given a string $r \in MR_n^\delta$ we will introduce an expression, for $CE_t(r)$, which depends only on the numbers of bits in each maximal substrings of consecutive equal bits. In other words, we will introduce a localized counting of $CE_t(r)$.

Definition: We say that b is a block (an all-σ block) of the string r if it is a maximal substring of equal bits. I.e. $b = \sigma^+$ and $r = \tau b \tau \alpha$, where $\tau \neq \sigma$ and α is an arbitrary string.

Denotations: Let q denote the number of all-zero [all-one] blocks in r. Beginning from an arbitrary position between an all-one block and an all-zero block and going cyclically from left to right; number the blocks of consecutive zeros [ones] by $0,1,2,...,(q-1)$. Denote by z_i the number of zeros in the i-th all-zero-block and by y_i the number of ones in the i-th all-one-block. I.e., $r = 0^{z_0}1^{y_0}0^{z_1}1^{y_1}0^{z_2}1^{y_2}...0^{z_{q-1}}1^{y_{q-1}}$.

Proposition 8: Overlines occur (in r) only either within a block or between two consecutive blocks (of the same bit).

Remark: Note that Prop. 8 holds even if $r \in R_n^\delta$.

This suggests to evaluate the number of overlines (in r) by counting the "contribution" of each (homogeneous) block to it. This counting is hereafter referred as the *Block-Localized Counting (BLC)* and proceeds as follows:

Block-Localized Counting (with respect to a block of length l in r):

(i) The number of overlines **within the block**, denoted I_l.

(ii) The number of overlines **between bits of the blocks** neighbouring this block (i.e the first block on its left and the first block on its right), denoted B_l.

Note that I_l and B_l are easy to evaluate and can be used to express $CE_t(r)$. Namely,

Proposition 9:

(i) $CE_t(r) = \sum_{i=0}^{q-1}((I_{y_i} + B_{y_i}) + (I_{z_i} + B_{z_i}))$, where $r = 0^{z_0}1^{y_0}0^{z_1}1^{y_1}...0^{z_{q-1}}1^{y_{q-1}}$.

(ii) For $l < t$, $I_l = \binom{l}{2}$ and $B_l = \sum_{i=1}^{t-l} i$.

(iii) For $l = t$, $I_l = \binom{t}{2}$ and $B_l = 0$.

Remark: Note that for $l > t$, $I_t = \binom{t}{2} + (l-t)t$ and $B_t = 0$. (Note that for $k > 0$, $CE_t(\sigma^{t+k}) = CE_t(\sigma^{t+k-1}) + t = CE_t(\sigma^t) + kt$.) However such substrings donot exist in a string which belongs to MR_n^δ.

Evaluating $I_l + B_l$ we get

Proposition 10: The contribution (to the BLC) of one l-bit long block (in r) is:

$$f(l) = l^2 - (t+1)l + \frac{t^2+t}{2}.$$

Note that the contribution of all the all-zero blocks to the number of overlines (in r) only depends on the way the zeros are partitioned among the all-zero blocks. (I.e. it is independent of the way the ones are partitioned among the all-one blocks.) This contribution amounts to:

$$g(z_0, z_1, .., z_{q-1}) = \sum_{i=0}^{q-1} f(z_i),$$

where $r = 0^{z_0}1^{y_0}0^{z_1}1^{y_1} ... 0^{z_{q-1}}1^{y_{q-1}}$.

Note that $g(\cdot, \cdot, \cdots, \cdot)$ is a quadratic form and therefore

Proposition 11: For fixed q, t and k, the minimum value of the function $g(x_0, x_1, .., x_{q-1})$ subject to the constraint $k = \sum_{i=0}^{q-1} x_i$, is obtained at $x_0 = x_1 = \cdots = x_{q-1} = \frac{k}{q}$.

Thus, the minimum number of overlines is achieved if all the all-zero-blocks [all-one-blocks] are of the same size. This yields

Proposition 12: Let $Q = \{q \in Integers: \frac{m}{t} \leq q \leq n - m\}$. Then:

$$nt\mathrm{Aver}_{MR}(n,\delta,t) \geq \min_{q \in Q}\{q \cdot (f(\tfrac{m}{q}) + f(\tfrac{n-m}{q}))\} \ .$$

We remind the reader that $m = (0.5 + \delta)n$.

Elaborating the r.h.s. expression of Prop. 12 we get

Proposition 13: $\mathrm{Aver}_{MR}(n,\delta,t) \geq \min_{q \in Q}\{h_n^\delta(q)\}$, where

$$h_n^\delta(q) = \frac{t+1}{n} \cdot q + \frac{(0.5+2\delta^2)n}{t} \cdot \frac{1}{q} - \frac{t+1}{t} \ .$$

Note that

Proposition 14: The minimum of the function $h_n^\delta(\cdot)$ is obtained at:

$$q_{min} = \sqrt{\frac{0.5+2\delta^2}{t(t+1)}} \cdot n \ ;$$

and the minimum value, $h_n^\delta(q_{min})$, is:

$$v_t^\delta = \sqrt{(2 + 8\delta^2) \cdot \frac{t+1}{t}} - \frac{t+1}{t} \ .$$

Thus, $\mathrm{Aver}_{MR}(n,\delta,t) \geq v_t^\delta$. All that is left is to derive a lower bound for $\mathrm{Aver}_R(n,\delta,t)$.

2.2.3. Lower bound for $\mathrm{Aver}_R(n,\delta,t)$ and $\mathrm{Aver}(n,\delta,t)$

In this subsection we show that a string, $r_0 \in R_n^\delta$, with minimum overlines can be transformed into a string $r_0' \in MR_{n'}^{\delta'}$, such that $n' \approx n$, $\delta' \approx \delta$ and $CE(r_0') \approx CE_t(r_0)$. We conclude by using this fact and the lower bound for $\mathrm{Aver}_{MR}(n,\delta,t)$, to introduce a lower bound for $\mathrm{Aver}_R(n,\delta,t)$.

Proposition 15: Let $r_0 \in R_n^\delta$ be a string with minimum number of overlines; i.e. $CE_t(r_0) = nt\mathrm{Aver}_R(n,\delta,t)$. Then:

(i) For $\sigma \in \{0,1\}$, either r_0 contains no substring of more than t consecutive σ's or r_0 contains no block of less than t consecutive σ's. Futhermore, w.l.o.g, r_0 contains atmost one substring of more than t consecutive σ's.

(ii) If $t > \frac{\frac{1}{2}+\delta}{\frac{1}{2}-\delta}$ then r_0 has no substring of the form σ^{2t}.

(iii) If $t \leq \frac{\frac{1}{2}+\delta}{\frac{1}{2}-\delta}$ then $\mathrm{Aver}(n,\delta,t)=2\delta$.

(iv) If $t > \frac{\frac{1}{2}+\delta}{\frac{1}{2}-\delta}$ then there exist a $k < t$, a $\delta' \geq \delta$ and a $r_0' \in MR_{n+k}^{\delta'}$ such that $CE_t(r_0) \geq CE_t(r_0') - kt$.

We conclude by using Prop. 15$_{(iv)}$ and the lower bound for $\mathrm{Aver}_{MR}(n,\delta,t)$, to introduce lower bounds for $\mathrm{Aver}_R(n,\delta,t)$ and $\mathrm{Aver}(n,\delta,t)$.

Proposition 16: If $t > \frac{\frac{1}{2}+\delta}{\frac{1}{2}-\delta}$ then

(i) There exist $0 \leq k < t$ and $\delta' \geq \delta$ such that
$\text{Aver}_R(n,\delta,t) > \text{Aver}_{MR}(n+k,\delta',t) - \frac{t}{n}$.

(ii) $\text{Aver}_R(n,\delta,t) > v_t^\delta - \frac{t}{n}$.

(iii) $\text{Aver}(n,\delta,t) > v_t^\delta - \frac{3t}{n}$.

2.3. The Main Results

Throughout this section we assume that $\frac{\frac{1}{2}+\delta}{\frac{1}{2}-\delta} < t \leq \frac{1}{2}(n-2)$.

Lower Bound Lemma: $\text{Aver}(n,\delta,t)$ is at least

$$\left(\sqrt{(2+8\delta^2)} \cdot \frac{t+1}{t} - \frac{t+1}{t}\right) - \frac{3t}{n} \ .$$

The proof follows immediately from Prop. 14 and 16$_{(iii)}$.

Upper Bound Lemma: $\text{Aver}(n,\delta,t)$ is at most

$$\left(\sqrt{(2+8\delta^2)} \cdot \frac{t+1}{t} - \frac{t+1}{t}\right) + \frac{t+1}{n} + \frac{1}{2t^2} \ .$$

The proof follows from observing that the proof of the lower bound specifies the structure of a string which achieves minimum $CE_t(\cdot)$ among all strings in MR_n^δ. The only problem in constructing such a string is that non-integer numbers, of blocks and block sizes, may appear. However, the overlap added by the round-up of the number of blocks is less than $\frac{t+1}{n}$; while the overline added by the round-up of the blocks' sizes is less than $\frac{1}{2t^2}$. For details see the full version of this paper.

Evaluating the expressions in the above lemmas we get

Corollary 1:

(i) $\sqrt{2}-1-O(\frac{1}{t}) < \text{Aver}(n,0,t) < \sqrt{2}-1+O(\frac{1}{t^2})+O(\frac{t}{n})$.

(ii) For $t \geq 2500$ and $n > 300000 \cdot t$, $\text{Aver}(n,0.177,t) > \frac{1}{2} + 0.0001$.

(iii) For $t \geq 500$ and $n > 10000 \cdot t$, $\text{Aver}(n,0.225,t) > 0.55 + 0.0001$.

(iv) For every $2500 < t < \frac{n}{10000}$ and $\delta \leq 0.176$, $\text{Aver}(n,\delta,t) < \frac{1}{2}$.

(v) For every $500 < t < \frac{n}{10000}$ and $\delta \leq 0.224$, $\text{Aver}(n,\delta,t) < 1 - 2\delta$.

2.4. Additional Definitions and Results

In this section we define a different, yet related, combinatorial problem. Instead of considering the average overlap over all "small"[4] shifts; we consider the maximum overlap obtained by one of the "small" shifts.

Let us define an *i-overline* to be a line which connects a pair of equal bits which are (exactly) at distance i apart.

---

[4] Here, "small" means not greater than t.

Denote by MaxOver(s,t) the maximum over the i-overlaps of s for $i \in \{1, 2, .., t\}$. I.e.

$$\text{MaxOver}(s,t) = max_{1 \leq i \leq t} \{ over_i(s) \} .$$

Denote by Max(n,δ,t) the minimum value of MaxOver(s,t) divided by n, when minimized over all strings in S_n^δ . I.e.

$$\text{Max}(n,\delta,t) = min_{s \in S_n^\delta} \{ \tfrac{1}{n} \cdot \text{MaxOver}(s,t) \}.$$

Clearly,

Proposition 17: Max$(n,\delta,t) \geq$ Aver(n,δ,t).

This establishes a trivial lower bound on Max(n,δ,t). We donot beleive that this bound is tight; however we failed to prove a better one. On the other hand the following proposition yields an upper bound on Max$(n,0,t)$.

Proposition 18: ((i) is folklore and (ii) appears in van Lint[L])

(i) For every De-Bruijn Sequence[5], s, of length 2^k and every i, $i \in \{1, 2, .., k-1\}$

$$over_i(s) = \tfrac{1}{2} \cdot 2^k .$$

(ii) For every k there exists a Shortened De-Bruijn Sequence[6], s, of length $2^k - 1$ such that for every i, $i \in \{1, 2, .., 2^k - 2\}$,

$$over_i(s) = 2^{k-1} - 1 \approx \tfrac{1}{2} \cdot (2^k - 1) .$$

Using Prop. 18 we also obtain an upper bound on Max(n,δ,t); i.e.

Proposition 19: [Here q is an integer.]

(i) For $t+1 = l = 2^k - 1$, $n = ql$ and $\delta = \frac{l+q-1}{2n}$, Max$(n,\delta,t) \leq \tfrac{1}{2} + \delta - \frac{1}{t+1} + \frac{1}{n}$.

(ii) Max$(n,\delta,t) \leq$ Max$(n,\delta,t+1)$.

(iii) Max$(n,\delta,t) < \tfrac{1}{2} + \delta + O(\frac{t}{n})$.

The proof appears in the full version of this paper.

---

[5] The 2^k-bit long string $(s_0, s_1, s_2, ..., s_{2^k-1})$ is a De-Bruijn Sequence if (when considered in circular order) it contain as substrings all possible bit-strings of length k.

[6] A Shortened De-Bruijn Sequence, of length $2^k - 1$, is a 2^k-long De-Bruijn Sequence in which a zero has been omitted from the all-zero block of length k .

3. On the Cryptographic Security of the RSA's L.S.B

In this section we apply the results of the privious section to the analysis of algorithms which invert the RSA encryption function when given access to an oracle for the least significant bit of the encrypted message. This implies results (concerning the security of RSA's l.s.b.) which fall into the following three categories:

(i) A 0.725-security result (for RSA's l.s.b)

(ii) Conditional improvements of the above result. I.e. results which will hold if some conjecture is proven.

(iii) Bounds on the possibility of improvements using current techniques.

3.1. Specific Background

Our 0.725-security result is based on Vazirani and Vazirani work [VV1], which is an improvement of Ben-Or Chor and Shamir [BCS] work. In this subsection we sketch some of the ideas used in these nice works.

3.1.1. A Sketch of Ben-Or Chor and Shamir Algorithmic Procedure

The essence of the Inverting Algorithm:

The plaintext is reconstructed, from its encryption, by running a g.c.d procedure on two multiples[7] of it. The values of these multiples (as well as the values of all multiples discussed hereafter) are "small"[8]. A Modified Binary G.C.D algorithm is used. To operate, this algorithm needs to know the parity of multiples of the plaintext. Thus, it is provided with a *subroutine* that determines the parity of these multiples.(see [BCS])

Determining Parity using an Oracle which may err:

The *subroutine* determines the parity of a multiple $,kx,$ of the plaintext $,x,$ by using an $(\frac{1}{2} + \delta)$-oracle for RSA's l.s.b as follows. It picks a random r and asks the oracle for the parity (i.e. l.s.b) of both rx and $rx + kx$ feeding it in turn with $E(rx) = E(r)E(x)$ and $E((r+k)x) = E(r+k)E(x)$[9] . The oracle's answers are processed according to the following observation. Since kx is "small" with very high probability $rx < rx + kx$. Then, the parity of kx is equel to 0 if the parities of rx and $rx + kx$ are identical; and equal to 1 otherwise. This is repeated many times; every repetition (instance) is called a kx-measurement (or a toss of the kx-coin). Note that the outcome of a kx-measurement is correct if the oracle was correct on both rx and $rx + kx$. The outcome is correct also if the oracle was wrong on both queries (but this fact is not used in [BCS]).

---

[7] All integers and operations are considered modulo $,N$, the RSA's modulus.

[8] Here and throughout the rest of the paper "small" means bounded by a very small fraction of the RSA's modulus.

[9] $E(M)$ denotes the RSA encryption function. Recall that $E(M) = M^e \ (mod \ N)$, where N and e are respectively the RSA's modulus and exponent.

(Trivial) Measurement Analysis:

A kx-coin toss is correct with probability at least 2δ .

(This suffices if $\delta = \frac{1}{4} + \epsilon$, see [BCS])

3.1.2. A Sketch of Vazirani and Vazirani Modification of the BCS-Procedure

Distinguishing a Good Coin from a Bad one:

For $\delta < \frac{1}{4}$; if when running a Monte-Carlo experiment on a kx-coin toss, more than a 1-2δ fraction of the answers agree on some value, then this is the correct value.(In such a case the coin is said to be *distinguishably good*. See [VV1])

Using Distinguishably Good Coins:

Let t be a fixed constant and K be a set of cardinality $O(\log N)$. If *for every* $k \in K$ *there exist a* $1 \leq j \leq t$ *such that the* $(j \cdot kx)$-*coin is distinguishably good* then one can determine the parity of kx. (This is done by replacing every kx-measurement, of the subroutine, by a set of $O(\log \log N)$ measurements, see [VV1]). (The above condition will be referred to as the *Distinguishability Condition*.)

Vazirani and Vazirani combined the above sketched ideas to an algorithm that inverts the RSA using a $(\frac{1}{2} + \delta)$-oracle. It remained to be shown that when given certain oracles for RSA's l.s.b the Distinguishability Condition holds. In [VV1] Vazirani and Vazirani proved that the Distinguishability Condition holds for any 0.741-oracle for RSA's l.s.b.; in [VV2] they improved their analysis and showed that this condition holds for any 0.732-oracle.

3.2. Cryptographic Implications of our Combinatorial Results

It is easy to show that the Distinguishability Condition is equivalent to the following condition, hereafter referred to as the *Big-Advantage Condition* : for some fixed t, $\text{Max}(N,\delta,t) > 1 - 2\delta + \epsilon$.

(Use oracle transformation through multiplication by the inverse of $kx \bmod N$. Note that if the inverse does not exist it is feasible to factor N and inverting the RSA becomes easy.) This was also observed by Vazirani and Vazirani [VV2].

Thus, we can summerize Vazirani and Vazirani's [VV1] work by the following

VV-Theorem: Let N be the RSA's modulus and t be a fixed constant. If $\text{Max}(N,\delta,t) > 1 - 2\delta + \epsilon$ then any $(\frac{1}{2} + \delta)$-oracle for RSA's l.s.b can be used to efficiently invert the RSA. (In other words: if the Big Advantage Condition holds for δ then RSA's l.s.b is $(\frac{1}{2} + \delta)$-secure.)

By our results, the Big-Advantage Condition holds for $\delta \geq 0.225$. Namely, using the VV-Theorem, Prop. 17 and Corollary $1_{(iii)}$ we get

Corollary 2: Any 0.725-oracle for the least significant bit of the RSA can be efficiantly used to invert the RSA.

In other words

Theorem: RSA's l.s.b. is 0.725-secure.

Note that the result of corollary $1_{(iii)}$ is tight. Thus under the condition $\text{Aver}(n,\delta,t) > 1 - 2\delta + \epsilon$, the result of Corollary 2 is optimal. However, $\text{Aver}(n,\delta,t) > 1 - 2\delta + \epsilon$, is more than is needed to satisfy the Big-Advantage Condition. (Recall that the Big-Advantage Condition requires only that $\text{Max}(n,\delta,t) > 1 - 2\delta + \epsilon$.) Thus, any improvement of the current lower bound on $\text{Max}(n,\delta,t)$ will yield an improvement of the result of Corollary 2. We beleive that $\text{Max}(n,\delta,t) > \text{Aver}(n,\delta,t)$ and thus that such an improvement is possible. Furthermore we conjecture that

Conjecture 1: $\text{Max}(n,\delta,t) \approx \frac{1}{2} + \delta$.

Combined with the VV-Theorem this implies

Corollary 3: If Conjecture 1 is valid then RSA's l.s.b. is $(\frac{2}{3} + \epsilon)$-secure, for arbitrary small fixed ϵ.

Note that under the **Big-Advantage Condition** the "result" of Corollary 3 is optimal. This is due to Prop. $19_{(iii)}$ which states that $\text{Max}(n,\delta,t) \leq \frac{1}{2} + \delta$. Thus, using the VV-Theorem (or any proof technique which requires that the Big-Advantage Condition holds) one cannot hope to prove that RSA's l.s.b is $\frac{2}{3}$-secure.

Let us conclude by pointing out that the full power of the results obtained in section 2.3 was not used; however, we conjecture that it can be used. Namely,

Conjecture 2: Let N be the RSA's modulus and $t << N$. If $\text{Aver}(N,\delta,t) > \frac{1}{2} + \epsilon$ then any $(\frac{1}{2} + \delta)$-oracle for RSA's l.s.b can be used to efficiently invert the RSA. (In other words: if $\text{Aver}(N,\delta,t) > \frac{1}{2} + \epsilon$ then RSA's l.s.b is $(\frac{1}{2} + \delta)$-secure.)

The condition of the statement of Conjecture 2 is hereafter referred to as the *Average-Advantage Condition*. By Corollary $1_{(ii)}$, the Average-Advantage Condition is satisfied by $\delta = 0.177$; thus

Corollary 4: If Conjecture 2 is valid then the RSA's l.s.b is 0.677-secure.

Note that $\delta = 0.177$ is the minimum for which the Average-Advantage Condition is satisfied. Thus no progress beyond the $\delta = 0.177$ point can be made through the Average-Advantage Condition; i.e. when relying on it one cannot hope to prove that RSA's l.s.b is 0.676-secure.

Note that in Corollary 4 the missing part to reach the stated result is the algorithm that will use the analysis. (The analysis of the question which oracles satisfy the Avarage-Advantage Condition is complete!) However, in the case of the Big-Advantage Condition improved results can still be achieved (just) by improving the analysis of the combinatorial problem (see Corollary 3).

4. Conclusion

We have solved a combinatorial problem and have shown how to use this solution to improve knowledge on the security of RSA's l.s.b . We have also pointed out possible directions for further improvement of our result. Improved results can be obtained by either conducting a better combinatorial analysis of $Max(\cdot,\cdot,\cdot)$ or by suggesting an inverting algorithm based on the Average-Advantage Condition.

However such improvements will not suffice to show that RSA l.s.b. is $\frac{2}{3}$-secure. We believe that any improvement in the results concerning the security of RSA's l.s.b , beyond the $\frac{2}{3}$ point (which is still out of reach), must make use of additional properties of the RSA.

5. Epilogue

Meanwhile, Schnorr and Alexi [SA84] proved that RSA l.s.b is $(\frac{1}{2} + \epsilon)$-secure, for every fixed ϵ. Thus, the above coclusions are no longer of interest.

Schnorr and Alexi's proof is based on guessing the parity of $O(\log \log N)$ randomly selected positions and using these positions in all measurements of Ben-Or, Chor and Shamir's algorithmic procedure. Thus, the oracle is queried only about one end-point of each measurement and the analysis is w.r.t single positions rather than being w.r.t pairs of close positions.

Further improvement was achieved by Chor and Goldreich [CG84], who proved that RSA l.s.b is $(\frac{1}{2} + \frac{1}{\log^c N})$-secure, for every fixed c.

6. Acknowledgements

I am indebted to Tom Leighton for teaching me how to count (overlaps).

I would like to thank Ron Rivest for guiding me with his insightful suggestions.

I thank Vijay Vazirani for a private presentation of the .741 result and for his remarks.

It is my pleasure to thank Michael Ben-Or, Benny Chor, Shafi Goldwasser, Hans Heller, Silvio Micali, Gary Miller and Avi Wigderson for very helpful discussions, useful ideas and consistent encouragement.

I am most thankful to Dassi Levi for her unique existence.

7. References

[BCS] Ben-Or,M., Chor,B., and Shamir,A., "On the Cryptogrsphic Security of Single RSA Bits", *15th ACM Symp. on Theory of Computation*, April 1983, pp. 421-430

[BM] Blum,M., and Micali,S., "How to Generate Cryptographically Strong Sequences of Pseudo-Random Bits", to appear in the *SIAM Jour. on Computing*

[CG84] Chor,B., and Goldreich,O., "RSA least significant bits are $\frac{1}{2} + \frac{1}{poly(\log N)}$ Secure, MIT/LCS/TM-260, May 1984

[DH] Diffie,W., and Hellman,M.E., "New Directions in Cryptography", *IEEE Trans. on Inform. Theory*, Vol. IT-22, No. 6, November 1976, pp. 644-654

[G84] Goldreich,O., "On the Number of Close-and-Equal Pairs of Bits in a String (with Implications on the Security of RSA's L.s.b.)", MIT/LCS/TM-256, March 1984

[GM] Goldwasser,S., and Micali,S., "Probabilistic Encryption", to appear in the *JCSS special issue from the 14th STOC*

[GMT] Goldwasser,S., Micali,S., and Tong,P., "Why and How to Establish a Private Code on a Public Network", *Proc. of the 23rd IEEE Symp. on Foundation of Computer Science*, November 1982, pp. 134-144

[L] van Lint,J.H., *Combinatorial Theory Seminar, Eindhoven University of Technology*, Lecture Notes in Mathematics, SpringVerlag, 1974, pp. 90-91.

[RSA] Rivest,R.L., Shamir,A., and Adleman,L., "A Method for Obtaining Digital Signature and Public Key Cryptosystems", *Comm. of the ACM*,Vol.21, February 1978, pp. 120-126

[SA84] Schnorr,C.P. and Alexi,W., "RSA Bits are $0.5 + \epsilon$ Secure", this proceedings

[VV1] Vazirani,U.V., and Vazirani,V.V., "RSA's l.s.b is .741 Secure", presented in *Crypto83*, August 1983.

[VV2] Vazirani,U.V., and Vazirani,V.V., "RSA Bits are .732 Secure", preprint, November 1983.

Fast Cryptanalysis of the Matsumoto-Imai Public Key Scheme

P. Delsarte

Philips Research Laboratory,
Avenue Van Becelaere, 2
B-1170 Brussels, Belgium

Y. Desmedt

Katholieke Universiteit Leuven,
Laboratorium ESAT, Kardinaal Mercierlaan, 94
B-3030 Heverlee, Belgium

A. Odlyzko

AT&T Bell Laboratories
Murray Hill, New Jersey 07974, U.S.A.

P. Piret

Philips Research Laboratory,
Avenue Van Becelaere, 2
B-1170 Brussels, Belgium

ABSTRACT

The Matsumoto-Imai public key scheme was developed to provide very fast signatures. It is based on substitution polynomials over $GF(2^m)$. This paper shows in two ways that the Matsumoto-Imai public key scheme is very easy to break. In the faster of the two attacks the time to cryptanalyze the scheme is about proportional to the binary length of the public key. This shows that Matsumoto and Imai greatly overestimated the security of their scheme.

Fast Cryptanalysis of the Matsumoto-Imai Public Key Scheme

P. Delsarte

Philips Research Laboratory,
Avenue Van Becelaere, 2
B-1170 Brussels, Belgium

Y. Desmedt

Katholieke Universiteit Leuven,
Laboratorium ESAT, Kardinaal Mercierlaan, 94
B-3030 Heverlee, Belgium

A. Odlyzko

AT&T Bell Laboratories
Murray Hill, New Jersey 07974, U.S.A.

P. Piret

Philips Research Laboratory,
Avenue Van Becelaere, 2
B-1170 Brussels, Belgium

1. INTRODUCTION

Several attempts have been made to use the fields $GF(2^m)$ [1] in cryptography. The motivation is that these fields allow very fast computation and are very easy to implement in hardware [2]. However, many such attempts quickly yielded to cryptanalytic attacks. For example, an extension of the RSA scheme to the fields $GF(2^m)$ [3] was immediately broken [4,10]. The security of the fields $GF(2^m)$ in public key distribution systems [5] was also overestimated [6]. Cryptanalysis is possible there if the dimension m of the field $GF(2^m)$ is less than 1000 [6].

The Matsumoto-Imai public key scheme [7] also uses the fields $GF(2^m)$. It allows generation of signatures much faster than the RSA scheme. Moreover the scheme is very easy to implement. However, in this paper we give two efficient algorithms to cryptanalyze the Matsumoto-Imai public key scheme.

First the details of the Matsumoto-Imai scheme are presented, based on our interpretation of [7]. Then an overview of the first and second cryptanalytic attack are given. Both attacks use the public knowledge of the construction algorithm for public keys, and find secret parameters used in the construction of the public key. These algorithms are then presented in detail.

2. THE MATSUMOTO-IMAI PUBLIC KEY SCHEME

The Matsumoto-Imai [7] enciphering is defined over $GF(2^m)$, the message space. The public key is a substitution polynomial [1]: $E(X) = \sum_{i=0}^{2^m-2} e_i X^i$. For a message Y, which belongs to $GF(2^m)$, the ciphertext is $E(Y)$. In order to have a "short" public key and to be able to encipher rapidly, most of the e_i must be zero. To that end, $E(X)$ is constructed as $E(X) \equiv a(b+X^\alpha)^\beta$ modulo $(X^{2^m}+X)$, where the Hamming weight [2] of β is r. One can then easily prove that only 2^r coefficients e_i will be non-zero. If r is small (e.g., 14, as suggested in [7]), the public key is not too long. $E(X)$ in expanded form is made public, while a, b, α, and β are kept secret in order to be able to decipher fast. In order to specify $E(X)$, the field $GF(2^m)$ has to be made public also, and r can be deduced from the number of non-zero coefficients. Therefore we have:

Remark: One can consider that m and r are given, so these values do not have to be deduced.

3. MAIN PRINCIPLES FOR THE CRYPTANALYSIS OF THE MATSUMOTO-IMAI PUBLIC KEY SCHEME

In order to allow a unique deciphering, the system designer has to chose $\gcd(\alpha, 2^m-1) = \gcd(\beta, 2^m-1) = 1$, and so from now on we will assume these conditions hold. The following theorems help to explain the cryptanalysis.

Theorem 1: If the public key is constructed as mentioned above and β is written as

$$\beta = \sum_{j=1}^{r} 2^{u_j}, \quad \text{with} \quad 0 \leqslant u_j < m, \tag{1}$$

then the exponents of X with non-zero coefficients can be expressed as

$$\alpha \sum_{j=1}^{r} z_j 2^{u_j} \pmod{2^m-1}, \quad \text{with} \quad z_j = 0 \text{ or } 1, \tag{2}$$

and their corresponding coefficients as

$$ab^k \quad with \quad k \equiv \sum_{j=1}^{r} (1-z_j)2^{u_j} \quad (mod \ 2^m - 1). \tag{3}$$

Proof: Using the construction algorithm for public keys and (1), we have $E(X) = a \prod_{j=1}^{r} (b+X^\alpha)^{2^{v_j}}$. Since the characteristic of $GF(2^m)$ is 2, $E(X) = a \prod_{j=1}^{r} (b^{2^{v_j}} + X^{\alpha 2^{v_j}})$, and using $X^{2^m} \equiv X$ modulo $X^{2^m} + X$ we obtain (2) and (3). ∎

Corollary 1: At least m different (a,b,α,β) determine the same enciphering key.

Proof: Choose $\alpha' \equiv 2^h \alpha$ and $\beta' \equiv 2^{m-h}\beta$ (modulo 2^m-1) and use the proof of Theorem 1. ∎

It is sufficient to find any one of these equivalent (a,b,α,β) in order to break the scheme. To simplify the description, all these equivalent keys will be called the secret key. We will sometimes suppose in the paper that $u_1 = 0$, which by Corollary 1 entails no loss of generality.

Corollary 2: If $u_1 = 0$ then $b = $ (coefficient of X to the power 0)/(coefficient of X to the power α) and $a = $ (coefficient of X to the power 0)/b^β.

Proof: Can be verified easily using Theorem 1. ∎

Theorem 2: If $\gcd(\alpha, 2^m-1) = 1$ and $\gcd(\beta, 2^m-1) = 1$, then the list of exponents of X in $E(X)$ with nonzero coefficients contains a unique subset of size r of the form $\{2^{v_1}\alpha_1, \ 2^{v_2}\alpha_1,...,2^{v_r}\alpha_1\}$ (modulo 2^m-1). Taking Corollary 1 into account one has $\alpha = \alpha_1$ and $\beta = \Sigma 2^{v_j}$.

Proof: In view of Theorem 1 this subset is actually present in the list of exponents. Let now γ be any other element of the list, say $\gamma \equiv (2^{p_1} + 2^{p_2} + ... + 2^{p_s})\alpha$ (modulo 2^m-1), where $\{p_1, p_2,...,p_s\}$ is a subset of $\{u_1, u_2,...,u_r\}$ with $s \geqslant 2$. We shall prove that the list contains fewer than r elements of the form $2^k \gamma$ (modulo 2^m-1). First it is clear there cannot be more than r such elements, because for each i, each sum p_i+k (modulo m) must coincide with one of the integers $u_1, u_2,...,u_r$. If there were exactly r elements, then one would necessarily have $p_1+k_j \equiv u_{\pi(j)}$ and $p_2+k_j \equiv u_{\sigma(j)}$ (modulo m), for $j = 1,2,...,r$, where π and σ are two permutations on $\{1,2,...,r\}$. Taking the binary exponential of these identities and adding the results together (for $j = 1, 2,...,r$)

one readily obtains $\beta(2^{p_2 - p_1} - 1) \equiv 0$ (modulo 2^m-1), which is impossible since $\gcd(\beta, 2^m-1) = 1$ and $p_2 \neq p_1$. ∎

If one finds an α_1 which satisfies the above property, then α will be chosen equal to α_1. The calculation of β is then trivial; it is in fact obtained at the same time as α. Once α and β have been found, a and b are calculated using Corollary 2. As a consequence of Theorem 2 and the remark at the beginning of this section, one does not need to check that the obtained α is correct! Two algorithms will now be presented which find α and β. The first algorithm uses the calculation of the inverse of elements modulo 2^m-1. The second one is based on shift operations and sorting algorithms.

4. CRYPTANALYSIS USING INVERSE CALCULATION

4.1 The Principles Of The Algorithm

Exponents of X with non-zero coefficients will be written as i_k, with $1 \leqslant k \leqslant 2^r$. For each k, $1 \leqslant k \leqslant 2^r$, we test whether $\alpha = i_k$. If $\gcd(i_k, 2^m-1)$ is not equal to one, a wrong choice for α was made. If $\gcd(i_k, 2^m-1) = 1$ then several techniques can be used to find β. In one of them the cryptanalyst first calculates

$$f_l \equiv i_l i_k^{-1} \pmod{2^m-1}, \ 1 \leqslant \ell \leqslant 2^r. \tag{4}$$

In view of Theorem 2, if r values of f_l are powers of 2, then i_k is α, and β is the sum of these r values of f_l. If no such r values are found, continue the exhaustive search. Because r is small this exhaustive search is fast.

4.2 Speed Evaluation Of The Algorithm

The number of elementary steps (such as additions and shifts) used in the above cryptanalytic algorithm will be analyzed. First the complexity of each step will be obtained; next this value will be multiplied by the number of times each step is executed.

The calculation of the $\gcd(i_k, 2^m-1)$ and the calculation of i_k^{-1}, if it exists, can be done at once. This requires $O(m)$ steps [8] (subtractions or shifts). This means in total $O(m2^r)$ steps during the exhaustive search for α. The calculation of (4) requires in practice $O(m^2)$ [8] elementary steps (additions and small multiplications). For larger values of m better algorithms (e.g., using the FFT) can be used [8]. This means for the exhaustive search that (4) is executed in worst case in $O(m^2 2^{2r})$ steps, while on average it takes $O(m^2 2^{2r}/r)$ steps. The calculation of β requires for each trial $O(\log_2 m)$ steps. We conclude that the cryptanalysis requires $O(m^2 2^{2r}/r)$ steps on average, and $O(m^2 2^{2r})$ in the worst case. The next algorithm has an improved speed performance.

5. CRYPTANALYSIS USING SHIFT OPERATIONS

5.1 The Principles Of The Algorithm

In the second method of attack we partition the exponents of X with nonzero coefficients into sets S_p. Two different exponents i_k and i_l of X, with non-zero coefficients, will belong to the same set S_p if and only if for some $s, \cdot i_k \equiv 2^s i_l \pmod{2^m-1}$. In other words, i_k and i_l belong to the same set S_p if one can obtain i_k from i_l by a suitable rotation of its binary representation. The cryptanalysis consists of determining all different sets S_p for all exponents of X with non-zero coefficients. Using Theorem 2 exactly one S_p, which we call S_r, will contain r elements. Using Corollary 2, any element of S_r can be chosen as α. Identifying the required rotation operations for going from α to obtain the other elements of S_r, we obtain β. We now describe how the above ideas can be carried out. The speed of the algorithm will be discussed later.

First we define a unique representative for each set S_p. A value v_p is the representative of the set S_p if it is the smallest of the m values obtained by rotating $0,1,2,...,m-1$ times an element of the set S_p. Note that v_p can be viewed as the value of a function $v(i)$ defined over the set $\{0,1,...,2^m-2\}$ and satisfying $v(i_1) = v(i_2)$ if and only if $i_1 \equiv 2^s i_2 \pmod{2^m-1}$, for a certain s. This function $v(i)$ will now be used to find α. We calculate $v(i_k)$ for all 2^r exponents i_k of X with non-zero coefficients. The $v(i_k)$ and i_k together are written in lists A and B of 2^r elements, in which each element contains m bits. There is a unique element w that appears r times in list A, and then α can be chosen as any of the corresponding elements in list B. This search for w and α can easily be performed by sorting [9, pp. 2] the list A while simultaneously permuting the list B in the same way.

5.2 Speed Evaluation Of The Algorithm

The calculation of $v_i(i)$ requires m steps. Doing this for all the exponents of X that appear in $E(X)$ takes $m2^r$ steps. The sorting of list A, together with the permutation of list B, requires $O(r2^r)$ steps in practice [9, pp. 181-198, p. 381].

In total this algorithm requires $O(m2^r)$ steps even in the worst case!

6. CONCLUSIONS

The Matsumoto-Imai public key scheme seems attractive from speed considerations, *but is totally insecure*! Matsumoto and Imai estimated the cryptanalysis of their scheme would require about 10^{20} steps if $m = 127$ and $r = 14$. However using our cryptanalytic attack using inverse calculation, on the same example, one needs only about $3*10^{11}$ steps, which is performable even on a small computer. If one step requires 10 μsec on a small computer, then the attack requires 36 days. If one step asks 100 ηsec on a fast computer, the attack can be performed in only 8 hours. Using the cryptanalysis based on shift operations, one needs only $2*10^6$ steps. Using the same small and fast computer, this requires 20 sec and 0.2 sec, respectively. On a fast computer, the cryptanalytic attack suggested by Matsumoto and Imai would require 3×10^5 years.

Remark: The second cryptanalytic attack requires about as many steps as the binary length of the public key!

One could increase the security of the Matsumoto-Imai scheme by increasing m and r. However, even disregarding the fact that this might entail impractically large storage requirements, this would not produce an acceptable system. Evaluation of the publicly known function $E(X)$ takes at least 2^r multiplications in $GF(2^m)$, and each such multiplication might be expected to take about m operation such as the shifts we utilize in our second attack. *Hence the time needed to cryptanalyze the Matsumoto-Imai system is essentially the same as the time needed to use it once!*

REFERENCES

1. R. Carmichael, *Introduction to the Theory of Groups of Finite Order*, Dover, New York, 1956.

2. E. R. Berlekamp, *Algebraic Coding Theory*, McGraw-Hill, 1968.

3. D. W. Kravitz and I. S. Reed, Extension of RSA Crypto-Structure: A Galois Approach, *Electronics Letters*, vol. 18, no 6, pp. 255-256, 18th March 1982.

4. P. Delsarte and P. Piret, Comment: Extension of RSA Crypto-Structure: A Galois Approach, *Electronics Letters*, vol. 18, no. 13, pp. 582-583, 24th June 1982.

5. K. Yiu and K. Peterson, A Single-Chip VLSI Implementation of the Discrete Exponential Public Key Distribution System, *Proc. Globecom '82 IEEE Global Telecommunications Conference*, vol. 1, pp. 173-179, Miami, USA, 1982.

6. D. Coppersmith, Fast Evaluation of Logarithms in Fields of Characteristic Two, *Research Report*, RC 10187 IBM Yorktown Heights. *IEEE Trans. Inform. Theory*, to appear.

7. T. Matsumoto and H. Imai, A Class of Asymmetric Crypto-Systems based on Polynomials over Finite Rings, *IEEE Intern. Symp. Inform. Theory*, St. Jovite, Quebec, Canada, September 26-30, 1983, Abstracts of Papers, pp. 131-132.

8. D. E. Knuth, *The Art of Computer Programming, Vol. 2, Seminumerical Algorithms*, Addison-Wesley, Reading, Massachusetts, 1981.

9. D. E. Knuth, *The Art of Computer Programming, Vol. 3, Sorting and Searching*, Addison-Wesley, Reading, Massachusetts 1975.

10. J. Gait, Short Cycling in the Kravitz-Reed Public Key Encryption System, *Electronics Letters*, vol. 18, no. 16, pp. 706-707, 5th August 1982.

A New Trapdoor Knapsack Public Key Cryptosystem.

R.M.F. Goodman, B.Sc., Ph.D., C.Eng., M.I.E.E.

Department of Electronic Engineering
University of Hull
HULL HU6 7RX
U.K.

20 July 1984

Keywords : cryptography, ciphers, codes, knapsack problem, public key.

Abstract

This paper presents a new trapdoor-knapsack public-key-cryptosystem. The
encryption equation is based on the general modular knapsack equation, but
unlike the Merkle-Hellman scheme the knapsack components do not have to have
a superincreasing structure. The trapdoor is based on transformations between
the modular and radix form of the knapsack components, via the Chinese
Remainder Theorem. The resulting cryptosystem has high density and has a typical
message block size of 2000 bits and a public key of 14K bits. The security is
based on factoring a number composed of 256 bit prime factors. The major
advantage of the scheme when compared with the RSA scheme is one of speed.
Typically, knapsack schemes such as the one proposed here are capable of
throughput speeds which are orders of magnitude faster than the RSA scheme.

List of Principal Symbols

a_i =   a published knapsack component.

a_i' =   a secret knapsack component.

$\underline{a}$ =   the public knapsack vector = (a_1 , a_2 , ... , a_n).

$\underline{a}'$ =   the secret knapsack vector = (a_1' , a_2' , ... , a_n') ,
also transformable to the secret knapsack matrix.

$a_j^{(i)}$ = $a_j \bmod p_i$ = residue of the j th knapsack component modulo the i th prime.

D =   density of the cryptosystem.

g =   number of bits in $x_{i,max}$, the message sub-blocks.

h =   number of bits in $p_{i,min}$.

K =   the number of distinct secret matrices $\underline{a}'$.

n =   the number of knapsack components,
also, the number of primes p_i .

p_i =   a prime number.

$\underline{p}$ =   a set of n distinct primes = (p_1 , p_2 , ... , p_n) .

p = $\prod_{i=1}^{n} p_i$ = the product of n distinct primes .

PK =   number of bits in the public key.

r =   number of bits in $\left\{ \sum_{j=1}^{n} a_j'^{(i)} \right\}_{max}$.

S =   the cryptogram = $\sum_{i=1}^{n} a_i \cdot x_i$.

S' =   the transformed cryptogram = $S \cdot W^{-1} \bmod p$.
also equal to ($S'^{(1)}, S'^{(2)}, \ldots , S'^{(n)}$) in modular form.

W =   a secret modular multiplier, relatively prime to p .

$\underline{x}$ =   the message vector = (x_1 , x_2 , ... , x_n).

Introduction

Public-key-cryptosystems have received considerable attention over the last few years (Diffie and Hellman 1976, ref.1.). This is because such systems offer secure communications without the need for prior key distribution, and the possibility of digital signatures. The two most important schemes are the RSA scheme (Rivest, Shamir, and Adelman 1978, ref.2.), and the Trapdoor-Knapsack scheme (Merkle and Hellman 1978, ref.3.). Of these the Knapsack scheme has fallen into disfavour because of successful attacks on the original Merkle-Hellman scheme. Specifically, the attacks have not been on the encryption equation which appears secure, but on the fact that the knapsack components are transformations of a superincreasing sequence (Desmet 1982, ref.4). In addition, it has been shown that if the density of the knapsack is low, where density is loosly defined as the ratio of messagetext bits to cryptogram bits, then even non-superincreasing knapsacks are insecure (Brickell 1983, ref.5., Lagarias and Odlyzko 1983, ref.6.). Despite these problems knapsack schemes have one major practical advantage over the RSA scheme, and that is speed. This is because the encryption and decryption processes used are intrinsically faster than performing the modular exponentiations needed in the RSA. Typically, knapsack schemes can operate at throughput rates of 20Mbits/sec, whereas the RSA is limited to about 50Kbits/sec, using current technology.

The new trapdoor-knapsack presented in this paper uses the general modular knapsack equation (eqn. 1) , and does not require the knapsack components to be superincreasing. In addition, the system parameters can be chosen to give a very high density secure cryptosystem. The trapdoor is based on being able to transform between the radix and modular representations of the subset sums via the Chinese Remainder Theorem (Knuth 1968, ref.7.). The system bears a resemblance to the Lu - Lee (1979, ref.8.) system, but whereas their cryptosystem is linear and has been shown to be insecure (Goethals and Couvreur, 1980, ref.9.), ours is based on the general modular knapsack equation, which to date has not been generally broken.

The New Trapdoor

The general modular knapsack equation is given by

$$S = \sum_{i=1}^{n} a_i \cdot x_i \mod p \ . \qquad\qquad \text{eqn. 1.}$$

When used for cryptography, the a's are the n published knapsack components, p is a published modulus, and the x's are the message bits. In the binary knapsack the x's are 0 or 1, but in the general knapsack they are g bit numbers. The subset sum S is the cryptogram which is sent to the legitimate user, who is the only one who can unwind the cryptogram back to the original x's.

Let (p_1 , p_2 , $\dots$, p_n) be a set of prime integers whose product is given by

$$p = \prod_{i=1}^{n} p_i \ , \quad \text{and where} \quad a_j^{(i)} = a_j \mod p_i$$

is the residue of the j th knapsack component modulo the i th prime.
Then by the Chinese Remainder Theorem

$$a_j \longleftrightarrow a_j^{(1)} , a_j^{(2)} , \dots , a_j^{(n)}$$

is a bijective mapping. That is, the transformation is one-to-one for all a's between 1 and p-1. Thus if the factorisation of p is kept secret, then only the legitimate user will be able to transform the radix representation of the knapsack components into their modular representation. This forms the trapdoor. Let us now choose a set of n knapsack components and express them in both radix and modular form:

$$\underline{a}' = \begin{matrix} a_1' \longleftrightarrow a_1'^{(1)}, a_1'^{(2)}, \dots , a_1'^{(n)} \\[4pt] a_2' \longleftrightarrow a_2'^{(1)}, a_2'^{(2)}, \dots , a_2'^{(n)} \\[4pt] \vdots \\[4pt] a_n' \longleftrightarrow a_n'^{(1)}, a_n'^{(2)}, \dots , a_n'^{(n)} \ . \end{matrix} \qquad \text{eqn. 2.}$$

Let us then disguise the trapdoor by forming a new set of knapsack components via the modular multiplication

$$a_j = a_j' \cdot W \mod p \qquad\qquad \text{eqn. 3.}$$

where W and p are relatively prime, and W^{-1} is the multiplicative inverse of W , modulo p.

We now publish p , and the modified knapsack components ($\underline{a}$) in radix form. This is the public key. The factorisation of p and and the integer W are kept secret, and hence so is the modular representation of the a'.

Now let $\qquad p_{i,min} \geq 2^h$ $\qquad$ eqn. 4.

that is, the primes are at least h+1 bit numbers.

Let $\qquad x_{i,max} < 2^g$ $\qquad$ eqn. 5.

that is, the message blocks are g bit numbers.

And let $\qquad \left\{ \sum_{i=1}^{n} a_j^{(i)} \right\}_{max} < 2^r$ $\qquad$ eqn. 6.

that is, the columns of $\underline{a}'$ sum to an r bit number.

In order to ensure that the encryption equation has a unique decryption, we must ensure that the message to ciphertext transformation $\underline{x} \longrightarrow S$ is injective. To guarantee this we must have

$$h \geq r + g \qquad \text{eqn. 7.}$$

which also ensures that modular multiplication is equivalent to matrix multiplication :

$$(S'^{(1)} , \ldots , S'^{(n)}) = (x_1 , \ldots , x_n) \begin{pmatrix} a_1'^{(1)} , & a_1'^{(2)} , & \ldots , & a_1'^{(n)} \\ \vdots & & & \\ a_n'^{(1)} , & a_n'^{(2)} , & \ldots , & a_n'^{(n)} \end{pmatrix}$$

i.e. $\qquad \underline{S}' = \underline{x} \cdot \underline{a}'$

and that the transformation can be inverted (provided the matrix $\underline{a}'$ is non-singular) via

$$\underline{x} = \underline{S} \cdot \underline{a}'^{-1}. \qquad \text{eqn. 8.}$$

The cryptosystem then operates as follows. A user wishing to send us a message forms the ciphertext

$$S = (x_1 \cdot a_1 + x_2 \cdot a_2 + \ldots + x_n \cdot a_n) \mod p$$

via equation 1. We compute S' via

$$S' = S \cdot W^{-1} \mod p$$

and express in modular form via our known factorisation of p :

$$S' \longleftrightarrow (S'^{(1)}, S'^{(2)}, \ldots , S'^{(n)})$$

we then apply $\underline{x} = \underline{S}' \cdot \underline{a}'^{-1}$ and hence recover the message. The cryptanalyst must either break the factorisation of p or attack the trapdoor in some other manner.

A Small Example

We now give an example of the above method using n=3. The example is of course too small for security.

Let n = 3 and define $\underline{p}$ = (37, 41, 43) , hence p = 65231, and h = 5 (eqn. 4). Choose g = 2 , that is, the message components are two bit numbers. This dictates that r = 3 via equation 7. (h = 5 $\geq$ 3 + 2). Choose n = 3 knapsack components which satisfy equation 6, that is, the columns of $\underline{a}'$ add to <8 , and express in both modular and radix form:

$$\underline{a}' = \begin{array}{l} a'_1 = (\ 3 \ , \ 1 \ , \ 1 \ ) \ \longleftrightarrow \ 125174 \\ a'_2 = (\ 1 \ , \ 5 \ , \ 3 \ ) \ \longleftrightarrow \ 151664 \\ a'_3 = (\ 2 \ , \ 1 \ , \ 2 \ ) \ \longleftrightarrow \ 122509 \ . \end{array}$$

Now choose W = 6553 which is relatively prime to p = 65231. Perform the modular multiplication of equation 3 , and publish the resulting knapsack components :

$$a_1 = 50628$$
$$a_2 = 59907$$
$$a_3 = 3560$$

and the modulus   p = 65231 .

Compute the inverse W^{-1} = 2618 via Euclid's algorithm and invert the matrix $\underline{a}'$:

$$\underline{a}'^{-1} = (\ 1/16 \ ) \begin{Bmatrix} +7 \ , \ -1 \ , \ -2 \\ +4 \ , \ +4 \ , \ -8 \\ -9 \ , \ -1 \ , \ +14 \end{Bmatrix} .$$

To transmit the 6 bit message $\underline{x}$ = (1 , 2 , 3) a user computes the ciphertext

$$\begin{aligned} S \ &= \ (\ 1 \ . \ 50628 \ ) + (\ 2 \ . \ 59907 \ ) + (3 \ . \ 3560 \ ) \\ &= \ 181122 \\ &= \ 50660 \ \ mod \ 65231 \ . \end{aligned}$$

Using the secret W^{-1} the receiver computes

$$\begin{aligned} S' \ &= \ 50660 \ . \ 2618 \ \ mod \ 65231 \\ &= \ 13257 \ \ mod \ 65231 \end{aligned}$$

and using the secret $\underline{p}$ is able to transform into modular form :

$$\underline{S}' = (\ 11 \ , \ 14 \ , \ 13 \ ) \ \longleftrightarrow \ 13257 \ .$$

From equation 8, the receiver computes :

$$16 \ . \ \underline{x} \ = \ (\ 11 \ , \ 14 \ , \ 13 \ ) \begin{Bmatrix} +7 \ , \ -1 \ , \ -2 \\ +4 \ , \ +4 \ , \ -8 \\ -9 \ , \ -1 \ , \ +14 \end{Bmatrix}$$

giving $\underline{x}$ = (1 , 2 , 3) as transmitted.

Practical Constraints

We now choose the values for n, r, g, and h needed to give a secure practical cryptosystem.

In order to present a large knapsack problem we set

$$n \cdot g \geq 256 \quad . \qquad \qquad \text{eqn. 9.}$$

The value of n is influenced by the fact that the general knapsack problem is not as secure as the binary knapsack because the least significant bits of the message are not as well hidden. We have reduced the problem by performing the reduction mod p , but we must still set a limit, say

$$n > 5 \quad . \qquad \qquad \text{eqn. 10.}$$

In order to protect the trapdoor and ensure that the published p is not factored we set

$$h \geq 255 \qquad \qquad \text{eqn. 11.}$$

so that the primes are at least 256 bit numbers.

To ensure sufficient randomness in the knapsack components we need to bound the number of valid matrices $\underline{a}'$, which we call K. If we assume that any number $1 \leq a_i' \leq 2^r$ can be chosen to be a knapsack component then the number of different column vectors that can be chosen is 2^{nr}, and thus

$$K = 2^{n^2 r} \quad .$$

However, because of the restriction on the sum of the column vectors imposed by equation 6, not all of these matrices are acceptable. Let us develop a conservative lower bound on K by employing an averaging argument. Assume that all knapsack components are chosen so that

$$1 \leq a_i' \leq \frac{2^r}{n} \quad .$$

This guarantees that all the resulting matrices will satisfy equation 6. The number of valid column vectors that can be chosen in this way is

$$2^{nr} \cdot \left\{ \frac{1}{n} \right\}^n \quad .$$

Which gives $\qquad K > 2^{n^2 r} \cdot \left\{ \frac{1}{n} \right\}^{n^2} \quad . \qquad \text{eqn. 12.}$

To ensure sufficient randomness in the choice of knapsack components we require say $K \geq 2^{128}$. Taking logs of equation 12 we get :

$$n^2 (r - \log_2 n) \geq 128 \quad . \qquad \qquad \text{eqn. 13.}$$

The value of r is influenced by several factors. If r is small then the
knapsack components will have a small remainder when divided by a factor
of p (Goethals and Couvreur 1980, ref. 9.) This has been allowed for by the
disguising modular multiplication (eqn. 3); but r must be large enough to
ensure that no knapsack component has the same remainder modulo any prime
factor. A loose lower bound falls out from equation 13. That is,

$$r > \log_2 n$$

but, if r is much less than n , then the choice of knapsack components is
severely reduced by equation 6. Thus we set

$$r \geq n .$$ eqn. 14.

The density of the cryptosystem is given by :

$$D = \frac{g}{(h + 1)}$$

if we assume the primes are all exactly h+1 bit numbers. Now, in order to
minimise the redundancy of the scheme and to increase the resistance to
low-density attacks, h should be as small as possible. Thus we set eqn. 7 to:

$$h = r + g$$

so that $$D = \frac{g}{g + r + 1}$$

Thus to maximise D, we must keep r small. From equation 14 we should set r = n,
and if we then set n = r = 7, we satisfy both equation 13 and equation 10.

The size of the public key is given by :

$$PK = n.(n + 1).(h + 1) ,$$

and in order to keep this small we must keep h small. So let us set eqn. 11 to

$$h = 255$$

which gives $$g = 255 - 7 = 248 .$$

The size of the basic message block is then :

$$n . g = 1736 \text{ bits} ,$$

which certainly satisfies eqn. 9.

The final system parameters are then : n = r = 7, g = 248, h = 255 which
gives D = 0.97 and PK = 14336 bits.

Conclusions

In this paper we have presented a new public key cryptosystem based on the
general modular knapsack problem. Its security is not based on disguising
a superincreasing sequence, but on the difficulty of factoring a number
with seven 256 bit prime factors, and on a knapsack problem with a typical

density of 0.97 and a block size of 1736. The knapsack nature of the system ensures that fast encryption and decryption are possible when compared with the RSA public-key-cryptosystem. In addition, the size of the public key which is typically 14Kbits is not excessive. It may be possible to attack the trapdoor information more directly, but we can see no productive method of doing this. The only successful attacks on dense trapdoor-knapsacks to date have been on the security of the superincreasing sequence. Our method does not require this. However, it may turn out that all injective trapdoor knapsacks are solvable in polynomial time, in which case all such schemes are useless for cryptography.

References

1. W. Diffie and M. Hellman, "New directions in cryptography", IEEE Trans. on Information Theory, IT-22, pp 644-654, Nov. 1976.

2. R. Rivest, A. Shamir, and L. Adelman, "On digital signatures and public key cryptosystems", Comm. of the ACM, Vol. 21, No. 2, pp 120-126, Feb 1978.

3. R.C. Merkle and M.E. Hellman, "Hiding information and signatures in trapdoor knapsacks", IEEE Trans. on Information Theory, IT-24, pp 525-530, Sept. 1978.

4. Y. Desmet, J. Vandewalle, and R. Govaerts, "A critical analysis of the security of knapsack public key cryptosystems", IEEE Symp. on Information Theory, Les Arcs, France, June 1982.

5. E.F. Brickell, "Solving low density knapsacks", Sandia National Laboratories, Albuquerque, New Mexico, USA, 13p, 1983.

6. J.C. Lagarias, and A.M. Odlyzko, "Solving low-density subset sum problems", Bell Laboratories, Murray Hill, New Jersey, USA, 38p, 1983.

7. D.E. Knuth, The Art of Computer Programming, Vol. 1., "Fundamental Algorithms", Addison-Wesley, 1968.

8. S.C. Lu, and L.N. Lee, "A simple and effective public key cryptosystem", Comsat Tech. Rev., Vol. 9., pp15-24, Spring 1979.

9. J.M. Goethals, and C. Couvreur, "A cryptanalytic attack on the Lu-Lee public key cryptosystem, Phillips J. Res., Vol. 35, pp. 301-306, 1980.

RSA Chips (Past/Present/Future)*

(Extended abstract)

Ronald L. Rivest
MIT Laboratory for Computer Science
Cambridge, Mass. 02139

Brief Abstract We review the issues involved in building a special-purpose chip for performing RSA encryption/decryption, and review a few of the current implementation efforts.

* This research was supported by NSF grant MCS-80-06938.

I. Review of the RSA Cryptosystem

The "RSA cryptosystem" [RSA78] was the first published solution to the problem of implementing a public-key cryptosystem [DH76] – a concept invented by Diffie and Hellman. It remains today as the preeminent proposal for practical use. In this paper we review some of the considerations involved in implementing the RSA cryptosystem with special-purpose VLSI chips.

We begin by reviewing the RSA cryptosystem itself. The reader who wishes a more detailed review of public-key cryptography might consult [De82], [DH76], [DH79], or [RSA78].

A user A of the RSA cryptosystem creates his keys as follows:

- He first chooses at random two large (e.g. 100 decimal digit) prime numbers p and q.
- He then multiplies them together to get his public modulus $n = p \cdot q$.
- He then chooses at random a large integer d which has no divisors in common with either $p-1$ or $q-1$.
- He then computes e as the multiplicative inverse of d, modulo $(p-1) \cdot (q-1)$.
- He publishes as his secret key the pair (e, n), and keeps as his secret key the pair (d, n). (He may also wish to keep as part of his secret key the primes p and q.)

Anyone else can then encrypt a message M for A using A's public key, resulting in ciphertext C, using the equation:

$$C = M^e \pmod{n}.$$

Similarly, A can decrypt the ciphertext C using the equation:

$$M = C^d \pmod{n}.$$

As an example, if we choose $p = 47$ and $q = 59$, we have $n = 2773$. If we then choose $d = 157$ we can compute $e = 17$ using the technique given in [RSA78]. The public key is then $(e, n) = (17, 2773)$ and the secret key is $(d, n) = (157, 2773)$. The message $M = 31$ can be encrypted using the public key to obtain the ciphertext $C = 31^{17} = 587 \pmod{2773}$; decrypting yields the original message back: $31 = 587^{157} = 31 \pmod{2773}$.

II. Security of the RSA Cryptosystem

The security of the RSA cryptosystem depends on the difficulty for the enemy of factoring the published modulus n. If the enemy can factor the number n, he can compute the secret key (d, n) and read all of A's private mail (or forge A's digital signatures).

The security of the RSA cryptosystem is not known to be *equivalent* to the problem of factoring; it may be possible to break the RSA cryptosystem without factoring n. However, the most efficient attacks found to date are all provably equivalent to factoring. One can prove that computing the secret key is equivalent to factoring, and some variations on the basic RSA scheme are provably equivalent to factoring for some attacks (see [Ra79, Wi80]).

One interesting result, due to Andy Yao, is that the RSA system is "uniformly secure" in the sense that there can be no large sets of "weak messages": if an enemy can decrypt a significant fraction of messages encrypted with the RSA cryptosystem, then he could effectively decrypt all messages. Putting it another way, if the RSA cryptosystem offers security for the encrypted messages, then it offers uniformly high security for all messages. This follows from the multiplicative nature of the RSA scheme.

Even stronger results along this line have been proven by a number researchers (see [ACGS84] and its extensive list of references). The essence of these results is that if the RSA cryptosystem is secure, then the enemy will not even be able to get various kinds of partial information about the message from the ciphertext. (If he could, he would be able to get the whole message.)

IIA. How Hard is Factoring?

The best available algorithms for factoring large composite integers have a running time which is proportional to:

$$e^{\sqrt{\ln(n)\cdot\ln(\ln(n))}}.$$

for factoring a k-bit number n. A very crude approximation to this, in the range we are interested in, is:

$$5 \cdot 10^{9+(\frac{k}{60})}.$$

In the range of interest, the difficulty of factoring seems to grow roughly one order of magnitude more difficult with each extra 50 bits (15 decimal digits) of modulus.

At the moment, using available supercomputers, numbers with 71 digits can be factored in a reasonable length of time. Numbers with up to 100 decimal digits are plausibly factorable in the future using the best available algorithms and special-purpose hardware.

If we take as a bench-mark data point that a 75-digit number can be factored in about one day with today's technology, and using the above formulas, we can derive the following table:

75 digits – $9 \cdot 10^{12}$ operations – 1 day
100 digits – $2 \cdot 10^{15}$ operations – 255 days
125 digits – $3 \cdot 10^{17}$ operations – 103 years
150 digits – $3 \cdot 10^{19}$ operations – 9,755 years
175 digits – $2 \cdot 10^{21}$ operations – 70 thousand years
200 digits – $1 \cdot 10^{23}$ operations – 36 million years
225 digits – $5 \cdot 10^{24}$ operations – 1 billion years
250 digits – $2 \cdot 10^{26}$ operations – 60 billion years
300 digits – $1 \cdot 10^{29}$ operations – $5 \cdot 10^{13}$ years

In our original paper [RSA78] we proposed that 200 decimal digits (around 664 bits) would be a reasonable modulus size; we still feel that this is a reasonable choice.

III. Implementation Basics and the Need for Special-Purpose VLSI

III.A. Implementation Basics

Multiplication of two k-bit integers takes time:

- $O(k^2)$ on a microcomputer using a standard algorithm,
- $O(k)$ with special-purpose serial/parallel multiplication hardware ($O(k)$ gates),
- $O(\log k)$ with special-purpose parallel-parallel multiplication hardware ($O(k^2)$ gates).

Using today's technology, the serial-parallel approach seems the best trade-off point.

Modular multiplication of two k-bit integers modulo a third k-bit integer takes time:

- $O(k^2)$ on a microcomputer using standard algorithms,
- $O(k)$ with special-purpose hardware ($O(k)$ gates),
- $O((\log k)^{1+\epsilon})$ with special-purpose hardware ($O(k^2)$ gates).

Again, with today's technology, the $O(k)$-time, $O(k)$-hardware approach seems best.

Modular exponentiation is an interesting computational problem in that it seems intrinsically "sequential": using extra hardware or extra parallelism doesn't seem to help beyond the amount it helps to speed up the underlying modular multiplications. To raise a k-bit number to a k-bit power modulo a k-bit modulus thus seems to require $O(k)$ multiplications. We have the available time/hardware tradeoff choices:

- $O(k^3)$ time on a microcomputer (e.g. 2 minutes for 200 digits),
- $O(k^2)$ time using $O(k)$ gates (e.g. 0.5 seconds for 200 digits),
- $O(k \cdot \log k)$ using $O(k^2)$ gates (e.g. 7 milliseconds for 200 digits).

The corresponding data rates would then be

- 5 bits/second on a microcomputer,
- 1330 bits/second with $O(k)$ gates, and
- 95K bits/second with $O(k^2)$ gates.

Key generation has two parts: finding large primes and computing e from d. The first part is the most expensive; it requires approximately $O(k)$ primality tests to locate a k-bit prime, and each primality test requires one modular exponentiation. We thus have that the expected time to find two large prime numbers is:

- $O(k^4)$ on a microcomputer (e.g. 20 minutes for 100-digit primes),
- $O(k^3)$ using $O(k)$ gates (e.g. 5 seconds for 100-digit primes),
- $O(k^2 \log k)$ using $O(k^2)$ gates (e.g. 70 milliseconds for 100-digit primes).

We note that so-called "strong" primes are not intrinsically more difficult to find that random primes. (See the paper by J. Gordon in this proceedings.)

The second step of generating an RSA key-set, finding e from d, is not harder than modular exponentiation, since we have the relation:

$$e = d^{\phi(\phi(n))-1} \pmod{n}.$$

Another approach, using the extended Euclidean algorithm for finding greatest common divisors, can also be used (see [RSA78] for details). The algorithm chosen here doesn't matter much since the bulk of work for key-generation will be in finding the large prime numbers.

III. B. Implementation ideas for speed.

The following ideas may help speed up an implementation, over and above the basic approach outlined above.

A *fast clock rate* may of course be very helpful.

Using a *short encryption exponent* (e.g. $e = 3$, as suggested by Knuth [Kn81, p. 386]) gives a 300-fold or so improvement in the speed of encryption and signature verifications (operations which use the public key), but does not help with decryption or signing (operations which use the secret key). This trick can not be used on d as well, since the length of e plus the the length of d should be approximately the length of n. Furthermore, if d is short it could be guessed, so a short d provides little security.

Using the *Chinese Remainder Theorem* – working modulo p and modulo q separately – can help speed up decryption and signing by a factor of 4 on a microcomputer and a factor of 2 to 4 using $O(k)$ hardware.

There are two basically different *exponentiation algorithms* one may use: the *left-to-right* algorithm and the *right-to-left* algorithm. These algorithms examine the bits of the exponent in different orders. Suppose the exponent e has a binary representation of $e_{k-1}e_{k-2}\ldots e_1 e_0$. Then the algorithms for computing a ciphertext C from a message M both begin by setting C to 1, and then proceed as follows:

- The *Left-to-Right* Algorithm: for i from $k-1$ down to 0, this algorithm first sets C to C^2 (mod n) and then, if $e_i = 1$, sets C to $C \cdot M$ (mod n).
- The *Right-to-Left* Algorithm: for i from 0 up to $k-1$, this algorithm first sets C to $C \cdot M$ (mod n) if $e_i = 1$, and then (in any case) sets M to M^2 (mod n).

If the *left-to-right* algorithm is used, then the number of modular multiplications required in the worst case can be reduced from $2 \cdot k$ to $k + (\frac{k}{t})$ by precomputing a table of $M^1, \ldots, M^{2^t - 1}$ (i.e. by modifying the left-to-right algorithm to consider the exponent e in radix 2^t instead of radix 2).

If the *right-to-left* algorithm is used, then by using twice as much hardware one can obtain a two-fold speed-up, since each squaring modular multiplication can be performed *in parallel* with the "accumulation" modular multiplication.

We note that the above two optimization techniques are incompatible, since they require different underlying exponentiation algorithms.

An elegant approach for speeding up the computation is to perform modular multiplication *directly*, rather than first performing an integer multiplication and then reducing the result modulo n as a separate step. This can yield a six-fold (approximately) speed-up, since the modular multiplication of two k-bit numbers can now be performed in approximately k clock cycles instead of approximately $6 \cdot k$. (see [Br82]).

IV. Overview of Existing/Planned Chips

In this section we review briefly six designs for RSA chips. These reviews are brief, and only itended to give the reader a feel for the kinds of chips possible with today's technology. For more details the reader should consult the references. Also, there are other chips in the design stage for which no references exist; these chips are not listed here.

IV.A. The "first" RSA chip

This chip was designed by Rivest, Shamir, and Adleman, and is described in [Ri80].

It was a single-chip nMOS design; using 4-micron design rules, the chip occupied 42 mm². It contained a 512-bit ALU in bit-slice design with eight 512-bit registers for storage of intermediate results, carry-save adder logic, and up-down shifter logic. The 224-word microcode ROM contained control routines for encryption, decryption, finding large primes, gcd, etc. It used a 5V supply, and drew approximately 1 watt of power. It contained approximately 40,000 transistors. It communicated with a host microprocessor using an 8-bit I/O port. The encryption rate was designed to be slightly in excess of 1200 bits/second. Due to an as yet undiagnosed error in the memory cell design, this chip never worked reliably.

IV.B. The NEC/Miyaguchi Design

This chip design was described in [Mi82]; I do not know if it was ever fabricated.

The design was for a cascadable chip set, with each chip having a 2-bit slice. (So 333 chips would be needed for a 200 decimal digit modulus.) Each chip would contain a 2 by 8 multiplier;

multiplication would be done byte-wise (8 by n). An encryption rate of 50,000 bits/second was claimed possible for a 512-bit modulus using this design, or 29,000 bits/second using a 200 decimal-digit modulus.

IV.C. The First Sandia Design

This chip, described in [RSWB82], used a two-chip set to work with numbers up to 336 bits in length. Each of the two chips is identical and could perform a modular multiplication of 336-bit numbers. Using the right-to-left exponentiation algorithm, one chip repeatedly squared the message while the other chip accumulated the product of the desired powers.

The chip was fabricated using 3-micron CMOS technology; the total area of the chip is 41 mm^2. With a 20Mhz clock rate the chip can encrypt one block in 0.8 second – a rate of 420 bits/second. The chip works correctly.

IV.D. The Second Sandia Design

This design is still in progress. The mathematics involved are described in [Br82]; the chip performs modular multiplications directly.

The chip will be cascadable; the first chips made are likely to be a 128-bit slice of the set. (For 512-bit moduli, four chips would be needed.)

IV.E. The "RSA Security" Design

RSA Security, Inc., a new start-up in the data-encryption area, is designing an RSA chip for commercial use [RSA84]. Currently in the design stage, the chip should be available in sample quantities in mid-1985.

Using 3-micron CMOS design rules, the chip should be approximately 47 mm^2 in size.

It will be able to handle numbers up to 200 decimal digits (664 bits) in length, and should be able to do one encryption in under 65 milliseconds (i.e. the data rate should be in excess of 9600 bits/second for a full-size modulus).

V. The Future...

It is interesting to observe that seven years ago, when the RSA cryptosystem was invented, the task of implementing the RSA scheme in a reasonably secure manner was quite expensive. (For example, we built a $3000 TTL implementation that could only handle numbers slightly over 300 bits in length.) Today, a very secure implementation (664 bits) fits nicely on one chip. Seven years from now we may move from a 3-micron technology to a submicron (say 0.3 micron) technology, giving a 100-fold reduction in area. In this case the same RSA implementation will take only 1% of a typical chip. The steady progess of technology will clearly make cryptography so cost-effective that no information system that handles data that is at all sensitive or that needs to be authenticated can afford to do without it.

REFERENCES

[ACGS84] Alexi, W., B. Chor, O. Goldreich, and C. P. Schnor, "RSA/Rabin Bits are $1/2 + \frac{1}{poly(\log N)}$ Secure," *Proc. 25th Annual IEEE Symposium on Foundations of Computer Science*, (Singer Island, 1984).

[Br82] Brickell, E. F., "A Fast Modular Multiplication Algorithm with Applications to Two-Key Cryptography," *Advances in Cryptology – Proceedings of CRYPTO 82*, (ed. by Chaum et. al) (Plenum 1983), 51-60.

[De82]   Denning, D. CRYPTOGRAPHY AND DATA SECURITY, (Addison-Wesley, Reading, Mass., 1982).

[DH76]   Diffie, W. and M. E. Hellman, "New Directions in Cryptography", *IEEE Trans. Info. Theory* IT-22 (Nov. 1976), 644-654.

[DH79]   Diffie, W. and M. E. Hellman, "Privacy and Authentication: An Introduction to Cryptography, *Proc. of the IEEE* 67,3 (March 1979), 397-427.

[Kn81]   Knuth, Donald E., SEMINUMERICAL ALGORITHMS – The Art of Computer Programming (Vol. 2 – Second Edition), (Addison-Wesley 1981).

[Mi82]   Miyaguchi, S., "Fast Encryption Algorithm for the RSA Cryptographic System," *Proceedings COMPCON 82*.

[Ra79]   Rabin, Michael. "Digitalized Signatures as Intractable as Factorization," MIT Laboratory for Computer Science Technical Report MIT/LCS/TR-212 (Jan. 1979).

[Ri80]   Rivest, R. L., "A Description of a Single-Chip Implementation of the RSA Cipher," Lambda 1 (Fourth Quarter 1980), 14-18.

[RSA78]   Rivest, R., A. Shamir, and L. Adleman, "A Method for Obtaining Digital Signatures and Public-Key Cryptosystems," *Comm. of the ACM* (Feb. 1978), 120-126.

[RSA84]   RSA Security, Inc. (1717 Karameos Drive, Sunnyvale, CA 94087) "Preliminary Data Sheet for the RSA Cryptochip," (1984).

[RSWB82]   Rieden, R. F., J. B. Snyder, R. J. Widman, and W. J. Barnard, "A Two-Chip Implementation of the RSA Public-Key Encryption Algorithm," Digest of Papers for the 1982 Government Microciruit Applications Conference (November 1982), 24-27.

[Wi80]   Williams, H. C., "A Modification of the RSA Public-Key Cryptosystem," *IEEE Trans. Info. Theory* IT-26 (Nov. 1980), 726-729.

[Wi84]   Williams, H. C., "Some Public-Key Crypto-Functions as Intractable as Factorization," *Proceedings of CRYPTO 84* (Springer 1984).

SECTION III

NUMBER THEORETICAL PAPERS

THE QUADRATIC SIEVE FACTORING ALGORITHM

by

Carl POMERANCE[*]
Department of Mathematics
University of Georgia
Athens, Georgia 30602 USA

The quadratic sieve algorithm is currently the method of choice to factor very large composite numbers with no small factors. In the hands of the Sandia National Laboratories team of James Davis and Diane Holdridge, it has held the record for the largest hard number factored since mid-1983. As of this writing, the largest number it has cracked is the 71 digit number $(10^{71} -1)/9$, taking 9.5 hours on the Cray XMP computer at Los Alamos, New Mexico. In this paper I shall give some of the history of this algorithm and also describe some of the improvements that have been suggested for it.

KRAITCHIK'S SCHEME

There is a large class of factoring algorithms that share a common strategy. If N is the number to be factored, then the idea is to multiply congruences $U \equiv V \bmod N$, where $U \neq V$ and complete or partial factorizations (depending on the algorithm) have been obtained for U and V, so as to produce a special congruence $X^2 \equiv Y^2 \bmod N$. Then one stands a good chance that the greatest common factor $(X-Y, N)$, found by Euclid's algorithm, is a non-trivial factor of N. If it is not, then another combination of congruences can be tried. Thus these algorithms have several parts :

(1) Generation of the congruences $U \equiv V \bmod N$,

(2) Determination of the complete or partial factorizations of U and V for some of the congruences,

(3) Determination of a subset of the factored congruences which can be multiplied to produce a special congruence $X^2 \equiv Y^2 \bmod N$,

(4) Computation of $(X-Y, N)$.

---

* supported in part by a grant from the National Science Foundation.

For example, say we try to factor $N = 91$ and we notice that

$$81 \equiv -10, \quad 90 \equiv -1, \quad 75 \equiv -16, \quad \text{and} \quad 64 \equiv -27.$$

Factoring these numbers completely we have

$$3^4 \equiv -2 \cdot 5, \quad 2 \cdot 3^2 \cdot 5 \equiv -1, \quad 3 \cdot 5^2 \equiv -2^4, \quad \text{and} \quad 2^6 \equiv -3^3.$$

Multiplying the last two congruences, we have

$$2^6 \cdot 3 \cdot 5^2 \equiv 2^4 \cdot 3^3,$$

or cancelling common factors,

$$2^2 \cdot 5^2 \equiv 3^2.$$

This gives $10^2 \equiv 3^2 \bmod 91$ and $7 = (10-3, 91)$. Or we might have multiplied the first two congruences, getting

$$2 \cdot 3^6 \cdot 5 \equiv 2 \cdot 5 \longrightarrow 3^6 \equiv 1,$$

so $27^2 \equiv 1^2 \bmod 91$ and $13 = (27-1, 91)$.

This general scheme for factoring was published by Kraitchik [4] in 1926. The numbers U, V are factored into primes except for squared factors. Since most of the congruences one is likely to generate will not successfully factor in step (2), one's chances are enhanced if one of U, V is arranged to be a square and the other has a large square factor. In [5], pp. 26-27, Kraitchik explains how this should be done. He lets $U = x^2$ where x is carefully chosen so that $V = -N + x^2$ has a large factor y^2. He can force y^2 to appear by choosing x as a solution of the quadratic congruence $x^2 \equiv N \bmod y^2$. However, V/y^2 need not be small and so easily factorable. This method has its problems.

Kraitchik opportunistically used other congruences $U \equiv V \bmod N$ that were suggested by the special form of N in question. These congruences would not be available for a "random" N. In his later work [5], the congruences $U \equiv V \bmod N$ were used to assist in finding X and Y with $X^2 - Y^2 = N$. This is an old factoring strategy that goes back to Fermat. I think Kraitchik preferred this method for two reasons. First, fewer congruences $U \equiv V \bmod N$ with multiplicative information about U and V are used. Second, when X, Y are found with $X^2 - Y^2 = N$, one could be assured of a non-trivial factorization of N, unlike with the other method where step (4) may produce a trivial factorization. Little did Kraitchik know that his largely abandoned method of producing "cycles" (the combination of congruences in step (3)) would be the basis of most modern factoring algorithms !

THE CONTINUED FRACTION ALGORITHM

Instead of finding $U \equiv V \bmod N$ with one of U, V a square and the other divisible by a large square factor, another strategy might be to choose one a square and the other *small* in absolute value. It thus would more likely factor in step (2). In 1931, Lehmer and Powers [6] suggested the use of the continued fraction expansion of $\sqrt{N}$ to generate the congruences $U \equiv V \bmod N$ in Kraitchik's scheme. This is done by a simple recursive procedure that creates pairs Q_n, A_n where

$$(1) \qquad Q_n \equiv A_n^2 \bmod N$$

and $|Q_n| < 2\sqrt{N}$. An old method of Legendre also suggested the use of the continued fraction expansion of $\sqrt{N}$, but his aim was to use the congruences (1) to find information on the quadratic character $\bmod Q_n$ of prime factors p of N. Then a direct search, such as trial division, could be greatly speeded up because many potential divisors would not have the proper character. In contrast, Lehmer and Powers advocated multiplying several congruences of the form (1) to produce congruent squares.

Morrison and Brillhart [10] were the first to try the continued fraction algorithm on a modern computer. In the implementation they made several major improvements and refinements that would be of use in any of the combination of congruences family of algorithms. First, they used a "factor base", or all of the primes to some point F, to dermine which of the congruences (1) were useful. When a congruence (1) was generated, the number Q_n was subjected to trial division by the primes $p \le F$. If a complete factorization could be obtained, the congruence was kept for later use -if not, it was discarded.

Step (3) of the algorithm, the actual combination of congruences was effected by a Gaussian elimination in a very large matrix over $\mathbb{Z}/2\mathbb{Z}$. Specifically, if the factor base consists of the primes $p_1, \ldots, p_f$, and if

$$Q_n = (-1)^{a_0} \prod_{i=1}^{f} p_i^{a_i}$$

where the a_i are non-negative integers, then we look at the vector

$$\vec{v}(n) = (a_0, a_1, \ldots, a_f) \bmod 2.$$

If we have enough vectors $\vec{v}(n)$, then Gaussian elimination will produce a linear dependency

$$\vec{v}(n_1) + \ldots + \vec{v}(n_k) = \vec{0},$$

so that $Q_{n_1} \ldots Q_{n_k}$ is a square, say X^2. If we compute $X \bmod N$ and $Y = A_{n_1} \ldots A_{n_k} \bmod N$, then $X^2 \equiv Y^2 \bmod N$ and we are ready for step (4).

Another improvement, called the "early abort strategy" was described in [11]. This improvement extended the useful range of the continued fraction algorithm on an ordinary main frame computer by about 10 digits —from the mid 40's to the mid 50's (see [14], [12]).

A special purpose, low cost processor has been designed by J.W. Smith and S.S. Wagstaff, Jr. and built at the University of Georgia to implement the continued fraction algorithm with the early abort strategy. It is designed to do the trial division step on a Q_n in parallel (several trial divisors can be tried at once) and the device has extended precision, so that this arithmetic done with long integers can be done in single precision. It should be fully operational soon and we await their results. It will probably be somewhat inferior to the results produced by the Sandia team, butthis should be weighed by the fact that the cost of the Smith-Wagstaff device is about three orders of magnitude less than the cost of a Cray X M P.

THE MILLER —WESTERN ALGORITHM

The issue of Mathematics of Computation which contains the Morrison-Brillhart paper is dedicated to D.H. Lehmer and has many interesting articles on computational number theory. In this issue there is an article by J.C.P. Miller [7] on factoring that also uses congruences $U \equiv V \bmod N$. He attributes the idea to A.E. Western. The aim is to find congruences with U and V completely factored. But rather than combine these congruences to produce congruent squares, each congruence is read as a linear relation of indices with respect to some primitive root g of p, where p is a prime factor of N. When enough congruences can be found there is a chance of finding p via created congruences of the form $a^t \equiv 1 \bmod N$. If some $q|t$ can be found with $a^{t/q} \not\equiv 1 \bmod N$, then perhaps $(a^{t/q}-1, N)$ is a non-trivial factor of N.

I see no particular advantage to this method over just combining the factored congruences to produce congruent squares in the Kraitchik scheme. I mention the algorithm here because of the very simple way Miller chooses the congruences $U \equiv V \bmod N$. Namely he just partitions N as $A+B$, letting $U = A$, $V = -B$. There is an interesting unsolved problem of Erdös that says that for each $\varepsilon > 0$ there is an $N_0(\varepsilon)$ such that for each integer $N > N_0(\varepsilon)$ there is a partition of N as $A+B$ where no prime in $A\,B$ exceeds N^ε. What we need is an *algorithmic* solution of Erdös's problem that gives many such pairs A,B. Perhaps this problem (and factoring itself) is not so hard !

SCHROEPPEL'S ASYMPTOTIC ANALYSIS

In the late 1970's some important advances on factoring were made by Richard Schroeppel. He never published his results, but they have become known through copies of his letters and through second hand published accounts (e.g. [8], [11]). First, Schroeppel began the systematic study of the asymptotic running time of factorization algorithms in the Kraitchik family. Second, he found an algorithm in the family where step (2) could be accomplished without time consuming trial division.

Schroeppel's asymptotic analysis hinged on the optimal choice of the parameter F, the upper bound for the primes in the factor base. A small choice of F means only few factored congruences are necessary to produce a linear dependency, but such congruences are very hard to find. With a large choice of F the situation is reversed. Somewhere between "large" and "small" is the optimal choice. Schroeppel realized that to study this situation asymptotically one needed to use the function $\psi(x,y)$ -the number of integers up to x divisible by no prime exceeding y. Specifically this was needed with x being the average size of the residues being trial divided and $y = F$. Thus $\psi(x,y)/x$ represents the "probability" that a residue will completely factor over the factor base.

For example, suppose we study the continued fraction algorithm. Then the typical Q_n will be approximately $\sqrt{N}$. Further, if f is the number of primes in the factor base, then we should have $f \approx F/2 \log F$ (only those odd primes p with $(N/p) = 1$ can divide a Q_n). We need to obtain about f completely factored Q_n's. Thus we should expect to have to generate

$$f(\psi(\sqrt{N},F)/\sqrt{N})^{-1} = f\sqrt{N}/\psi(\sqrt{N},F)$$

values of Q_n before enough factored ones are found. More, we need to do about f trial divisions on the average Q_n produced, so the total number of trial division steps needed to factor N with the continued fraction algorithm should be about

$$f^2\sqrt{N}/\psi(\sqrt{N},F).$$

Ignoring other steps in the algorithm, we thus choose F so as to minimize this quantity. Schroeppel assumed that

$$\psi(x,x^{1/u})/x = u^{-(1+o(1))u} \quad \text{for} \quad (\log x)^\epsilon < u < (\log x)^{1-\epsilon}$$

(a result which was subsequently proved in [1]) and found that the optimal choice of F is $L(N)^{1/\sqrt{8}+o(1)}$ where

$$L(N) = \exp(\sqrt{\log N \log \log N})$$

(natural logs) and that the expected running time is $L(N)^{\sqrt{2}+o(1)}$. Of course, this argument is only *heuristic* -for one, it is assumed without proof that the numbers Q_n factor over the primes to F as frequently as random numbers of the same approximate size.

SCHROEPPEL'S LINEAR SIEVE

Schroeppel's new algorithm with by-passed trial division is also in Kraitchik's family. Let

$$(2) \quad \begin{aligned} S(A,B) &= (\lfloor\sqrt{N}\rfloor+A)(\lfloor\sqrt{N}\rfloor+B) - N \\ T(A,B) &= (\lfloor\sqrt{N}\rfloor+A)(\lfloor\sqrt{N}\rfloor+B). \end{aligned}$$

If $|A|$, $|B|$ are less than N^ε, then $|S(A,B)| \lesssim 2N^{1/2+\varepsilon}$ so that the $S(A,B)$ are relatively small, not much larger than the Q_n's given by (1). More, we evidently have

$$S(A,B) \equiv T(A,B) \bmod N$$

so that we use these as the congruences in Kraitchik's scheme. We attempt to completely factor the $S(A,B)$'s over a factor base, but we do not try to factor the $T(A,B)$'s. Note that (2) already gives a partial factorization of $T(A,B)$. We could thus arrange for a product of $T(A,B)$'s to be a square if each A and each B is used an even number of times in the product. Thus we treat the variables A,B as if they were primes in the Gaussian elimination step.

Thus the Gaussian elimination step is harder and the residues $S(A,B)$ are a bit larger than in the continued fraction algorithm. There is an advantage here, though, and it is that the numbers $S(A,B)$ can be factored *without* trial division. The idea is that for a fixed value A_o for A we can let B run over consecutive integers. These numbers form an arithmetic progression, so that if $p|S(A_o,B_o)$, then $p|S(A_o,B_o+p)$, $p|S(A_o,B_o+2p)$, etc. That is, we know beforehand exactly which values of B have $S(A_o,B)$ divisible by p. No more do we need to waste a trial division step on a number where the trial divisor does not go.

Schroeppel's asymptotic analysis suggested the running time of his algorithm was $L(N)^{1+o(1)}$. However, his analysis neglected the time for the Gaussian elimination. This is not a mistake in the continued fraction algorithm analysis because it really takes less time than the trial division step. But in Schroeppel's algorithm we have given the Gaussian elimination a larger task to accomplish and it can be shown (heuristically) that it takes $L(N)^{3/2+o(1)}$ steps, worse than the running time of the continued fraction algorithm.

THE QUADRATIC SIEVE

In 1981 I suggested taking $A=B$ in Schroeppel's linear sieve algorithm, calling the resulting method the quadratic sieve algorithm. This simple move changes things drastically. Let

$$(3) \quad Q(A) = S(A,A) = (\lfloor\sqrt{N}\rfloor+A)^2 - N.$$

Thus we are back in the game of producing quadratic residues as in the continued fraction algorithm, so the Gaussian elimination step should not be a major difficulty. In addition, we can still sieve as Schroeppel did. If $p|Q(A_0)$, then $p|Q(A_0+p)$, $p|Q(A_0+2p)$, etc. This property of the function $Q(A)$ follows from the fact that it is a polynomial with integer coefficients. Heuristically, the running time for the algorithm is $L(N)^{\sqrt{9/8}+o(1)}$, including the matrix step, an improvement over the continued fraction algorithm. This analysis and a description of the algorithm is found in [11].

The idea in (3) is to choose A with $|A| < N^\varepsilon$. Since for small A we have

$$Q(A) \approx 2A\sqrt{N},$$

We thus have $|Q(A)| \lesssim 2N^{1/2+\varepsilon}$, as with Schroeppel. It is amusing to note that the method (3) of choosing quadratic residues $\bmod N$ is very similar to that of Kraitchik discussed above. There is a difference though. Kraitchik carefully prepared values of x so that x^2-N had a large square factor. In (3) we indiscriminately choose all values of x near $\sqrt{N}$.

The advantage is clear, because now we can use a sieve. For each odd prime p in the factor base (p is in the factor base if $(N/p)=1$) we solve the quadratic congruence

$$(\lfloor\sqrt{N}\rfloor+A)^2 \equiv N \bmod p,$$

labelling the solutions $A_1^{(p)}$, $A_2^{(p)}$ (for $p=2$, special treatment is required). We then compute very crude logs of each of the $Q(A)$ for A in a long interval (these logs are all approximately equal). These logs are stored in an array indexed by the values of A. We then pull out each log that has its index $A \equiv A_1^{(p)}$ or $A_2^{(p)} \bmod p$ and subtract $\log p$ from the number in the location. (Again, $\log p$ is a low precision log). This is done for each p in the factor base and for some of the higher powers of the smaller primes p. At the end, we scan the array for residual logs that are close to 0. These locations correspond to values of $Q(A)$ that completely factored. The number $Q(A)$ may now be computed and factored by trial division. Of course, very few numbers $Q(A)$ completely factor, so the amount of trial division in the algorithm is negligible. Note that not only does the quadratic sieve algorithm have asymptotically fewer steps than the continued fraction algorithm, but each step is simpler. In the quadratic sieve a typical step is a single precision subtraction , while in the continued fraction algorithm a typical step is a divide with remainder of a single precision integer into a long dividend.

Asymptotically, the algorithm of Schnorr and Lenstra [13] (which is not in the Kraitchik family) should be faster than the quadratic sieve : its heuristic run time is $L(N)^{1+o(1)}$. However it has not yet proved computer practical and the crossover point may be very large. A typical step in the Schnorr-Lenstra algorithm is composition of binary quadratic forms with multi-precision entries and finding a reduced form in the class.

THE DAVIS VARIATION

Davis and Holdridge [2] have written a very clear article on the implementation of the quadratic sieve algorithm and there is no need to duplicate their work here. But I would like to mention an important improvement Davis made on the method. It seems clear that the quadratic sieve algorithm majorizes the continued fraction algorithm in every respect but in the size of the quadratic residues. Namely, in the latter method, each $|Q_n|$ is less than $2\sqrt{N}$ but in the former, the numbers $|Q(A)|$ are about $N^{1/2+\varepsilon}$ (where $\varepsilon > 0$ is small and tends to 0 slowly as $N \to \infty$). Of course, the larger the residue, the less likely it is to factor over the factor base.

The Davis variation is simply to sieve over various arithmetic progressions of A's so that the $Q(A)$'s are guaranteed to have a fixed factor. Specifically, if p is some large prime *not* in the factor base and $p|Q(A_o)$ where $0 < A_o < p$, then p divides every $Q(A_o + Ap)$ as noted before. Let

$$Q_p(A) = Q(A_o + Ap).$$

Then

$$Q_p(A)/p \approx 2A\sqrt{N},$$

so that after the known factor p is divided out of $Q_p(A)$, the cofactor is about the same size as $Q(A)$. Thus instead of having just one polynomial to work with, we have a large family of polynomials —one (in fact, two) for each possible p. For each p used we consider p as a new prime in the factor base. Thus if k factored values of $Q_p(A)$ are found, after eliminating p we have $k-1$ vectors left over the original factor base. However, Davis avoids losing even one vector. He does this by finding a factored $Q_p(A)$ for "free". This magic is accomplished as follows. If in the original polynomial $Q(A)$ a location A_1 is found after sieving where the residual log is not near 0, but less than $2 \log F$, then the cofactor after $Q(A_1)$ is divided by all primes in the factor base is a prime p with $F < p < F^2$. We thus use this p' to form $Q_p(A)$ (and we can choose $A_o \equiv A_1 \bmod p$). We start with one factored value before sieving the new polynomial, so any new factored values found are all to the good.

THE MONTGOMERY VARIATION

Independently of Davis, Peter Montgomery [9] has come up with another strategy for fighting the drift to infinity of the quadratic residues $Q(A)$. His method tailor makes polynomials to custom fit not only the number N to be factored, but the length of the interval we sieve over before we change polynomials.

Suppose we sieve over intervals of length 2M before we change polynomials.
We are looking for polynomials

$$F(x) = ax^2+2bx+c \quad \text{where} \quad N \mid b^2-ac,$$

for then

(4) $$aF(x) = a^2X^2+2abx+ac = (ax+b)^2 - (b^2-ac)$$
$$\equiv (ax+b)^2 \bmod N.$$

Further, we would like the values of $F(x)$ to be small in absolute value on an
interval of length 2M. It thus seems reasonable to center this interval on the
vertex of the parabola $F(x)$ -so we specify the interval as

$$I = (-b/a-M, -b/a+M)$$

and choose a,b,c so that

$$-F(-b/a) \approx F(-b/a-M) = F(-b/a+M).$$

To be specific, we choose a,b,c so that

(5) $$b^2-ac = N .$$

Then from (4),

$$-aF(-b/a) = N, \quad aF(-b/a-M) = aF(-b/a+M) = a^2M^2-N.$$

Thus we should choose a so that $N \approx a^2M^2-N$, i.e.,

(6) $$a \approx \sqrt{2N}/M.$$

Montgomery suggests then that we decide first on 2M, the length of the interval
sieved. Next an integer a is chosen satisfying (6) and then integers b and c
are found satisfying (5). (For example, we could choose a as a prime satisfying
$(N/a) =1$. Then the quadratic congruence $b^2 \equiv N \bmod a$ is solved for b and c is
chosen as $(b^2-N)/a$.)

We thus have constructed a quadratic polynomial $F(x)$ so that on the interval
I

$$|F(x)| \lesssim \frac{1}{\sqrt{2}} M\sqrt{N}.$$

This is better than the polynomials $Q(A)$ and $Q_p(A)/p$. For them on the interval
$(-M,M)$ their absolute values are bounded by $2M\sqrt{N}$. Thus the largest of Montgomery's
residues are about $2\sqrt{2}$ times smaller and so somewhat more likely to factor over
the factor base.

Here is an idea which should improve Montgomery's basic plan. If $k \geq 1$ values
of $F(x)$ are found which factor over the factor base, we only end up with k-1
vectors because the factor a must be eliminated from the congruences (4). This
could be serious if the expected value of k were much smaller than 1, for then in
the rare instances we had k >0, it would be likely that k =1 and nothing would

be gained. To solve this problem, we choose $a = g^2$ where g is a prime with $(N/g) = 1$ and $g \approx \sqrt{\sqrt{2N}/M}$. Then everything is as before, but we do not have to eliminate a from (4) because it is a square. All factored values of $F(x)$ are now to the good.

The quadratic congruence

$$(7) \qquad\qquad b^2 \equiv N \bmod g^2$$

can be solved very simply if $g \equiv 3 \bmod 4$ and $(N/g) = 1$. Just take

$$b = N^{(g^2-g+2)/4} \bmod g^2.$$

This involves arithmetic mod g^2. Instead, by first solving (7) mod g by taking $b_1 \equiv N^{(g+1)/4} \bmod g$ and next determine x so that $(b_1+xg)^2 \equiv N \bmod g^2$, all of the arithmetic can be done mod g. (This idea was suggested by Wagstaff -it is an elementary application of Hensel's lemma).

Above we chose a satisfying (6) to minimize the maximum value of $|F(x)|$ on I. Instead, it may be more appropriate to minimize the *average* value of $|F(x)|$. For this we should choose

$$a \approx (1.5127453)\sqrt{N}/M.$$

However, it probably makes very little difference whether we choose a by this scheme or by (6).

In the implementation of Montgomery's variation (which has not yet been done) one should compute how costly it is to produce new polynomials $F(x)$. If it is very costly, a larger value should be chosen for M; if it is not so costly, a smaller value should be chosen for M. That is, we should sieve over as *short* an interval as possible, where the overhead of producing new polynomials and computing the starting points for each prime used in the sieve says it should not be *too* short.

LARGE PRIME VARIATION

In [11] the large prime variation was suggested for the quadratic sieve. This variation is commonly used with the continued fraction algorithm. As mentioned above, if the residual log after sieving is not close to 0, but less than $2 \log F$, then we have produced a quadratic residue that completely factors over the factor base except for one large prime factor p with $F < p < F^2$. Not only do we receive this information for free, but such residues are simple to process. If the large prime p is never seen again in another factored residue, it is useless for us and this line may be discarded. If it appears k times, we can eliminate it, being left with $k-1$ vectors over the factor base. The "birthday paradox" suggests that the event $k \geqslant 2$ will not be that uncommon.

If this method is used together with the Davis variation, another method should be used to produce the polynomials $Q_p(A)$. We can instead use (7). Let $g > F$ be a prime with $g \equiv 3 \bmod 4$ and $(N/g) = 1$. If b is the solution of (7), we let $A_o = b - \lfloor \sqrt{N} \rfloor \bmod g^2$. Then we can use the polynomial

$$Q_{g^2}(A) = Q(A_o + g^2 A)$$

in the Davis variation. (We can also use $A_o \equiv -b - \lfloor \sqrt{N} \rfloor \bmod g^2$.)
Every value factored over the factor base is useful and we can use the large prime variation on all of the $Q_{g^2}(A)$ for various choices of g^2. Note that there is less overhead with producing the polynomials $Q_{g^2}(A)$ than the $\tilde{F}(x)$ in Montgomery's variation because g can be chosen smaller with Davis.

SMALL MODULI

In trial division it takes just as long to test divisibility by 3 as by 101. But sieving by 3 takes 101/3 times *longer* than 101 since it has more frequent "hits". Thus a considerable percentage of sieving time is spent with the very smallest moduli. This seems a waste since these small moduli contribute the least information. One idea is to skip sieving with them completely. Say we do not sieve with any modulus below 30. Then if 3 is in the factor base, for example, we will not sieve mod 3, mod 9, nor mod 27. But we will sieve mod 81, subtracting 4 log3 (instead of log 3) at hits for this modulus. If P is the product of the highest powers of the moduli skipped and if $P < F$, then we lose nothing by this strategy. Indeed, the maximal error introduced in skipping the small moduli is at most $\log P < \log F$. Thus if the residual log is less than $\log F$ the number has factored completely and every completely factored number will have a residual log less than $\log F$.

If this idea proves good, one might "live dangerously" and let P be somewhat bigger than F. In fact if we let P be around F^2 and use the large prime variation too, the only residues lost will be some of the residues which factored with a large prime. Of course, you may prefer not to lose anything.

USE OF A MULTIPLIER

The factor base for N in the quadratic sieve algorithm consists of those primes $p \leqslant F$ with $p = 2$ or $(N/p) = 1$. If we replace N by λN where λ is a small positive square-free integer (Kraitchik again –see [4], p. 208 and [5], Ch. 2) then the factor base changes. The expected contribution to $\log(x^2 - \lambda N)$ by the power of p in $x^2 - \lambda N$ is

$$E_p = (2 \log p)/(p-1)$$

if x is a random integer and $(\lambda N/p) = 1$. For $p = 2$ the expected contribution is

$$E_2 = \begin{cases} \frac{1}{2}\log 2 \, , & \text{if } \lambda N \equiv 3 \bmod 4 \\ \log 2 \, , & \text{if } \lambda N \equiv 5 \bmod 8 \\ 2\log 2 \, , & \text{if } \lambda N \equiv 1 \bmod 8. \end{cases}$$

If $p|\lambda$ the expected contribution E_p is $(\log p)/p$. Thus we wish to choose the value of λ so as to maximize the function

$$F(\lambda,N) = -\frac{1}{2}\log|\lambda| + \sum_{p \leq F} E_p$$

where the sum is over those primes $p \leq F$ with $p=2$, $(\lambda N/p)=1$, or $p|\lambda$. This function is very similar to one associated with the continued fraction algorithm (see [3], p. 391, Ex. 28 or [12]).

SPECIAL PURPOSE PROCESSORS

J.W. Smith, S.S. Wagstaff, Jr., and I have discussed the feasibility of building a special purpose processor to implement the quadratic sieve algorithm. We are encouraged by the prospects. For a budget of perhaps #25,000 in parts, we believe a "quadratic siever" could be built that would rival a Cray in speed. For ten or twenty times as much money a machine could be built that could factor 100 digit numbers in a month. Perhaps these figures are way off, it is hard to tell unless one tries.

The basic idea of the "quadratic siever" would be to construct a sequence of $16 \times 4K$ units each of which would sieve over an interval of length 4096. The largest moduli (fastest through the sieve) would be started one after the other through the sequence of units. There would never be interference of moduli because we have let the fastest racers start first.

Another idea is to use many unextraordinary computers each using a different batch of polynomials with one central computer which is fed the factored residues.

With all of these ideas we may begin to approach the 100 digit level in factoring. But 150 digit numbers should be about 100,000 times harder and it seems clear that current methodology is insufficient for factoring such huge numbers. However, until someone proves that factoring *must* be hard, there will always be some doubt about the security of R SA. When R SA was introduced 40 digit numbers were considered hard to factor, while now we are doing 70 digit numbers and talking about 100 digit numbers. As always, the future is hard to predict.

ACKNOWLEDGEMENTS

I would like to thank the Département de Mathématiques-Informatique at the U.E.R. des Sciences de Limoges for their hospitality while this paper was written. I would also like to thank H.J.J. te Riele for helping me track down the Kraitchik references and Peter Montgomery for his kind permission to describe his improvement to the quadratic sieve alogorithm.

REFERENCES

[1]   E.R. Canfield, P. Erdös and C. Pomerance, On a problem of Oppenheim concerning "Factorisatio Numerorum", J. Number Theory, 17 (1983), 1-28.

[2]   J.A. Davis and D.B. Holdridge, Factorization using the quadratic sieve algorithm, Sandia Report Sand 83-1346, Sandia National Laboratories, Albuquerque, New Mexico, 1983.

[3]   D.E. Knuth, The Art of Computer Programming, vol. 2, Seminumerical Algorithms, 2nd edition, Addison Wesley, Reading, Mass., 1981.

[4]   M. Kraitchik, Théorie des Nombres, Tome II, Gauthier-Villars, Paris, 1926.

[5]   M. Kraitchik, Recherches sur la Théorie des Nombres, Tome II, Factorisation, Gauthier-Villars, Paris, 1929.

[6]   D.H. Lehmer and R.E. Powers, On factoring large numbers, Bull. Amer. Math. Soc. 37 (1931), 770-776.

[7]   J.C.P. Miller, On factorisation with a suggested new approach, Math. Comp. 29 (1975), 155-172.

[8]   L. Monier, Algorithmes de factorisation d'entiers, thèse de 3e cycle, Orsay (1980).

[9]   P. Montgomery, private communication.

[10]   M.A. Morrison and J. Brillhart, A method of factoring and the factorization of F_7, Math. Comp. 29 (1975), 183-205.

[11]   C. Pomerance, Analysis and comparison of some integer factoring algorithms, in Computational Methods in Number Theory, H.W. Lenstra, Jr. and R. Tijdeman, eds., Math. Centrum Tract 154 (1982), 89-139.

[12] C. Pomerance and S.S. Wagstaff, Jr., Implementation of the continued fraction algorithm, Cong. Numerantium 37 (1983), 99-118.

[13] C.P. Schnorr and H.W. Lenstra, Jr., A Monte Carlo factoring algorithm with finite storage, preprint.

[14] M.C. Wunderlich, A report on the factorization of 2797 numbers using the continued fraction algorithm, unpublished manuscript.

Status Report on Factoring
(At the Sandia National Laboratories)*

James A. Davis, Diane B. Holdridge and Gustavus J. Simmons

Sandia National Laboratories
Albuquerque, New Mexico 87185

Introduction

It is well known that the cryptosecurity of the RSA (Rivest-Shamir-Adleman) two key cryptoalgorithm [1] is no better than the composite modulus is difficult to factor. Except for one special case, the converse statement is still an open and extremely important question. It is not so well known, perhaps, that there are several other crypto-like schemes whose performance is also bounded by the difficulty of factoring large numbers: the digital signature schemes of Ong-Schnorr [2], of Ong-Schnorr-Shamir [3] and of Schnorr [4], the oblivious transfer channel of Rabin [5] and the subliminal channel of Simmons [6] to name only a few. The point is that the difficulty of factoring large integers has become a vital parameter in estimating the security achievable in many secure data schemes -- and conversely factoring techniques are potentially a tool for the cryptanalyst if the cryptographer misjudges the difficulty of factoring a composite number on which he bases a system.

The Sandia National Laboratories have already fielded several secure data systems that are dependent on the difficulty of factoring for their security [7,8,9] and at least as many other applications are approaching

---

* This work performed at Sandia National Laboratories supported by the U. S. Department of Energy under contract No. DE-AC04-76DP00789.

realization. As a result, a concerted research effort was initiated in 1982 in the Mathematics Department at Sandia to define as sharply as possible the bounds on the computational feasibility of factoring large numbers, using the most powerful computers available -- as efficiently as possible -- with the factoring algorithms being carefully matched to the architecture of the machine on which the algorithm was to be run [10]. Our primary objective in this paper will be to present an overview of the advances in factoring resulting from this research. Later, we shall discuss in detail the mathematical and coding advances themselves. Suffice it to say that a roughly three-order of magnitude improvement in factoring -- as measured by the time required to factor a particular size number -- has been achieved by the Sandia researchers over what was possible (and well benchmarked) a few years ago. This is a combined effect due in part to a new generation of computers with much increased computing power and especially due to the unique architecture of the Cray family of machines, in part due to substantial advances in factoring algorithms and finally -- and equally significant -- in part attributable to the efficiency with which the algorithms have been coded for the specific computers. Our secondary objective will be to separate out the contributions of these three factors (to factoring progress) in order to both understand how the improvements of the past three years were achieved as well as to project what the state of the art in factoring is likely to be 5 to 10 years from now.

An Overview

The easiest question to ask concerning integer factoring and the hardest to answer, is; "How large a number is it computationally feasible to factor using a general purpose factoring routine?" Figure 1 gives one

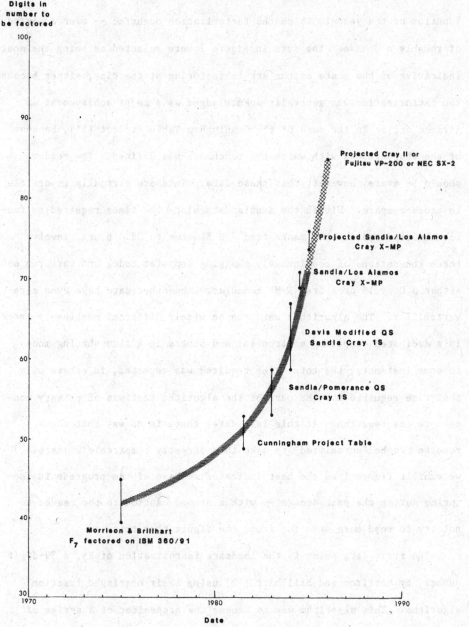

Progress in Factoring

Digits in
number to
be factored

Projected Cray II or
Fujitsu VP-200 or NEC SX-2

Projected Sandia/Los Alamos
Cray X-MP

Sandia/Los Alamos
Cray X-MP

Davis Modified QS
Sandia Cray 1S

Sandia/Pomerance QS
Cray 1S

Cunningham Project Table

Morrison & Brillhart
F_7 factored on IBM 360/91

Date

Figure 1.

answer showing the record size numbers that were factored as an approximate
function of the year in which the factorization occurred -- over a period
of roughly a decade. The data in Figure 1 were selected as being the most
indicative of the state of the art in factoring at the time, either because
the factorization was generally acknowledged as a major achievement or
advance or, as in the case of the Cunningham Table Project [11], because
of the thoroughness with which the benchmark was defined. The reader
should be aware, however, that these data points are virtually impossible
to cross-compare. Within the Sandia data alone the times required to factor the reported numbers range from 7.2 minutes to 32.3 hours, involve
three generations of continuously changing computer codes and were run on
either a Cray 1S or a Cray X-MP computer. The other data have even more
variability. The algorithms were run on widely different machines -- some
in a dedicated computing environment and others in a time sharing mode.
In some instances, the total time required was reported, in others only
that time required for the part of the algorithm that was of primary concern to the research. At this late date, there is no way that these
results can be "normalized" to make them directly comparable. Instead,
we exhibit Figure 1 as the best indicator we have of the progress in factoring during the past decade -- with a strong caution to the reader to
not try to read more into (or from) the figure than this.

The first data point is the landmark factorization of F_7, a 39-digit
number, by Morrison and Brillhart [12] using their continued fraction
algorithm. This algorithm was to become the progenitor of a series of
steadily improving continued fraction algorithms that dominated the factoring scene until Pomerance's quadratic sieve [13] was first implemented at
Sandia in 1982 [10]. Using an IBM 360/91 over a period of several weeks,

Morrison and Brillhart found the necessary number of completely factored quadratic residues in a total CPU time of only 90 minutes. They don't report the time required to carry out the Gaussian elimination (in 2700 variables -- primes) but it must have been large. Based on recent discussions with John Brillhart, it appears that their technique and machine could have factored numbers in the mid-forty digit range in times comparable to the average of the times required for the two dozen or so factorizations that make up the Sandia data points. The error bar on the Morrison and Brillhart data point therefore reflects a rough attempt to show the true capability of this factorization technique.

Unquestionably, the most extensive -- and up to date -- compilation of integer factorizations ever made is the Cunningham Project Table [11] published by the AMS in 1983. As the authors say in the introduction, "The present tables are now at the limit of what can be done by factoring through 50 digits ...." The mid-1981 data point representing this benchmark in Figure 1 indicates the spread above and below this 50-digit figure accounted for by the variation in difficulty of specific numbers. Roughly speaking, the Cunningham Project Table established a well defined standard of the computational feasibility of factoring any 50-digit number in at most one day's computing time. This was the state of the art in the fall of 1982 when the quadratic sieve in the form originally proposed by Carl Pomerance [13] was implemented by Davis and Holdridge at Sandia on a Cray 1S. The Sandia effort was prompted by the recognition by Simmons, Tony Warnock of Cray Research and Marvin Wunderlich that the Cray's ability to efficiently pipeline vector operations on vectors containing thousands of elements could be matched to the sieving operation that was the heart of the quadratic sieve factoring algorithm. The immediate results were startling. A pair of 51 and 52-digit numbers -- taken from the composite cofactor list in the Cunningham Project Table that gave them a recognized certificate of difficulty -- were factored in under two hours. This represented a speed improvement of better than an order of magnitude on the first attempt over what had been possible only a year earlier when the Cunningham Project Table was sent to press. This algorithm, using a very memory efficient Gaussian elimination routine for binary matrices devised by Parkinson and Wunderlich [16], was found to have a feasible range of 50-58 digits, i.e., it could factor up to 58-digit numbers in approximately a day's CPU time.

The next big advance occurred in 1983 when Davis discovered the special q variation to the basic quadratic sieve [10]. This innovation is so vital to the Sandia advances, and to the most recent factoring results shown in Figure 1, that it will be discussed in detail later. We also give some precise cross-comparisons of the time required to factor numbers using the quadratic sieve, both with and without the special q variation, later in this section, but roughly speaking this improvement bought another order of magnitude improvement in the speed of factoring.

The last two data points in Figure 1 are another factor of six or seven removed from the points in the error bar for the special q algorithm. This is due to the optimization of the coding of the special q algorithm for the Cray -- attributable in large part to an improved search algorithm developed by Tony Warnock. In addition, Holdridge found that by "unrolling" the nested loops in the code the running times could be substantially improved. In other words, the six-fold improvement between the special q case and the 69 and 71-digit examples is primarily due to the substantially improved efficiency with which the computers were coded and used.

The research on factoring at the Sandia National Laboratories has been proof tested at each stage of algorithm development on numbers that were left unfactored in [11] and which were cited as being of either extraordinary interest or difficulty to factor or both. For example, in [11], there is a table of the "Ten 'Most Wanted' Factorizations" that included as the first two entries the composite cofactors of the only two surviving unfactored composite numbers from Mersenne's 1640 list; $2^{211}-1$ and $2^{251}-1$. Since this list was essentially an open challenge to the factoring community, we have responded by factoring all ten of them (nine of them for the first time). In the "shorthand" notation of [11], the numbers and the vital statistics of their factorization are shown in Table I. 2,211- C60 denotes the 60-digit composite cofactor of $2^{211}-1$, etc. The cofactors themselves are

Table I.

10 Most Wanted Factorizations

CPT No.	Digits	Cunningham Designation	Sieve Time (hrs)	Process Time (hrs)	Program Configuration
1	60	2,211-	22	.25	(a)
2	69	2,251-	31.9	.4	Sq
3*	54	2,212+	.1	.9	Sq, SGE
4	55	10,64+	4.3	.1	BQS
5	61	10,67-	1.0	.22	Sq
6	71	10,71-	8.75	.75	Sq, SGE
7	58	3,124+	1.6	.2	Sq
8	53	3,128+	5.9	.15	BQS
9	67	11,64+	15	.34	Sq
10	55	5,79-	.66	.33	Sq

*   This number originally factored by Sam Wagstaff. The times shown for 3 are for the Sandia factorization. The other nine were all first factored at Sandia.

(a) 18.5 hours sieving using basic algorithm obtained 1/2 needed relations 3.5 hours using special q's conpleted the sieving.

BQS = Basic Quadratic Sieve (+)

Sq = Special q ($\square$)

SGE - Segmented Gaussian Elimination ($\triangle$)

tabulated in [11]. Figure 2 plots the total computing time required to factor these numbers. As already mentioned, there have been three distinct generations of quadratic sieving algorithms, although refinements and improvements have occurred steadily in each generation of software. The + symbol denotes factorizations made with the original quadratic sieve, □ the special q algorithm and △, the segmented (partioned matrix) Gaussian elimination codes that make it possible to handle much larger prime bases than would otherwise be possible. The 54-digit outlier (2,212+) is the result of factoring a small number using the partitioned matrix code, so that almost all of the time shown was overhead spent in moving blocks of the matrix into and out of memory. It is included for completeness, but

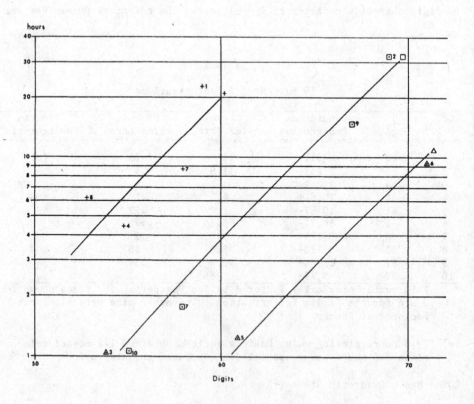

Figure 2.

would have taken roughly the same time to factor using only the special
q algorithm. Incidentally, the approximating curves are simply fits of
$(L(n))^c$ where $L(n) = e^{\sqrt{\log n \times \log\log n}}$ is the bound that most of the
general purpose factoring algorithms seem to obey [13].

Especially noteworthy is the 58-digit number (#7, 3,124+ from [11])
that was factored twice; first using the basic quadratic sieve in a time
of 8.78 hours and then again using the special q algorithm in 1.76 hours
with a five-fold improvement in speed. This provides a crisp cross-
comparison of the algorithms since both factorizations were done on the
Cray 1S with codes developed by Holdridge within a very short time span.
Hence, the improvement in this case is directly attributable to the mathematics (special q algorithm). An even more spectacular, but also more
difficult to interpret cross-comparison is possible. In [13] Pomerance
discusses the benchmark 49-digit number $\dfrac{3^{121} - 1}{(3^{11}-1)11617}$ factored by Sam
Wagstaff in 70 hours of computing and projects that it might be possible
by various refinements (such as the early abort technique) to reduce the
running time to as little as 20 hours. The latest generation of Sandia
algorithms factored this number in 4 minutes and 34 seconds: a ratio of
920 to 1 in computing time! Admittedly, this timing comparison is hard to
interpret since different machines and different factoring algorithms were
used, but the comparison supports our earlier statement that a roughly
three-order of magnitude overall improvement in the speed of factorization
has been achieved. Other comparisons yield similar results.

Twenty-five large numbers (>40 digits) have been factored at Sandia --
plus many other smaller numbers for which the overhead obscures the time
actually spent in factoring. Figure 3 shows a least squares fit of $(L(n))^c$
to the data on numbers of at least forty digits for the three generations
of algorithms; marked +, □ and △ as before. Note, however, that in an

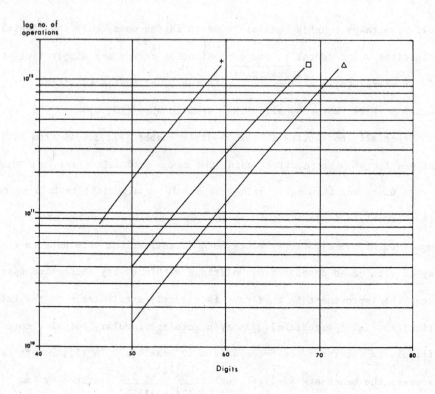

Figure 3.

effort to make the data machine independent, we have plotted the number of
elementary machine operations (shifts, adds, XOR, etc.) rather than the
total time required to factor a number. The △ curve is translated upward
in Figure 3 compared to the same curve in Figure 2 since the Cray X-MP has
a basic clock frequency of 105 MHz compared to the 80 MHz clock frequency
for the Cray 1S, so that the elapsed time (Figure 2) for a given number of
elementary operations on the X-MP is roughly 3/4 of what it would be on
the 1S. The most obvious conclusion to be drawn from Figure 3 is that the
Sandia work has -- for a given number of machine operations -- roughly
increased the size of the number that can be factored by thirteen digits.
This may not sound like much of an improvement, but over the range from 40
to 75 digits -- essentially independent of the algorithm used -- for each

three-digit increase in the size of the number to be factored, the time
required roughly doubles. This translates into slightly more than a 20-
fold improvement in factoring resulting from the Sandia work, independent
of the machine. This latter statement assumes that the machine is vectorized so that the quadratic sieve can be accommodated efficiently and also
that the memory is organized in such a way that data can be "streamed"
through an arithmetic unit and back into memory, etc., as is needed for
an efficient implementation of a quadratic sieve. The Crays have this
type of architecture, but so does the NEC SX-2, the Fujitsu VP-200 and the
Hitachi S-810 [14,15].

A sort of "sound barrier" in computing is 10^{12} operations. At present
this is a generally accepted dividing line between what is computationally
feasible and infeasible. Figure 4, taken from the same data shown in Fig-

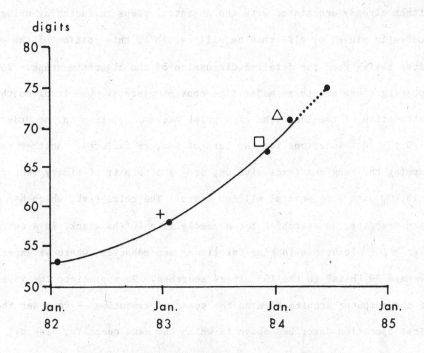

Figure 4. Size of composite "hard" number
factorable by 10^{12} operations.

ures 1 and 3, shows how large a composite "hard" number could be factored using 10^{12} operations with the various generations of Sandia quadratic sieving algorithms and codes. Again, the roughly thirteen-digit overall improvement mentioned earlier can be seen to hold at 10^{12} operations decreasing to roughly ten digits improvement at 10^{10} operations -- the difference being due to the relative effect of the fixed overhead in the computation.

The third factor, in addition to the algorithmic improvements and the advances in the speed and power of the machines on which the algorithms are run, that has made a major contribution to speeding up the factorization of large numbers is the architecture of the Cray family of computers (or of the Cray-like vectorized machines such as the NEC SX-2, the Fujitsu VP-200 and the Hitachi S-810). We presuppose here that the reader is either already acquainted with the essential steps in factoring using a quadratic sieve, or else that he will return to this portion of the paper after having read the detailed discussion of the algorithm steps. Roughly speaking there are three major time-consuming steps. One involves the subtraction of the logarithm of a prime number, p_i, from on the order of $(1/p_i) \times 10^{10}$ locations for the largest numbers factored. Another requires forming the ring sum (exclusive OR, or $\oplus$) of a pair of binary vectors 7-15,000 bits long several million times. The third task, which has often been described as searching for a needle in a 10^9 haystack, is a search over $\approx 10^{10}$ locations looking for linear dependencies, where we expect on average 20 "hits" in the 10^{10} items searched. To appreciate the impact of the computer architecture on the speed of execution -- consider the first operation described above in which the same quantity, $-\log p_i$, is to be added to a string of memory locations that can be indexed in such a way that the locations to which $-\log p_i$ is to be added differ by a constant

p_i^j. The total string length is $\approx 10^{10}$. In a machine of more or less conventional architecture in which data is fetched from memory, operated on in the arithmetic unit (AU) and the result then returned to memory, this sort of operation is slow. Programmed optimally on a CDC 7600 only a 1 megabit per second effective throughput is possible. The Cray however has the ability to "stream" information from memory through the AU and back into memory for a fixed operation without pausing for fetch, store or interpret states. As a result, we can carry out this operation,

$$\text{DO 10, I = J, N, } p_i^j \qquad N \approx 10^{10}$$
$$10 \quad A(I) = A(I) - X(p_i) \quad ,$$

where $X(p_i)$ is the logarithm of p_i, at 1/2 the clock rate of 80 MHz on the Cray 1S and at the full clock rate of 105 MHz on the Cray X-MP. In other words, the architecture alone has accounted for a speed up of nearly forty times (Cray X-MP with 105 MHz clock versus CDC 7600 with a 37 MHz clock rate) for this type of operation! In order to exploit the capability to stream information from the memory through the AU and back into memory, the algorithm must have many long strings on which a fixed operation needs to be performed. The recognition that quadratic sieving could be organized in such a way that this feature of the Crays could be exploited is what prompted the Sandia research in the first place.

The exclusive or operation

$$A(I) = A(I) \oplus B(I)$$

goes at the same rate as the subtraction, i.e., the Cray 1S streams at $1/2 \times 80$ MHz while the Cray X-MP can stream data at 1×105 MHz. The search operation in either of the Crays has an overhead that only allows a throughput of 2/3 of the clock rate, i.e., $2/3 \times 80$ MHz for the Cray 1S or 2/3 × 105 MHz for the Cray X-MP.

In addition to using the ability of the Crays to stream data, Holdridge did a timing analysis and found that if the major sieving loop was "unrolled" that the same computation could be carried out even faster.

As a result of the timing analysis of the sieving code it was also determined that a great deal of time was spent in searching. Once the sieving is done those vector entries that have reached a specified limit must be found and saved. The search, written in Fortran with an "if" statement was not vectorized by the Cray compiler. The search is now done by a Cray Assembly Language (CAL) subroutine which does use the vectorization capability and is much faster.

The bottom line, when all of these refinements are included and when one weighs the efficiencies for the various operations with the relative times spent in carrying out the associated calculation, is that the Cray 1S, running the quadratic sieve, has a throughput (bits of meaningful information processed per second) of 1/4 × 80 MHz while the Cray X-MP achieves 3/4 × 105 MHz. Both of these figures are quite impressive since they indicate that the coding is exceptionally taut -- so much so that Cray scientists have said that these codes come the closest to running the Crays "flat out" of any codes they know of. The point is that since no code can have a throughput greater than the clock rate, and since the throughput with these codes (especially on the X-MP) is so close to the clock rate, there is only a marginal improvement possible from further refinements of the coding -- for the present factoring algorithms. Almost an order of magnitude of the total advance in factoring achieved at Sandia is attributable to the efficiency with which the Crays are being used, i.e., to the tautness of the codes.

We can extrapolate the future of factoring a short distance into the

future with relatively high confidence. First, the Cray X-MP is a dual
processor machine in which the present Sandia code has only used one of
the processors. Preliminary work on splitting up the main parts of the
quadratic sieving calculation so that two processors can be efficiently
employed -- a nontrivial task incidentally -- suggests that it may be possible to gain a factor of ≈ 1.7 in computing effectiveness by using the
X-MP to its fullest. Using the rule of thumb that doubling the computing
time roughly equates to increasing the size of the number that can be
factored with a fixed amount of work by three digits -- taking advantage
of the dual processor capability of the Cray X-MP should make it possible
to factor numbers of 73-74 digits in the same time required to factor the
71-digit number using a single processor. Another way of stating this
result is; with the present code and using the Cray X-MP, 75-digit numbers
should be factorable in roughly a day's computing time.

Looking at the next generation of vectorized machines -- especially
the Cray II and also the Fujitsu VP-200 or the NEC SX-2 [14,15], all will
have a 256 million word high-speed memory compared to the four million word
memory on the Cray X-MP used in the research reported here. The Cray II
has a projected arithmetic capability of 2000 megaflops (millions of floating point operations per second) while the Japanese machines have 533 and
1300 megaflops respectively compared to ≈ 100 megaflops for the Cray X-MP.
Perhaps more significantly for the quadratic sieve algorithm, all have an
improved vectorization capability; 80 K for the SX-2 and 64 K for the VP-200
compared to the 4 K capability of the Cray 1S or 2 × 4K of the Cray X-MP.
All of these factors when combined suggest that the Cray II and probably
the Fujitsu VP-200 or the NEC SX-2 will be roughly eight to nine times
more effective in factoring using the quadratic sieve than is the Cray
X-MP. This translates into an increase in the size of the numbers that
can be factored of ≈ 10 digits. We therefore feel quite confident in pro-

jecting that 85-digit numbers will be factorable in a day's time using
the machines that will be available in the next year or so as indicated in
Figure 1.

Beyond that point, we leave it to the reader to draw his own conclusions. It is unlikely, however, that either of the curves in Figures 1 or
4 showing recent progress in factoring will suddenly go "flat", but whether
the exponential rate of change will continue is impossible to predict.
What does appear plausible to predict, though, is that it will be feasible
to factor 100 digits by the end of the decade, i.e., by 1990.

Fanciful Factoring

Most general purpose factoring algorithms (continued fraction,
Schroeppel's sieve and the various quadratic sieves) depend for their
success on the following simple observation. In the ring of residues
modulo a composite number n, any quadratic residue, y, i.e., a residue
that is the square of some other element in the ring, has at least four
"square roots" -- and perhaps many more depending on the choice of y and
on the prime decomposition of n. If there existed an oracle that when
presented with a quadratic residue, y, would pronounce a square root of y,
then n could be factored with probability that goes to 1 exponentially
fast. For example, if $n = pq$, p and q distinct primes, and $y = x^2$ (mod n)
where x has the unique representation $x = ap + bq$ (mod n), where $0 < a < q$
and $0 < b < p$, then y has the four square roots $(\pm a)p + (\pm b)q$ where we
interpret $-a = q-a$ and $-b = p-b$. To factor n using the services of the
oracle, choose $x = ap + bq$ (at random) and compute the quadratic residue y
$\equiv x^2 \equiv a^2p^2 + b^2q^2$ (mod n). We, of course, do not know a, p, b or q since
we don't yet know the factorization of n, but we do know x and y. The
oracle when presented with y, would with probability 1/2 pronounce either
$y^{1/2} = ap + bq$ or $y^{1/2} = (-a)p + (-b)q$ in which case we learn nothing

about the factorization of n. On the other hand, with probability 1/2 the oracle would pronounce either $y^{1/2} = ap + (-b)q$ or $y^{1/2} = (-a)p + bq$. In which case the two greatest common divisors;

$$(x+y^{1/2}, n) \qquad \text{and} \qquad (x-y^{1/2}, n)$$

would be either p and q or else q and p, respectively, depending on which root the oracle chose.

All of the general purpose factoring algorithms mentioned cause the computer to function (ultimately) in the same way as our fancied oracle. The main difference is that instead of getting back a square root as the response to a submitted quadratic residue, the algorithm yields a sequence of intermediate answers, that ultimately amount to one of the oracle's responses. Just as in the case of the oracle, a quadratic residue, Q_i, is presented to the algorithm -- but the response is not (except in the rarest of cases) a square root of Q_i, but rather the prime decomposition of Q_i, in which some of the prime factors may occur to an odd power. Hence it is computationally infeasible to infer a square root of Q_i from the response, since this would be equivalent to being able to factor n. If after sufficiently many responses, however, a subset of the Q's can be found for which each of the primes that has occured as a factor in some one of the Q's has occurred an even number of times in all, then we are able to effectively recreate one of the oracle's responses. Since the product of the Q's is a quadratic residue of a root that we know and the square root of the product of the primes is trivially the product of each of the primes raised to half of its even exponent, it is also feasible to calculate a square root. Just as in the case of the oracle, when n = pq there is only a 50-50 chance that this will lead to a factorization of n with comparable probabilities for other composite n, but this is the essential notion underlying the various factoring schemes.

Quadratic Sieving: Plain

Given an odd number, n, to be factored, the basic quadratic sieving

scheme [13] calculates a sequence of (relatively) small quadratic residues

$$Q(x) = (x+m)^2 - n \tag{1}$$

where m = $[\sqrt{n}]$. If $|x| \leq B$ and $B \ll \sqrt{n}$, then Q(x) will be "close" to

$\sqrt{n}$. It is important to keep Q(x) small since the algorithm attempts to

factor Q(x) over a prescribed -- but restricted -- set of primes. This

set of possible factors of Q(x) consists of precisely those primes for

which n is a quadratic residue, i.e., 2 and the odd primes, p, for which

the Legendre symbol (n/p) = 1. Fortunately, the Legendre symbol is easy

to calculate in a manner similar to the Euclidean algorithm for finding

the greatest common divisior, so that it is computationally easy to find

the t-1 smallest odd primes, p_i, for which $(n/p_i) = 1$. The set of t+1

elements $(-1, 2, p_i)$ we shall refer to as the factor base. In order for

the algorithm to succeed, we must find sufficiently many quadratic residues,

Q(x), that factor completely into factors in the factor base so that it is

possible to find some subset of the Q(x) among which the prime factors

have all occurred an even number of times. The justification for referring

to the procedure as a sieve is now easy to see. If $p^\alpha | Q(x)$ for some x,

then $p^\alpha | (Q(x \pm hp^\alpha)$, h = 0,1,2,..., hence the division of the resulting

sequence of quadratic residues can be performed by a sieve-like operation

at argument values indexed in an arithmetic progression with spacing of

p^α. One of the primary reasons for the speed of the quadratic sieving

algorithm is that instead of having to carry out multiple precision trial

divisions as is required in some of the other general purpose factoring

algorithms, we can use single precision subtraction of approximate logar-

ithms on the $Q(x \pm hp^\alpha)$, i.e., at only those positions where it is already known that p^α is a divisor.

Since we must ultimately be able to combine a subset of the factored residues by multiplication to form a perfect square, i.e., to simulate a response by the oracle, we need to find a linear combination of the exponents for the primes appearing in the various factorizations such that the sum is even in each entry (for each prime). In order to have a reasonable chance of finding such a dependency we should have approximately as many completely factored residues as we have primes in the factor base. One might conclude from this, that t should be small. However, if we take t to be too small, then a given residue is not likely to factor. On the other hand, if we take t to be too large, we spend more time sieving and will have to find many more factorizations in order to be able to find a linearly dependent subset. It is clear, though, that qualitatively speaking as the magnitude of n increases, the number of entries, t, in the factor base should also increase. If one had no storage constraints, it would be possible to optimize the size of the factor base in order to minimize running time. In fact Wunderlich has analyzed, partly theoretically and partly empirically, the optimum size of the factor base as a function of the size of n, but the conclusion is that this optimum is so large that using a t of this size would result in an impractically large matrix even for the Cray X-MP; hence, we simply use as large a factor base as we can accommodate.

A detailed discussion of the coded implementation of quadratic sieves is inappropriate to the objectives of this paper, however, it is necessary to understand the essential steps involved in using sieves for factoring in order to appreciate why and how the Cray machines can be so well matched to the algorithm. For the Q(x) defined in (1), we wish to find solutions, x, to the related congruences

202

$$Q(x) \equiv 0 \qquad (\bmod \ p_i) \tag{2}$$

for p_i an element in the factor base. As already remarked (2) has solutions
precisely when $(n/p_i) = 1$, $p_i | n$ or $p_i = 2$. If $(n/p_i) = 1$ then (2) has two
solutions, which are usually represented as A_{i1} and $B_{i1} = -(A_{i1} + 2m)$ $(\bmod \ p_i$
The sieving process depends on the fact that if we had a list of consecu-
tive values of $Q(x)$ indexed by x, that for all indices $x = A_{i1} \pm hp_i$ and
$x = B_{i1} \pm hp_i$ the associated $Q(x)$ would be divisable by p_i. The sieving
procedure consists of dividing out (effectively) p_i from only these $Q(x)$
while leaving all other $Q(x)$ unaffected. This requires two sievings of
the array per solution to (2) -- but as we shall see, the whole procedure
can be implemented very efficiently.

As a matter of fact, we actually wish to solve a slightly more general
version of (2)

$$Q(x) \equiv 0 \qquad (\bmod \ p_i^j) \tag{3}$$

since the smaller primes may occur to some power > 1 in the factorization
of $Q(x)$ over the factor base. We therefore choose a bound L and sieve for
all $p_i^j < L$ where p_i is in the factor base. We have generally taken L
to be the length of one sieving block (8×10^5 on the Cray 1S). This gives
at least one successful division per prime power per sieving interval.

For each odd prime p_i in the factor base and each exponent j such
that $p_i^j < L$ compute and save the two integers A_{ij} and B_{ij}, that are
obvious generalizations of the A_{i1} and B_{i1} defined in connection with
(2). A_{ij} is the least nonnegative residue $(\bmod \ p_i^j)$ that satisfies (3)
and $B_{ij} = -(A_{ij} + 2m)$ $(\bmod \ p_i^j)$ is its paired solution. These starting
addresses for sieving are stored along with the associated weight log p_i.
In the same way that $Q(x)$ was sieved for p_i, we sieve at $x = A_{ij} \pm hp_i^j$
and $x = B_{ij} \pm hp_i^j$ by subtracting the weight log p_i, $i > 1$. If ℓ is

the highest power of p_i that divides $Q(x)$ for some particular argument
x and $p_i^{\ell} < L$, then $\log p_i$ will be subtracted from $Q(x)$ precisely ℓ times
as it should be by this procedure.

The prime 2, of course, has every odd integer as a quadratic residue
but $x^2 \equiv n \bmod 4$ has a solution if and only if $n \equiv 1 \bmod 4$. Also for
$k > 3$, $x^2 \equiv n \bmod 2^k$ has solutions if and only if $n \equiv 1 \bmod 8$. Thus, the
indices for sieving with powers of 2 must be chosen in a somewhat dif-
ferent fashion depending on the residue class of n mod 8. Following a
suggestion of Pomerance, these sieving parameters are assigned as follows:

In all cases

$$A_{11} \equiv (1-m) \qquad (\bmod\ 2)$$
$$A_{12},\ B_{11},\ B_{12} \quad \text{undefined}$$

The other values of A_{1j}, B_{1j} must be treated as three distinct cases:

1) $n \equiv 1 \bmod 8$

   For $j = 3,4,\ldots,\ell$, $\dfrac{B}{2} < 2^{\ell} < B$, A_{1j} is chosen such that

   $$(A_{1j}-m)^2 \equiv n \qquad (\bmod\ 2^{j+1}) \quad \text{and} \quad 0 < A_{1j} < 2^j$$

   $$B_{1j} \equiv -(A_{1j} + 2m) \qquad (\bmod\ 2^j)\ .$$

   A_{11} is assigned weight 3 log 2. All other defined A_{1j}, B_{1j}
   have weight log 2.

2) $n \equiv 3 \bmod 4$

   A_{11} is assigned weight log 2. Other A_{1j}, B_{1j} are undefined.

3) $n = 5 \bmod 8$

   A_{11} is assigned weight 2 log 2. Other A_{1j}, B_{1j} are undefined.

In sieving, start from the origin (x = 0) and sieve in both positive and negative directions until approximately t of the Q(x) have factored completely over the factor base. Because of some overhead in the initializing of arrays and the pipelining capability of the Cray's, we sieve on intervals which are as large as possible, say of length k, [0,k), [-k,0), [k,2k),... : k = 765,000 on the Cray 1S and 1.5×10^6 on the Cray X-MP.

In order to be able to carry out the factorization by subtraction, we need to first fill the arrays with approximate (single precision) values of $\log|Q(x)|$, $x \in [\ell k,(\ell+1)k)$. After the first positive and negative blocks, these logarithms are taken as constant in a given sieving interval. When an array has been initialized in this way, we sieve on p_i^j by subtracting the assigned weight (usually $\log p_i$ as discussed above) from each $\log Q(x)$ in the arithmetic progression of indices

$$x = A_{ij} \pm hp_i^j \qquad \text{and} \qquad x = B_{ij} \pm hp_i^j$$

and in the sieving interval $[k\ell, k(\ell+1))$.

When the sieving procedure is completed for a given block, the contents remaining in each location are compared with $\log p_t$: where p_t is the largest prime in the factor base. Values that are smaller then $\log p_t$ indicate the residues corresponding to these locations have been factored entirely into the primes in the factor base and these addresses are stored. Occasional false alarms due to approximations are eliminated later. Notice that very little multiple precision arithmetic is needed. The sieving procedure is repeated block-by-block until the desired number of Q's have been found that factored completely over the factor base. Once this has been done, it should be possible to find a subset of the Q's among which each of the primes has occurred an even number of times in total. The

problem of finding such a subset can best be treated as a problem of finding a linear dependency among vectors over GF(2). For each address x_i at
which $Q(x_i)$ factored completely over the factor base as indicated by the
entry being less than log p_t, $Q(x_i)$ is now actually factored by dividing
out the factors in the prime base to get

$$Q(x_i) = \prod_{j=0}^{t} p_j^{\alpha_{ij}}$$

with which we associate a binary, t+1 element, vector $V_i = (v_{ij})$ where
$v_{ij} = 1$ if α_{ij} is odd and 0 otherwise. This results in a roughly $t \times t$
binary array, in which all of the essential information concerning the
factorization of each $Q(x_i)$ is stored in t+1 bits, or $2^{-6}(t+1)$ words
in the Cray. Now we need to find a subset, S, of the V_i such that
$\bigoplus_S V_i = \phi$ where $\oplus$ denotes exclusive OR and ϕ denotes the zero vector.
This is a straightforward problem in Gaussian elimination over GF(2).
We use an improved version of a code developed by Parkinson and Wunderlich
for this part of the calculation [16]. Once such a subset S is found, and
w and z are calculated from

$$w \equiv \prod_S (x+m) \pmod{n}$$

where

$$Q(x) = (x+m)^2 - n \quad \text{and} \quad Q(x) \ \varepsilon \ S \ .$$

and

$$z \equiv \prod_{j=0}^{t} \prod_S p_j^{\frac{1}{2}\Sigma\alpha_{ij}} \pmod{n}$$

if $w \not\equiv \pm z$, n can be factored by calculating the greatest common divisors

$$(w+z, n) \quad \text{and} \quad (w-z, n) \ ,$$

both of which will be proper divisors of n. It may be the case that neither is a prime and that the procedure will have to be iterated to eventually obtain the prime decomposition of n, however the factor base remains the same and the factorizations of the Q(x) have already been done, so that only the end calculation would need to be repeated with some other linear dependent subset.

For Example

Since this has been -- unavoidably -- a rather lengthy discussion, we illustrate the basic quadratic sieve factoring algorithm using a small example.

Let $n = 37 \cdot 137 = 5069$, so that $m = \left[\sqrt{5069}\right] = 71$.

This example was "cooked" so as to have many small primes in the factor base, i.e., 5069 is a quadratic residue of 5,7,11 and 13, hence the factor base for $t = 5$ consists of -1,2,5,7,11,13.

First $5069 \equiv 5 \pmod 8$, so that $2^2 | Q(0 \pm 2h)$ and no other values of $Q(x)$ are divisable by a power of 2 from the earlier discussion of A_{1j} and B_{1j}. Similarly, it is easy to show that for $p_2 = 5$, $A_{21} = 1$ and hence that $B_{21} = -(1 + 2m) \equiv -3 \equiv 2 \pmod 5$. Thus $5 | Q(1 \pm 5h)$ and $5 | Q(2 \pm 5h)$, etc. Similar results hold for $p = 7$, 11 and 13. Table II shows the

Table II

x	1	2	3	4	5	6	7	8	9
x+m	72	73	74	75	76	77	78	79	80
Q(x)	115	260	407	556	707	860	1015	1172	1331
Factors from base	5	$2^2 \cdot 5 \cdot 13$	11	2^2	7	$2^2 \cdot 5$	$5 \cdot 7$	2^2	11^3
Residual	23		37	139	101	43	29	293	

x	0	-1	-2	-3	-4	-5	-6	-7	-8
x+m	71	70	69	68	67	66	65	64	63
Q(x)	-28	-169	-308	-445	-580	-713	-844	-973	-1100
Factors from base	$-1 \cdot 2^2 \cdot 7$	$-1 \cdot 13^2$	$-1 \cdot 2^2 \cdot 7 \cdot 11$	$-1 \cdot 5$	$-1 \cdot 2^2 \cdot 5$	-1	$-1 \cdot 2^2$	$-1 \cdot 7$	$-1 \cdot 2^2 \cdot 5^2 \cdot 11$
Residual				89	29	713 (23·31)	211	139	

shows the quadratic residues $Q(x)$ for $-8 \leqslant x \leqslant 9$, six of which factor completely over the factor base. The periodic appearance of the factors on which sieving is based is easy to see. The corresponding binary matrix V is of the form.

	-1	2	5	7	11	13
V_9					1	
V_2			1			1
V_0	1			1		
V_{-1}	1					
V_{-2}	1			1	1	
V_{-8}	1				1	

Three subsets of the V_i sum (exclusive OR) to ϕ:

$$V_0 \oplus V_{-1} \oplus V_{-2} \oplus V_{-8} = \phi \qquad (a)$$

$$V_9 \oplus V_{-1} \oplus V_{-8} = \phi \qquad (b)$$

$$V_9 \oplus V_0 \oplus V_{-2} = \phi \qquad (c)$$

The relationship in (a) corresponds to having presented the quadratic residue 3625 to the oracle:

$$3625 \equiv Q(0)Q(-1)Q(-2)Q(-8) \qquad (\text{mod } 5069)$$

$$\equiv (71)^2(70)^2(69)^2(63)^2 \qquad (\text{mod } 5069) \ .$$

In this case the algorithm (oracle) returns the result that

$$z \equiv 2^3 \cdot 5 \cdot 7 \cdot 11 \cdot 13 \equiv 4557 \qquad (\text{mod } 5069)$$

while we can calculate

$$w \equiv 71 \cdot 70 \cdot 69 \cdot 63 \equiv 512 \qquad (\text{mod } 5069)$$

which tells us nothing whatsoever about the factorization of n, since $4557 \equiv -512 \pmod{5069}$.

If however we use either of the other two linear dependencies, we have: corresponding to b;

$$80 \cdot 70 \cdot 63 \not\equiv \pm 2 \cdot 5 \cdot 11^2 \cdot 13 \quad (\text{mod } 5069)$$
$$3039 \not\equiv \pm 523 \quad (\text{mod } 5069)$$

and hence

$$(3039 + 523, 5069) = 137$$
$$(3039 - 523, 5069) = 37 \quad .$$

While corresponding to c;

$$80 \cdot 71 \cdot 69 \not\equiv \pm 2^2 \cdot 7 \cdot 11^2 \quad (\text{mod } 5069)$$
$$1067 \not\equiv \pm 3388 \quad (\text{mod } 5069)$$

and hence

$$(3388 + 1607, 5069) = 37$$
$$(3388 - 1607, 5069) = 137$$

either of which leads to the factorization of n.

It is this "plain" quadratic sieve factoring algorithm that was first implemented at Sandia, with the results documented in earlier portions of this paper. In attempting to use this technique to factor numbers larger than 57 to 58 digits, it was found that as the sieving interval became large enough to find $\approx$ t residues that factored completely that the magnitudes of the quadratic residues to be factored themselves became prohibitively large. Eventually the frequency with which a quadratic residue could be completely factored over the prime base became so small that the sieving times were intolerable. For the largest numbers factored, we were examining many tens of millions of residues to find even one complete factorization.

Quadratic Sieving: Fancy

If it is the case that after all of the prime factors from the prime base have been factored out of a quadratic residue,

$$Q(x) = q \prod_{i=0}^{t} p_i^{\alpha_1} ,$$

the residual factor, q, is bounded by $p_t < q < p_t^2$, then q is necessarily a prime. Use of these "large" primes in the factorization by simply adding them to the prime base has been suggested and implemented [13], since if two quadratic residues, $Q(x_1)$ and $Q(x_2)$ can be found such that

$$Q(x_1) \equiv q \prod_{i=0}^{t} p_i^{\alpha_{1i}} \pmod{n} ,$$

and

$$Q(x_2) \equiv q \prod_{i=0}^{t} p_i^{\alpha_{2i}} \pmod{n} ,$$

then

$$Q(x_1) \cdot (x_2) q^{-2} \equiv \prod_{i=0}^{t} p_i^{\alpha_{1i} + \alpha_{2i}} \pmod{n} ,$$

i.e., a quadratic residue that can be factored over the prime base can be constructed.

Although this approach, known as the large prime variation, does improve the performance of the algorithm over the "plain" quadratic sieve, the improvement isn't great enough to asymptotically make any difference. The reason that one only gets a marginal improvement from augmenting the prime base with a large prime is that for all intents and purposes we are randomly generating the quadratic residues -- at least so for as their divisability by a particular prime is concerned. Therefore the probability that we will find another quadratic residue, $Q(x')$, -- by sequentially indexing on x -- such that

$$q \mid Q(x')$$

is $\approx 1/q$ per trial, which is a very small quantity. If instead of simply searching for a $Q(x')$ such that $q \mid Q(x')$, we could systematically generate a new sequence of Q's, such that $q \mid Q(x)$, and in which $Q(x)/q$ is small, then we could recover the same comparatively high probability that the resulting quotients would completely factor over the factor base that we had for $Q(x)$ when x, and the $Q(x)$, were small. This is the essential idea behind Davis' special q variation or "quadratic sieving; fancy."

Assume that we have found in the regular quadratic sieving an x for which

$$Q(x) = q \prod_{i=0}^{t} p_i^{\alpha_i}$$

where $p_t < q < p_t^2$.

A candidate for such an x is found when the quantity remaining in one of the indexed entries after the sieveing is completed lies between $\log p_t$ and $2 \log p_t$. If by chance some of these candidate $Q(x)$'s actually factor over the factor base because of large prime powers that were not considered in the original sieving, they are identified later and included among the complete factorizations. If q is actually prime, which is almost always the case, then note that:

$$Q(x \pm hq) = (x \pm hq + m)^2 - n = Q(x) \pm 2hq(x + m) + h^2 q^2 \quad ,$$

where each term on the right is divisible by q, and the magnitude $Q(x + hq)/q$ is essentially that of $Q(h)$, i.e., $\dfrac{Q(x \pm hq)}{q} \approx 2hm$ for $x \ll \sqrt{n}$. We can then form subsequences of residues starting at x and at $-(x + 2m) \pmod{q}$

whose magnitudes are comparable to those of $Q(x)$ at the start of the original sieve. The sieving on the subsequences is done exactly as in the plain quadratic sieve. One problem that may be encountered when using special q's is that the arguments may become larger than single precision words in the computer. We overcame this by using the pairs (x,h) to represent $x + hq$ and thus temporarily avoid multiprecision operations.

These special q's are relatively easy to find compared to finding complete factorizations. Thus in order to keep reduced residues "small", for each special q we sieve the subsequence for only a short interval: typically for a few blocks. When dealing with a single special q any complete factorization of a quadratic residue contains the factor q, which can be eliminated before going to the Gaussian reduction by combining pairs of factorizations to get quadratic residues in which q occurs an even number of times.

The sieving property is not dependent on the primality of the divisor, q, so why require the special q's to be prime? This is to prevent "collisions" between special q subsequences; that is, to prevent the same factorization being generated by two subsequences. If $q_1|Q(x)$ and $q_2|Q(x)$ and $p_t^2 > q_1 > q_2 > p_t$, then we would have $q_1 \cdot q_2|Q(x)$. But then $Q(x)$ could not have passed the factorization criterion in the first place.

The special q modification introduced a few complications to the computation such as multiprecision arguments, and required writing a new computer code, but the increased capability was dramatic. The bottom line is that the special q variation enabled factorization of 63-64 digit integers in times comparable to those required by the original sieve to factor 55-56 digits. Furthermore, the relatively constant success rate for complete factorizations within the subsequences enables an accurate

early estimation to be made of how much computing time will be required
for a given factorization.

Examining the residuals in Table II we see that 23, 29 and 31 are
all candidate special q's. We let q = 23 be the special q in the example
used earlier. Table III shows the resulting quadratic residues S_x based

Table III

Sieve on special q = 23

$$Q'(x) = Q(x_0 + xq) = (x_0 + xq + m)^2 - n$$

	S_x $x_0 = 1$					T_x $x_0 \equiv -(1-2m) \equiv -5 \pmod{23}$				
x	-2	-1	0	1	2	-2	-1	0	1	2
$x_0 + xq + m$	26	49	72	95	118	20	43	66	89	112
$Q'(x)/q$	-191	-116	5	172	385	-203	-140	-31	124	325
Factors from base	-1	$-1 \cdot 2^2$	5	2^2	$5 \cdot 7 \cdot 11$	$-1 \cdot 7$	$-1 \cdot 2^2 \cdot 5 \cdot 7$	-1	2^2	$5^2 \cdot 13$
Residual	191	29		43		29		31	31	

on $x_0 = 1$ and T_x based on the paired $x_0 \equiv -(1-2m) \equiv -5 \pmod{23}$ for
$|x| < 2$. Four residues factor completely over the prime base -- extended
by 23.

	-1	2	5	7	11	13	23
S_2			1	1	1		1
S_0			1				1
T_{-1}	1		1	1			1
T_2						1	1

Eliminating 23 by multiplying each row by the first we get;

	-1	2	5	7	11	13
S_2S_0				1	1	
S_2T_{-1}	1				1	
S_2T_2			1	1	1	1

Referring to Table II, we see that

$$V_0 \oplus V_{-8} \oplus S_2S_0 = \phi \qquad \text{(a)}$$

$$V_{-1} \oplus V_{-2} \oplus S_2S_0 = \phi \qquad \text{(b)}$$

$$V_{-1} \oplus V_0 \oplus V_9 \oplus S_2S_0 = \phi \quad . \qquad \text{(c)}$$

From (a) we find

$$w = 71 \cdot 63 \cdot 118 \cdot 72 \equiv 315 \qquad (\text{mod } 5069)$$

and

$$z = 2^2 \cdot 5^2 \cdot 7 \cdot 11 \equiv 4754 \qquad (\text{mod } 5069) \quad .$$

where

$$w \equiv -z \qquad (\text{mod } 5069) \quad .$$

Similarly from (b) we find

$$w = 70 \cdot 69 \cdot 118 \cdot 72 \equiv 2125 \qquad (\text{mod } 5069)$$

and

$$z = 2 \cdot 5 \cdot 7 \cdot 11 \cdot 13 \cdot 23 \equiv 2125 \qquad (\text{mod } 5069)$$

neither of which tells us anything about the factorization of n. On the other hand, from (c)

$$w = 70 \cdot 71 \cdot 80 \cdot 118 \cdot 72 \equiv 2655 \qquad (\text{mod } 5069)$$

and

$$z = 2 \cdot 5 \cdot 7 \cdot 11^2 \cdot 13 \cdot 23 \equiv 3099 \qquad (\text{mod } 5069)$$

where $w \not\equiv \pm z$. Hence

$$(3099 + 2655, 5069) = 137$$

and

$$(3099 - 2655, 5069) = 37 \quad .$$

One cannot expect such a small example to illustrate the advantages
of using special q's -- although the range of the parameters is slightly
smaller in the example with the special q than without.

References

1.   R. Rivest, A. Shamir and L. Adleman, "A Method for Obtaining Digital Sig
     tures and Public-key Cryptosystems," Commun. ACM 21, 2 (Feb. 1978), 120-

2.   H. Ong and C. P. Schnorr, "Signatures through Approximate Representa-
     tions by Quadratic Forms," Proceedings of Crypto 83, Santa Barbara, CA,
     August 21-24, 1983, to be published by Plenum Press.

3.   H. Ong, C. P. Schnorr and A. Shamir, "An Efficient Signature Scheme
     Based on Quadratic Equations," to appear Proceedings of 16th Symposium
     on Theory of Computing, Washington D.C., April 1984.

4.   C. P. Schnorr, "A Cubic OSS-Signature Scheme," private communication,
     May 1984.

5.   S. Even, O. Goldreich and A. Lempel, "A Randomized Protocol for Signing
     Contracts," in Advances in Cryptology, Proceedings of Crypto 82, Ed. by
     David Chaum, Ronald L. Rivest and Alan T. Sherman, Plenum Press, New
     York (1983).

6.   G. J. Simmons, "The Prisoners' Problem and the Subliminal Channel,"
     Proceedings of Crypto 83, Santa Barbara, CA, August 21-24, 1983, to
     be published by Plenum Press.

215

7.   P. D. Merillat, "Secure Stand-Alone Positive Personnel Identity Verifi-
      cation System (SSA-PPIV)," Sandia National Laboratories Tech. Rpt.
      SAND79-0070 (March 1979).

8.   G. J. Simmons, "A System for Verifying User Identity and Authorization
      at the Point-of-Sale or Access," Cryptologia, Vol. 8, No. 1 (January,
      1984), pp. 1-21.

9.   G. J. Simmons, "Verification of Treaty Compliance -- Revisited,"
      Proceedings of the 1982 Symposium on Security and Privacy, Oakland,
      CA (April 25-27, 1983), pp. 61-66.

10.   J. A. Davis and D. B. Holdridge, "Factorization Using the Quadratic Sieve
      Algorithm," Sandia National Laboratories Tech. Rpt. SAND83-1346 (Dec. 1983).

11.   J. Brillhart, D. H. Lehmer, J. L. Selfridge, B. Tuckerman and S. S.
      Wagstaff, Jr., Factorizations of $b^n \pm 1$ b = 2, 3, 5, 6, 7, 10, 11, 12
      up to High Powers," AMS Contemporary Mathematics, Vol. 22 (1983).

12.   M. A. Morrison, J. Brillhart, "A Method of Factoring and the Factor-
      ization of F_7," Math. Comp. 29 (1975), 183-205.

13.   C. Pomerance, "Analysis and Comparison of Some Integer Factoring
      Algorithms," in Number Theory and Computers, Ed. by H. W. Lenstra, Jr.,
      and R. Tijdeman, Math. Centrum Tracts, No. 154, Part I, Amsterdam
      (1982), pp. 89-139.

14.   R. H. Mendez, "The Japanese Supercomputer Challenge," SIAM News, Vol. 17,
      No. 1 (January 1984), pp. 1 and 5.

15.   R. H. Mendez, "Benchmarks on Japanese and American Supercomputers --
      Preliminary Results," IEEE Trans. Comp, Vol. C-33, No. 4 (April 1984).
      pp. 374-375.

16.   D. Parkinson, M. C. Wunderlich, "A Memory Efficient Algorithm for
      Gaussian Elimination over GF(2) on Parallel Computers," private com-
      munication (Feb. 1983).

Strong Primes are Easy to Find

John Gordon, Cybermation Ltd

Summary

A simple method is given for finding *strong*, random, large
primes of a given number of bits, for use in conjunction with the
RSA Public Key Cryptosystem. A *strong* prime p is a prime
satisfying:

* p = 1 mod r

* p = s-1 mod s

* r = 1 mod t,

where r,s and t are all large, random primes of a given number of
bits. It is shown that the problem of finding *strong*, random,
large primes is only 19% harder than finding random, large
primes.

Introduction

The most promising public key cryptosystem (PKC) since the idea
was first published [1] is almost certainly the RSA scheme [2].

A brief description of the RSA scheme will now be given, but the
interested reader should consult [2] for more details. In what
follows, the terms *number*, and *integer* are both to be
taken as indicating either a positive integer or zero.

In implementing this scheme a person (say Bob) makes for himself
a set of three large numbers: m, E and D, (respectively the
modulus, *Public key* and *Secret key*) with the properties:

if $y = x^E$ mod m   then $x = y^D$ mod m

for all numbers x in the range (0, m-1).

The numbers E and m are published, and someone else (say Alice)
wishing to send a secret message x (regarded for the purpose of
encryption as a large integer) to Bob, calculates y from x and
sends to Bob the *cryptogram* y. Since Bob knows D he can
recover the message. Anyone else wishing to eavesdrop must find D,
or else discover x some other way. Both of these recourses appear
to be *computationally infeasible* for suitable choices of
parameters.

Bob makes m, E and D as follows. He chooses two very large primes
p and q at random with p and q of roughly equal size (of say 256

bits each). This choice of p and q is the subject of this paper.
He chooses E at random, relatively prime to (p-1)(q-1) and then
finds D from the relationship:

$$ED = 1 \bmod (p-1)(q-1)$$

which he can do easily and quickly using *Euclid's algorithm*
[3], [4]. Finally he forms m using:

$$m = pq.$$

A potential eavesdropper must it seems first find D, which appears
to require the determination of p and q, which in turn seems to
imply that he must be able to factorise m. To factorise a product
m=pq where p and q are very large primes of say 256 bits each is
one of the hardest known common problems [2], [3].

The advanced techniques a cryptanalyst might use to factor m [3]
break down when p (and similarly q) is not only prime but also has
the properties that p-1 has a large prime factor say r, and p+1
has a large prime factor say s. To make the problem really hard
r-1 should have a large prime factor as well. For logistical
reasons it is also necessary to be able to choose p in some sense
at random but with a given number of bits.

There is thus a considerable interest in the problem of finding
primes with these desirable properties. However there does not
appear to be any published way of finding primes with all these
properties, and in this paper we show how to satisfy all the
requirements. In particular it is shown that the extra conditions
imposed upon p add only 19% to the cost of the task of finding p.

The Technique

We seek therefore a computationally economical construction for a
large, randomly seedable integer p of given number of bits and
with the following properties:

* p is prime.

* p-1 has a large, prime factor, say r.

* p+1 has a large, prime factor, say s.

* r-1 has a large, prime factor, say t.

Numbers sastisfying these criteria will be known as *Strong
Primes*. We now show, explicitly how to contruct strong primes.
We begin with the following observations.

If p-1 has a large, prime factor r, then p = Kr + 1 for some K. If
K is odd (and assuming that r is greater than 2 and hence an odd
prime), then p will be even (since a product of odd numbers is
odd), which is ridiculous since p is greater than r. Therefore K
must be even. Since p, r s and t are all assumed to be large we

are only interested in *odd* primes p whose properties are in effect:

    (1) p = 2jr + 1   (or p = 1 mod 2r)

    (2) p = 2ks − 1   (or p = s−1 mod 2s)

    (3) r = 2Lt + 1   (or r = 1 mod 2t)

for some j, k, L where r,s and t are primes.

Our order of events will be:

* choose random seeds a and *b*

* from a and *b* generate random primes s and t

* from t construct r

* from r and s construct p.

It will be assumed that choosing random seeds with any required number of bits does not present any special problems and this aspect will not be addressed further.

Find s and r

Finding s (and t) which are just random primes greater than a given seed and of specified number of bits is relatively straightforward. Starting from random seed a, we will find the first prime s (or t) greater than a. We now estimate the computational effort and the time to complete tasks of this type.

We know from the *Prime Number Theorem* [4], that x/Ln(x) is a very good estimate of the number of primes less than x. Hence the density of primes in the neighbourhood of x is given by:

$$d/dx \ (x/Ln(x)) = (1/Ln(x)-1/Ln(x)^2)$$

which is close to 1/Ln(x) for large x. The mean separation between primes of magnitude x is therefore about Ln(x). If we search through only *odd* numbers for the next prime greater than s we will need to examine on average no more than Ln(x)/2 numbers. If $x=2^n$ this amounts to 0.35n integers. We are thus unlikely to need to examine say n integers before finding a prime.

Eliminating multiples of 3 reduces the search by a further factor of two-thirds and so on. Continuing in this way we find that eliminating multiples of the first 54 primes, (2,3,5,...,251), leaves only 10.035% of all integers for serious further examination. The reason for being interested in the first 54 primes resides in the fact that these are precisely those primes which can be represented in one 8-bit byte or less. They can be stored in single bytes and permit extremely rapid elimination using a division algorithm which efficiently exploits a 1-byte divisor. This algorithm need not form a quotient. The typical search will then pay serious attention to only $0.10035Ln(x)$ integers. If x is a n-bit number this amounts to less than $0.07n$ integers.

Our technique is to test these remaining, uneliminated integers using an efficient, statistical technique, for example *Algorithm-P* in [3]. Each such test consists of v passes through a procedure whose complexity is dominated by the need to perform a modular exponentiation $u^q(mod.x)$ where v is about 5, and q and x are n-bit quantities.

In point of fact, non-primes are almost invariably eliminated on the *first* pass and so $v=5$ only for the number finally chosen. If most numbers are eliminated then $v=1$ is a more realistic estimate.

Modular exponentiation on a normal computer where multiprecision arithmetic must be used requires triple-nested loops at the bit or word level and the time to perform such an exponentiation is of order $O(n^3)$. Experiments on small computers using very efficient assembly language programming indicate that the time to exponentiate for large n is about

$$T_{exp}(n) = cTn^3/w$$

where c is a constant of size about 8, T is the time for one instruction and w is the word size. (On a special-purpose n-bit machine the time would be of the order $O(n^2)$). The time therefore needed to find s (or t) (ignoring the time for quick eliminations) is about $0.07n$ times $cvTn^3/w$ i.e. about:

$$T_{prime}(n) = 0.07cvTn^4/w.$$

When we have found s (or t), it is unlikely to have more bits than the seed a. We can virtually ensure this by picking our value of a in the range $(2^{n-1}, 2^{n-1}+2^{n-2}-1)$. This ensures that a starts with the two digits 10 which leaves a run of 2^{n-2} integers in which to find a prime before increasing the number of bits.

Find r

We now seek a prime r of the form $2Lt+1$. Our technique is to search through $(2Lt+1)$-space for successive values of L. Since we will only be examining odd numbers, primes will appear to be twice as dense as among all numbers, but conversely twice as many will have non-trivial divisors. Thus the time to find r will again be be $T_{prime}(n)$ where n in the number of bits in r.

Controlling the size of r

We are likely to use about $n Ln(2)/2 = 0.35n$ successive values of L
before finding r. Every time L doubles another bit is added to
$2Lt+1$. If this process is not to leave great uncertainties in the
final number of bits in r we should start with a value L_o of
of about n, so that L will increase on average by a factor of 1.35
which is less than 2. The final size of r will be very close to
$Log_2(2L_o) + n$ bits. We can increase the certainty of
this by increasing L_o.

A more sophisticated approach is to arrange for 2t to be say
$Log_2(n)$ bits shorter than the desired length of r, then
starting with unity, add in successive multiples or 2t until the
desired length of r is reached, and then begin checking for
primality at each subsequent addition of 2t.

Find p

We now come to the final part of the technique namely, given
primes r and s, find a prime p, close in size to a given number of
bits, and satisfying:

$$p = 2jr+1 = 2ks-1, \text{ for some j and k}$$

or

$$p = 1 \bmod 2r = 2s-1 \bmod 2s. \tag{1}$$

The key to solving the problem of finding primes with these
properties is contained in the following theorem.

Theorem 1:

If r and s are odd primes, then p satisfies:

$$p = (1 \bmod 2r) = (s-1 \bmod 2s)$$

if and only if p is of the form:

$$p = p_o + 2krs \tag{2}$$

where

$$p_o = u(r,s) \qquad \qquad :u(r,s) \text{ odd}$$

$$= u(r,s) + rs \qquad :u(r,s) \text{ even}$$

$$\text{and } u(r,s) = (s^{r-1} - r^{s-1}) \bmod rs. \tag{3}$$

Proof:

Integers, prime or otherwise, satisfying {1} clearly also satisfy the weaker condition:

$$p = jr + 1 = ks - 1 \qquad \text{for some } j,k. \qquad \{4\}$$

Numbers satisfying {4} are alternately odd and even. Integers satisfying {1} are just the odd valued numbers satisfying {4}. The remainder of the proof consists in showing that numbers satisfying {4} are of the form $u(r,s) + krs$. Solving {4} is just a special case of an application of the *Chinese Remainder Theorem* [4].

Consider the number $u(r,s)$ of the form {3} above.

Now by *Fermat's Theorem* [4], namely:

if q is prime and $0 <= x < q$, then

$$x^{q-1} = 1 \bmod q \qquad = kq + 1, \qquad \text{for some k,}$$

it is clear that $s^{r-1} = 1 \bmod r$, and similarly $r^{s-1} = 1 \bmod s$.

Also of course $s^{r-1} = 0 \bmod s$, and $r^{s-1} = 0 \bmod r$.

Finally $rs = (0 \bmod r) = (0 \bmod s)$.

Thus $u(r,s)$ satisfies {4}.

We now show that numbers not of the form $u(r,s) + ksr$ cannot satisfy {4}.

Let u and u' satisfy {4} and consider the difference:

$$u - u' \;=\; (1 \bmod r) = (1 \bmod r) = 0 \bmod r \qquad = kr$$

$$= (s-1 \bmod s) - (s-1 \bmod s) = 0 \bmod s = k's$$

for some k and k'. Thus $u-u'$ is a multiple of $LCM(r,s)$ which is rs since r and s are prime. Since $u(r,s)$ satisfies {4}, u and u' must be of the form $u(r,s) + ksr$. QED.

Finding $u(r,s)$ and hence p_0 requires two exponentiations at a cost of $2T_{exp}$. Finding p amounts to finding a prime in (p_0+2krs)-space and the same considerations apply here as did to the search for r in $(2Lt+1)$-space, namely that we should start with p_0 and add in successive multiples of $2rs$ until the desired size is reached, then check for primality at each subsequent addition.

Size of p,r,s and t

The size of p is a few bits larger than the size of 2rs. The
difference is entirely due to the need to excercise some control
in the size of p. Thus we should start with 2rs of a suitable
size, say $Log_2(n)$ bits less than n, the desired number of
bits in p. This in turn tells us the size for r and s. Presumably
it is desirable for r and s to be of about equal size which will
be a few bits less than half the size of p. There is no problem
with s, and the method of finding r of suitable size has already
been dealt with earlier.

Time to Find p

The time spent searching for primes dominates. We need to mount
searches for p, of n bits, and for t, r and s, each roughly of n/2
bits. Altogether, ignoring all times except those spent searching
for primes, the time to find p should average

$$T_{prime}(n) + 3T_{prime}(n/2)$$

$$= 1^3/_{16}T_{prime}(n)$$

$$= 1.19 \times 0.07cvTn^4/w.$$

This represents an increase of only 3/16 (=19%) over the time to
find a random prime of given size n bits.

Example

Using the technique described here, *strong* primes of about 256
bits such as:

$$p=7,918,324,333,004,779,287,780,879,909,121,159,911,537,$$
$$551,977,796,076,554,305,607,309,994,905,870,203$$

where t=   83,106,713,586,449,986,154,292,642,419,182,973
       r= 7,645,817,649,953,398,726,194,923,102,564,833,517
and s=10,638,156,841,358,536,678,090,874,848,207,317,901

can be generated in about 20 minutes on a small microcomputer with
1MHz clock (Apple-II) using an extremely efficient modular
arithmetic package (CyMAS).

Acknowledgements

I am indebted to Donald Davies of the National Physical
Laboratories, England for his encouragement in this matter and for
one or two observations incorporated above. I am also indebted to
British Telecom for suggesting and sponsoring the problem.

223

References

[1] W Diffie and M.E. Hellman, *"New Directions in Cryptography"*, IEEE Trans. Inform. Theory, vol. IT-22, No.6, 1976, 644-54.

[2] R.L. Rivest, A. Shamir and L. Adleman, *"A Method for obtaining Digital Signatures and Public Key Cryptosystems"*, Comms ACM, 21,2, 121-126, 1978.

[3] D.E. Knuth, *"The Art of Computer Programming Volume 2; Seminumerical Algorithms"*, 2nd Ed., Addison-Wesley, 1982.

[4] D.M. Burton, *"Elementary number theory"*, Allyn and Bacon, 1980

J Gordon
Cybermation Ltd
High St
Wheathampstead, Herts
England

Discrete logarithms in finite fields and their cryptographic significance

A. M. Odlyzko

AT&T Bell Laboratories
Murray Hill, New Jersey 07974

ABSTRACT

Given a primitive element g of a finite field $GF(q)$, the discrete logarithm of a nonzero element $u \in GF(q)$ is that integer k, $1 \leqslant k \leqslant q-1$, for which $u = g^k$. The well-known problem of computing discrete logarithms in finite fields has acquired additional importance in recent years due to its applicability in cryptography. Several cryptographic systems would become insecure if an efficient discrete logarithm algorithm were discovered. This paper surveys and analyzes known algorithms in this area, with special attention devoted to algorithms for the fields $GF(2^n)$. It appears that in order to be safe from attacks using these algorithms, the value of n for which $GF(2^n)$ is used in a cryptosystem has to be very large and carefully chosen. Due in large part to recent discoveries, discrete logarithms in fields $GF(2^n)$ are much easier to compute than in fields $GF(p)$ with p prime. Hence the fields $GF(2^n)$ ought to be avoided in all cryptographic applications. On the other hand, the fields $GF(p)$ with p prime appear to offer relatively high levels of security.

Discrete logarithms in finite fields and their cryptographic significance

A. M. Odlyzko

AT&T Bell Laboratories
Murray Hill, New Jersey 07974

1. Introduction

The multiplicative subgroup of any finite field $GF(q)$, q a prime power, is cyclic, and the elements $g \in GF(q)$ that generate this subgroup are referred to as *primitive elements*. Given a primitive element $g \in GF(q)$ and any $u \in GF(q)^* = GF(q)-\{0\}$, the *discrete logarithm* of u with respect to g is that integer k, $0 \leqslant k \leqslant q-1$, for which

$$u = g^k .$$

We will write $k = \log_g u$. The discrete logarithm of u is sometimes referred to as the index of u.

Aside from the intrinsic interest that the problem of computing discrete logarithms has, it is of considerable importance in cryptography. An efficient algorithm for discrete logarithms would make several authentication and key-exchange systems insecure. This paper briefly surveys (in Section 2) these cryptosystems, and then analyzes the known algorithms for computing discrete logarithms. As it turns out, some of them, including the most powerful general purpose algorithm in this area, have not been analyzed in complete detail before. Moreover, some of the analyses in the literature deal only with fields $GF(p)$, where p is a prime. In cryptographic applications, on the other hand, attention has been focused on the fields $GF(2^n)$, since arithmetic in them is much easier to implement, with respect to both software and hardware. Therefore we concentrate on the fields $GF(2^n)$.

Several proposed algorithms for computing discrete logarithms are known. We briefly discuss most of them (including some unsuccessful ones) in Section 3. In Section 4 we present the most powerful general purpose algorithm that is known today, called the index-calculus algorithm, and analyze its asymptotic performance. Recently a dramatic improvement in its performance in fields $GF(2^n)$ was made by Coppersmith [18,19], and we discuss it in detail. In Section 5 we discuss several technical issues that are important to the performance of the index-calculus algorithm, such as rapid methods to solve the systems of linear equations that arise in it. In that section we also present several suggested modifications to the Coppersmith algorithm which appear to be unimportant asymptotically, but are of substantial importance in practice. We discuss them in order to obtain a reasonable estimate of how fast this algorithm could be made to run in practice. In Section 6 we estimate the running time of that algorithm for fields $GF(2^n)$ that might actually be used in cryptography. In Section 7 we briefly discuss the performance of the index-calculus algorithms in fields $GF(p)$ for p a prime. Finally, we discuss the implications of these algorithms for cryptography in Section 8. It turns out, for example, that the MITRE scheme [38,59] and the Hewlett-Packard chip [69], both of which use the field $GF(2^{127})$, are very insecure. Depending on the level of security that is desired, it seems that fields $GF(2^n)$ to be used ought to have n large, no smaller than 800 and preferably at least 1500. Furthermore, these values of n have to be very carefully chosen. On the other hand, it appears at this moment that the fields $GF(p)$, where p is a prime, offer a much higher level of security, with $p \geq 2^{500}$ adequate for many applications and $p \geq 2^{1000}$ being sufficient even for extreme situations. The fields $GF(p)$ appear at this moment to offer security comparable to that of the RSA scheme with modulus of size p.

It has to be stressed that this survey presents the current state of the art of computing discrete logarithms. Since the state of the art has been advancing very rapidly recently, this paper has already gone through several revisions. The most important of the new developments has certainly been the Coppersmith breakthrough in fields $GF(2^n)$. Even more recently, there has been much less spectacular but still important progress in fields $GF(p)$, which is briefly described in Section 7, and in methods for dealing with sparse systems of equations, which are discussed in Section 5, and which are crucial for the index-calculus algorithms. It is quite likely that further progress will take place in discrete logarithm algorithms and so the cryptographic schemes described below will require the use of even larger fields than are being recommended right now.

2. Cryptographic systems related to discrete logarithms

One of the first published cryptosystems whose security depends on discrete logarithms being difficult to compute appears to be an authentication scheme. In many computer systems, users' passwords are stored in a special file, which has the disadvantage that anyone who gets access to that file is able to freely impersonate any legitimate user. Therefore that file has to be specially protected by the operating system. It has been known for a long time (cf. [54]) that one can eliminate the need for any secrecy by eliminating the storage of passwords themselves. Instead, one utilizes a function f that is hard to invert (i.e., such that given a y in the range of f, it is hard to find an x in the domain of f such that $f(x) = y$) and creates a file containing pairs $(i, f(p_i))$, where i denotes a user's login name and p_i the password of that user. This file can then be made public. The security of this scheme clearly depends on the function f being hard to invert. One early candidate for such a function was discrete exponentiation; a field $GF(q)$ and a primitive element $g \in GF(q)$ are chosen (and made public), and for x an integer, one defines

$$f(x) = g^x .$$

Anyone trying to get access to a computer while pretending to be user i would have to find p_i knowing only the value of g^{p_i}; i.e., he would have to solve the discrete logarithm problem in the field $GF(q)$.

Public key cryptography suffers from the defect that the systems that seem safe are rather slow. This disadvantage can be overcome to a large extent by using a public key cryptosystem only to distribute keys for a classical cryptosystem, which can then be used to transmit data at high speeds. Diffie and Hellman [23] have invented a key-exchange system based on exponentiation in finite fields. (This apparently was the very first public key cryptosystem that was proposed.) In it, a finite field $GF(q)$ and a primitive element $g \in GF(q)$ are chosen and made public. Users A and B, who wish to communicate using some standard encryption method, such as DES, but who do not have a common key for that system, choose random integers a and b, respectively, with $2 \leqslant a, b \leqslant q-2$. Then user A transmits g^a to B over a public channel, while user B transmits g^b to A. The common key is then taken to be g^{ab}, which A can compute by raising the received g^b to the a power (which only he knows), and which B forms by raising g^a to the b power. It is clear that an efficient discrete logarithm algorithm would make this scheme insecure, since the publicly transmitted g^a would enable the cryptanalyst to determine a, and he could then determine the key used by A and B. Diffie and Hellman [23] have even conjectured that breaking their scheme is equivalent in difficulty to computing discrete logarithms. This conjecture remains unproved, and so we cannot exclude the possibility that there might be some way to generate g^{ab} from knowledge of g^a and g^b only, without computing either a or b, although it seems unlikely that such a method exists.

The Diffie-Hellman key-exchange scheme seems very attractive, and it has actually been implemented in several systems, such as a MITRE Corp. system [38,59]. Moreover, Hewlett-Packard has built a special purpose VLSI chip which implements this scheme [69]. However, these implementations have turned out to be easily breakable. It appears possible, though, to build a Diffie - Hellman scheme that is about as secure as an RSA scheme of comparable key size. This will be discussed at some length in Section 8.

Systems that use exponentiation in finite fields to transmit information have also been proposed. One is based on an idea due to Shamir [37; pp. 345-346] and has been advocated in the context of discrete exponentiation by Massey and Omura [63]. For example, suppose user A wishes to send a message m (which we may regard as a nonzero element of the publicly known field $GF(q)$) to user B. Then A chooses a random integer c, $1 \leqslant c \leqslant q-1$, $(c,q-1) = 1$, and transmits $x = m^c$ to B. User B then chooses a random integer d, $1 \leqslant d \leqslant q-1$, $(d,q-1) = 1$, and transmits $y = x^d = m^{cd}$ to A. User A now forms $z = y^{c'}$ where $cc' \equiv 1 \pmod{q-1}$, and transmits z to B. Since

$$z = y^{c'} = m^{cdc'} = m^d ,$$

B only has to compute $z^{d'}$ to recover m, where $dd' \equiv 1 \pmod{q-1}$, since

$$z^{d'} = m^{dd'} = m .$$

In this scheme it is again clear that an efficient method for computing discrete logarithms over

$GF(q)$ would enable a cryptanalyst to recover the plaintext message m from the transmitted ciphertext messages m^c, m^{cd}, and m^d.

Another scheme for transmission of information has been proposed by T. ElGamal [26] and is in essence a variant of the Diffie-Hellman key distribution scheme. User A publishes a public key $g^a \in GF(q)$, where the field $GF(q)$ and a primitive root g are known (either they are also published by A or else they are used by everyone in a given system), but keeps a secret. User B, who wishes to send $m \in GF(q)$ to A, selects k at random, $1 \leqslant k \leqslant q-2$ (a different k has to be chosen for each m) and transmits the pair (g^k, mg^{ak}) to A. User A knows a and therefore can compute $g^{ak} = (g^k)^a$ and recover m. An efficient discrete logarithm algorithm would enable a cryptanalyst to compute either a or k, and would therefore make this scheme insecure also.

T. ElGamal [26] has also proposed a novel signature scheme that uses exponentiation in fields $GF(p)$, p a prime. User A, who wishes to sign messages electronically, publishes a prime p, a primitive root g modulo p, and an integer y, $1 \leqslant y \leqslant p-1$, which is generated by choosing a random integer a, which is kept secret, and setting $y = g^a$. (The prime p and the primitive root g can be the same for all the users of the system, in which case only y is special to user A.) To sign a message m, $1 \leqslant m \leqslant p-1$, user A provides a pair of integers (r,s), $1 \leqslant r,s \leqslant p-1$, such that

$$g^m \equiv y^r \, r^s \pmod{p}. \tag{2.1}$$

To generate r and s, user A chooses a random integer k with $(k, p-1) = 1$ and computes

$$r = g^k.$$

Since $y = g^a$, this means that s has to satisfy

$$g^m \equiv g^{ar + ks} \pmod{p}, \tag{2.2}$$

which is equivalent to

$$m \equiv ar + ks \pmod{p-1}. \tag{2.3}$$

Since $(k, p-1) = 1$, there is a unique solution to (2.3) modulo $p-1$, and this solution is easy to find for user A, who knows a, r, and k. An efficient discrete logarithm algorithm would make this scheme insecure, since it would enable the cryptanalyst to compute a from y. No way has been found for breaking this scheme without the ability to compute discrete logarithms, and so the scheme appears quite attractive. It is not as fast as the Ong-Schnorr-Shamir signature scheme [50], but since several versions of that scheme were recently broken by Pollard, it should not be considered for use at the present time. The ElGamal scheme appears to be about as secure as the RSA scheme for moduli of the same length, as we will see later, although it does expand bandwidth, with the signature being twice as long as the message.

The presumed intractability of the discrete logarithm problem is crucial also for the Blum-Micali construction [9] of a cryptographically strong random number generator. What they show is that it is possible to compute a long sequence that is obtained deterministically from a short random sequence, and in which successive bits cannot be predicted efficiently from the preceding ones without the ability to compute discrete logarithms efficiently.

A scheme whose security is essentially equivalent to that of the Diffie - Hellman scheme was recently published by Odoni, Varadharajan, and Sanders [49]. These authors proposed taking a matrix B over $GF(p)$ which is the companion matrix of an irreducible polynomial $f(x)$ of degree m over $GF(p)$. The Diffie - Hellman scheme would then be implemented by replacing the primitive element g by the matrix B, so that pairs of users would transmit matrices B^a and B^b to each other, where a and b are the two random integers chosen by the two users. However, the matrix ring generated by B is isomorphic to the field $GF(p^m)$, so this scheme does not provide any additional security. The more sophisticated scheme proposed in [49], with the matrix B being obtained from several companion matrices of irreducible polynomials of degrees $m_1, \ldots, m_s$ can also be shown to be reducible to the problem of computing discrete logarithms in the fields $GF(p^{m_i})$ separately.

Finally, we mention that the ability to compute quantities generalizing discrete logarithms in rings of integers modulo composite integers would lead to efficient integer factorization algorithms [5,40,45,52].

3. Some special algorithms

In this section we discuss briefly some algorithms that apparently don't work very well and then we discuss a very useful algorithm that works well only when all the prime divisors of $q-1$ are of moderate size.

The first method we discuss was not designed as an algorithm at all. In a field $GF(p)$, p a prime, any function from the field to itself can be represented as a polynomial. Wells [64] has shown that for any u, $1 \leqslant u \leqslant p-1$, if g is a primitive root modulo p, then one can write

$$\log_g u \equiv \sum_{j=1}^{p-2} (1-g^j)^{-1} u^j \pmod{p}. \tag{3.1}$$

This formula is clearly useless computationally, but it is interesting that such an explicit form for the discrete logarithm function exists.

The Herlestam-Johannesson method [32] was designed to work over the fields $GF(2^n)$, and was reported by those authors to work efficiently for fields as large as $GF(2^{31})$. However, the heuristics used by those authors in arguing that the method ought to work efficiently in larger fields as well seem to be very questionable. As usual, $GF(2^n)$ is represented as polynomials over $GF(2)$ modulo some fixed irreducible polynomial $f(x)$ of degree n over $GF(2)$. In order to compute the logarithm of $h(x)$ to base x, Herlestam and Johannesson proposed to apply a combination of the transformations

$$h(x) \rightarrow h(x)^{2^r},$$
$$h(x) \rightarrow x^{-2^r} h(x)$$

so as to minimize the Hamming weight of the resulting polynomial, and apply this procedure iteratively until an element of low weight, for which the logarithm was known, was reached. There is no reason to expect such a strategy to work, and considerable numerical evidence has been collected which shows that this method is not efficient [13,67], and is not much better than a random walk through the field. However, some unusual phenomena related to the algorithm have been found whose significance is not yet understood [13,57]. In particular, the algorithm does not always behave like a random walk, and its performance appears to depend on the choice of the polynomial defining the field. These observations may be due to the small size of the fields that were investigated, in which case their significance would be slight.

Another approach to computing discrete logarithms in fields $GF(2^n)$ was taken by Arazi [3]. He noted that if one can determine the parity of the discrete logarithm of u, then one can quickly determine the discrete logarithm itself. Arazi showed that one can determine the parity of discrete logarithms to base g fast if g satisfies some rather complicated conditions. Since being able to compute discrete logarithms to one base enables one to compute them to any other base about equally fast (as will be discussed in Section 5), it would suffice to find any g that satisfies Arazi's condition. However, so far no algorithm has been found for finding such primitive elements g in large fields $GF(2^n)$, nor even a proof that any such elements exist. It was shown by this author that primitive elements g satisfying another set of conditions originally proposed by Arazi, which were more stringent than those of [3], do exist in fields $GF(2^n)$ for $2 \leqslant n \leqslant 5$, but not for $6 \leqslant n \leqslant 9$. Thus while the ideas of [3] are interesting and may be useful in future work, they appear to be of little practical utility at this moment.

We next discuss a very important algorithm that was published by Pohlig and Hellman [51], and whose earlier independent discovery they credit to Roland Silver. This algorithm computes discrete logarithms over $GF(q)$ using on the order of $\sqrt{p}$ operations and a comparable amount of storage, where p is the largest prime factor of $q-1$. In fact, there is a time-memory tradeoff that can be exploited, and Pohlig and Hellman [51] showed that if

$$q-1 = \prod_{i=1}^{k} p_i^{n_i},\tag{3.2}$$

where the p_i are distinct primes, and if $r_1,...,r_k$ are any real numbers with $0 \leqslant r_i \leqslant 1$, then logarithms over $GF(q)$ can be computed in

$$O(\sum_{i=1}^{k} n_i(\log q + p_i^{1-r_i}(1+\log p_i^{r_i})))$$

field operations, using

$$O\left(\log q \sum_{i=1}^{k} (1+p_i^{r_i'})\right)$$

bits of memory, provided that a precomputation requiring

$$O\left(\sum_{i=1}^{k} (p_i^{r_i'}\log p_i^{r_i'}+\log q)\right)$$

field operations is carried out first.

We now present a sketch of the above algorithm. Suppose that g is some primitive element of $GF(q)$, $x \in GF(q)-\{0\}$, and we wish to find an integer a, $1 \leqslant a \leqslant q-1$, such that

$$x = g^a . \tag{3.3}$$

Because of the Chinese Remainder Theorem, we only need to determine a modulo each of the $p_i^{n_i}$. Suppose that $p = p_i$ and $n = n_i$ for some i. Let

$$a \equiv \sum_{j=0}^{n-1} b_j p^j \pmod{p^n} .$$

To determine b_0, we raise x to the $(q-1)/p$ power:

$$y = x^{\frac{q-1}{p}} = g^{a\frac{q-1}{p}} = (q^{\frac{q-1}{p}})^{b_0} ,$$

and note that y is one of only p elements, namely

$$h^0 = 1, h^1, h^2,...,h^{p-1} ,$$

where

$$h = g^{(q-1)/p} .$$

How one determines b_0 we will describe below. Once we have determined b_0, we can go on to determine b_1 by forming

$$(xg^{-b_0})^{(q-1)/p^2} = h^{b_1} ,$$

and so one.

The value of b_0 is determined using Shanks' "baby steps-giant steps" technique. We are given y, and we need to find m such that $y = h^m, 0 \leqslant m \leqslant p-1$. If $r \in \mathbf{R}$ is given, $0 \leqslant r \leqslant 1$, we form

$$u = \lceil p^r \rceil .$$

Then there exist integers c and d such that

$$m = cu+d, \quad 0 \leqslant d \leqslant u-1, \quad 0 \leqslant c < p/u .$$

Hence finding m is equivalent to finding integers c and d in the above ranges which satisfy

$$h^d \equiv yh^{-cu} .$$

To find such c and d, we can precompute h^d for $0 \leqslant d \leqslant n-1$ and then sort the resulting values. We then compute yh^{-cu} for $c = 0,1,...,$ and check each value for a match with the sorted table of values of y^d. The precomputation and sorting take $O(p^2 \log p)$ operations (note that these steps have to be done only once for any given field), and there are $O(p^{1-r})$ values of yh^{-cu} to be computed.

The Silver-Pohlig-Hellman algorithm is efficient whenever all the prime factors of $q-1$ are reasonably small. (It is most efficient in fields in which q is a Fermat prime, $q = 2^m + 1$, for which there is another polynomial-time discrete logarithm method [41].) Therefore great care has to be taken in selecting the fields $GF(q)$ for use in cryptography. This question will be discussed further in Section 8.

We conclude this section by mentioning two interesting randomized algorithms due to Pollard [52]. One of them computes discrete logarithms in fields $GF(q)$ in time roughly $q^{1/2}$. The other algorithm finds the discrete logarithm of an element in time roughly $w^{1/2}$, if that logarithm is known to lie in an interval of size w.

4. A subexponential discrete logarithm method

This section presents the fastest known general purpose discrete logarithm method. The basic ideas are due to Western and Miller [65] (see also [47]). The algorithm was invented independently by Adleman [1], Merkle [46], and Pollard [52], and its computational complexity was partially analyzed by Adleman [1]. We will refer to it as the index-calculus algorithm. Previous authors were concerned largely with the fields $GF(p)$, where p is a prime. Here the method will be presented as it applies to the fields $GF(2^n)$, since they are of greatest cryptographic interest. An extensive asymptotic analysis of the running time of the algorithm in this and the related cases $GF(p^n)$ with p fixed and $n \to \infty$ was given recently by Hellman and Reyneri [30]. As will be shown below, their estimates substantially overestimate the running time of this algorithm.

Recently some improvements on the index-calculus method as it applies to the fields $GF(2^n)$ were made by I. Blake, R. Fuji-Hara, R. Mullin, and S. Vanstone [8] which make it much more efficient, although these improvements do not affect the asymptotics of the running time. Even more recently, D. Coppersmith [18,19] has come up with a dramatic improvement on the $GF(2^n)$ version of the algorithm (and more generally on the $GF(p^n)$ version with p fixed and $n \to \infty$) which is much faster and even has different asymptotic behavior. More recently, a whole series of improvements on the basic algorithm have been discovered [20]. They do not approach the Coppersmith algorithm in asymptotic performance, but they do apply to fields $GF(p)$ as well as $GF(2^n)$ and they can be used to motivate Coppersmith's algorithm (although they did not perform this function, having come afterwards), so we briefly sketch them as well.

The model of computation we will assume in this section is that of the Random Access Machine (RAM), with no parallel computation. In Section 6 we will discuss what effect lifting this restriction might have. The index-calculus algorithm, at least in the form presented here is a probabilistic method in that the analysis of its running time relies on assumptions about randomness and independence of various polynomials which seem reasonable but at present cannot be proved.

Before presenting the algorithm, it is necessary to specify the notation that will be used. As usual, we regard the field $GF(2^n)$ as the ring of polynomials over $GF(2)$ modulo some irreducible polynomial $f(x)$ of degree n. Hence all elements $g \in GF(2^n)$ can be regarded as polynomials $g(x)$ over $GF(2)$ of degree $< n$.

One very important factor in analyzing the performance of the index-calculus algorithm over $GF(2^n)$ is that polynomials over $GF(2)$ are very easy to factor. Algorithms are known [7,16,36,55] that can factor $g(x)$ in time polynomial in the degree of $g(x)$. Since the running time of the index-calculus algorithm in $GF(2^n)$ is much higher (of the form $\exp(c(n \log n)^{1/2})$ for the basic version and of the form $\exp(c'n^{1/3}(\log n)^{2/3})$ for the Coppersmith version), we will neglect the time needed to factor polynomials in this section, since we will be concerned here with asymptotic estimates. In Section 6 we will perform a more careful analysis for some specific values of n.

Suppose that $g(x)$, a polynomial of degree $< n$ over $GF(2)$, is a primitive element of $GF(2^n)$. The index-calculus method for computing discrete logarithms in $GF(2^n)$ with respect to the base $g(x)$ consists of two stages. The first stage, which is by far the more time and space consuming, consists of the construction of a large data base. This stage only has to be carried out once for any given field. The second stage consists of the computation of the desired discrete logarithms.

We now present the basic version of the index-calculus algorithm. The initial preprocessing stage, which will be described later, consists of the computation of the discrete logarithms (with respect to $g(x)$) of a set S of chosen elements of $GF(2^n)$. The set S usually consists of all or almost all the irreducible polynomials over $GF(2)$ of degrees $\leqslant m$, where m is appropriately chosen. Once the preprocessing stage is completed, logarithms can be computed relatively rapidly. The basic idea is that given $h - h(x)$, to find $a \in Z^+$ such that

$$h \equiv g^a \pmod{f},$$

one chooses a random integer s, $1 \leqslant s \leqslant 2^n-1$, and computes

$$h^* \equiv h \, g^s \pmod{f}, \quad \deg h^* < n. \tag{4.1}$$

The reduced polynomial h^* is then factored into irreducible polynomials and if all its factors are elements of S, so that

$$h^* \equiv h \, g^s \equiv \prod_{v \in S} v^{b_v(h^*)} \pmod{f}, \tag{4.2}$$

then

$$\log_g h \equiv \sum_{v \in S} b_v(h^*) \log_g v - s \pmod{2^n-1}. \tag{4.3}$$

In the form in which we have presented it so far, it is possible to obtain a fully rigorous bound for the running time of the second stage. The polynomials h^* in (4.1) behave like random polynomials over $GF(2)$ of degree $< n$. Let $p(k, m)$ denote the probability that a polynomial over $GF(2)$ of degree exactly k has all its irreducible factors of degrees $\leqslant m$; i.e., if $N(k,m)$ is the number of polynomials $w(x) \in GF(2)[x]$ such that $\deg w(x) = k$ and

$$ w(x) = \prod_i u_i(x)^{c_i}, \quad \deg u_i(x) \leqslant m , $$

then

$$ p(k,m) = \frac{N(k,m)}{N(k,k)} = \frac{N(k,m)}{2^k} . \tag{4.4} $$

We expect that if S does consist of the irreducible polynomials of degrees $\leqslant m$, the reduced polynomial h^* in (4.1) will factor as in (4.2) with probability approximately $p(n,m)$, and that approximately $p(n,m)^{-1}$ of the polynomials of the form (4.1) will have to be generated before the second stage of the algorithm succeeds in finding the discrete logarithm of $h(x)$. (This reasoning explains why the set S is usually chosen to consist of all irreducible polynomials of degrees $\leqslant m$ for some fixed m; any other set of polynomials of equal cardinality is expected to have a smaller chance of producing a factorization of the form (4.2).)

The function $p(n,m)$ can be evaluated fairly easily both numerically and asymptotically. Appendix A presents the basic recurrences satisfied by $N(n,m)$ (from which $p(n,m)$ follows immediately by (4.4)), and shows that as $n \to \infty$ and $m \to \infty$ in such a way that $n^{1/100} \leqslant m \leqslant n^{99/100}$, (which is the range of greatest interest in the index calculus algorithm),

$$ p(n,m) = \exp((1+o(1)) \frac{n}{m} \log_e \frac{m}{n}) . \tag{4.5} $$

Appendix B consists of a table of $p(n, m)$ for a selection of values of n and m, which was computed using the recurrences in Appendix A. Approximations better than that of (4.5) for $p(n,m)$ can be obtained with more work, but for practical purposes the table of Appendix B is likely to be quite adequate and is more accurate to boot. The analysis of Hellman and Reyneri [30] relied on an estimate of $p(n, m)$ that was essentially equivalent to

$$p(n, m) \geqslant \exp((1+o(1)) \frac{n}{m} \log_e \frac{2e}{n}) \, ,$$

which while true, is much weaker than (4.5).

The polynomials h^* are always of degree $\leqslant n-1$, and have degree $n-k$ with probability 2^{-k}. Hence the probability that h^* factors in the form (4.2) is better approximated by

$$\sum_{k=1}^{n} 2^{-k} p(n-k, m) \, ,$$

which is approximately

$$p(n, m) \frac{(ne/m)^{1/m}}{2-(ne/m)^{1/m}} \, ,$$

as follows from the results of Appendix A. The last quantity above is $\sim p(n, m)$ as $n \to \infty$, $n^{1/100} \leqslant m \leqslant n^{99/100}$. Hence asymptotically this effect is unimportant, although for small values of n and m it can make a difference; for example, for $n = 127$ and $m = 17$ we obtain $1.51 p(127, 17)$ as the correct estimate of the probability that h^* will factor in the form (4.2).

The relation (4.5) shows that the expected running time of the second stage of the algorithm, as it has been presented so far, is approximately

$$p(n,m)^{-1} = (\frac{n}{m})^{(1+o(1))n/m} \, . \tag{4.6}$$

It was recently observed by Blake, Fuji-Hara, Mullin, and Vanstone [8] that this stage can be speeded up very substantially, although at the cost of not being able to provide an equally rigorous bound for the running time. Their idea is not to factor the polynomial h^* defined by (4.1) directly, but instead to find two polynomials w_1 and w_2 such that

$$h^* \equiv \frac{w_1}{w_2} \pmod{f} \, , \tag{4.7}$$

and such that $\deg w_i \leq n/2$ for $i = 1,2$. Once that is done, the w_i are factored, and if each is divisible only by irreducibles from S, say

$$w_i = \prod_{v \in S} v^{c_v(i)} , \qquad (4.8)$$

then

$$\log_g h \equiv \sum_{v \in S} (c_v(1) - c_v(2)) \log_g v - s \pmod{2^n - 1} . \qquad (4.9)$$

The advantage of this approach is that if the w_i behave like independently chosen random polynomials of degree $\sim n/2$, as seems reasonable, then the probability that both will factor into irreducibles of degrees $\leqslant m$ is approximately $p([n/2], m)^2$, and therefore the expected number of polynomials h^* that have to be tested is on the order of

$$p([n/2], m)^{-2} = (\frac{n}{2m})^{(1 + o(1))n/m} . \qquad (4.10)$$

This is smaller than the quality in (4.8) by a factor of approximately $2^{n/m}$, and so is very important, provided the w_i can be generated fast.

The polynomials w_i can be generated very rapidly (in time polynomial in n) by applying the extended Euclidean algorithm [36,42] to h^* and f. This algorithm produces polynomials α and β over $GF(2)$ such that $\alpha h^* + \beta f = 1$, the greatest common divisor of h^* and f, and such that $\deg \alpha < \deg f = n$, $\deg \beta < \deg h^* < n$. To do this, the algorithm actually computes a sequence of triples of polynomials $(\alpha_j, \beta_j, \gamma_j)$ such that

$$\alpha_j h^* + \beta_j f = \gamma_j , \qquad (4.11)$$

where the final $(\alpha_j, \beta_j, \gamma_j) = (\alpha, \beta, 1)$, $\deg \gamma_1 > \deg \gamma_2 > ...$, and where $\deg \alpha_j \leqslant n-1 - \deg \gamma_j$. If we choose that j for which $\deg \gamma_j$ is closest to $n/2$, then $w_1 = \gamma_j$ and $w_2 = \alpha_j$ will satisfy the congruence (4.7), and their degrees will be relatively close to $n/2$ most of the time. These w_1 and w_2 are not completely independent (for example, they have to be relatively prime), but on the other hand their degrees will often be less than $n/2$, so on balance it is not unreasonable to expect that the probability of both having a factorization of the form (4.8) should be close to $p([n/2], m)^2$.

The above observations justify the claim that the second stage of the index-calculus algorithm, as modified by Blake et al., ought to take on the order of $p([n/2], m)^{-2}$ operations on polynomials of degree $\leqslant n$ over $GF(2)$, where each such polynomial operation might involve on the order of n^3 bit operations. For small values of n, $p([n/2],m)$ can be found in Appendix B, while for very large n, the quantity on the right side of (4.10) ought to be a reasonable approximation to the running time of the second stage.

It is clear that the running time of the second stage can be decreased by increasing m. Doing that, however, increases both storage requirements and the running time of the first (preprocessing) stage of the algorithm. It is well known (see Appendix A) that the number of irreducible polynomials of degree $\leqslant m$ is very close to $m^{-1}2^{m+1}$, and for each one it is necessary to store roughly n bits, namely its logarithm (which is in the range $[1,2^n-1]$). This already puts a limit on how large m can be, but this limit is not very stringent, since these discrete logarithms can be stored on slow storage devices, such as tape. This is due to the fact that they are needed only once in the computation of each discrete logarithm by stage two, when both of the polynomials w_i are discovered to have factorizations of the form (4.8). Thus this argument does not exclude the use of values of m on the order of 40.

A much more severe limitation on the size of m and n is placed by the preprocessing first stage, which we now discuss. The basic idea there is to choose a random integer s, $1 \leqslant s \leqslant 2^n-1$, form the polynomial

$$h^* \equiv g^s \pmod{f}, \quad \deg h^* < n ,$$

and check whether h^* factors into irreducible factors from S. If it does, say

$$h^* = \prod_{v \in S} v^{b_v(h^*)} , \tag{4.12}$$

then we obtain the congruence

$$s \equiv \sum_{v \in S} b_v(h^*)\log_g v \pmod{2^n-1} . \tag{4.13}$$

Once we obtain slightly more than $|S|$ such congruences, we expect that they will determine the $\log_g v$, $v \in S$, uniquely modulo 2^n-1, and the first stage will be completed. There is a complication here in that 2^n-1 is not in general a prime, so that solving the system (4.13) might require working separately modulo the different prime power divisors of 2^n-1 and using the Chinese Remainder Theorem to reconstruct the values of $\log_g v$. This complication is not very serious, and if it does occur, it should lead to a speedup in the performance of the algorithm, since arithmetic would have to be done on smaller numbers. In any case this complication does not arise when 2^n-1 is a prime. A general linear system of the form (4.13) for the $\log_g v$ takes on the order of $|S|^3$ steps to solve if we use straightforward gaussian elimination. (We neglect here multiplicative factors on the order of $O(n^2)$.) This can be lowered to $|S|^r$ for $r = 2.495548...$ using known fast matrix multiplication algorithms [21], but those are not practical for reasonably sized $|S|$. The use of Strassen's matrix multiplication algorithm [10] might be practical for large n, and would lower the running time to about $|S|^r$ with $r = \log_2 7 = 2.807...$. However, the systems of linear equations that arise in the index-calculus algorithms are quite special in that they are quite sparse. (i.e., there are only a few nonzero coefficients). It was only recently discovered that this sparseness can be effectively exploited, and systems (4.13) can be solved in time essentially $|S|^2$. This development will be described in Section 5.7.

Generation of $|S|$ congruences of the form (4.13) takes about

$$|S| \; p(n,m)^{-1}$$

steps if we use the algorithm as described above. If instead we use the Blake et al. modification described in connection with the second stage, in which instead of factoring h^* right away, we first express it in the form (4.7) with $\deg w_i \leq n/2$, $i = 1,2$, and then factor the w_i, then generation of $|S|$ of the congruences (4.13) ought to take on the order of

$$|S| \; p([n/2], m)^{-2} \tag{4.14}$$

steps, where each step takes a polynomial number (in n) of bit operations. Thus the first stage of the algorithm takes on the order of

$$|S| \; p([n/2], m)^{-2} + |S|^2 \tag{4.15}$$

steps. Hence using our approximations to $p(k, m)$ and $|S|$ and discarding polynomial factors yields an estimate of the running time of the form

$$2^m \left(\frac{n}{2m}\right)^{n/m} + 2^{2m} .\qquad\qquad (4.16)$$

(To be precise, the exponents in (4.16) should be multiplied by $1+o(1)$.) The quantity

$$2^m \left(\frac{n}{2m}\right)^{n/m}$$

is minimized approximately for $m \sim c_1 (n \log_e n)^{1/2}$, where

$$c_1 = (2 \log_e 2)^{-1/2} = 0.8493... ,$$

in which case

$$2^m \left(\frac{n}{2m}\right)^{n/m} = \exp\left((c_2 + o(1)) \sqrt{n \log_e n}\right) \quad \text{as } n \to \infty , \qquad (4.17)$$

where

$$c_2 = c_1 \log_2 2 + (2c_1)^{-1} = (2 \log_e 2)^{1/2} = 1.1774... .$$

For $m \sim c_1 (n \log_e n)^{1/2}$, 2^{2m} is also of the form (4.17), so the time to solve the system of linear equations is of the same asymptotic form as the time needed to generate them.

If we modify the notation used by Pomerance [53] in his survey of integer factorization and let $M = M(n)$ represent any quantity satisfying

$$M = \exp((1+o(1)) (n \log_e n)^{1/2}) \quad \text{as } n \to \infty ,$$

then our analysis shows that the first stage of the basic index-calculus algorithm can be carried out in time $M^{1.178}$.

The time required by the second stage of the index-calculus algorithm to compute a single discrete logarithm is

$$M^{(2c_1)^{-1}} = M^{0.588...} .$$

This running time estimate is much lower than for the first stage. The space requirements of the second stage are essentially negligible. It is necessary to have access to the logarithms of the elements of S, which requires

$$\exp\left((c_1 \log_e 2 + o(1))\,(n \log_e n)^{1/2}\right)$$

bits of storage, but these logarithms are needed only once, and so they can be stored on a cheap slow-access device, such as tape.

Our estimates for the running time of the basic index-calculus algorithm for the fields $GF(2^n)$ are substantially smaller than those of Hellman and Reyneri [30]. This is due primarily to our use of a more accurate estimate for $p(n, m)$. The Blake et al. innovation which replaces the polynomial h^* by the quotient of two polynomials, each of roughly half the degree of h^* turns out not to affect the asymptotic estimate, since it improves the running time only by the factor $2^{n/m}$, which is $M^{o(1)}$ for $m \sim c(n \log_e n)^{1/2}$. However, for values of n that might be of practical interest, say $200 \leqslant n \leqslant 1000$, and best possible choices of m, this factor $2^{n/m}$ is very important, speeding up the algorithm by between two and ten orders of magnitude.

We next describe several algorithms that improve on the asymptotic performance of the basic index-calculus algorithm to an extent greater than the Blake et al. [8] modification. They are nowhere near as fast as the Coppersmith version, since they still run in time M^c for some constant $c > 0$, but they have the property that $c < c_2$. They are presented here very briefly in order to show the variety of methods that are available, and also to motivate the Coppersmith algorithm. Like the Coppersmith method, these variants depend on the polynomial $f(x)$ that defines the field being of a somewhat special form, namely

$$f(x) = x^n + f_1(x), \tag{4.18}$$

where the degree of $f_1(x)$ is small. Since approximately one polynomial of degree n out of n is irreducible (cf. Appendix A), we can expect to find $f(x)$ of the form (4.18) with $\deg f_1(x) \leq \log_2 n$. (The $f_1(x)$ of smallest degrees for which $x^n + f_1(x)$ is irreducible for some interesting values of n are $f_1(x) = x+1$ for $n = 127$, $f_1(x) = x^9+x^6+x^5+x^3+x+1$ for $n = 521$, $f_1(x) = x^9+x^7+x^6+x^3+x+1$ for $n = 607$, and $f_1(x) = x^{11}+x^9+x^8+x^5+x^3+x^2+x+1$ for $n = 1279$.) As is explained in Section 5.2, this is not a severe restriction, since being able to compute logarithms rapidly in one representation of a field enables one to compute logarithms in any other representation just about as fast.

The first algorithm we discuss is one of several that have the same asymptotic performance. (The other algorithms in this group are described in [20], at least in the form applicable to fields $GF(p)$.) It is basically an adaptation of the Schroeppel factorization algorithm [20,53]. We assume that $f(x)$ is of the form (4.18) with $\deg f(x) \leqslant n/2$, say. This time we let $S = S_1 \cup S_2$, where S_1 consists of the irreducible polynomials of degrees $\leqslant m$, and S_2 of polynomials of the form

$$x^k + g(x), \quad \deg g(x) \leqslant m, \tag{4.19}$$

where $k = \lceil n/2 \rceil$ is the least integer $\geqslant n/2$. Consider any $h_1(x), h_2(x) \in S_2$. If

$$h_i(x) = x^k + \bar{h}_i(x), \quad i=1,2,$$

then, if we write $2k = n+a$, $a = 0$ or 1, we have

$$h_1(x) h_2(x) = x^{2k} + x^k(\bar{h}_1(x) + \bar{h}_2(x)) + \bar{h}_1(x)\bar{h}_2(x)$$
$$= x^a(f(x) + f_1(x)) + x^k(\bar{h}_1(x)+\bar{h}_2(x)) + \bar{h}_1(x)\bar{h}_2(x) \tag{4.20}$$
$$\equiv x^k(\bar{h}_1(x)+\bar{h}_2(x)) + \bar{h}_1(x)\bar{h}_2(x) + x^a f_1(x) \pmod{f(x)},$$

and so the polynomial on the right side of (4.20) is of degree roughly $n/2$ (for $m = o(n)$, as will be the case). If that polynomial, call it $h^*(x)$, factors into irreducible polynomials of degrees $\leqslant m$, say

$$h^*(x) = \prod_{v \in S_1} v(x)^{b_v(h^*)},$$

then (4.20) yields a linear equation for the logarithms of the elements of S:

$$\log_g h_1 + \log_g h_2 \equiv \sum_{v \in S_1} b_v(h^*) \log_g v \pmod{2^n-1}. \tag{4.21}$$

Since each of S_1 and S_2 has on the order of 2^m elements, once we obtain about 2^m equation of the form (4.21), we ought to be able to solve them and obtain the discrete logarithms of the elements of S_1, which is what is desired. Now there are approximately 2^{2m} different pairs h_1,h_2 that can be tested, and if the h^* behave like random polynomials of degrees about $n/2$, each will factor into irreducibles of degrees $\leqslant m$ with probability approximately $p(\lceil n/2 \rceil, m)$. Hence we will have to perform about 2^{2m} polynomial time factorizations and obtain about $2^{2m} p(\lceil n/2 \rceil, m)$ equations of the form (4.21). Therefore we need

$$2^{2m} p([n/2], m) \geq 2^m,$$ (4.22)

and the work we do is on the order of 2^{2m}, since the linear equations can also be solved in this much time. To minimize the running time, we choose the smallest m for which (4.22) is satisfied, and a brief computation shows that the right choice is $m \sim c_3(n \log_e n)^{1/2}$ as $n \to \infty$, with $c_3 = (4 \log_e 2)^{-1/2}$, so that the running time of the first stage of this algorithm is

$$M^{c_4} = M^{0.8325...}, \quad c_4 = (\log_e 2)^{1/2}.$$ (4.23)

The improvement in the exponent of M is the running time estimate of the first stage from 1.177... in the basic algorithm to 0.832... in the version above was due to the fact that this time, in order to obtain a linear equation we only had to wait for a single polynomial of degree about $n/2$ to split into low degree irreducibles, instead of a single polynomial of degree n or two polynomials of degree $n/2$. In the next algorithm, we obtain a further improvement by reducing to the problem of a single polynomial of degree about $n/3$ splitting into low degree irreducibles. The method is an adaptation of the so-called "cubic sieve" for factoring integers, which was invented by J. Reyneri some years ago and rediscovered independently several times since then (see [20] for further details). This time we assume that $f(x)$ has the form (4.18) with $\deg f_1(x) \leq n/3$. We set $k = \lceil n/3 \rceil$ and let $S = S_1 \cup S_2$ with S_1 consisting of the irreducible polynomials of degrees $\leq m$ and S_2 of polynomials of the form $x^k + h(x)$, $\deg h(x) \leq m$. We consider pairs $h_1(x)$ and $h_2(x)$ with each $h_i(x)$ of degree $\leq m$, and let

$$h^*(x) \equiv (x^k+h_1(x))\,(x^k+h_2(x))\,(x^k+h_1(x)+h_2(x)) \pmod{f(x)},$$ (4.24)

$0 \leq \deg h^*(x) < n$. We then have

$$h^*(x) \equiv x^{3k} + x^k(h_1^2+h_1h_2+h_2^2) + h_1h_2(h_1+h_2) \pmod{f},$$ (4.25)

and since

$$x^{3k} \equiv x^a f_1(x) \pmod{f(x)}$$

for some a, $0 \leq a \leq 2$, we find that $h^*(x)$ is of degree about $k \sim n/3$ if $m = o(n)$. If $h^*(x)$ is divisible only by irreducibles in S_1, we obtain a linear equation relating logarithms of three elements of S_2 to those of elements of S_1. There are about 2^{2m} pairs $h_1(x), h_2(x)$ to test, and so if the $h^*(x)$ behave like random polynomials of degrees $\sim n/3$, we expect to obtain about $2^{2m} p([n/3], m)$ equations. Since there are about 2^m elements of S, we therefore need to choose m so that

$$2^{2m} p([n/3], m) \geq 2^m . \tag{4.26}$$

The time to run the algorithm is (within polynomial factors of n) 2^{2m}, both to form and factor the polynomials $h^*(x)$, and to solve the system of linear equations. A simple computation shows that the smallest m that satisfies (4.26) has $m \sim c_5(n \log_e n)^{1/2}$, where $c_5 = (6 \log_e 2)^{-1/2}$, and the running time of the first phase of this algorithm is

$$M^{c_6} = M^{0.6797...} , \text{ where } c_6 = (2(\log_e 2)/3)^{1/2} . \tag{4.27}$$

The running times of the second phases of the two algorithms presented above can be improved beyond what is obtained by using the strategy of the basic variant, but we will not discuss that subject. Details can be found in [20], in the case of fields $GF(p)$, p a prime, and it is easy to adapt those methods to the fields $GF(2^n)$.

The variants of the index-calculus algorithm presented above raise the question of whether they can be generalized so as to give even faster algorithms. The obvious idea is to use more than three factors and choose those factors in such a way that the product will reduce modulo $f(x)$ to a polynomial of low degree. A very clever way to do this was found by Coppersmith [18,19]. However, his work was motivated by different considerations.

We next present the Coppersmith variation [18,19] on the index-calculus algorithm. Unlike the basic algorithm, which runs in time roughly of the form $\exp(n^{1/2})$ in fields $GF(2^n)$, this new variation runs in time which is roughly of the form $\exp(n^{1/3})$. Unlike the basic version, though, the Coppersmith variant does not apply to the fields $GF(p)$ with p prime. Just like the algorithms presented above, the Coppersmith algorithm relies on several unproved assumptions. Since these assumptions are supported by both heuristic reasoning and empirical evidence, though, there seems to be no reason to doubt the validity of the algorithm.

The Coppersmith algorithm was inspired to a large extent by the Blake et al. [8] method of systematic equations, which is explained in Section 5.1, and which yields many linear equations involving logarithms at very low cost. Like the systematic equations method, it depends on the polynomial $f(x)$ being of a the special form (4.18) with $f_1(x)$ of very low degree.

We now discuss the first stage of the Coppersmith variant of the index-calculus algorithm. We assume that the field $GF(2^n)$ is defined by a polynomial $f(x)$ that is of the form (4.18) with $\deg f_1(x) \leq \log_2 n$. The first stage consists again of the computation of logarithms of $v \in S$, where S consists of irreducible polynomials of degrees $\leq m$, but now m will be much smaller, on the order of $n^{1/3}(\log_e n)^{2/3}$. We will also assume that $g(x) \in S$, since it follows from Section 5.2 that this restriction does not affect the running time of the algorithm.

The essence of the Blake et al. [8] improvement of the basic index-calculus algorithm is that it replaced the factorization of a single polynomial of degree about n by the factorization of two polynomials of degrees about $n/2$ each. The essence of the two improvements discussed above was that they rely on the factorization of polynomials of degrees about $n/2$ and $n/3$, respectively, into low degree irreducibles. The essence of the Coppersmith [18,19] improvement is that it instead relies on factorization of two polynomials of degrees on the order of $n^{2/3}$ each. The lower the degree of the polynomials being factored, the greater the probability that they will consist only of small degree irreducible factors. To accomplish this lowering of the degree, take $k \in Z^+$ (k will be chosen later so that 2^k is on the order of $n^{1/3}(\log_e n)^{-1/3}$) and define

$$h = \lfloor n\, 2^{-k} \rfloor + 1 . \tag{4.28}$$

Pick $u_1(x)$ and $u_2(x)$ of degrees $\leq B$ (B will be chosen later to be on the order of $n^{1/3}(\log_e n)^{2/3}$) with $(u_1(x), u_2(x)) = 1$, and set

$$w_1(x) = u_1(x)x^h + u_2(x) . \tag{4.29}$$

Next let

$$w_2(x) \equiv w_1(x)^{2^k} \pmod{f(x)} , \quad \deg w_2(x) < n . \tag{4.30}$$

We then have

$$w_2(x) \equiv u_1(x^{2^k})x^{h2^k} + u_2(x^{2^k}) \pmod{f(x)},$$

$$= u_1(x^{2^k})x^{h2^k-n}f_1(x) + u_2(x^{2^k}). \tag{4.31}$$

If B and 2^k are on the order of $n^{1/3}$, then h is on the order of $n^{2/3}$, $h\,2^k-n$ is on the order of $n^{1/3}$, and so both $w_1(x)$ and $w_2(x)$ have degrees on the order of $n^{2/3}$. Since

$$\log_g w_2(x) \equiv 2^k \log_g w_1(x) \pmod{2^n-1},$$

if both $w_1(x)$ and $w_2(x)$ have all their irreducible factors in S we obtain a linear equation for the $\log_g v$, $v \in S$. (The restriction $(u_1(x), u_2(x)) = 1$ serves to eliminate duplicate equations, since the pairs $u_1(x)$, $u_2(x)$ and $u_1(x)t(x)$, $u_2(x)t(x)$ produce the same equations.)

We next consider the Coppersmith algorithm in greater detail. We need to obtain about $|S|$ linear equations for the $\log_g v$, $v \in S$. Now

$$\deg w_1(x) \leqslant B+h,$$

$$\deg w_2(x) \leqslant B \cdot 2^k + 2^k + \deg f_1(x),$$

so if $w_1(x)$ and $w_2(x)$ behave like independent random polynomials of those degrees, then the probability that both $w_1(x)$ and $w_2(x)$ have all their irreducible factors in S is approximately

$$p(B+h, m)p(B2^k+2^k, m). \tag{4.32}$$

Of course $w_1(x)$ and $w_2(x)$ are neither independent nor random. However, as far as their factorizations are concerned, it does not appear unreasonable to expect that they will behave like independent random polynomials, and this does turn out to hold in the case $n = 127$ studied by Coppersmith [18,19]. Therefore to obtain $|S| \sim m^{-1}2^{m+1}$ equations we need to satisfy

$$2^{2B} p(B+h, m)p(B2^k+2^k, m) \geq 2^m. \tag{4.33}$$

The work involved consists of generating approximately 2^{2B} polynomials $w_1(x)$ and testing whether both $w_1(x)$ and $w_2(x)$ have all their irreducible factors in S. Once these roughly 2^m equations are generated, it becomes necessary to solve them, which takes about 2^{2m} operations. The estimate (4.5) shows that to minimize the running time, which is approximately

$$2^{2B} + 2^{2m} ,$$

subject to (4.33), it is necessary to take

$$2^k \sim \alpha \, n^{1/3} \, (\log_e n)^{-1/3} , \tag{4.34a}$$

$$m \sim \beta \, n^{1/3} \, (\log_e n)^{2/3} , \tag{4.34b}$$

$$B \sim \gamma \, n^{1/3} \, (\log_e n)^{2/3} , \tag{4.34c}$$

as $n \to \infty$, where α, β, and γ are bounded away from both zero and infinity. Under these conditions we find that the running time of the first stage of the algorithm is

$$K^{2\gamma \log_e 2} + K^{2\beta \log_e 2} , \tag{4.35}$$

where $K = K(n)$ denotes any quantity that satisfies

$$K = \exp \left((1+o(1)) \, n^{1/3} \, (\log_e n)^{2/3} \right) , \tag{4.36}$$

and this is subject to the condition

$$2 \, \gamma \log_e 2 - \frac{1}{3\alpha\beta} - \frac{\alpha\gamma}{3\beta} \geq (1+o(1)))\beta \log_e 2 . \tag{4.37}$$

Let us now regard α, β, and γ as continuous variables. Since the estimate (4.35) does not depend on α, we can choose α freely. The quantity on the left side of (4.37) is maximized for

$$\alpha = \gamma^{-1/2} , \tag{4.38}$$

and for this choice of α, (4.37) reduces to (after neglecting the $1+o(1)$ factor)

$$2\gamma \log_e 2 \geq \beta \log_e 2 + \frac{2}{3} \beta^{-1}\gamma^{1/2} . \tag{4.39}$$

To minimize the asymptotic running time of the algorithm, we have to choose β and γ so that (4.39) is satisfied and $\max(2\gamma, 2\beta)$ is minimized. A short calculation shows that the optimal choice is obtained when $\gamma = \beta$ and equality holds in (4.37), which yields

$$\beta = 2^{2/3}3^{-2/3} \, (\log_e 2)^{-2/3} = 0.9743... . \tag{4.40}$$

The running time for this choice is

$$K^{2\beta \log_e 2} = K^{1.3507...},$$

and the space required is $K^{\beta \log_e 2} = K^{0.6753...}$.

The analysis above assumed that α, β, and γ could all be treated as continuous variables. This is essentially true in the case of β and γ, but not in the case of α, since (4.34a) has to hold with k a positive integer. Since the analysis is straightforward but tedious, we do not discuss the general situation in detail but only mention that the running time of the Coppersmith algorithm and the space required are of the form K^u, where u is a function of $\log_2 (n^{1/3} (\log_e n)^{2/3})$ which is periodic with period 1. The minimal value of u is $2\beta \log_e 2$, with β given by (4.40), while the maximal value of u is $3^{2/3}\beta \log_e 2 = (2.08008...) \beta \log_e 2$. Thus we are faced with the not uncommon situation in which the running time of the algorithm does not satisfy a simple asymptotic relation but exhibits periodic oscillations.

We next discuss the second stage of the Coppersmith algorithm, which computes logarithms of arbitrary elements. It is somewhat more involved than the second stage of the basic version of the algorithm. If h is a polynomial whose logarithm is to be determined, then Coppersmith's second stage consists of a sequence of steps which replace h by a sequence of polynomials of decreasing degrees. The first step is similar to the second stage of the basic algorithm and consists of selecting a random integer s, forming h^* as in (4.1), and checking whether h^* has all its irreducible factors of degrees $\leqslant n^{2/3} (\log_e n)^{1/3}$, say. (In practice, one would again replace h^* by w_1/w_2, where the degrees of the w_i are $\leq h/2$, and the bound on the degrees of the irreducible factors might be somewhat different, but that is not very important.) The probability of success is approximately $p(n, n^{2/3}(\log_e n)^{1/3})$, so we expect to succeed after

$$p(n, n^{2/3}(\log_e n)^{1/3})^{-1} = K^{\log_e 3} = K^{1.098...} \tag{4.41}$$

trials. When we do succeed with some value of s, we obtain

$$h \equiv g^{-s} \prod_i u_i \pmod{f(x)},$$

where the u_i are of degrees $\leqslant n^{2/3} (\log n)^{1/3}$, and there are $< n$ of them (since their product is a polynomial of degree $< n$). This then yields

$$\log_g h \equiv -s + \sum_i \log_g u_i \pmod{2^n - 1} , \tag{4.42}$$

and so if we find the $\log_g u_i$, we obtain $\log_g h$.

Suppose next that u is a polynomial of degree $\leqslant B \leqslant n^{2/3} (\log n)^{1/3}$ (say one of the u_i above, in which case $B = n^{2/3} (\log n)^{1/3}$). We again reduce the problem of computing $\log_g u$ to that of computing logarithms of several polynomials of lower degrees. We select 2^k to be a power of 2 close to $(n/B)^{1/2}$ (precise choice to be specified later), and let

$$d = \lfloor n 2^{-k} \rfloor + 1 . \tag{4.43}$$

Consider polynomials

$$w_1(x) = v_1(x) x^d + v_2(x) , \tag{4.44}$$

where $\deg v_1(x)$, $\deg v_2(x) \leqslant b$ (b to be specified later), $(v_1(x), v_2(x)) = 1$, and $u(x) | w_1(x)$. If

$$w_2(x) \equiv w_1(x)^{2^k} \pmod{f(x)} , \quad \deg w_2(x) < n , \tag{4.45}$$

then (for b small)

$$w_2(x) = v_1(x^{2^k}) x^{d 2^k - n} f_1(x) + v_2(x^{2^k}) ,$$

and thus $w_1(x)$ and $w_2(x)$ both have low degrees. If $w_1(x)/u(x)$ and $w_2(x)$ both factor into irreducible polynomials of low degree, say

$$w_1(x) = u(x) \prod_i s_i(x) ,$$

$$w_2(x) = \prod_j t_j(x) ,$$

then we obtain

$$\sum_j \log_g t_j(x) \equiv \log_g w_2(x) \equiv 2^k \log_g w_1(k)$$

$$\equiv 2^k \left(\log_g u(x) + \sum_i \log_g s_i(x) \right) \pmod{2^n - 1} .$$

This reduces the computation of $\log_g u$ to the computation of the $\log_g t_j$ and the $\log_g u_i$. We next analyze how much of a reduction this is. The probability that $w_1(x)/u(x)$ and $w_2(x)$ both factor into irreducible polynomials of degrees $\leqslant M$ is approximately

$$p(d+b-\deg u(x), M)\, p(b2^k+2^k+\deg f_1(x), M)\,,$$

and the number of pairs of polynomials $v_1(x)$, $v_2(x)$ of degrees $\leqslant b$ with $(v_1(x), v_2(x)) = 1$ and $u(x) \mid w_1(x)$ is approximately

$$2^{2b-\deg u(x)}\,.$$

(Divisibility by $u(x)$ is determined by a set of $\deg u(x)$ linear equations for the coefficients of $v_1(x)$ and $v_2(x)$.) Hence to find $v_1(x)$ and $v_2(x)$ such that $w_1(x)$ and $w_2(x)$ factor in the desired fashion we select b to be approximately

$$(n^{1/3}\,(\log_e n)^{2/3}(\log_e 2)^{-1} + \deg u(x))/2\,, \tag{4.46}$$

and select 2^k to be the power of 2 nearest to $(n/b)^{1/2}$. We then expect to obtain the desired factorization in time

$$K = \exp((1+o(1))n^{1/3}(\log_e n)^{2/3})\,,$$

with M being the largest integer for which

$$Kp(d+b-\deg u(x), M)p(b2^k+2^k+\deg f_1(x), M) \geqslant 1\,. \tag{4.47}$$

If $B \sim n^{2/3}(\log_e n)^{1/3}$ (as occurs in the first step of the second stage of the Coppersmith algorithm), we find that we can take $M \sim cn^{1/2}(\log_e n)^{3/2}$, and if $B \sim cn^{1/2}(\log_e n)^{3/2}$, then we can take $M \sim c'n^{5/12}(\log_e n)^{25/12}$. More generally, it is also easy to show that if $B \geqslant n^{1/3}(\log_e n)^{2/3}$, say, then we can take $M \leqslant B/1.1$, so that each iteration decreases the degrees of the polynomials whose logarithms we need to compute by a factor $\geqslant 1.1$, while raising the number of these polynomials by a factor $\leqslant n$. When $B \leqslant (1.1)^{-1}n^{1/3}(\log_e n)^{2/3}$, the polynomial $u(x)$ is already in our data base, and we only need to read off its logarithm. Thus we expect to perform

$$\leqslant \exp(c''(\log n)^2) = K^{o(1)}$$

iterations of this process, each iteration taking K steps.

We have shown that the second stage of the Coppersmith algorithm can compute individual logarithms in time $K^{1.098...}$. In fact, with slightly more care the exponent of K can be lowered substantially. We do not do it here, since the main point we wish to make is that as in the basic algorithm, the second stage of the Coppersmith variant requires very little time and negligible space, compared to the first stage.

This section was devoted almost exclusively to the asymptotic analysis of the index-calculus algorithms on a random access machine. In Section 6 we will consider the question of estimating the running time of this algorithm for some concrete values of n, including the possible effects of the use of parallel processors. In the next section we will discuss several variations on the algorithm as it has been presented so far.

5. Further modifications of the index-calculus algorithm

Section 4 was concerned largely with the asymptotic behavior of the index-calculus algorithm in fields $GF(2^n)$. This section will discuss several technical issues related to both the basic algorithm and the Coppersmith version. The most important of them is that of efficient solutions to systems of linear equations, discussed in Section 5.7. The fact that the equations that occur in index-calculus algorithms can be solved fast is a recent discovery which affects the estimates of the running time both asymptotically and in practice.

This section also presents a variety of modifications of both the basic algorithm and of the Coppersmith version, which do not affect the asymptotics of the running times very much, but which are very important in practice. The most significant of these variations is that of Section 5.6. That variation speeds up the first phase of the Coppersmith algorithm by two or three orders of magnitude in fields that might be of practical interest. The variations presented here are not analyzed in exhaustive detail because their exact contributions depend on the hardware and software in which the algorithm is implemented. The purpose here is to obtain rough estimates of the performance of the algorithm with the best currently conceivable techniques. These estimates will be used in the next section to evaluate how large n ought to be to offer a given level of security.

5.1 Systematic equations

The first stage of the index-calculus algorithm involves the collection of slightly over $|S|$ linear equations for the logarithms of the polynomials $v \in S$ and then the solution of these equations. The reason the Coppersmith version is so much faster than the Blake et al. version is that by dealing with pairs of polynomials of degree around $n^{2/3}$ as opposed of degree about $n/2$, it increases the probability of finding an additional equation for the $\log_g v$, $v \in S$. In fact, for the fields $GF(2^n)$, Blake et al. had some methods for obtaining large numbers of equations at very low cost per equation. They called the equations obtained this way "systematic." They were able to obtain upwards of one half of the required number of equations that way, but never all. Their methods in fact inspired Coppersmith to invent his version of the algorithm. We will now explain the Blake et al. methods and explore their significance. These methods work best when the polynomial $f(x)$ which defines the field has the special property that it divides some polynomial of the form

$$x^{2^k} + f_1(x) , \tag{5.1}$$

where the degree of $f_1(x)$ is very small, and where the primitive element $g = g(x) = x$. In general, it appears likely that the degree of $f_1(x)$ will be relatively high, which will make these new approaches of Blake et al. of little significance. In some cases, however, these methods produce startling improvements. This happens, for example, in the case of $n = 127$, when we take the defining polynomial to be $f(x) = x^{127}+x+1$, since here

$$xf(x) = x^{2^7}+x^2+x ,$$

and $f_1(x)$ has degree 2.

The first of the observations made by Blake and his collaborators is that if $f_1(x)$ is of low degree, the polynomials x^{2^r}, $1 \leqslant r \leqslant n-1$, will often have low degree when reduced modulo $f(x)$. When this degree is low enough to make that polynomial a product of polynomials from S, we obtain a linear equation of the desired kind, since $\log_x x^{2^r} = 2^r$. As an example, for $n = 127$ and $f(x) = x^{127}+x+1$, we find that for $7 \leqslant i \leqslant 126$,

$$x^{2^i} = (x^{2^7})^{2^{i-7}} = (x^2+x)^{2^{i-7}} = x^{2^{i-6}}+x^{2^{i-7}},$$

and repeated application of this result shows that each x^{2^r}, $0 \leqslant r \leqslant 126$, can be expressed in the form

$$\sum_{i=0}^{6} \epsilon_i x^{2^i}, \quad \epsilon_i = 0, 1,$$

and so the logarithms of all such elements can be quickly computed, and are of the form 2^r for some r. Furthermore, since

$$1+x^{2^r} = (1+x)^{2^r} = x^{127.2^r},$$

one can also obtain the logarithms of all elements of the form

$$\epsilon_{-1} + \sum_{i=0}^{6} \epsilon_i x^{2^i}, \quad \epsilon_i = 0, 1.$$

In particular, these will include the logarithms of 31 nonzero polynomials of degrees $\leqslant 16$. In general, for other values of n, $f_1(x)$ will not have such a favorable form, and we can expect fewer usable equations.

Another observation of Blake et al., which is even more fruitful, is based on the fact that if $u(x)$ is any irreducible polynomial over $GF(2)$ of degree d, and $v(x)$ is any polynomial over $GF(2)$, then the degrees of all irreducible factors of $u(v(x))$ are divisible by d. To prove this, note that if $w(x)$ is an irreducible factor of $u(v(x))$, and α is a root of $w(x) = 0$, then $v(\alpha)$ is a zero of $u(x)$, and thus is of degree d over $GF(2)$. Since $v(x)$ has its coefficients in $GF(2)$, this means that α must generate an extension field of $GF(2^d)$, which means that its degree must be divisible by d, as we wished to show.

To apply the above fact, Blake et al. take an irreducible $u(x)$ of low degree, $u(x) \in S$, and note that by (5.1),

$$u(x)^{2^k} = u(x^{2^k}) = u(f_1(x)) .$$

If $u(f_1(x))$ factors into polynomials from S, one obtains another equation for the logarithms of the $v \in S$. The result proved in the preceding paragraph shows that all the factors of $u(f_1(x))$ will have degrees divisible by $\deg u(x)$, and not exceeding $(\deg u(x))(\deg f_1(x))$. Blake and his collaborators noted that in many cases all the irreducible factors have degrees actually equal to $\deg u(x)$. We will now discuss the likelihood of this happening.

Suppose that

$$f(x) \mid x^{2^d} + f_1(x) . \tag{5.2}$$

We can assume without loss of generality that not all powers of x appearing in $f_1(x)$ are even, since if they were, say $f_1(x) = f_2(x^2) = f_2(x)^2$, we would have

$$f(x) \mid x^{2^d} + f_2(x)^2 = (x^{2^{d-1}} + f_2(x))^2 ,$$

and since $f(x)$ is irreducible, we would obtain

$$f(x) \mid x^{2^{d-1}} + f_2(x) ,$$

and we could replace $f_1(x)$ by $f_2(x)$ in (5.2). Therefore we will assume $f_1(x)$ does have terms of odd degree, and so $f_1'(x) \neq 0$.

The polynomial

$$F_d(x) = x^{2^d} + x \tag{5.3}$$

is the product of all the irreducible polynomials of all degrees dividing d. When we substitute $f_1(x)$ for x in $F_d(x)$, we obtain

$$F_d(f_1(x)) = f_1(x)^{2^d} + f_1(x) = f_1(x^{2^d}) + f_1(x) . \tag{5.4}$$

But

$$f_1(x^{2^d}) + f_1(x) \equiv f_1(x) + f_1(x) = 0 \pmod{F_d(x)} ,$$

and so each irreducible polynomial whose degree divides d has to divide some $u(f_1(x))$ for another irreducible $u(x)$ of degree dividing d. Since

$$\frac{d}{dx} F_d(f_1(x)) = f_1'(x)$$

by (5.4), only a small number of irreducibles can divide $F_d(f_1(x))$ to second or higher powers.

Hence we conclude that at most only about one in deg $f_1(x)$ of the irreducible polynomials $u(x)$ of degree d can have the property that $u(f_1(x))$ factors into irreducible polynomials of degree d. Thus if we have only one pair $(k, f_1(x))$ for which (5.2) holds, then we can expect at most about $|S|/(\deg f_1(x))$ systematic equations from this method. We also obtain useful equations from all $u(x)$ for which $\deg u(f_1(x)) \leqslant m$, but there are relatively few such polynomials $u(x)$. If $\deg f_1(x) = 2$ (as it is for $n = 127$, $f(x) = x^{127}+x+1$), it is easy to see that almost exactly one half of the irreducible polynomials $u(x)$ of a given degree d will have the property that $u(f_1(x))$ factors into irreducible polynomials of degree d. If $\deg f_1(x) > 2$, the situation is more complicated, in that the $u(f_1(x))$ can factor into products of irreducible polynomials of several degrees, and so the number of useful equations obtained this way is typically considerably smaller than $|S|/(\deg f_1(x))$.

One factor which is hard to predict is how small can one take the degree of $f_1(x)$ so that (5.2) holds for some k and some primitive polynomial $f(x)$ of degree n. The situation for $n = 127$, where we can take $f_1(x) = x^2+x$, is extremely favorable. For some n, it is possible to take $\deg f_1(x) = 1$. Condition (5.2) with $f_1(x) = x$ is not useful, since it holds precisely for the irreducible polynomials of degrees dividing k, and the resulting discrete logarithm equations simply say that

$$2^k \log_x v \equiv \log_x v \pmod{2^d - 1}$$

for $d | k$, $d = \deg v(x)$, which is trivial. Condition (5.2) with $f_1(x) = x+1$ is somewhat more interesting. If it holds, then

$$f(x) \mid x^{2^{2k}} + x ,$$

and thus $\deg f(x) \mid 2k$. On the other hand, because of (5.2), $\deg f(x) \nmid k$. Thus this condition can hold only for even n, which, as we will argue later, ought to be avoided in cryptographic applications. For these even n, however, it gives relations of the form

$$2^{n/2} \log_x v \equiv \log_x v^* \pmod{2^n - 1} ,$$

for all irreducible $v(x)$, where $v^*(x) = v(x+1)$, and then gives about $|S|/2$ useful equations.

In many cases it is impossible to find $f(x)$ of a given degree such that (5.2) holds for some $f_1(x)$ of low degree. When such $f(x)$ can be found, it sometimes happens that (5.2) holds for several pairs $(k, f_1(x))$. For example, when $n = 127$, $f(x) = x^{127}+x+1$, condition (5.2) holds for $k = 7$, $f_1(x) = x^2+x$ and also for $k = 14$, $f_1(x) = x^4+x$.

The significance of these systematic equations is not completely clear. Our arguments indicate that unless (5.2) is satisfied with $f_1(x)$ of low degree, few systematic equations will be obtained. No method is currently known for finding primitive $f(x)$ of a given degree n for which (5.2) is satisfied with some $f_1(x)$ of low degree. It is not even known whether there exist such $f(x)$ for a given n. Even in the very favorable situation that arises for $n = 127$, $f(x) = x^{127}+x+1$, Blake et al. [8] found only 142 linearly independent systematic equations involving the 226 logarithms of the irreducible polynomials of degrees $\leqslant 10$. (They reported a very large number of linear dependencies among the systematic equations they obtained.) Thus it seems that while systematic equations are a very important idea that has already led to the Coppersmith breakthrough and might lead to further developments, at this time they cannot be relied upon to produce much more than $|S|/2$ equations, and in practice probably many fewer can be expected.

5.2 Change of primitive element and field representation

The Coppersmith algorithm requires that the polynomial $f(x)$ that generates the field $GF(2^n)$ be of the form (4.18) with $f_1(x)$ of low degree. Section 4.1 showed that if the $f(x)$ satisfies (5.2) with $f_1(x)$ if low degree, and x is a primitive element of the field, one can obtain many systematic equations. On the other hand, it is often desirable that $f(x)$ satisfy other conditions. For example, if $f(x)$ is an irreducible trinomial,

$$f(x) = x^n+x^k+1 , \qquad (5.5)$$

where we may take $k \leqslant n/2$, since $x^n+x^{n-k}+1$ is irreducible if and only if $f(x)$ is, then reduction of polynomials modulo $f(x)$ is very easy to implement; if

$$h(x) = \sum_{i=0}^{2n-2} a_i x^i$$

(as might occur if $h(x)$ is the product of two polynomials reduced modulo $f(x)$), then

$$h(x) \equiv \sum_{i=0}^{n-1} a_i x^i + \sum_{i=0}^{n-2} a_{i+n} x^i + \sum_{i=k}^{k+n-2} a_{i+n-k} x^i \pmod{f(x)}, \tag{5.6}$$

a reduction that can be accomplished using two shifts and two exclusive or's of the coefficient strings, and another iteration of this procedure applied to the polynomial on the right side of (4.6) yields the fully reduced form of $h(x)$. It is often also desirable that $f(x)$ be primitive, since then x can be used as a primitive element of the field. (Extensive tables of primitive trinomials are available, see [28,71,72].) In some cases, of which $n = 127$ and $f(x) = x^{127}+x+1$ is the example par excellence, it is possible to satisfy all these desirable conditions. In general, though, some kind of compromise might be necessary, and the choice to be made might depend both on n (and thus on what kinds of polynomials exist) and on the hardware and software that are being used. Our purpose here is to show that the security of a cryptosystem is essentially independent of the choices that are made; the cryptosystem designer and the cryptanalyst can choose whichever $f(x)$ and $g(x)$ suit them best.

To show that changing only the primitive element $g(x)$ does not affect the security of a system, suppose that we have a way to compute discrete logarithms to base $g(x)$ efficiently. If another primitive element $g_1(x)$ and a nonzero polynomial $h(x)$ are given, and it is desired to compute the logarithm of $h(x)$ to base $g_1(x)$, we compute the logarithms of $g_1(x)$ and $h(x)$ to base $g(x)$, say

$$g_1(x) \equiv g(x)^a \pmod{f(x)},$$
$$h(x) \equiv g(x)^b \pmod{f(x)},$$

and obtain immediately

$$h(x) \equiv g_1(x)^{a^*b} \pmod{f(x)},$$

where a^* is the integer with $1 \leqslant a^* \leqslant 2^n-1$ for which

$$aa^* \equiv 1 \pmod{2^n-1}.$$

(Since $g(x)$ and $g_1(x)$ are primitive, $(a_1 2^n-1) = 1$, and so a^* exists.)

Changing the representation of the field, so that it is given as polynomials modulo $f_1(x)$, as opposed to modulo $f(x)$, also does not affect the difficulty of computing discrete logarithms, as was first observed by Zierler [70]. The two fields are isomorphic, with the isomorphism being given by

$$x \pmod{f_1(x)} \rightarrow h(x) \pmod{f(x)},$$

where

$$f_1(h(x)) \equiv 0 \pmod{f(x)}.$$

Thus to construct the isomorphism we have to find a root $h(x)$ of $f_1(x)$ in the field of polynomials modulo $f(x)$. Such a root can be found in time polynomial in n [7,16,36,55,70], which establishes the isomorphism and enables one to transfer logarithm computations from one representation to another.

5.3 Faster generation and processing of test polynomials

As we described the basic index-calculus algorithm, the polynomials h^* are generated (in the first stage of the algorithm, say) by selecting a random integer s and reducing g^s modulo $f(x)$. Typically this involves on the order of $3n/2$ polynomial multiplications and reductions modulo $f(x)$. This work can be substantially reduced by choosing the h^* in succession, say $h_1^* = 1$, h_2^*, h_3^*,..., with

$$h_{k+1}^* \equiv h_k^* v_s \pmod{f(x)},$$

where v_s is chosen at random from S. This requires only one polynomial multiplication (in which one factor, namely v_s, is of low degree) and one reduction. Since each h_k^* is of the form

$$h_k^* \equiv \prod_{v \in S} v^{a_v} \pmod{f(x)},$$

any time we find that both w_1 and w_2 have all their irreducible factors in S, we obtain another equation for the $\log_g v$, $v \in S$. Heuristic arguments and some empirical evidence [58] indicate that the sequence h_k^* ought to behave like a random walk in $GF(2^n) \backslash \{0\}$, which means that the modified algorithm ought to produce linear equations about as efficiently as the old one.

Once h^* is computed, the (w_1, w_2) pair that satisfies (4.7) is produced by the extended

Euclidean algorithm applied to the polynomials h^* and f, which are each of degree about n. It might be advantageous to decrease the cost of this relatively slow operation by generating several pairs (w_1, w_2) that satisfy (4.7). This can be done by choosing $w_1 = \gamma_j$ and $w_2 = \alpha_j$ for several values of j such that (4.11) holds and the degrees of the w_i are not too far from $n/2$. As is shown in Appendix A,

$$p(r+s, m)p(r-s, m) \approx p(r, m)^2$$

for s small compared to r (for example, $p(105, 18)p(95, 18) = 1.07 \times 10^{-8}$, while $p(100, 18)^2 = 1.09 \times 10^{-8}$) so that if the neighboring pairs (γ_j, α_j) that satisfy (4.11) are independent with regard to factorization into small degree irreducible polynomials, as seems reasonable, we can cheaply obtain additional pairs (w_1, w_2) satisfying (4.7) which will be just as good in producing additional equations.

The two modifications suggested above can also be applied to the second stage of the basic index-calculus algorithm, where they will lead to a similar improvements in running time. They can also be used in the first step of the second stage of the Coppersmith algorithm.

Blake et al. [8] used the Berlekamp algorithm [7] to factor the polynomials w_i. However, what is really needed initially is only to check whether all the irreducible factors of the w_i are of degrees $\leqslant m$. The complete factorization of the w_i is needed only when the w_i are both composed of low degree factors, and this happens so infrequently that the time that is needed in those cases to factor the w_i is an insignificant fraction of the total running time. Now to rapidly check whether a polynomial $w(x)$ has all its irreducible factors of degrees $\leqslant m$, we can proceed as follows. Since the greatest common divisor, $(w'(x), w(x))$, of $w(x)$ and its derivative equals

$$(w'(x), w(x)) = \prod_i y_i(x)^{2[a_i/2]}, \tag{5.7}$$

where

$$w(x) = \prod_i y_i(x)^{a_i},$$

and the $y_i(x)$ are distinct irreducible polynomials, we can compute

$$w^{(0)}(x) = \prod_i y_i(x)$$

in a few greatest common divisor and square root operations. Then, for $i = 1,2,..., m$ we compute

$$w^{(i)}(x) = \frac{w^{(i-1)}(x)}{(w^{(i-1)}(x), x^{2^i}+x)} . \tag{5.8}$$

Since $x^{2^k} + x$ is the product of all the irreducible polynomials of degrees dividing k, $w^{(m)}(x) = 1$ if and only if all the irreducible factors of $w(x)$ are of degrees $\leqslant m$.

The above procedure ought to be quite fast, since the greatest common divisor of two polynomials of degrees $\leqslant n$ can be computed using at most n shifts and exclusive or's of their coefficient sequences and since the degrees of the $w^{(i)}$ are likely to decrease rapidly. The above procedure can be simplified some more by noting that it suffices to define $w^{(i_0)}(x) = w^{(0)}(x)$ for $i_0 = [(m-1)/2]$ and apply (5.8) for $i = i_0+1,..., m$, since any irreducible polynomial of degree d, $d \leqslant m$, divides at least one of the $x^{2^i}+x$, $i_0+1 \leqslant i \leqslant m$. Furthermore, the $x^{2^i}+x$ do not have to be computed at each stage separately, but instead, if we save

$$u_i(x) \equiv x^{2^i}+x \quad (\text{mod } w^{(i-1)}(x)) ,$$

with $u_i(x)$ reduced modulo $w^{(i-1)}(x)$, then

$$u_i(x) \equiv x^{2^i}+x \quad (\text{mod } w^{(i)}(x)) ,$$

and so

$$u_{i+1}(x) \equiv u_i(x^2)+x^2+x \quad (\text{mod } w^i(x)) ,$$

which is a much simpler operation.

Another fast way to test whether a polynomial $w(x)$ has all its irreducible factors of degrees $\leqslant m$ was suggested by Coppersmith [19]. It consists of computing

$$w'(x) \prod_{i = \lceil m/2 \rceil}^{m} (x^{2^i}+x) \quad (\text{mod } w(x)) ,$$

and checking whether the resulting polynomial is zero or not. This method avoids the need for many greatest common division computations, and so may be preferable in some implementations.

It is not completely foolproof, since polynomials in which all irreducible factors of degrees $> m$ appear to even powers will pass the test. However, such false signals will occur very infrequently, and will not cause any confusion, since polynomials $w(x)$ that pass the Coppersmith test have to be factored in any case.

5.4 Large irreducible factors

This section discusses a variation on both the basic index-calculus algorithm and the Coppersmith variation that was inspired by the "large prime" variation on the continued fraction integer factoring method (cf. [53]). In practice, as will be discussed in greater length later, the w_i would probably be factored by removing from them all irreducible factors of degree $\leqslant m$, and discarding that pair (w_1, w_2) if either one of the quotients is not 1. If one of the quotients, call it $u(x)$, is not 1, but has degree $\leqslant 2m$, then it has to be irreducible. The new variation would use such pairs, provided the degree of $u(x)$ is not too high ($\leqslant m+6$, say). The pair (w_1, w_2) that produced $u(x)$ would be stored, indexed by $u(x)$. Then, prior to the linear equation solving phase, a preprocessing phase would take place, in which for each irreducible $u(x)$, $\deg u(x) > m$, the pairs (w_1, w_2) that are associated to it would be used to obtain additional linear equations involving logarithms of the $v \in S$. For example, in the basic algorithm, if there are k pairs associated to $u(x)$, say

$$h_i^* \equiv u^{a_i} \prod_{v \in S} v^{b_v(i)} \pmod{f} , \quad 1 \leqslant i \leqslant k , .$$

where each $a_i = \pm 1$, then we can obtain $k-1$ equations for the logarithms of the $v \in S$ by considering the polynomials

$$h_i^*(h_1^*)^{-a_i/a_1} \equiv \prod_{v \in S} v^{b_v(i)-b_v(1)a_i/a_1} \pmod{f} , \quad 2 \leqslant i \leqslant k .$$

A similar method works with the Coppersmith variation.

We now consider the question of how many equations we are likely to obtain by this method. Suppose that we generate N different pairs (w_1, w_2), where each of the w_i is of degree approximately M (which would be $\sim n/2$ for the basic algorithm and on the order of $n^{2/3}$ in the

Coppersmith variation). We then expect to obtain about

$$Np(M, m)^2$$

pairs (w_1, w_2), where each of the w_i factors into irreducibles from S. Consider now some $k > m$. The probability that a random polynomial of degree $\sim M$ has exactly one irreducible factor of degree k and all others of degrees $\leqslant m$ is about

$$p(M-k, m)I(k)2^{-k} ,$$

where $I(k)$ is the number of irreducible polynomials of degree k. Therefore we expect that the probability that exactly one of w_1 and w_2 has one irreducible factor of degree k and all other factors of both w_1 and w_2 are of degrees $\leqslant m$ is about

$$2p(M-k, m)p(M, m)I(k)2^{-k} .$$

(The probability that both w_1 and w_2 have one irreducible factor of degree k and all others of degree $\leqslant m$ is negligible.) Hence among our N pairs (w_1, w_2) we expect about

$$N_k \sim 2N\, p(M, m)p([n/2]-k, m)I(k)2^{-k} \qquad (5.9)$$

pairs that would be preserved. The number of equations that we expect to obtain from these N_k pairs is $N_k - M_k$, where M_k is the number of irreducible polynomials of degree k that appear in the stored list.

To estimate M_k, we make the assumption that the irreducible polynomials $u(x)$ of degree k that appear in the factorization of the w_i behave as if they were drawn at random from the $I(k)$ such polynomials. When N_k balls are thrown at random into $I(k)$ buckets, the expected number of buckets that end up empty is $I(k)$ times the probability that any single bucket ends up empty. Since the probability that a particular bucket ends up with no balls is

$$\frac{(I(k)-1)^{N_k}}{I(k)^{N_k}} ,$$

the expected number of buckets that we expect to be occupied is

$$I(k)-I(k)(I(k)-1)^{N_k} I(k)^{-N_k} .$$

Therefore we expect to obtain approximately

$$N_k + I(k)((1-I(k)^{-1})^{N_k}-1) \qquad (5.10)$$

additional equations from polynomials of degree k. Since N_k will be comparable to $I(k)$ in magnitude in applications to the index-calculus algorithm, we can approximate (5.10) by

$$N_k + I(k) (\exp(-N_k/I(k))-1) . \qquad (5.11)$$

Since (see Appendix A) $I_k \sim 2^k k^{-1}$ and

$$p(M-k, m) \sim p(M, m) (Mm^{-1} \log_e M/m)^{k/m} ,$$

(5.9) gives us

$$N_k \sim 2 Nk^{-1}p(M, m)^2 (Mm^{-1} \log_e M/m)^{k/m} . \qquad (5.12)$$

Since $|S| \sim 2^{m+1}m^{-1}$, we are interested in N for which $Np(M, m)^2$ is on the order of $2^m m^{-1}$. For such N, though, (5.11) and (5.12) show that the number of additional equations is negligible for $k-m \to \infty$. For $k \sim m$, on the other hand, (5.12) shows that

$$N_k \sim 2 M m^{-2}N \, p(M, m)^2 \, (\log_e M/m) ,$$

which is

$$\sim c'Np(M, m)^2$$

for $m \sim c(M \log_e M)^{1/2}$, which is the case for both the basic algorithm and the Coppersmith variant. Hence we also have

$$N_k \sim c''I(m) ,$$

and (5.11) then shows that we can expect

$$[c''-2^{k-m}(1-\exp(-c''2^{m-k}))]I(m)$$

additional equations, where the implied constants are absolute. Hence when we sum over k, we find that the total number of additional equations we can expect the large irreducible factor variation to generate is proportional to the number that have to be obtained.

The large irreducible factor variation can be quite important for moderate values of n, especially when m is relatively low, as it might have to be to make the solution of the system of linear equations feasible. For example, for $M \sim 65$, $m = 18$, without the large irreducible factor variation we might expect to test about $N \approx 1.04 \times 10^8$ pairs (w_1, w_2), whereas with this variation we expect to need only about 6.7×10^7. For $M \sim 65$ and $m = 12$, the difference is even more dramatic, since without the variation we expect to need $N \approx 1.3 \times 10^{10}$, while with it we need only $N \approx 3.5 \times 10^9$. For $M \sim 100$ and $m = 20$ the figures are $N \approx 4.9 \times 10^{11}$ and $N \approx 2.3 \times 10^{11}$, respectively, while for $M \sim 100$ and $m = 18$ they are $N \approx 2.7 \times 10^{12}$ and $N \approx 1.1 \times 10^{12}$. Thus for values that are of cryptographic significance, the large irreducible variation can shorten the running time of the equation generating phase by a factor of between 2 and 3. Furthermore, it can speed up the second stage of the index-calculus algorithm by an even greater factor, since in addition to the logarithms of the $v \in S$, the cryptanalyst will possess the logarithms of many polynomials of degrees $m+1$, $m+2$,... .

5.5 Early abort strategy

Like the large irreducible factor variation discussed in the preceding section, the early abort strategy is also inspired by a similar technique used in factoring integers. Most of the pairs (w_1, w_2) that are generated turn out to be ultimately useless, whether the large irreducible factor variation is used or not. It would obviously be of great advantage to be able to select those pairs (w_1, w_2) in which both of the w_i are likely to factor into irreducible polynomials from S. The idea behind the early abort strategy is that a polynomial is unlikely to have all its factors in S unless it has many factors of small degree. Asymptotically this variation is unimportant, since factorization of binary polynomials can be accomplished in time polynomial in their degree. For small values of n, though, this variation can be important, as will be shown below.

Let $p_k(r, m)$ denote the probability that a polynomial of degree r has all its irreducible factors of degrees strictly larger than k but at most m. It is easy to obtain recurrences for $p_k(r, m)$

similar to those for $p(r, m)$ derived in Appendix A, which enables one to compute the $p_k(r, m)$ numerically. (It is also possible to obtain asymptotic expansions for the $p_k(r, m)$, but since we know a priori that the early abort strategy is unimportant asymptotically, we will not do it here.) For a polynomial $w(x)$, let $w^*(x)$ denote the product of all the irreducible factors of $w(x)$ of degrees $\leqslant k$ (with their full multiplicity). Let $Q(r, R, m, k)$ denote the probability that a polynomial $w(x)$ of degree r has all its irreducible factors of degrees $\leqslant m$, that deg $w^*(x) \geqslant R$. Then we easily obtain

$$Q(r, R, m, k) = \sum_{j \geqslant R} p(j, k)p_k(r-j, m) .$$

Let $Q^*(r, R, k)$ denote the probability that a random polynomial $w(x)$ of degree r has the property that deg $w^*(x) \geqslant R$. Then we similarly obtain

$$Q^*(r, R, k) = \sum_{j \geqslant R} p(j, k)p_k(r-j, r-j) .$$

The early abort strategy with parameters (k, R) is to discard the pair (w_1, w_2) if either $w_1^*(x)$ or $w_2^*(x)$ has degree $< R$. Let A represent the time needed to check whether both $w_1(x)$ and $w_2(x)$ have all their irreducible factors are of degrees $\leqslant m$, and let B represent the time involved in testing whether the degrees of $w_1^*(x)$ and $w_2^*(x)$ are both $\geqslant R$. Then to obtain one factorization that gives a linear equation for the logarithms of the $v \in S$, the standard index-calculus algorithm has to test about $p([n/2], m)^{-2}$ pairs (w_1, w_2) at a cost of approximately

$$A\, p([n/2], m)^{-2} \tag{5.13}$$

units of time. The early abort strategy has to consider about $Q([n/2], R, m, k)^{-2}$ pairs (w_1, w_2), but of these only about $Q^*([n/2], R, k)^2\, Q([n/2], R, m, k)^{-2}$ pairs have to be subjected to the expensive test of checking if all their irreducible factors have degrees $\leqslant m$. Hence the work involved in obtaining an additional linear equation under the early abort strategy is about

$$\{B + A\, Q^*([n/2], R, k)^2\}\, Q([n/2], R, m, k)^{-2} . \tag{5.14}$$

In Table 1 we present some values of the ratio of the quantity in (5.14) to that in (5.13):

Table 1. Evaluation of the early abort strategy.

n	m	k	R	ratio of (5.14) to (5.13)
128	16	4	5	$2.47\, B/A + 0.412$
128	16	5	5	$1.73\, B/A + 0.452$
200	20	4	5	$2.67\, B/A + 0.445$
200	20	5	6	$2.32\, B/A + 0.396$

We see from this that if $B/A \leq 1/10$, then one can reduce the work required to obtain an additional equation by 30-40%, which might speed up the algorithm by a factor of approximately 1.5.

The success of the early abort strategy is crucially dependent on the ability to quickly find the divisors w_i^* of the w_i that are composed only of irreducible factors of degrees $\leq k$. If we use the procedure suggested in Section 5.3, this can be accomplished quite easily. Given a polynomial $w(x)$ to be tested, we compute its square-free part $w^{(0)}(x)$ and go through the first k steps of the procedure described by (5.8). If $k = 4$, this can be simplified further. Here we only need to know

$$(w^0(x), x^8+x) \quad \text{and} \quad (w^0(x), x^{16}+x) ,$$

and these can be computed by reducing $w^{(0)}(x)$ modulo $x^8 + x$ and modulo $x^{16} + x$, respectively and looking up the greatest common divisors in precomputed tables. We could then decide not to reject $w(x)$ if the difference of the degree of $w^{(0)}(x)$ and the sum of the degrees of the two divisors is small enough. It might also be advantageous to avoid computing $w^{(0)}(x)$ on the first pass compute

$$(w(x), x^8+x) , \quad (w(x), x^{16}+x) ,$$

and accept or reject $w(x)$ depending on how small the difference between the degree of $w(x)$ and the sum of the degrees of those factors is.

One can obtain some further slight gains by using additional conditions further along in the computation of the $w^{(i)}(x)$ defined by (5.8). It seems safe to say, though, that the early abort strategy is unlikely to speed up the linear equation collection phase of the index-calculus algorithm by more than a factor of 2 or so.

5.6 Faster generation of equations in Coppersmith's method

It is possible to significantly speed up the first stage of Coppersmith's variant of the index-calculus algorithm by applying some of the ideas that occur in the second stage of that version. Asymptotically, the improvements are not important, but in practice they are likely to be much more important than all the other variations we have discussed so far, and could speed up the equation-collecting phase of the algorithm by factors of 10 to 20 for $n = 127$, by up to 300 for $n = 521$, and by over 1000 for $n = 1279$.

The idea behind the new variation is that instead of selecting $u_1(x)$ and $u_2(x)$ to be any pair of relatively prime polynomials of degrees $\leqslant B$ each, we select them to increase the chances of $w_1(x)$ and $w_2(x)$ splitting into low degree irreducible factors. To do this, we select a pair $v_1(x)$ and $v_2(x)$ of polynomials of degrees $\leqslant B-1$ (but close to B) such that each is composed of irreducible factors of degrees $\leqslant m$. We then select $u_1(x)$ and $u_2(x)$ of degrees $\leqslant B$ so that $v_1(x) \mid w_1(x)$ and $v_2(x) \mid w_2(x)$. The divisibility condition gives us $\deg v_1(x) + \deg v_2(x) \leqslant 2B-2$ homogeneous linear equations for the $2B$ coefficients of $u_1(x)$ and $u_2(x)$, and so we obtain at least 3 nonzero solutions. Moreover, these solutions can be found very fast, by using gaussian elimination on the $GF(2)$ matrix of size $\leqslant 2B-2$ by $2B$.

When $u_1(x)$ and $u_2(x)$ are selected by the above procedure, the probability of $w_1(x)$ splitting into irreducible factors of degrees $\leqslant m$ ought to be close to $p(h, m)$, and the probability of $w_2(x)$ splitting in this way ought to be close to

$$p(h\,2^k - n + B(2^k - 1) + \deg f_1(x), m) .$$

Since $B = O\,(n^{1/3}\,(\log_e n)^{2/3})$, the form of the asymptotic estimate for the probability of both $w_1(x)$ and $w_2(x)$ splitting is not affected by this improvement. In practice, however, the improvements can be vital.

Some care has to be used in the application of the idea proposed above. The first stage of the index-calculus algorithm requires the generation of $|S| \sim m^{-1}2^{m+1}$ linearly independent equations. The equations generated by the basic version of the algorithm and by the Coppersmith variation are expected to be largely independent of the preceding ones (as long as there are $< |S|$ of them) on heuristic grounds, and this is confirmed by computational experience. That is not the case, however, with the variation proposed above, because in general many pairs $(v_1(x), v_2(x))$ will give rise to the same pair $(w_1(x), w_2(x))$. To circumvent this difficulty, we select B so that the standard Coppersmith algorithm without the variation proposed here would generate about $1.6|S|$ equations. (This involves increasing B by at most 1.) We then implement the present variation, with the new value of B. Essentially all of the $1.6|S|$ equations that would be generated by the standard Coppersmith algorithm can be generated by the new variation with appropriate choices of $v_1(x)$ and $v_2(x)$, and most can be generated in roughly the same number of ways. Hence we can again model this situation in terms of the "balls into buckets" problem described in Section 5.4; we have about $1.6|S|$ buckets corresponding to the equations we can possibly obtain, and we are throwing balls into them corresponding to the equations our variation actually produces. If we obtain about $1.6|S|$ equations all told, approximately $1.6(1-e^{-1})|S| > 1.01|S|$ of them will be distinct, and so it will be overwhelmingly likely that $|S|$ of them will be independent.

In our new variation we do not need to check whether $(u_1(x), u_2(x)) = 1$, and thus whether $(v_1(x), v_2(x)) = 1$. Therefore we can prepare beforehand a list of all polynomials of degrees $\leqslant B-1$ that are composed of irreducible factors of degrees $\leqslant m$, and this will generate a slight additional saving over the standard Coppersmith algorithm. (In order to take full advantage of the sparse matrix techniques of Section 5.7, it might be best to use only irreducible factors of degrees $\leqslant m-5$, say.) The effort needed to compute $u_1(x)$ and $u_2(x)$ (i.e., to solve a small linear system of equations), which is comparable to the work needed to test whether a polynomial has all its irreducible factors of degrees $\leqslant m$, can be amortized over more test polynomials by requiring that degrees of $v_1(x)$ and $v_2(x)$ be $\leqslant B-2$, since that will produce at least 15 nonzero solutions each time.

. There are other ways to speed up the Coppersmith algorithm. One way would be to fix $2B+2-b$ of the coefficients of $u_1(x)$ and $u_2(x)$, where b is maximal subject to being able to store about 2^b small integers. Then, for all irreducible polynomials $u(x)$ of degrees $\leqslant m$, one could quickly compute those choices of the remaining b coefficients for which $w_1(x)$ or $w_2(x)$ is divisible by $u(x)$. All that would need to be stored for each of the 2^b combinations would be the sum of the degrees of the divisors that were found. This variation, however, does not appear as promising as the one discussed above, and it would require some very novel architectures to implement it on a parallel processing machine of the type we will discuss later. Hence we do not explore this variation further.

A slight improvement on the basic idea of this section is to allow $v_1(x)$ and $v_2(x)$ to have different degrees, subject to the requirement that their sum be $\leqslant 2B-2$, so as to make the degrees of $w_1(x)/v_1(x)$ and $w_2(x)/v_2(x)$ more nearly equal.

Another modification to the Coppersmith algorithm was suggested by Mullin and Vanstone [48]. It consists of choosing $w_1(x)$ to be of the form

$$w_1(x) = u_1(x)\, x^{h-a} + u_2(x)$$

for $a = 1$ or 2, say, and selecting

$$w_2(x) \equiv w_1(x)^{2^a}\, x^b \pmod{f(x)},$$

where b is chosen so as to give small degree for $w_2(x)$ after reduction modulo $f(x)$. This might allow the use of slightly lower degree polynomials for $u_1(x)$ and $u_2(x)$ than would otherwise be required, since if $u_1(0) = 1$, the equations this method yields ought to be idependent of those the basic method produces. This modification can be combined with the others suggested here.

5.7 Sparse matrix techniques

So far we have concentrated on variations on the linear equation collection phase of the index-calculus algorithm. However, as we noted in Section 4, the difficulty of solving systems of linear equations seemed for a long time to be an important limiting factor on the algorithm and affected the asymptotic estimate of its running time. For example, in the basic algorithm, if the term 2^{2m} in

(4.16) were replaced by 2^{rm} for any $r > 2$ ($r = 3$ corresponding to the use of gaussian elimination, for example), then the minimum of (4.16) would occur not at $m \sim c_1(n \log_e n)^{1/2}$, but at a smaller value, $m \sim c_1(r) (n \log_e n)^{1/2}$, and would be larger, with c_2 replaced by

$$c_2(r) = r(2(r-1))^{-1/2} (\log_e 2)^{1/2} .$$

In this section, though, we will show that the linear equations produced by the index-calculus algorithm can be solved in time essentially $|S|^2$, where $|S|$ is roughly the number of equations.

The matrices of coefficients of the linear equations generated by the first stage of the index-calculus algorithm are special in that they are very sparse. The reason is that the coefficient vector of each equation is obtained by adding several vectors $(b_v(h))$, indexed by $v \epsilon S$, coming from factorizations of polynomials

$$h = \prod_{v \epsilon S} v^{b_v(h)} .$$

Since the polynomials h are always of degrees $< n$, there can be at most n nonzero $b_v(h)$, and so each equation has at most n nonzero entries. This is a very small number compared to the total number of equations, which is around $\exp(n^{1/3})$ or $\exp(n^{1/2})$. The literature on sparse matrix techniques is immense, as can be seen by looking at [4,6,11,27,61] and the references cited there. Many of the techniques discussed there turn out to be very useful for the index-calculus problem, even though we face a somewhat different problem from the standard one in that we have to do exact computations modulo 2^n-1 as opposed to floating point ones. In the worst case, the problem of solving sparse linear systems efficiently is probably very hard. For example, it is known that given a set of 0−1 vectors $v_1,...,v_r$, each of which contains exactly three 1's, to determine whether there is a subset of them of a given size that is dependent modulo 2 is NP-complete [35]. Thus we cannot hope to find the most efficient worst case algorithm. However, very efficient algorithms can be found.

There are several methods for solving the systems of linear equations that arise in the index-calculus algorithms that run in tone $O(N^{2+\epsilon})$ for every $\epsilon > 0$, where N is the number of equations.

The first ones were developed by D. Coppersmith and the author from an idea of N. K. Karmarkar. This idea was to adapt some of the iterative algorithms that have been developed for solving real, symmetric, positive definite systems of equations [6,11,33,39]. For example, in the original version of the conjugate gradient method [33], in order to solve the system $Ax = y$, where A is a symmetric positive definite real matrix of size N by N, and y is a given real column vector of length N, one can proceed as follows. Let x_0 be an arbitrary vector of length N, and let $P_0 = r_0 = y - Ax_0$. The algorithm then involves $\leqslant N-1$ iterations of the following procedure: given x_i, r_i, and p_i, let

$$a_i = \frac{(r_i, r_i)}{(p_i, Ap_i)} , \tag{5.15a}$$

$$x_{i+1} = x_i + a_i p_i , \tag{5.15b}$$

$$r_{i+1} = r_i - a_i Ap_i , \tag{5.15c}$$

$$b_i = \frac{(r_{i+1}, r_{i+1})}{(r_i, r_i)} , \tag{5.15d}$$

$$p_{i+1} = r_{i+1} + b_i p_i . \tag{5.15e}$$

It can be shown [33] that if the computations are done to infinite precision, the algorithm will find $r_i = 0$ for some $i \leqslant N-1$, and $x = y_i$ will then solve the original system $Ax = y$.

There are several problems with trying to use the conjugate gradient method to solve the systems of linear equations that arise in the index-calculus algorithms. One is that the system is not symmetric, and one has to solve $Bx = y$ where B is not even a square matrix. This problem can be bypassed (as is well known, cf. [33]) by solving the system $Ax = z$, where $A = B^T B$ and $z = B^T y$. Since B will in general be of almost full rank, solutions to $Ax = z$ will usually give us solutions to $Bx = y$. The matrix A will not in general be sparse, but its entries do not have to be computed explicitly, since it is only necessary to compute the vectors Ap_i, and that can be done by multiplying p_i first by B and then B^T. The matrix B can be stored in the sparse form, with rows and columns being given by lists of positions and values of nonzero coefficients.

The main difficulty with the use of the conjugate gradient method is that the basic theory was based on minimizing a quadratic functional, and this does not apply in finite fields. However, as was suggested by Karmarkar, the most important property of the algorithm is that the direction vectors p_i are mutually conjugate (i.e., $(p_i, Ap_j) = 0$ for $i \neq j$), and this is a purely algebraic property. Therefore the algorithm will terminate after at most $n-1$ iterations and will find a solution unless at some stage a vector p_i is encountered such that $(p_i, Ap_i) = 0$. This cannot happen if A is a real positive-definite matrix and $p_i \neq 0$, but can occur over finite fields. If the computations are being done over a large finite field, the probability of this occurring if x_0 is choosen at random is quite low. If the field is small, say $GF(q)$ with small q, this probability is much more significant, and the way to avoid the problem is to choose x_0 to have entries in a larger field, say $GF(q^t)$ for some small $t \epsilon Z^+$.

The adaptation of the conjugate gradient algorithm outlined above has been tested successfully by the author on some small systems. The advantages of the method include not only speed, since only about NQ operations in the field $GF(q^t)$ are required, where Q is the number of nonzero entries in B, and thus $O(\log N)$ or $O((\log N)^2)$ in our problems, but also very modest storage requirements, since aside from the matrix B it is necessary to store the vectors x_i, p_i, r_i for only two consecutive values of i at a time.

An algorithm due to Lanczos [39], somewhat different from the conjugate gradient algorithm, was similarly adapted by Coppersmith to solve the linear systems arising in the index-calculus algorithm. Coppersmith used that method to obtain another solution to the linear system that arose in the implementation of his attack on discrete logarithms in $GF(2^{127})$.

A more elegant method for dealing with the index-calculus linear systems was invented recently by Wiedemann [66]. Suppose first that we wish to solve for x in $Ax = y$, where A is a matrix of size N by N (not necessarily symmetric) over a field $GF(q)$. Let $v_0, v_1, \ldots, v_{2N}$ be vectors of length K, which might be 10 or 20, with v_j consisting of the first K coefficients of the vector $A^j y$. Since to compute the v_j we need only start with y and keep multiplying it by A, without storing all the vectors $A^j y$, we need only $O(KN)$ storage locations, each one capable of storing an element of $GF(q)$, and the number of $GF(q)$ operations to carry out this computation is $O(NQ)$. Now the matrix A satisfies a polynomial equation of degree $\leqslant N$:

$$\sum_{j=0}^{N} c_j A^j = 0, \tag{5.16}$$

and therefore also for any $k \geqslant 0$,

$$\sum_{j=0}^{N} c_j A^{j+k} y = 0 . \tag{5.17}$$

Eq. (5.17) implies that any single component of the $v_0, \ldots, v_{2N}$ satisfies the linear recurrence with characteristic polynomial

$$\sum_{j=0}^{N} c_j z^j . \tag{5.18}$$

Given any sequence of length on the order of N, the Berlekamp-Massey algorithm [29,44,56] finds its minimal characteristic polynomial in $O(N^2)$ operations in the field $GF(q)$. Hence if we apply the Berlekamp-Massey algorithm to each of the K coordinates of the vectors $v_0, \ldots, v_{2N}$, we will in $O(KN^2)$ steps obtain K polynomials whose least common multiple is likely to be the minimal polynomial of A. When we do find that minimal polynomial, and it is of the form (5.18) with $c_0 \neq 0$, then we can easily obtain the desired solution to $Ax = y$ from

$$y = A^0 y = -c_0^{-1} \sum_{j=1}^{N} c_j A^j y$$

$$\tag{5.19}$$

$$= A \left(-c_0^{-1} \sum_{j=1}^{N} c_j A^{j-1} y \right) .$$

If A is nonsingular, then $c_0 \neq 0$, as is easy to see. Conversely, if $c_0 \neq 0$, then A is nonsingular, since we can then write

$$A \sum_{j=1}^{N} c_j A^{j-1} = -c_0 I .$$

In general in index-calculus algorithms, we have to solve a system of the form $Ax = y$, where A is of size M by N, with $M > N$ (but $M-N$ small). One way to reduce to the earlier case of a nonsingular square matrix is to take a submatrix A' of A of size N by N, and apply the algorithm presented above to $(A')^T x = z$ for some random vector z. If A' turns out to be nonsingular, we can then go back and search for solutions to $A'x = y$, which is what we are interested in. If A' is singular, though, we will obtain a linear dependency among the rows of A'. This means we can discard one of the rows of A' that was involved in that dependency and replace it with another row of that part of A that has not been used yet. After a few steps, we ought to obtain a nonsingular A', and this will enable us to solve for x in $Ax = y$. Wiedemann [66] also has a deterministic algorithm, which may not be as practical, however.

We conclude this section by discussing some very simple methods for solving sparse systems of equations. Some of these methods can be used as a preliminary step before the application of Wiedemann's algorithm, say, since they serve to reduce the effective size of the matrix that has to be dealt with. In some cases these methods by themselves could be just about as efficient as the techniques described above. These methods are based on a simple observation that has often been made in the work on sparse matrices (cf. [6]), namely that if a matrix is noticeably sparser on one end than on the other, then it is better to start gaussian elimination from the sparse end. In our case, if we arrange the matrix of coefficients so that the columns correspond to polynomials $v \in S$ sorted by increasing degree, then the right side of the matrix will be very sparse. (If we use the fast version for generating the h^* that is presented in Section 5.3, it is necessary to choose the random $v_r \in S$ to have only low degrees for this to remain true.) To see just how sparse that matrix is, consider the Coppersmith algorithm in $GF(2^n)$, with k, m, and B chosen to satisfy (4.34a-c) with α satisfying (4.38), and β and γ satisfying $\beta = \gamma$ and (4.40). If we take $M \sim m^{-1}2^m$, then the matrix of coefficients will have about $2M$ rows and $2M$ columns, with columns $M+1, \ldots, 2M$ (approximately) corresponding to the irreducible polynomials of degree m. We now consider those columns. Any row in the matrix comes from adding two vectors of discrete logarithm coefficients from factorization of two polynomials of degrees about $B \cdot 2^k$, both of which are divisible only by irreducible factors of degrees $\leqslant m$. The probability that a polynomial of degree $B \cdot 2^k$, which factors into irreducibles of degrees $\leqslant m$, also is divisible by a particular chosen irreducible polynomial of degree exactly m is approximately

$$\frac{2^{-m}p(B2^k-m,m)}{p(B2^k,m)},$$

which, by Lemma A.3 of Appendix A, is

$$\sim 2^{-m}m^{-1}B2^k\log(B2^k/m).$$

Therefore the probability that any particular entry in the last M columns of the matrix is nonzero is about

$$2^{-(m-1)}m^{-1}B2^k\log(B2^k/m). \tag{5.20}$$

(The factor 2 comes from the fact that we are adding two vectors.) For the choices of $B, 2^k$, and m that were specified, this becomes δM^{-1}, where

$$\delta = 2\alpha\gamma\beta^{-2}/3 = 2\beta^{-3/2}/3 = \log 2 = 0.6931....$$

(Exactly the same asymptotic result also applies to the basic index-calculus algorithm.) Therefore, by the "balls into buckets" model, we expect that with probability about

$$(1-\delta M^{-1})^{2M} \approx \exp(-2\delta) = 1/4,$$

any column among the last M will contain only zeros. This means that about $M/4$ of the M irreducible polynomials of degree m will not appear in any of the factorizations and so the data base obtained from the first phase will be missing those values. More importantly, it means that it was not necessary to obtain all of the $2M$ equations, as $7M/4$ would have sufficed. (In fact fewer than $7M/4$, since with that few equations, the chances of obtaining a zero column would be even larger, and in addition we would also have some irreducible polynomials of degrees $m-1, m-2$, etc., which would not appear in the equations.) In addition, the probability of a particular column among the last M having just a single nonzero coefficient is about

$$2M\cdot\delta M^{-1}(1-\delta M^{-1})^{2M-1} \approx 2\delta\exp(-2\delta) = (\log 2)/2 = 0.346...$$

Thus an additional 0.346M of the last M columns would have a single nonzero coefficient, so that we could remove those columns together with the rows in which those columns have nonzero coefficients, solve the remaining system, and then obtain the values of logarithms corresponding to the deleted columns by back substitution. (Occasionally a row might contain two nonzero coefficients which are the only such in their columns, which would prevent recovery of the values of the corresponding logarithms, but that is not a significant problem.) Furthermore, removal of those rows and columns would create more columns with only a single nonzero coefficient, so that the size of the matrix could be cut down by more than 0.35M. However, both simulations and heuristic arguments show that if we proceed to carry out standard gaussian elimination, proceeding from the sparse end, then very rapid fill-in occurs. Therefore one does have to be careful about algorithms that are used.

The above discussion of just how sparse the index-calculus algorithms matrices are was meant to motivate the following method. It will be helpful to explain it in terms of operating on the full matrix, although in practice the matrix would be stored in the sparse encoding, using lists of nonzero coefficients and their positions for rows and columns, just as in the case of the algorithms discussed above. The algorithm is as follows:

Step 1:   *Delete all columns which have a single nonzero coefficient and the rows in which those columns have nonzero coefficients.*

Step 1 is repeated until there are no more columns with a single nonzero entry.

Step 2:   *Select those αM columns which have the largest number of nonzero elements for some α > 0. Call these columns "heavy," the others "light."*

A typical value of α might be 1/32. The entries in the "heavy" columns for every given row might be stored on a disk, with a pointer attached to the row list indicating the storage location. These pointers would have coefficients attached to them, which are set to 1 initially. The weight of a row is then defined as the number of nonzero coefficients in its "light" columns.

Step 3:   *Eliminate variables corresponding to rows of weight 1 by subtracting appropriate multiples of those rows from other rows that have nonzero coefficients corresponding to those variables.*

During execution of Step 3, if u times row i is to be subtracted from row j, the pointers attached to row j are to have added to them the pointers of row i, with their coefficients multiplied by u. Step 3 is to be repeated until there are no more rows of weight 1. At the end of this process there are likely to be many more equations than unknowns. We can then perform the following operation.

Step 4: If r rows are excess, drop the r rows with highest weight.

We now iterate Step 1, and then Step 3. We then go on to the next procedure. Note that if a variable indexed by j, say, appears in rows of weights $2 \leqslant w_1 \leqslant w_2 \leqslant \cdots \leqslant w_k$, then eliminating that variable using a row of weight w_i will increase the number of nonzero entries in the matrix (after deletion of the row of weight w_i and the column corresponding to our variable) by

$$(w_i-1)(k-1) - w_i - (k-1) = (w_i-2)(k-1) - w_i . \tag{5.21}$$

Hence to minimize the amount of fill-in, we need to choose that variable and that w_i (which clearly equals w_1) for which (5.21) is minimized. Keeping track of this quantity is fairly easy if we use a priority queue data structure.

Step 5: Eliminate that variable which causes the least amount of fill-in.

The algorithm outlined above can be implemented to run very fast, and it reduces the problem of solving a roughly $2M$ by $2M$ system to that of solving an αM by αM system. What is perhaps most remarkable, if the original system is sufficiently sparse, only the first few steps of the algorithm are needed. For example, if the elements of the matrix are chosen independently at random, so that the probability of an entry in the last M columns being nonzero is δM^{-1}, in the next $M/2$ column is $2\delta M^{-1}$, etc., where $\delta \leqslant 0.85$ (compared to $\delta = 0.693...$ for the optimal case of Coppersmith's algorithm), and $\alpha = 1/32$, than Steps 1-4 of the algorithm are all that is needed, since by the time they are completed, there is nothing left of the "light" portion of the matrix. This result is confirmed by simulations (with systems of sizes up to 96,000) and by heuristic arguments.

The method presented above draws on ideas that are well known in the literature on sparse matrices (cf. [11]). Moreover, some of these ideas have already been used in the factoring integers and computing discrete logarithms. For example, J. Davenport in his computations related to Coppersmith's algorithm [19] used some heuristic methods to minimize fill-in. Such methods were also used during the execution of the Blake et al. [8] version of the basic index-calculus algorithm in $GF(2^{127})$. According to R. Mullin (private communication), the system of about 16,500 equations in about that many variables ($m=17$ was used) was reduced by methods similar to those presented above to a system of size under 1000, which was then solved by ordinary gaussian elimination. Moreover, their procedure did not involve such tricks as always choosing the equation with fewest nonzero entries during elimination, which appear to result in dramatic improvements in performance. Therefore we expect these methods to be quite useful.

6. Practical and impractical implementations

Blake, Fuji-Hara, Mullin, and Vanstone [8] have successfully tested the basic index-calculus algorithm on fields up to $GF(2^{127})$. They estimated that with their VAX 11/780, a relatively slow minicomputer, it would have taken them many CPU months to carry out the first stage of the algorithm for $GF(2^{127})$ with $m = 17$. On the HEP, a powerful multiprocessor to which they obtained access, their implementation of the algorithm took about 8 hours for the first stage, of which about one hour was devoted to solving linear equations. (Their systematic equations method produced a substantial fraction of all the required equations.) Once the first stage is completed, the second stage is expected to take around 1 CPU hour per logarithm even on the VAX 11/780. On the IBM 3081K, Coppersmith estimated that the equation collecting phase for $GF(2^{127})$ would take around 9 hours with the basic algorithm. Using his own variation, Coppersmith was able to find all the necessary polynomials (for $m = 12$) in 11 minutes [19]. (The factorization of the polynomials to obtain the actual equations took 8 minutes, and solution of the equations took 20 minutes, but these tasks were performed with a general purpose symbolic manipulation program, and so could undoubtedly be speeded up very substantially.) Further speedups, perhaps by a factor of 30 to 50, could be obtained by combining the variation proposed in Section 5.6, which might gain a factor of 10 to 20, with those of sections 5.4 and 5.5, which together might gain a factor of 2 or 3. Using the Cray-1 might gain an additional factor of 10 or so, because it is perhaps 5 times faster than the IBM 3081K and because it could store and manipulate the test polynomials (of degrees ≤ 42) in single words. Thus we can expect that with current supercomputers the equation collecting part of the first phase of the algorithm can be completed in around one second. Since the database produced by the algorithm is not very large (16,510 127-bit numbers for $m = 17$ in the basic algorithm and 747 numbers for $m = 12$ in the Coppersmith variation), this means that individual logarithms in $GF(2^{127})$ can now be computed even on personal computers. Therefore $GF(2^{127})$ ought to be regarded as completely unsuitable for cryptographic applications. Our intention here is to explore what other fields might be appropriate.

We first consider the basic algorithm. Although it has been made obsolete by the Coppersmith variation in applications to the fields $GF(2^n)$, it is worth analyzing in detail, since by comparing our estimates to actual running times we will obtain a better idea of how accurate the estimates are.

In Section 5 we presented briefly a number of variations on the basic index-calculus algorithm. These variations were not analyzed very carefully, since we were interested only in the order of magnitude of the improvements that can be obtained from such techniques. The general conclusion to be drawn from that section is that the time to generate the pairs (w_1, w_2), can probably be neglected. The work needed to obtain $|S|$ equations is probably no more than and at least 1/5 of the work needed to test

$$|S| \, p([n/2], m)^{-2}$$

pairs (w_1, w_2) by the procedure outlined in Section 4.3 to see whether all the irreducible factors of each of the w_i are in S. To test each w_i takes about $m/2$ operations of the form (4.8), each of which involves a squaring modulo a polynomial of degree perhaps $n/3$ on average (since the degrees of the $w^{(i)}(x)$ will be decreasing, especially if we use the early abort strategy with additional test along the way to discard pairs (w_1, w_2) that are not factoring satisfactorily), a greatest common divisor operation or two polynomials of degrees around $n/3$, and a division, which will usually be trivial.

To evaluate the significance of the index-calculus algorithm for cryptographic schemes, we have to look at the effect of parallel processing and at speeds of modern circuits. We will assume that no exotic algorithms, such as fast integer multiplication using the Fast Fourier Transform [10] are to be used, since they are probably not practical for n on the order of several hundred. Since a cryptographic scheme ought to be several orders of magnitude too hard to break, we will only try to be accurate within a factor of 10 or so.

It appears that at present, custom VLSI chips could be built that would perform about 10^8 operations per second, where each operation would consist of a shift of a register of length 200 to 300 or else an exclusive or of two such registers. Semi-custom chips, which would be much easier to design and cheaper to produce, could operate at about 10^7 operations per second. Within the next decade or so, these speeds might increase by a factor of 10, so custom chips might do 10^9 operations per second, while semi-custom ones do 10^8. General purpose supercomputers like the Cray-1 can do about 10^8 operations per second when running in vector mode to take advantage of parallel processing, where each operation consists of a shift or exclusive or of 64-bit words. The structure of the index-calculus algorithm lends itself to parallel processing, but the fact that coefficients of polynomials would often take more than a single machine word to store would cause a substantial slowdown in operations, perhaps to a level of 10^7 operations per second. The next generation of supercomputers, such as the Cray-2, will be about 10 times faster, and might run at the equivalent of 10^8 operations per second.

The number of shifts and exclusive or's that are involved in squaring a polynomial of degree $\sim n/3$ modulo another polynomial of roughly that same degree and then in taking the greatest common divisor of two polynomials of degrees $\sim n/3$ can be roughly estimated by $3n$. Therefore each of the roughly $|S| \, p([n/2], m)^{-2}$ pairs (w_1, w_2) that are generated can be expected to require about $3mn$ operations. (Various branchings and the like would make the actual algorithm slower, but this would be compensated somewhat by the factor of 3 or more that we might gain from using the large irreducible factor and the early abort variations, and the method of systematic equations. Note also that almost always it is only necessary to test w_1, since when it turns out not to factor in the desired way, there is no need to test w_2.) We therefore expect that about

$$n \, 2^{m+3} p([n/2], m)^{-2} \qquad (6.1)$$

operations might be needed to generate the linear equations for the $\log_g v$, $v \in S$. Below we give approximations to the minimal values of (6.1) for various values of n as m varies (only values of $m \leqslant 40$ were considered):

Table 2. Operation count for the basic algorithm.

n	minimum of (6.1)	m
120	3.3×10^{11}	19
160	2.9×10^{13}	23
200	1.6×10^{15}	26
240	6.5×10^{16}	29
280	2.0×10^{18}	32
320	5.2×10^{19}	35
360	1.1×10^{21}	37
400	2.1×10^{22}	40
500	3.5×10^{25}	40

We will now temporarily neglect the effort needed to solve the linear equations that are generated, and discuss for which n and m one could hope to generate the required linear equations with various hardware configurations. We will assume that the equations are to be generated within one year, roughly 3×10^7 seconds. If we use a single supercomputer, we can hope to carry out between 3×10^{14} and 3×10^{15} operations in that year. If we use a massively parallel machine with M special chips, we can expect to carry out between $3 \times 10^{14} M$ and $3 \times 10^{16} M$ operations in a year, depending on the technology that is used. Comparing these figures with those in the table in the preceding paragraph we see that even under our very optimistic assumptions, a general supercomputer could not assemble the required set of linear equations in under a year if $n \geq 240$, say, whereas it probably could for $n \leq 180$. On the other hand, even a relatively modest special purpose processor using 10^4 semi-custom chips based on current technology could perform about 3×10^{18} operations per year, and so could probably cope with $n \geq 260$, and perhaps with $n \geq 280$, but probably not much beyond it. A very ambitious processor, using 10^6 custom designed chips operating at speeds that might become attainable in the next decade could do about 3×10^{22} operations per year, and could probably generate the needed equations for $n \leq 380$, but probably not for $n \geq 420$.

The estimates made above are probably quite accurate, as is confirmed by comparing the numbers in Table 2 with the results of the $GF(2^{127})$ computations of [8]. Interpolating between the values in Table 2, we might expect that $GF(2^{127})$ might require about 10^{12} operations on a modern supercomputer, which is roughly what can be done in a day to a week. On the HEP, which is one of the modern multiprocessor supercomputers, the actual running time was about 7 hours, even though the method of systematic equations yielded about half of the equations practically for free.

The discussion in the preceding paragraph dealt only with the equation collection phase of the algorithm. The main reason for this is that the methods discussed in Section 5.7 make solving those equations rather negligible. However, in some cases this part of the algorithm might be nontrivial, since it would require doing arithmetic modulo 2^n-1. It is possible to envisage VLSI chips that multiply n-bit integers very fast, but such chips have impractically large areas. At the present time the best practical designs appear to be able to multiply two n-bit integers modulo another n-bit integer in about n clock periods (cf. [12]). Therefore we can expect that special purpose chips could perform between $n^{-1}10^7$ and $n^{-1}10^9$ multiplications modulo 2^n-1 per second, depending on the technology. In the case of a modern supercomputer, which could possibly perform about 10^8 multiplications on 32-bit words per second, we could expect about $10^8/(10(n/32)^2) \approx 10^{10}n^{-2}$ modular multiplications per second, and this will probably go up to $10^{11}n^{-2}$ in the next generation of supercomputers. (The factor 10 is there largely to compensate for the difficulty of working with multi-word numbers. We ignore the fact that many modern computers, such as the Cray-1, only allow 24-bit integer multiplication.)

In many situations, solving linear equations should be regarded as a limiting factor not so much due to its high operation count, but rather due to its requirements for a large memory and operation synchronization. A special purpose multiprocessor for the collection of equations is relatively simple to build. Each of the processors in it is quite simple, with essentially no storage, and these processors can operate independently of each other. Every once in a while one of these processors will find a factorization of the desired kind, which will then be sent to a central processor for storage. This also means that a multiprocessor of this kind would be fault-tolerant, since any factorization obtained by a small processor could be easily checked either by the central processor or by other processors without affecting the running time significantly. Therefore it would be very easy to build a multiprocessor to collect equations. On the other hand, a multiprocessor built for solving linear equations would require a very large memory, all the processors in it would have to operate synchronomsly under the control of the central unit, and it would have to operate essentially without errors. Such a multiprocessor would be much harder to build, and so we will often consider the use of a supercomputer for the equation solving phase together with a modest special purpose multiprocessor for the equation collecting phase.

In the case of the basic algorithm, the estimates derived from Table 2 for the running time of the algorithm do change somewhat if we consider using a modern supercomputer to solve the equations. For example, for $n = 400$, the value 2.1×10^{22} for the number of operations to find the needed equations requires the use of $m = 40$, which means that the number of unknowns (and equation) is around 5×10^{10}. Moreover, each equation might involve around 20 nonzero coefficients (which are usually equal to 1, though). Thus even with the use of the method described at the end of Section 5.7 to reduce the number of equations, of sorting on a disk, and sophisticated data structures, it seems that $m = 40$ would not be practical. However, use of $m = 35$ would reduce the size of the storage required by a factor of about 30, while increasing the number of operations to obtain the linear equations to only 3.5×10^{22}. Further reduction of m, to ≤ 30, would bring solution of the linear equations within practical reach without drastically increasing the effort needed for the equation collection phase.

The basic conclusion to be drawn from the preceding discussion is that using the basic algorithm, a supercomputer could probably be used to complete the first phase for $n \leq 200$, but almost certainly not for $n \geq 300$. Using a relatively simple special purpose multiprocessor to assemble the equation and a supercomputer to solve them might be feasible for $n \leq 300$. Finally, even a very ambitious special purpose machine with 10^6 chips operating at 1 nanosecond per operation would not suffice for $n \geq 500$.

The above discussion applied to the basic index-calculus algorithm. We next analyze the Coppersmith variation. In this case the performance of the algorithm can again be improved through use of the large irreducible factor variation and the early abort strategy, but again probably only by a factor of 3 to 5. Hence we will neglect these techniques. On the other hand, the method described in Section 5.6 leads to a speedup by two or three orders of magnitude, and so we will take it into account. As before, we first neglect the effort needed to solve the linear equations, and estimate only the work involved in finding those equations.

In the first stage of the Coppersmith algorithm, the time to generate the polynomials $w_1(x)$ and $w_2(x)$ can probably be neglected, especially since for each choice of $v_1(x)$ and $v_2(x)$ in the variation of Section 5.6 we will typically obtain several $(w_1(x), w_2(x))$ pairs. The main work consists of testing the pairs (w_1, w_2) to see whether all the irreducible factors of the w_i are in S. By a reasoning almost identical to that used in analyzing the basic algorithm (but with n replaced by $2h$), we see that this ought to take about $6mh$ exclusive or's and shifts. Hence the total number of such operations might be around

$$h 2^{m+4} p(h, m)^{-1} p(M, m)^{-1} ,$$
(6.2)

with

$$M = \max \left(h 2^k - n + 2^k d_1 - d_2 + \deg f_1(x), (2^k - 1) d_2 \right) ,$$

where we select $\deg u_i(x) \approx \deg v_i(x) \approx d_i$, $i = 1, 2$. (There is occasionally some slight advantage in allowing different degree bounds for u_1 and u_2.) We also have to satisfy

$$p(h+d_1, m) p(M+d_2, m) 2^{d_1+d_2+1} \geq m^{-1} 2^{m+2}$$

in order to have enough possible equations.

In the table below we present approximate values for the minimal number of operations that these estimates suggest. In the preparation of this table, $\deg f_1(x)$ was taken to be 10, since that is approximately what it is for such cryptographically important values of n as 521, 607, 881, and 1279. Also, only values of $m \leqslant 40$ were considered.

Table 3. Operation count for Coppersmith's algorithm (equation collecting phase only).

n	approximate minimum of (6.2)	2^k	h	m	d_1	d_2
280	4.5×10^{11}	4	70	20	14	16
400	4.8×10^{13}	4	100	23	17	20
520	3.0×10^{15}	4	130	27	20	22
700	7.3×10^{17}	4	175	31	24	26
880	3.8×10^{18}	8	110	36	27	29
1060	6.0×10^{20}	8	133	38	29	31
1280	1.3×10^{22}	8	160	39	32	33

The above table dealt with the equation collection phase of Coppersmith's algorithm. As in the case of the basic algorithm, the equation solution phase would be limited more by the large memory size needed then by the number of operations. If we consider somewhat smaller values of m, we obtain Table 4.

There are two entries in the table for each n. It is possible to obtain finer estimates than in Table 4 by using what are in effect fractional values of m. What that would mean, in practice, is that S might consist of all the irreducible polynomials of degrees $\leqslant m'$ and one third of those of degree $m'+1$, say. However, since Table 4 is meant to be used only as a rough guide, accurate only to within an order of magnitude, there is no point in doing this.

Table 4. Operation count for Coppersmith's algorithm (taking into account limitations of equation solving pha

n	value of (6.2)	2^k	h	m	d_1	d_2
280	2.7×10^{12}	4	70	16	17	20
280	4.7×10^{11}	4	70	19	14	17
400	1.3×10^{14}	4	100	20	19	22
400	7.3×10^{13}	4	100	21	18	21
520	1.3×10^{16}	4	130	22	23	25
520	7.0×10^{15}	4	130	23	22	24
700	1.2×10^{19}	4	175	24	28	31
700	2.6×10^{18}	4	175	26	26	29
880	2.0×10^{21}	4	220	27	32	34
880	4.3×10^{20}	4	220	29	30	32
1060	2.4×10^{24}	8	133	30	38	40
1060	1.2×10^{23}	8	133	31	35	37
1280	4.3×10^{26}	8	160	31	43	44
1280	1.1×10^{24}	8	160	33	37	38
2000	1.7×10^{30}	8	250	36	48	50
2000	1.3×10^{29}	8	250	37	46	47

If we neglect the time needed to solve the system of linear equations, we see that a single supercomputer could probably compute the database for $n \leq 460$ in about a year, and the next generation might be able to do it for $n \leq 520$. On the other hand, $n \geq 800$ would be safe from such attacks. If we assume that methods such as those of Section 5.7 are to be used to solve the linear equations, then Table 4 suggests that $n \geq 700$ is safe even from the next generation of supercomputers, while $n \leq 500$ probably isn't.

A special purpose processor using 10^4 chips running at 100 nanoseconds per cycle might be able to assemble the equations for $n \leq 700$ in about a year, and these equations could probably be solved in about that much time on a supercomputer. For $n \approx 520$, though, a processor consisting of only about 100 chips of this kind might be able to find the equations in about a year (with $m = 22$), and they could then be solved in about a month on a supercomputer like the Cray-2. (Alternatively, with 10^3 chips in the equation collecting phase, a supercomputer might be needed for only a couple of days.) A very fanciful multiprocessor with 10^6 chips running at 1 nanosecond per cycle might be able to assemble the required equations for $n \leq 1280$ and solve them in between 1 and 10 years. Since even relatively small improvements to presently known algorithms could lower the operation count by a factor of 10 or 100, this means that even $n = 1279$ should not be considered safe, since it could then be broken using a less ambitious machine. (Note that a machine using 10^6 chips running at around 10 nanoseconds per cycle was proposed by Diffie and Hellman [24] for finding a DES key in about a day through exhaustive search. Such a machine was generally thought to be too ambitious for the then current technology, but it seems to be generally accepted that it could be built for some tens of millions of dollars by 1990.) On the other hand, $n \geq 2200$ is about 10^6 times harder than $n \sim 1280$, and so can be considered safe, barring any new major breakthroughs in discrete logarithm algorithms.

7. Algorithms in $GF(p)$, p prime

The Silver-Pohlig-Hellman algorithm presented in Section 2 obviously applies directly to prime fields. The basic version of the index-calculus algorithm that has been presented so far can also be applied mutatis mutandis to the computation of discrete logarithms in fields $GF(p)$, p a prime. However, its simplest adaptation, even with the use of the early abort strategy [53], results in a running time for the first phase of about

$$L^{(5/2)^{1/2}} = L^{1.581\ldots}, \tag{7.1}$$

where L stands for any quantity that is

$$L = \exp((1+o(1))\ (\log_e p\ \log_e \log_e p)^{1/2})\ \text{as}\ n \to \infty\ . \tag{7.2}$$

It was recently found, however, that there are several algorithms which run in time L [20]. The second phases of those algorithms can be used to find individual logarithms in time $L^{1/2}$ [20].

The discovery of the new algorithms for computing discrete logarithms in fields $GF(p)$ means that discrete logarithms in these fields are just about as hard to compute as it is to factor integers of size about p, provided that the field $GF(p)$ is changing. If the field were to stay fixed, then there would be an initial phase that would be about as hard to do as factoring a general integer around p, but then each individual logarithm would be relatively easy to compute.

Until recently, it was thought that the Schnorr-Lenstra algorithm [60] was the only factorization algorithm that ran in time L, with various other methods, such as the Pomerance quadratic sieve [53] requiring time $L^{1+\delta}$ for various $\delta > 0$. Those conclusions were based on the assumption that one had to use general matrix inversion algorithms to solve systems of linear equations. Now, with the methods described in Section 5.7 that take advantage of the sparseness of those systems, there are several algorithms, including the quadratic sieve and the Schroeppel linear sieve, and the new ones proposed in [20], which factor integers of size around p in time L.

It is quite possible that further progress in both discrete logarithm and factorization algorithms could be made in the near future. For example, if one can find, for a given p, integers a, b, and c such that they are all $O(p^{1/3+\epsilon})$ and such that

$$a^3 \equiv b^2 c \pmod{p},\ a^3 \neq b^2 c\ , \tag{7.3}$$

then one obtains a discrete logarithm algorithm and a factorization algorithm with running time

$$L^{(2/3)^{1/2}} = L^{0.8164\ldots} \tag{7.4}$$

for the first phase [20]. Such a, b, and c are expected to exist for all p, and the problem is to construct an algorithm that finds them. In some cases they can be found. For example, if $p = a^3 - c$ for $c = O(p^{1/3})$, then (7.3) is satisfied with $b=1$. (This version is the "cubic sieve" of Reyneri.) Any algorithm for constructing a, b, and c satisfying (7.3) would help about equally in factoring integers and computing discrete logarithms. In general, while there are algorithms for factorization that do not generalize to give discrete logarithm algorithms (the Schnorr-Lenstra algorithm [60], for example), the converse is not the case. Therefore it seems fairly safe to say that discrete logarithms are at least as hard as factoring and likely to remain so.

The idea behind the Coppersmith variant cannot be extended to the fields $GF(p)$ with p prime. That idea is based on the fact that squaring is a linear operation in $GF(2)$, so that if the difference of two polynomials over $GF(2)$ is of low degree, so is the difference of the squares of those polynomials. Nothing like this phenomenon seems to hold in the fields $GF(p)$, p prime.

8. Cryptographic implications

The preceding sections presented descriptions of the most important known algorithms for computing discrete logarithms in finite fields. The conclusions to be drawn from the discussion of these algorithms is that great care should be exercised in the choice of the fields $GF(q)$ to be used in any of the cryptosystems described in the Introduction. The Silver-Pohlig-Hellman algorithm presented in Section 2 has running time on the order of $\sqrt{p}$, where p is the largest prime factor of $q-1$. It is possible to decrease the $\sqrt{p}$ running time in cases where many discrete logarithms in the same field are to be computed, but only at the cost of a substantially longer preprocessing stage. Of the cryptosystems based on discrete logarithms, probably the most likely ones to be implemented are the authentication and key exchange ones (cf. [38,59,69]). To crack one of these systems, it is only necessary to compute one discrete logarithm, since that gives the codebreaker a valid key or password, with which he can then either impersonate a valid user or forge enciphered messages. Thus it can be expected that any discrete logarithm method would be used relatively infrequently in cryptanalysis, so that optimizing the form of the Silver-Pohlig-Hellman algorithm would yield both the preprocessing stage and the average running time on the order of $\sqrt{p}$, or at least within a factor of 100 or so of $\sqrt{p}$. The Silver-Pohlig-Hellman algorithm can be parallelized to a very large extent, the main limitation arising from the need to have a very large memory, on the order of $\sqrt{p}$ bits, which would be accessible from all the independent elements. This means that values of $p \leq 10^{25}$, say, ought to be avoided in cryptographic applications. On the other hand, for $p \geq 10^{40}$, the Silver-Pohlig-Hellman algorithm appears impractical for the foreseeable future.

The limitation that $q-1$ have at least one large prime factor, which is imposed by the Silver-Pohlig-Hellman algorithm, has led to suggestions that fields $GF(2^n)$ be used for which 2^n-1 is a prime. Primes of the form 2^n-1 are known as Mersenne primes, and the known ones are listed in Table 5. One disadvantage of Mersenne primes is that there are relatively few of them. In particular, there are wide gaps between the consecutive Mersenne primes $2^{607} - 1$, $2^{1279} - 1$, and $2^{2203}-1$. The index-calculus algorithm is not very sensitive to the factorization of 2^n-1, and so it seems safe to use values of n for which 2^n-1 is not prime, provided it has a large prime factor ($\geq 10^{40}$, preferably, for reasons discussed above). Table 6 presents a selection of values of n between 127 and 521 for which the complete factorization of $2^n - 1$ is known and includes a very large prime factor. (This table is drawn from [14], except that the primality of the 105-digit factor of $2^{373} - 1$ was proved by the author using the Cohen-Lenstra [17] version of the Adleman-Pomerance-Rumely primality test [2].) Also included are the two values $n = 881$ and $n = 1063$, for which the cofactors have not been shown to be prime, although they almost definitely are, since they pass pseudoprime tests. Any one of these values of n will give a cryptosystem that is resistant to attacks by the Silver-Pohlig-Hellman algorithm.

It would be very desirable to have some additional entries in Table 6 to fill in the gap in Table 5 between $n = 1279$ and $n = 2203$. Unfortunately no prime values of n in that range are known for which 2^n-1 has been shown to contain a very large prime factor. It is possible to obtain composite values of n with this property (any multiple of 127 or 241 will do), but these are probably best avoided, since logarithms in these fields $GF(2^n)$ might be easy to compute. More generally, it might be advisable to avoid fields $GF(q)$ which have large subfields. Hellman and Reyneri [30] raised the possibility that the fields $GF(p^2)$ with p prime might be more secure than the fields $GF(p)$, since the index-calculus algorithm did not seem to extend to them. However, ElGamal [25] has shown how to modify the index-calculus algorithm to apply to most of the fields $GF(p^2)$. Furthermore, ElGamal's approach can be extended to all the fields $GF(p^2)$, and in fact to fields

$GF(p^n)$ with n bounded. Thus fields of this kind appear not to offer increased security. In fact, these fields may be very weak because of the possibility of moving between the field and its subfields. As an example of the danger that exists, it can be shown that if $p+1$ is divisible only by small primes, computing logarithms in $GF(p^2)$ is only about as hard as in $GF(p)$.

In the case of $GF(2^{127})$, the first stage of the index-calculus algorithm can now be carried out in a matter of hours on a minicomputer. Furthermore, once the database is generated, individual logarithms can be computed rapidly even on today's personal computers. For that reason the field $GF(2^{127})$ should be regarded as very unsafe for cryptographic applications.

Once n moves up to 400 or so, the first stage of the index-calculus algorithm becomes infeasible to carry out in the fields $GF(2^n)$ by anyone not having access to computing resources comparable to those of a modern supercomputer. However, if somebody does use a supercomputer or a large number of smaller machines to carry out the first stage, and makes the database widely available, anyone with access to even a medium speed computer can rapidly compute individual logarithms.

When n reaches 700 or so, the first stage becomes infeasible even with a supercomputer. However, a relatively modest special purpose device consisting of about 10^4 semi-custom chips would enable a cryptanalyst to assemble the desired database even in these ranges. Such a special purpose computer might be assembled as part of a university project (cf. [62]). Furthermore, computations of individual logarithms could still be performed on any relatively fast computer. Special purpose machines of this kind, but either with more special chips or with faster chips could probably be used to assemble the databases for n up to perhaps 1200, but might have difficulty solving the system of linear equations.

The fields $GF(2^n)$ have been preferred for cryptographic applications because of ease of implementation. There are penalties for this gain, though. One is that the codebreaker's implementation is correspondingly easy to carry out. Another is that logarithms in the fields $GF(2^n)$ are much easier to compute than in the fields $GF(p)$ for p a prime, $p \sim 2^n$, especially now

Table 5. Known Mersenne primes $2^p - 1$.

VALUES OF p FOR WHICH
$2^p - 1$ IS PRIME

2
3
5
7
13
17
19
31
61
89
107
127
521
607
1,279
2,203
2,281
3,217
4,253
4,423
9,689
9,941
11,213
19,937
21,701
23,209
44,497
86,243
132,049

that the Coppersmith algorithm is available [18,19]. Still another disadvantage of the fields $GF(2^n)$ as compared with the prime fields of the same order is that there are very few of them. All of the fields $GF(2^n)$ with a fixed value of n are isomorphic, and so can be regarded as essentially the same field. On the other hand, there are many primes p with $2^{n-1} < p < 2^n$. This is important, since in the index-calculus algorithm (and to some extent also in the Silver-Pohlig-Hellman algorithm) the initial preprocessing stage has to be done only once, and once it's done, individual logarithms are computable relatively fast. If the field can be changed, say every month or every year, the cryptanalyst will have only that long on average to assemble his database. (This may not be a serious strengthening of security in the case of information that has to be kept secret for extended periods of time.) Therefore having only a few fields to choose from makes a cryptosystem less

Table 6. Factorization of Mersenne numbers $2^p - 1$ (p prime) which contain a very large prime factor. Pn denotes a prime of n decimal digits, $PRPn$ a probable prime of n digits.

p	Factorization of $2^p - 1$
167	$2349023 \cdot P44$
197	$7487 \cdot P56$
227	$269863334377777017 \cdot P52$
241	$220000409 \cdot P66$
269	$13822297 \cdot P74$
281	$80929 \cdot P80$
307	$14608903 \cdot 85798519 \cdot 23487583308 \cdot$ $78952752017 \cdot P57$
331	$16937389168607 \cdot 865118802936559 \cdot P72$
373	$25569151 \cdot P105$
409	$4480666067023 \cdot 76025626689833 \cdot P97$
881	$26431 \cdot PRP261$
1063	$1485761479 \cdot PRP311$

secure.

The algorithms presented here show that great care has to be exercised in the choice of the fields $GF(2^n)$ for cryptographic applications. First of all, n should be chosen so that 2^n-1 has a large prime factor, preferably larger than 10^{40}. Secondly, n should be quite large. Even to protect against attackers possessing small but fast computers of the kind that might be widely available within the next ten years, it seems best to choose $n \geqslant 800$. To protect against sophisticated attacks by opponents capable of building large special purpose machines, n should probably be at least 1500. In fact, to guard against improvements in known algorithms or new methods, it might be safest to use $n \geqslant 2000$ or even larger.

Given a bound on the size of the key, one can obtain much greater security by using the fields $GF(p)$ with p prime then the fields $GF(2^n)$. In this case p also has to be chosen so that $p-1$ contains a large prime factor. If this precaution is observed, fields with $p \geq 2^{750}$ provide a level of security that can only be matched by the fields $GF(2^n)$ with $n \geq 2000$.

The requirement that p be changed frequently is not an onerous one. It is easy to construct large primes p for which $p-1$ have a large prime factor (cf. [68]). Moreover, it is easy to construct them in such a way that the complete factorization of $p-1$ is known, which makes it easy to find primitive roots g modulo p and prove that they are primitive.

The discrete logarithm problem in fields $GF(p)$ for which $p-1$ does have a large prime factor appears to be about as hard as the problem of factoring integers of size about p. The comparison of the asymptotic complexity of the two problems was presented in Section 7. As far as values of practical use are concerned, the best current factorization programs appear to be capable of factoring integers around 2^{250} in about 1 day on a supercomputer like the Cray-XMP [22]. In applications where one is only interested in exchanging keys for use with ordinary cryptographic equipment, the Diffie-Hellman scheme presented in the Section 2 seems comparable to the Rivest-Shamir-Adleman (RSA) scheme, provided one uses fields $GF(p)$. However, the best choice is not totally obvious. The Diffie-Hellman scheme has the advantage that the parties exchanging keys do not have to keep their private keys secret (since there are no private keys). It has the disadvantage that there is no authentication. Furthermore, if the Diffie-Hellman scheme is to be used with the same field shared by many people for a prolonged time, the discrete logarithm problem being as hard as factorization loses some of its significance because the cryptanalyst can afford to spend much more time compiling the database. If the field to be used does change from one session to another, though, the Diffie-Hellman scheme appears as a good choice among key distribution systems.

Acknowledgement

The author thanks D. Coppersmith, J. Davenport, J. Davis, D. Ditzel, G. Gonnet, D. Holdridge, J. Jordan, N. K. Karmarkar, L. Kaufman, H. W. Lenstra, Jr., R. Mullin, C. Pomerance, J. Reyneri, B. Richmond, N. Sollenberger, J. Todd, S. Vanstone, and D. Wiedemann for helpful conversations.

Appendix A: Computation and estimation of $N(n,m)$, the number of polynomials over $GF(2)$ of degree n, all of whose irreducible factors are of degrees $\leqslant m$.

Let $I(k)$ denote the number of irreducible polynomials over $GF(2)$ that are of degree k. Then it is well-known [38] that

$$I(k) = \frac{1}{k} \sum_{d/k} \mu(d) 2^{k/d} , \qquad (A.1)$$

where $\mu(d)$ is the Möbius μ-function. The formula (A.1) provides an efficient method for computing $I(k)$, the first few values of which are shown in Table 7. In addition, (A.1) shows immediately that

$$I(k) = k^{-1}2^k + O(k^{-1}2^{k/2}) . \qquad (A.2)$$

We define $N(k,0) = 1$ if $k = 0$ and $N(k,0) = 0$ if $k \neq 0$. Also, we adopt the convention that $N(k,m) = 0$ if $k < 0$ and $m \geqslant 0$. With these conventions, we obtain the following recurrence, valid for n, $m > 0$:

$$N(n,m) = \sum_{k=1}^{m} \sum_{r \geqslant 1} N(n-rk,k-1) \binom{r+I(k)-1}{r} . \qquad (A.3)$$

To prove the validity of (A.3), note that any polynomial $f(x)$ of degree n, all of whose irreducible factors are of degrees $\leqslant m$, can be written uniquely as

$$f(x) = g(x) \prod_{u(x)} u(x)^{a(u(x))} ,$$

where the $u(x)$ are all of degree k for some k, $1 \leqslant k \leqslant m$, $\Sigma\, a(n(x)) = r$ for some $r \in Z^+$, and $g(x)$ is a polynomial of degree $n-rk$, all of whose irreducible factors are of degrees $\leqslant k-1$. Given k and r, there are $N(n-rk,k-1)$ such polynomials $g(x)$. The number of $\prod u(x)^{a(n(x))}$ is the number of $I(k)$-tuples of nonnegative integers which sum to r, which is easily seen to equal

$$\binom{r+I(k)-1}{r} .$$

This proves (A.3).

Table 7. Values of $I(n)$, the number of irreducible binary polynomials of degree n.

n	$I(n)$
1	2
2	1
3	2
4	3
5	6
6	9
7	18
8	30
9	56
10	99
11	186
12	335
13	630
14	1161
15	2182
16	4080
17	7710
18	14532
19	27594
20	52377

The recurrence (A.3) was used to compute the probabilities $p(n,m)$ listed in Appendix B. To estimate $N(n,m)$ asymptotically, we use different techniques. The method we use differs from those used to study the analogous problem for ordinary integers (see [29,31,39,46]), and relies on the saddle point method [15]. With extra effort, it is capable of producing much more refined estimates than we obtain over much greater ranges of n and m. However, in order to keep the presentation simple, we consider only the ranges most important for cryptographic applications.

Theorem A1. Let

$$f_m(z) = \prod_{k=1}^{m}(1-z^k)^{-I(k)} \qquad (A.4)$$

and

$$b(z) = \left[\frac{f'_m}{f_m}(z)\right]' = \sum_{k=1}^{m}I(k)\left\{\frac{k(k-1)z^{k-2}}{1-z^k} + \frac{k^2z^{2k-2}}{(1-z^k)^2}\right\}. \qquad (A.5)$$

Then, for $n^{1/100} \leqslant m \leqslant n^{99/100}$, we have

$$N(n,m) \sim \left[2\pi b\,(r_0)\right]^{-1/2} f_m(r_0) r_0^{-n} \quad as\; n \to \infty, \tag{A.6}$$

where $r = r_0 = r_0(m,n)$ is the unique positive solution to

$$r\,\frac{f'_m}{f_m}(r) = n\,. \tag{A.7}$$

Corollary A2. If $n^{1/100} \leqslant m \leqslant n^{99/100}$, then

$$N(n,m) = 2^n \left(\frac{m}{n}\right)^{(1+o(1))n/m} \quad as\; n \to \infty. \tag{A.8}$$

Corollary A3. If $n^{1/100} \leqslant m \leqslant n^{99/100}$, and $0 \leqslant k \leqslant 2m$, then

$$\frac{N(n+k,m)}{N(n,m)} \sim 2^k \left[\frac{n}{m}\log_e \frac{n}{m}\right]^{k/m} \quad as\; n \to \infty. \tag{A.9}$$

Proof of Theorem A1. It is immediate from (A.4) that

$$f_m(z) = \prod_{k=1}^{m} (1+z^k+z^{2k}+\dots)^{I(k)} = \sum_{n=0}^{\infty} N(n,m)z^n\,. \tag{A.10}$$

Hence, by Cauchy's theorem,

$$N(n,m) = \frac{1}{2\pi i} \int_{|z|=r} f_m(z) z^{-n-1} dz \tag{A.11}$$

$$= \frac{1}{2\pi} \int_{-\pi}^{\pi} f_m(re^{i\theta}) r^{-n} e^{-in\theta} d\theta\,,$$

where r is any real number with $0 < r < 1$. As usual in the saddle point method, we determine $r = r_0$ by the condition (A.7), which is equivalent to

$$\sum_{k=1}^{m} I(k)\,\frac{kr^k}{1-r^k} = n\,. \tag{A.12}$$

Since $I(k) > 0$, it is clear that (A.12) has a unique solution $r = r_0$ with $0 < r_0 < 1$. We next estimate r_0 and $f_m(r_0)$. We consider $n^{1/100} \leqslant m \leqslant n^{99/100}$, $n \to \infty$, and take

$$r = \exp(\frac{\alpha \log n}{m} - \log 2), \quad 10^{-3} \leqslant \alpha \leqslant 10^3\,, \tag{A.13}$$

say. (All logrithms are to base e in this appendix.) Then, by (A.2),

$$\sum_{k=1}^{m} \frac{I(k)kr^k}{1-r^k} - \sum_{k=1}^{m} \frac{2^k r^k}{1-r^k} + O(1)$$

as $n \to \infty$ (uniformly in m satisfying $n^{1/100} \leqslant m \leqslant n^{99/100}$, as will be the case throughout the rest of the exposition), and so

$$\sum_{k=1}^{m} \frac{I(k)kr^k}{1-r^k} - \sum_{k=1}^{m} 2^k r^k + O(1)$$

$$= 2r \frac{2^m r^m - 1}{2r-1} + O(1) \tag{A.14}$$

$$= \frac{m(1+O(n^{-\alpha}+m^{-1} \log n))}{\alpha \log n} n^\alpha .$$

We conclude that $r = r_0$ is given by (A.13) with $\alpha = \alpha_0$ satisfying

$$\alpha_0 = (\log n/m + \log \log n/m + o(1)) (\log n)^{-1} , \tag{A.15}$$

so that

$$\alpha_0 \sim \frac{\log n/m}{\log n} \quad \text{as } n \to \infty , \tag{A.16}$$

and that

$$2^m r_0^m \sim \alpha_0 nm^{-1} \log n . \tag{A.17}$$

From (A.17) and (A.2) we easily conclude that

$$\sum_{k=1}^{m} - I(k) \log (1-r_0^k) = \sum_{k=1}^{m} k^{-1} 2^k r_0^k + O(1) , \tag{A.18}$$

$$b(r_0) = (\frac{f_m'}{f_m} (r))'|_{r=r_0} = \sum_{k=1}^{m} \left\{ \frac{I(k)k(k-1)r_0^{k-2}}{1-r_0^k} + \frac{I(k)k^2 r_0^{2k-2}}{(1-r_0^k)^2} \right\} \sim 4mn , \tag{A.19}$$

$$(\frac{f_m'}{f_m} (r))''|_{r=r_0} = O(m^2 n) . \tag{A.20}$$

We now use the above estimates to carry out the saddle point approximation, which proceeds along very standard lines (cf. [15]). We choose

$$\theta_0 = m^{-1/2} n^{-599/1200} .$$

If we let

$$a(r_0) = \log f_m(r_0) - n \log r_0,$$

then by (A.12), (A.19), and (A.20) we obtain, for $|\theta| \leqslant \theta_0$,

$$\log f_m(re^{i\theta}) - n \log r - in\theta = a(r_0) - \frac{1}{2}b(r_0)\theta^2 + O(m^2 n|\theta|^3)$$

$$= a(r_0) - \frac{1}{2}b(r_0)\theta^2 + O(m^{1/2}n^{-199/400}).$$

Therefore

$$\frac{1}{2\pi}\int_{-\theta_0}^{\theta_0} f_m(r_0e^{i\theta})r_0^{-n}e^{-in\theta}d\theta$$

$$= (2\pi b(r_0))^{-1/2}f_m(r_0)r_0^{-n}(1+O(m^{1/2}n^{-199/400})).$$

It remains only to show that the integral over $\theta_0 < |\theta| \leqslant \pi$ is negligible. Now for $z = re^{i\theta}$, $r = r_0$, and $m^* = [999m/1000]$, we have

$$\log f_m(r) - \log |f_m(z)| = \sum_{k=1}^{m} I(k) \log \left|\frac{1-z^k}{1-r^k}\right|$$

$$= \sum_{k=1}^{m} k^{-1}2^k \{\log|1-z^k| - \log(1-r^k)\} + O(1)$$

$$= \sum_{k=1}^{m} k^{-1}2^k r^k (1-\cos k\theta) + O(1)$$

$$\geqslant m^{-1}2^{m^*}r^{m^*} \sum_{k=m^*}^{m} (1-\cos k\theta) + O(1). \tag{A.21}$$

If $|\theta| \geqslant 10^4 m^{-1}$, say, the right side above is

$$= m^{-1}2^{m^*}r^{m^*}\left\{m-m^* + \frac{\sin(m+\frac{1}{2})\theta - \sin(m^*+\frac{1}{2})\theta}{2\sin\theta/2}\right\} + O(1)$$

$$\geqslant 10^{-4}2^{m^*}r^{m^*} + O(1)$$

$$\geqslant 10^{-5}(n/m)^{999/1000} + O(1). \tag{A.22}$$

If $\theta_0 \leqslant |\theta| \leqslant 10^4 m^{-1}$, on the other hand,

$$1-\cos k\theta \geqslant 1-\cos k\theta_0 \geqslant 10^{-3}mn^{-599/600}, \quad m^* \leqslant k \leqslant m,$$

and the last quantity in (A.21) is

$$\geqslant 10^{-6}m^{1/1000}n^{1/1500} + O(1). \tag{A.23}$$

Combining the estimates (A.22) and (A.23), we conclude that for $\theta_0 < |\theta| \leqslant \pi$,

$$\log f_m(r) - \log |f_m(z)| \geqslant \epsilon n^\delta$$

for some $\epsilon, \delta > 0$, and so the integral over that range is indeed negligible compared to the integral over $|\theta| \leqslant \theta_0$.

When we combine all the results obtained above, we obtain the estimate (A.6) of the theorem.

Proof of Corollary A2. By (A.19), we know that $b(r_0)\sim 4mn$. Now

$$-n \log r_0 = n \log 2 - \frac{n}{m} \alpha_0 \log n \tag{A.24}$$

$$= n \log 2 - (1+o(1))\frac{n}{m} \log \frac{n}{m}.$$

Furthermore, by (A.17),

$$2^k r_0^k = O(n^{1/2}m^{-1/2}\log n), \quad k \leqslant m/2,$$

so

$$\sum_{k=1}^{m} k^{-1}2^k r_0^k = O(n^{1/2}m^{-1/2}(\log n)^2) + O(nm^{-1}),$$

and so by (A.18),

$$\log f_m(r) = o\left(\frac{n}{m} \log\frac{n}{m}\right).$$

This proves the estimate (A.8) of the corollary.

Proof of Corollary A3. We first study how $r_0 = r_0(n, m)$ varies with n. Letting n be a continuous variable defined by (A.12) (with m fixed and r varying), we find that (as in (A.19) and (A.20))

$$\left.\frac{\partial n}{\partial r}\right|_{r-r_0} \sim 2mn \, , \qquad\qquad\qquad \text{(A.25)}$$

and for $|r-r_0| = O(n^{-1})$,

$$\frac{\partial^2 n}{\partial r^2} = O(m^2 n) \, .$$

Hence for $0 \leqslant k \leqslant 2m$,

$$\delta = r_0(n+k, m) - r_0(n, m) \sim k\,(2mn)^{-1} \, . \qquad\qquad \text{(A.26)}$$

Therefore

$$\log f_m(r_0(n+k, m)) - \log f_m(r_0(n, m))$$

$$= \delta \, \frac{f_m'}{f_m}\,(r_0(r, k)) + O(\delta^2 M) \, ,$$

where

$$M = \max_{r_0(n, k) \leqslant r \leqslant r_0(n, k)+\delta} |(\frac{f_m'}{f_m})'\,(r)| = O(mn) \, ,$$

and so

$$\log f_m(r_0(n+k, m)) - \log f_m(r_0(n, m)) \sim k/m \, .$$

Since by (A.19),

$$b(r_0(n+k, m)) \sim b(r_0(n, m)) \sim 4mn \, ,$$

we finally obtain, for $r = r_0(n, m)$,

$$\frac{N(n+k, m)}{N(n, m)} \sim \exp\,(k/m)\; r^{-k}\,(1+\delta r^{-1})^{-n}$$

$$\sim r^{-k}$$

$$\sim 2^k\,(\frac{n}{m}\,\log\,\frac{n}{m})^{-k/m} \, , \qquad\qquad \text{(A.27)}$$

which yields the desired result.

Appendix B. Values of $p(n,k)$, the probability that a random polynomial over $GF(2)$ of degree n will have all its irreducible factors of degrees $\leqslant k$, for various values of n and for $1 \leqslant k \leqslant 40$.

$n = 10$

1	1.07422E-02	3.51562E-02	1.08398E-01	2.22656E-01	3.95508E-01
6	5.36133E-01	6.76758E-01	7.93945E-01	9.03320E-01	1.00000E+00
11	1.00000E+00	1.00000E+00	1.00000E+00	1.00000E+00	1.00000E+00
16	1.00000E+00	1.00000E+00	1.00000E+00	1.00000E+00	1.00000E+00
21	1.00000E+00	1.00000E+00	1.00000E+00	1.00000E+00	1.00000E+00
26	1.00000E+00	1.00000E+00	1.00000E+00	1.00000E+00	1.00000E+00
31	1.00000E+00	1.00000E+00	1.00000E+00	1.00000E+00	1.00000E+00
36	1.00000E+00	1.00000E+00	1.00000E+00	1.00000E+00	1.00000E+00

$n = 20$

1	2.00272E-05	1.15395E-04	8.44955E-04	3.95012E-03	1.65253E-02
6	4.19769E-02	9.27200E-02	1.58895E-01	2.41888E-01	3.33941E-01
11	4.24762E-01	5.06549E-01	5.83453E-01	6.54315E-01	7.20904E-01
16	7.83160E-01	8.41983E-01	8.97418E-01	9.50049E-01	1.00000E+00
21	1.00000E+00	1.00000E+00	1.00000E+00	1.00000E+00	1.00000E+00
26	1.00000E+00	1.00000E+00	1.00000E+00	1.00000E+00	1.00000E+00
31	1.00000E+00	1.00000E+00	1.00000E+00	1.00000E+00	1.00000E+00
36	1.00000E+00	1.00000E+00	1.00000E+00	1.00000E+00	1.00000E+00

$n = 30$

1	2.88710E-08	2.38419E-07	3.20468E-06	2.89446E-05	2.70738E-04
6	1.30629E-03	5.32556E-03	1.46109E-02	3.27337E-02	6.05388E-02
11	9.95504E-02	1.46035E-01	2.00105E-01	2.59328E-01	3.23701E-01
16	3.85957E-01	4.44780E-01	5.00215E-01	5.52846E-01	6.02797E-01
21	6.50413E-01	6.95845E-01	7.39323E-01	7.80979E-01	8.20979E-01
26	8.59436E-01	8.96473E-01	9.32185E-01	9.66668E-01	1.00000E+00
31	1.00000E+00	1.00000E+00	1.00000E+00	1.00000E+00	1.00000E+00
36	1.00000E+00	1.00000E+00	1.00000E+00	1.00000E+00	1.00000E+00

$n = 40$

1	3.72893E-11	4.01087E-10	8.58199E-09	1.33864E-07	2.58580E-06
6	2.33114E-05	1.79979E-04	8.13273E-04	2.79863E-03	7.24926E-03
11	1.58528E-02	2.93316E-02	4.89490E-02	7.46204E-02	1.05880E-01
16	1.41606E-01	1.81373E-01	2.24427E-01	2.70539E-01	3.19242E-01
21	3.66858E-01	4.12290E-01	4.55768E-01	4.97424E-01	5.37424E-01
26	5.75881E-01	6.12918E-01	6.48630E-01	6.83113E-01	7.16445E-01
31	7.48703E-01	7.79953E-01	8.10256E-01	8.39667E-01	8.68239E-01
36	8.96016E-01	9.23043E-01	9.49359E-01	9.75000E-01	1.00000E+00

$n = 50$

1	4.52971E-14	6.00409E-13	1.87370E-11	4.64628E-10	1.72661E-08
6	2.83341E-07	4.15352E-06	3.15683E-05	1.70819E-04	6.37026E-04
11	1.89641E-03	4.51306E-03	9.32956E-03	1.69499E-02	2.80019E-02
16	4.27905E-02	6.17055E-02	8.43781E-02	1.10392E-01	1.39255E-01
21	1.70678E-01	2.04341E-01	2.40042E-01	2.77562E-01	3.16762E-01
26	3.55219E-01	3.92256E-01	4.27968E-01	4.62450E-01	4.95783E-01
31	5.28041E-01	5.59290E-01	5.89593E-01	6.19005E-01	6.47576E-01
36	6.75354E-01	7.02381E-01	7.28697E-01	7.54338E-01	7.79338E-01

$n = 60$

1	5.29091E-17	8.33535E-16	3.57405E-14	1.32500E-12	8.91426E-11
6	2.58718E-09	7.15988E-08	9.24769E-07	8.00984E-06	4.38229E-05
11	1.80902E-04	5.62442E-04	1.45972E-03	3.20781E-03	6.25179E-03
16	1.10167E-02	1.79110E-02	2.71835E-02	3.91011E-02	5.38207E-02
21	7.13458E-02	9.13458E-02	1.13563E-01	1.37747E-01	1.63715E-01
26	1.91288E-01	2.20330E-01	2.50714E-01	2.82341E-01	3.15118E-01
31	3.47376E-01	3.78625E-01	4.08928E-01	4.38340E-01	4.66911E-01
36	4.94689E-01	5.21716E-01	5.48032E-01	5.73673E-01	5.98673E-01

$n = 70$

1	6.01393E-20	1.09775E-18	6.19062E-17	3.27368E-15	3.78790E-13
6	1.88957E-11	9.76926E-10	2.15538E-08	3.02670E-07	2.46433E-06
11	1.43153E-05	5.88968E-05	1.94202E-04	5.22033E-04	1.21092E-03
16	2.47391E-03	4.57774E-03	7.79633E-03	1.24157E-02	1.86403E-02
21	2.66552E-02	3.65932E-02	4.85857E-02	6.26843E-02	7.87250E-02
26	9.65101E-02	1.15878E-01	1.36683E-01	1.58803E-01	1.82129E-01
31	2.06566E-01	2.32034E-01	2.58460E-01	2.85782E-01	3.13945E-01
36	3.41723E-01	3.68750E-01	3.95065E-01	4.20706E-01	4.45706E-01

$n = 80$

1	6.70016E-23	1.39049E-21	9.97836E-20	7.25067E-18	1.38122E-15
6	1.15256E-13	1.09894E-11	4.14853E-10	9.53139E-09	1.16815E-07
11	9.66482E-07	5.31900E-06	2.25093E-05	7.46852E-05	2.07615E-04
16	4.95625E-04	1.05199E-03	2.01760E-03	3.56457E-03	5.87520E-03
21	9.14845E-03	1.35494E-02	1.92187E-02	2.62653E-02	3.47883E-02
26	4.48677E-02	5.65725E-02	6.98314E-02	8.45073E-02	1.00477E-01
31	1.17636E-01	1.35888E-01	1.55151E-01	1.75351E-01	1.96424E-01
36	2.18311E-01	2.40962E-01	2.64330E-01	2.88376E-01	3.13064E-01

$n = 90$

1	7.35092E-26	1.70929E-24	1.52104E-22	1.47329E-20	4.45086E-18
6	6.05742E-16	1.05018E-13	6.77815E-12	2.56475E-10	4.77572E-09
11	5.68482E-08	4.22404E-07	2.31429E-06	9.54889E-06	3.20299E-05
16	8.99488E-05	2.19926E-04	4.77206E-04	9.41494E-04	1.71113E-03
21	2.90283E-03	4.64261E-03	7.06931E-03	1.03132E-02	1.44861E-02
26	1.96783E-02	2.59683E-02	3.34221E-02	4.20997E-02	5.20539E-02

| 31 | 6.32769E-02 | 7.56710E-02 | 8.91447E-02 | 1.03616E-01 | 1.19013E-01 |
| 36 | 1.35270E-01 | 1.52328E-01 | 1.70136E-01 | 1.88646E-01 | 2.07817E-01 |

$n = 100$

1	7.96750E-29	2.05183E-27	2.21718E-25	2.79208E-23	1.29509E-20
6	2.80812E-18	8.72341E-16	9.60294E-14	6.01224E-12	1.71395E-10
11	2.96075E-09	2.99434E-08	2.14020E-07	1.10537E-06	4.50209E-06
16	1.49474E-05	4.23006E-05	1.04387E-04	2.30656E-04	4.63358E-04
21	8.60536E-04	1.49335E-03	2.44477E-03	3.80487E-03	5.67219E-03
26	8.14723E-03	1.13206E-02	1.52676E-02	2.00530E-02	2.57320E-02
31	3.23535E-02	3.99608E-02	4.85939E-02	5.82726E-02	6.89360E-02
36	8.05132E-02	9.29404E-02	1.06160E-01	1.20121E-01	1.34775E-01

$n = 120$

1	9.10303E-35	2.79937E-33	4.24841E-31	8.51575E-29	8.58548E-26
6	4.43640E-23	4.23359E-20	1.33993E-17	2.31621E-15	1.57566E-13
11	5.85613E-12	1.12008E-10	1.38923E-09	1.14391E-08	6.97729E-08
16	3.28256E-07	1.26087E-06	4.06533E-06	1.13862E-05	2.82395E-05
21	6.33049E-05	1.30082E-04	2.48115E-04	4.43550E-04	7.50092E-04
26	1.20819E-03	1.86404E-03	2.76800E-03	3.97434E-03	5.54048E-03
31	7.52560E-03	9.98318E-03	1.29596E-02	1.64949E-02	2.06246E-02
36	2.53799E-02	3.07891E-02	3.68775E-02	4.36690E-02	5.11857E-02

$n = 140$

1	1.01163E-40	3.61674E-39	7.33734E-37	2.19965E-34	4.41316E-31
6	5.04962E-28	1.39814E-24	1.24688E-21	5.97886E-19	9.87955E-17
11	8.08426E-15	2.99212E-13	6.58221E-12	8.81292E-11	8.19347E-10
16	5.55000E-09	2.93431E-08	1.25224E-07	4.49650E-07	1.39106E-06
21	3.80057E-06	9.32833E-06	2.08939E-05	4.32132E-05	8.34419E-05
26	1.51678E-04	2.61437E-04	4.29945E-04	6.78498E-04	1.03218E-03
31	1.51926E-03	2.17048E-03	3.01880E-03	4.09904E-03	5.44782E-03
36	7.10258E-03	9.09777E-03	1.14637E-02	1.42271E-02	1.74120E-02

$n = 160$

1	1.10161E-46	4.48922E-45	1.17344E-42	5.01669E-40	1.86681E-36
6	4.44249E-33	3.38239E-29	8.30467E-26	1.10376E-22	4.48551E-20
11	8.22931E-18	6.00596E-16	2.38665E-14	5.28278E-13	7.59978E-12
16	7.51169E-11	5.53295E-10	3.15918E-09	1.46872E-08	5.71758E-08
21	1.91933E-07	5.66887E-07	1.50111E-06	3.61395E-06	8.01344E-06
26	1.65279E-05	3.19895E-05	5.85387E-05	1.01940E-04	1.69814E-04
31	2.71850E-04	4.19968E-04	6.28482E-04	9.13982E-04	1.29497E-03
36	1.79151E-03	2.42504E-03	3.21815E-03	4.19454E-03	5.37894E-03

$n = 180$

1	1.18108E-52	5.40360E-51	1.76869E-48	1.03860E-45	6.76840E-42
6	3.17410E-38	6.32280E-34	4.17015E-30	1.52942E-26	1.54164E-23
11	6.43456E-21	9.40765E-19	6.85942E-17	2.54621E-15	5.74207E-14
16	8.37861E-13	8.68865E-12	6.70002E-11	4.06745E-10	2.00783E-09
21	8.33948E-09	2.98308E-08	9.39352E-08	2.64665E-07	6.77278E-07
26	1.59242E-06	3.47604E-06	7.10546E-06	1.37023E-05	2.50828E-05
31	4.38309E-05	7.34728E-05	1.18633E-04	1.85151E-04	2.80190E-04
36	4.12329E-04	5.91651E-04	8.29679E-04	1.13916E-03	1.53389E-03

$n = 200$

1	1.25083E-58	6.34810E-57	2.54336E-54	1.99006E-51	2.16542E-47
6	1.90979E-43	9.50701E-39	1.64269E-34	1.65088E-30	4.15085E-27
11	3.98840E-24	1.18400E-21	1.60566E-19	1.01212E-17	3.61920E-16
16	7.87667E-15	1.16065E-13	1.21882E-12	9.73478E-12	6.13504E-11
21	3.17240E-10	1.38215E-09	5.20253E-09	1.72365E-08	5.11289E-08
26	1.37605E-07	3.40048E-07	7.79144E-07	1.66938E-06	3.36899E-06
31	6.44534E-06	1.17526E-05	2.05210E-05	3.44554E-05	5.58425E-05
36	8.76481E-05	1.33598E-04	1.98241E-04	2.87013E-04	4.06290E-04

$n = 250$

1	1.38731E-73	8.77490E-72	5.40876E-69	7.83967E-66	2.60927E-61
6	9.43320E-57	3.88248E-51	6.69001E-46	8.02116E-41	2.00422E-36
11	1.60958E-32	2.94386E-29	1.97886E-26	4.90886E-24	5.79891E-22
16	3.56248E-20	1.30783E-18	3.06590E-17	5.00010E-16	5.95292E-15
21	5.44802E-14	3.96906E-13	2.37961E-12	1.20333E-11	5.24971E-11
26	2.01111E-10	6.87289E-10	2.12261E-09	5.99202E-09	1.56105E-08
31	3.78515E-08	8.60400E-08	1.84519E-07	3.75441E-07	7.28331E-07
36	1.35288E-06	2.41546E-06	4.15966E-06	6.93046E-06	1.12015E-05

$n = 300$

1	1.47764E-88	1.11932E-86	9.83244E-84	2.37616E-80	2.02941E-75
6	2.48750E-70	6.82386E-64	1.01320E-57	1.35211E-51	3.35347E-46
11	2.33703E-41	2.77543E-37	9.78889E-34	1.00885E-30	4.14030E-28
16	7.51397E-26	7.16126E-24	3.88900E-22	1.33922E-20	3.10487E-19
21	5.17007E-18	6.45934E-17	6.31276E-16	4.97725E-15	3.25700E-14
26	1.80862E-13	8.69349E-13	3.67642E-12	1.38762E-11	4.73123E-11
31	1.47287E-10	4.22472E-10	1.12559E-09	2.80512E-09	6.57962E-09
36	1.46051E-08	3.08299E-08	6.21540E-08	1.20132E-07	2.23377E-07

$n = 350$

1	1.53041-103	1.35060-101	1.60284E-98	5.99444E-95	1.15598E-89
6	4.15490E-84	6.36291E-77	7.12431E-70	9.81396E-63	2.38010E-56
11	1.47173E-50	1.17990E-45	2.28345E-41	1.02142E-37	1.51735E-34
16	8.44461E-32	2.16145E-29	2.80349E-27	2.09567E-25	9.70161E-24
21	3.00716E-22	6.57878E-21	1.06830E-19	1.33657E-18	1.33338E-17
26	1.08953E-16	7.46950E-16	4.38196E-15	2.23833E-14	1.01023E-13

31	4.08092E-13	1.49196E-12	4.98491E-12	1.53517E-11	4.39066E-11
36	1.17397E-10	2.95185E-10	7.01651E-10	1.58406E-09	3.41082E-09

$n = 400$

1	1.55291-118	1.56457-116	2.41161-113	1.32035-109	5.21575-104
6	4.90260E-98	3.61544E-90	2.70641E-82	3.56518E-74	8.25910E-67
11	4.58566E-60	2.55583E-54	2.81416E-49	5.66577E-45	3.15379E-41
16	5.55533E-38	3.93027E-35	1.24956E-32	2.07597E-30	1.96036E-28
21	1.15333E-26	4.49726E-25	1.23335E-23	2.48551E-22	3.83276E-21
26	4.66781E-20	4.61886E-19	3.80070E-18	2.65470E-17	1.60138E-16
31	8.47073E-16	3.98086E-15	1.68143E-14	6.44748E-14	2.26456E-13
36	7.34282E-13	2.21339E-12	6.24107E-12	1.65527E-11	4.14991E-11

$n = 450$

1	1.55124-133	1.75679-131	3.41223-128	2.61980-124	1.96368-118
6	4.40044-112	1.37925-103	6.19409E-95	7.23803E-86	1.55644E-77
11	7.79521E-70	3.08892E-63	1.99379E-57	1.86331E-52	4.00361E-48
16	2.29399E-44	4.59937E-41	3.66621E-38	1.38170E-35	2.71137E-33
21	3.07933E-31	2.17355E-29	1.02106E-27	3.35795E-26	8.10087E-25
26	1.48691E-23	2.14569E-22	2.50052E-21	2.40980E-20	1.95927E-19
31	1.36783E-18	8.32458E-18	4.47600E-17	2.15115E-16	9.33645E-16
36	3.69290E-15	1.34195E-14	4.51235E-14	1.41305E-13	4.14464E-13

$n = 500$

1	1.53052-148	1.92464-146	4.59900-143	4.78471-139	6.39731-133
6	3.16656-126	3.79129-117	9.26531-108	8.93129E-98	1.72679E-88
11	7.79518E-80	2.23403E-72	8.66735E-66	3.86142E-60	3.28692E-55
16	6.27531E-51	3.64507E-47	7.43141E-44	6.46943E-41	2.68186E-38
21	5.96843E-36	7.73090E-34	6.29946E-32	3.42003E-30	1.30459E-28
26	3.64471E-27	7.74067E-26	1.28847E-24	1.72694E-23	1.90660E-22
31	1.76903E-21	1.40341E-20	9.66536E-20	5.85587E-19	3.15796E-18
36	1.53163E-17	6.74271E-17	2.71643E-16	1.00884E-15	3.47656E-15

References

1. L. M. Adleman, A subexponential algorithm for the discrete logarithm problem with applications to cryptography, *Proc. 20th IEEE Found. Comp. Sci. Symp.* (1979), 55-60.

2. L. M. Adleman, C. Pomerance and R. S. Rumely, On distinguishing prime numbers from composite numbers, *Annals Math. 117* (1983), 173-206.

3. B. Arazi, Sequences constructed by operations modulo 2^n-1 or modulo 2^n and their application in evaluating the complexity of a log operation over $GF(2^n)$, preprint.

4. C. P. Arnold, M. I. Parr, and M. B. Dewe, An efficient parallel algorithm for the solution of large sparse linear matrix equations, *IEEE Trans. on Computers, C-32* (1983), 265-272.

5. E. Bach, Discrete logarithms and factoring, to be published.

6. V. A. Barker, ed., *Sparse Matrix Techniques,* Lecture Notes in Mathematics #572, Springer-Verlag, 1977.

7. E. R. Berlekamp, Factoring polynomials over large finite fields, *Math. Comp. 24* (1970), 713-735.

8. I. F. Blake, R. Fuji-Hara, R. C. Mullin, and S. A. Vanstone, Computing logarithms in finite fields of characteristic two, *SIAM J. Alg. Disc. Methods, 5* (1984), 276-285.

9. M. Blum and S. Micali, How to generate cryptographically strong sequences of pseudo random bits, *SIAM J. Comp.*, to appear.

10. A. Borodin and I. Munro, *The Computational Complexity of Algebraic and Numeric Problems,* American Elsevier, 1975.

11. A. Brameller, R. N. Allan, and Y. M. Hamam, *Sparsity*, Pitman 1976.

12. E. F. Brickell, A fast modular multiplication algorithm with applications to two key crytography, pp. 51-60 in *Advances in Cryptology: Proceedings of CRYPTO '82*, D. Chaum, R. Rivest, and A. Sherman, eds., Plenum Press, 1983.

13. E. F. Brickell and J. H. Moore, Some remarks on the Herlestam-Johannesson algorithm for computing logarithms over $GF(2^n)$, pp. 15-20, in *Advances in Cryptology: Proceedings of CRYPTO '82*, D. Chaum, R. Rivest and A. Sherman, eds., Plenum Press, 1983.

14. J. Brillhart, D. H. Lehmer, J. L. Selfridge, B. Tuckerman, and S. S. Wagstaff, Jr., *Factorizations of $b^n \pm 1$, $b = 2, 3, 5, 6, 7, 10, 11, 12$ up to High Powers*, Am. Math. Society, 1983.

15. N. G. de Bruijn, *Asymptotic Methods in Analysis*, North-Holland. 1958,

16. D. G. Cantor and H. Zassenhaus, A new algorithm for factoring polynomials over finite fields, *Math. Comp. 36* (1981), 587-592.

17. H. Cohen and H. W. Lenstra, Jr., Primality testing and Jacobi sums, *Math. Comp., 42* (1984), 297-330.

18. D. Coppersmith, Evaluating logarithms in $GF(2^n)$, pp. 201-207 in *Proc. 16th ACM Symp. Theory of Computing*, 1984.

19. D. Coppersmith, Fast evaluation of logarithms in fields of characteristic two, *IEEE Trans. Inform. Theory* IT-30 (1984), 587-594.

20. D. Coppersmith and A. M. Odlyzko, manuscript in preparation.

21. D. Coppersmith and S. Winograd, On the asymptotic complexity of matrix multiplication, *SIAM J. Comp. 11* (1982), 472-492.

22. J. A. Davis, D. B. Holdridge, and G. J. Simmons, Status report on factoring (at the Sandia National Laboratories), to appear in Proc. EUROCRYPT 84.

23. W. Diffie and M. E. Hellman, New directions in cryptography, *IEEE Trans. Inform. Theory*, IT-22 (1976), 644-654.

24. W. Diffie and M. E. Hellman, Exhaustive cryptanalysis of the NBS Data Encryption Standard, *Computer 10* (1977), 74-84.

25. T. ElGamal, A subexponential-time algorithm for computing discrete logarithms over $GF(p^2)$, *IEEE Trans. Inform. Theory*, to appear.

26. T. ElGamal, A public key cryptosystem and a signature scheme based on discrete logarithms, *IEEE Trans. Inform. Theory*, to appear.

27. A. George and J. W.-H. Liu, *Computer Solution of Large Sparse Positive Definite Systems*, Prentice-Hall, 1981.

28. S. Golomb, *Shift-register Sequences*, Holden-Day, 1967.

29. F. G. Gustavson, Analysis of the Berlekamp-Massey feedback shift-register synthesis algorithm, *IBM J. Res. Dev. 20* (1976), 204-212.

30. M. E. Hellman and J. M. Reyneri, Fast computation of discrete logarithms in $GF(q)$, pp. 3-13 in *Advances in Cryptography: Proceedings of CRYPTO '82*, D. Chaum, R. Rivest, and A. Sherman, eds., Plenum Press, 1983.

31. D. Hensley, The number of positive integers $\leqslant x$ and free of prime factors $> y$, preprint.

32. T. Herlestam and R. Johannesson, On computing logarithms over $GF(2^p)$, *BIT 21* (1981), 326-334.

33. M. R. Hestenes and E. Stiefel, Methods of conjugate gradients for solving linear systems, *J. Res. Nat. Bureau of Standards 49* (1952), 409-436.

34. A. Hildebrand, On the number of positive integers $\leqslant x$ and free of prime factors $>y$, to be published.

35. J. Ja' Ja' and S. Venkatesan, On the complexity of a parity problem related to coding theory, Pennsylvania State Univ. Computer Sci. Report CS-81-5 (1981).

36. D. E. Knuth, *The Art of Computer Programming: Vol. 2*, Seminumerical Algorithms, 2nd ed., Addison-Wesley 1981.

37. A. G. Konheim, *Cryptography: A Primer*, Wiley, 19981.

38. J. Kowalchuk, B. P. Schanning, and S. Powers, Communication privacy: Integration of public and secret key cryptography, *NTC Conference Record*, Vol. 3, pp. 49.1.1-49.1.5, Dec. 1980.

39. C. Lanczos, Solution of systems of linear equations by minimized iterations, *J. Res. Nat. Bureau of Standards 49* (1952), 33-53.

40. D. L. Long, Random equivalence of factorization and computation of orders, *Theoretical Comp. Sci.*, to appear.

41. D. L. Long and A. Wigderson, How discreet is the discrete log?, pp. 413-420 in *Proc. 15-th ACM Symp. Theory of Computing*, 1983.

42. F. J. MacWilliams and N. J. A. Sloane, *The Theory of Error-Correcting Codes*, North-Holland, 1977.

43. H. Maier, On integers free of large prime divisors, to be published.

44. J. L. Massey, Shift-register synthesis and BCH decoding, *IEEE Trans. Inform. Theory IT-15* (1969), 122-127.

45. J. L. Massey, Logarithms in finite cyclic groups - cryptographic issues, pp. 17-25 in *Proc. 4th Benelux Symp. on Inform. Theory*, Leuven, Belgium, May 1983.

46. R. Merkle, Secrecy, authentication, and public key systems, Ph.D. dissertation, Dept. of Electrical Engineering, Stanford Univ., 1979.

47. J. C. P. Miller, On factorization, with a suggested new approach, *Math. Comp. 29* (1975), 155-172.

48. R. C. Mullin and S. A. Vanstone, manuscript in preparation.

49. R. W. K. Odoni, V. Varadharajan, and P. W. Sanders, Public key distribution in matrix rings, *Electronics Letters 20* (1984), 386-387.

50. H. Ong, C. P. Schnorr, and A. Shamir, An efficient signature scheme based on quadratic forms, pp. 208-216 in *Proc. 16th ACM Symp. Theory of Comp.*, 1984.

51. S. C. Pohlig and M. Hellman, An improved algorithm for computing logarithms over $GF(p)$ and its cryptographic significance, *IEEE Trans. Inform. Theory* IT-24 (1978), 106-110.

52. J. Pollard, Monte Carlo methods for index computations (mod p), *Math. Comp. 32* (1978), 918-924.

53. C. Pomerance, Analysis and comparison of some integer factoring algorithms, pp. 89-139 in *Computational Methods in Number Theory: Part 1*, H. W. Lenstra, Jr., and R. Tijdeman, eds., Math. Centre Tract 154, Math. Centre Amsterdam, 1982.

54. G. B. Purdy, A high security log-in procedure, *Comm. ACM 17* (1974), 442-445.

55. M. O. Rabin, Probabilistic algorithms in finite fields, *SIAM J. Comp. 9* (1980), 273-280.

56. J. A. Reeds and N. J. A. Sloane, Shift-register synthesis (modulo m), *SIAM J. Comp.*, to appear.

57. J. E. Sachs and S. Berkovits, Probabilistic analysis and performance modelling of the "Swedish" algorithm and modifications, to be published.

58. J. Sattler and C. P. Schnorr, Generating random walks in groups, preprint.

59. B. P. Schanning, Data encryption with public key distribution, *EASCON Conf. Rec.*, Washington, D.C., Oct. 1979, pp. 653-660.

60. C. P. Schnorr and H. W. Lenstra, Jr., A Monte Carlo factoring algorithm with linear storage, *Math. Comp. 43* (1984), 289-311.

61. R. Schreiber, A new implementation of sparse gaussian elimination, *ACM Trans. Math. Software 8* (1982), 256-276.

62. J. W. Smith and S. S. Wagstaff, Jr., An extended precision operand computer, pp. 209-216 in *Proc. 21st Southeast Region. ACM Conference*, 1983.

63. P. K. S. Wah and M. Z. Wang, Realization and application of the Massey-Omura lock, pp. 175-182 in *Proc. Intern. Zurich Seminar*, March 6-8, 1984.

64. A. L. Wells, Jr., A polynomial form for logarithms modulo a prime, *IEEE Trans. Inform. Theory*, to appear.

65. A. E. Western and J. C. P. Miller, *Tables of Indices and Primitive Roots*, Royal Society Mathematical Tables, vol. 9, Cambridge Univ. Press, 1968.

66. D. Wiedemann, Solving sparse linear equations over finite fields, manuscript in preparation.

67. R. M. Willett, Finding logarithms over large finite fields, in prepration.

68. H. C. Williams and B. Schmid, Some remarks concerning the M.I.T. public-key system, *BIT* *19* (1979), 525-538.

69. K. Yiu and K. Peterson, A single-chip VLSI implementation of the discrete exponential public key distribution system, *Proc. GLOBCOM-82*, IEEE 1982, pp. 173-179.

70. N. Zierler, A conversion algorithm for logarithms on $GF(2^n)$, *J. Pure Appl. Algebra 4* (1974), 353-356.

71. N. Zierler and J. Brillhart, On primitive trinomials (mod 2), *Inform. Control 13* (1968), 541-554.

72. N. Zierler and J. Brillhart, On primitive trinomials (mod 2), II., *Inform. Control 14* (1969), 566-569.

SECTION IV

CHANNELS, NETWORKS, KEY DISTRIBUTION PROTOCOLS

User Functions for the Generation and Distribution of Encipherment Keys

R.W. Jones
International Computers Ltd.
Lovelace Road,
Bracknell, Berks,
U.K.

Abstract

It is generally accepted that data encipherment is needed for
secure distributed data processing systems. It is accepted,
moreover, that the enciphering algorithms are either published or
must be assumed to be known to those who wish to break the
security. Security then lies in the safe keeping of the
encipherment keys, which must be generated and stored securely
and distributed securely to the intending users.

At an intermediate level of detail of a system it may be useful
to have functions which manipulate keys explicitly but which hide
some of the details of key generation and distribution, both for
convenience of use and so that new underlying techniques can be
developed. This paper offers a contribution to the discussion. It
proposes key manipulation functions which are simple from the
user's point of view. It seeks to justify them in terms of the
final secure applications and discusses how they may be
implemented by lower level techniques described elsewhere. The
relationship of the functions to telecommunication standards is
discussed and a standard form is proposed for encipherment key
information.

1. Introduction

It is generally accepted that data encipherment is needed for secure distributed data processing systems. It is accepted, moreover, that the enciphering algorithms are either published or must be assumed to be known to those who wish to break the security. Security then lies in the safe keeping of the encipherment keys, which must be generated and stored securely and distributed securely to the intending users. A number of schemes have been proposed, and in some cases implemented, to manipulate keys securely. For example refs. 1, 2 and 3 describe different methods and offer different but overlapping sets of facilities to the user. It is likely that new methods will be developed and that some part of these methods should be hidden from the user. Since the subject has clearly not reached a stable point it is very likely that any attempt at present to establish a standard user interface will soon need revision. Nevertheless, this paper is written on the assumption that a discussion of such an interface is useful, since it helps to identify the common features of different schemes and to gain some idea of which features will become generic and which become part of the underlying mechanisms.

At some level the user does not concern himself with the manipulation of keys or with explicit commands to encipher and decipher data. He asks for a secure connection to another user or for a securely stored file and can assume that such details are thereby taken care of. At a lower level software and hardware logic exists which deals with things such as how keys are generated, how data encipherment keys and key encipherment keys are kept distinct and the manner of transporting a data encipherment key to a remote user.

At an intermediate level of detail it may be useful to have functions which manipulate keys explicitly but which hide some of the details, both for convenience of use and so that new underlying techniques can be developed. This paper discusses this intermediate level. In doing so it must make assumptions about which functions are primitive at this level. For example, since a digital signature may be achieved by enciphering a message digest, using the secret member of a public key pair, one might decide that it is an application to be programmed in terms of encipherment primitives and does not give rise to specific primitive operations. This view is invalidated by signature techniques which do not depend upon encipherment. Similarly there is implicit in such an interface a judgement of which of the details which should be hidden. Ref. 4 describes a key distribution centre. In an appropriate context software at some level submits a request to a key distribution centre (KDC) for a key which can be used to communicate securely with an intended correspondent. We may wish to produce software which needs no modification when moved from such an environment to one where the system supporting the application user keeps records to enable it to issue keys securely to all members of the community. If this is so we should hide the use or non use of the KDC, but we judge in doing so that the user at that level has not lost needed flexibility. Such judgements as these are made in what follows and the reasons for them are discussed.

2. The Functions

This section describes a set of functions to generate and manipulate keys. The intention is that they appear simple to the user. The user is somewhat ill defined, but well enough, it is hoped, for the benefit of the discussion. One candidate is certainly an application process which makes use of an application service as defined in the Open Systems Interconnection model (see ref. 8) and which wishes to perform explicit data encipherment. Another candidate is the logic of a transport layer entity in the Open Systems Interconnection model which offers a secure service to users of the transport service and which, therefore, sends a data enciphering key to a remote transport entity. The functions are as follows.

i) <u>Generate key(t,s)</u>   meaning generate for me a key or a
   pair of keys of type t and return to me, as the result
   of this function, the local name of the item containing
   the key or keys. The type shows, among other things,
   whether a symmetric or asymmetric algorithm is
   involved. In the former case a single key is generated
   and returned as the result of the function. In the
   latter case the enciphering and deciphering pair is
   generated and returned. The local name is subsequently
   used subscripted by 1 or 2 to indicate an individual
   member of a key pair thus generated or unsubscripted to
   mean the single key generated or the complete item
   containing the key pair.   s is a 64 bit string,
   supplied by the caller, which is to be used by the key
   generation function. The caller does not know the
   cleartext value of the key generated but is assured
   that the same t and s values in a subsequent call
   generate the same key or keys. s may be omitted, in
   which case the values generated, as far as the caller
   is concerned, are random. His chance of generating
   them again is random. The type t is an integer.
   Possible meanings assigned to its values are:
   a key enciphering key (KEK) for DEA1,
   a data enciphering key (DEK) for DEA1.
   an RSA key pair to be used for enciphering keys.
   Other meanings, to which values might be assigned, are
   discussed in section 3.

   N.B. this function and the next two have a result. The
   assumption is that the user has a notation which
   enables him to write something like
        x := generate key (y, z).
   The variable which is to hold the result could be
   written as another parameter. This is a matter of
   taste.

ii) <u>Give key(k,q)</u>   meaning send my key whose local name is k
    securely to the user known to me as q. Assign to the
    key a common reference number which we may use in
    messages to each other and in communicating with our
    local encipherment services (of which this function
    forms a part). Make the reference number available to q

and return it to me as the result of this function.
N.B. the exact manner of making it known to q that the
key is available for him is not considered here. In an
implementation it would not be a trivial issue.
Similarly although we may assume that the services at
the users' locations acknowledge receipt to each other
there is need to consider whether the end user should
do so as well. The assumption here is that if this is
done it is separate from the basic functions needed for
key distribution.

iii) Mutual key(t,q,s)   meaning generate a mutual key for me
and user q. Use seed s and give the key type t.   t and
s are as in "generate key".   s may be omitted to obtain
a random key.   Assign to the key a common reference
number and make it available to q and return it to me
as the result of this function.

iv) Take key(r,q)   meaning make the key whose reference
number is r unavailable to user q.

v) Destroy key(K)   meaning destroy the key identified by K.
K may be a local name of a key, created by "generate
key" or a reference number created by "give key" or
"mutual key"

3. Use of the Functions

This section considers the functions of section 2 in the light of
applications of encryption and related techniques.

3.1 Connection Establishment and User Authentication

When establishing a connection between two users so that they may
exchange messages protected by encryption (for example if they
use an insecure telecommunication link) both users (or their
local services) must be provided with a key and the users must be
authenticated to each other's satisfaction. "Give key" and
"mutual key" may both be used to send a key to a remote user (the

reason why both exist is discussed in section 4). A reasonable
requirement of either of these functions is that it delivers the
key, guarantees to the initiator that the recipient is the user
requested, tells the recipient from whom the key came and
guarantees that he, in his turn, is who he claims to be, i.e. not
just a legitimate user of the service. This is illustrated in
figure 1., where A is one of a number of users of the A service
and B is one of a number of users of the B service. The A
service is used by A in a controlled environment in which the
identity of A is assured (for example the process which
represents him has been initiated after the submission of a
password to a control program which controls access to resources,
one of which is the A service). B has the same relationship to
the B service. The route between the A service and the B service
is assumed to be insecure in the absence of encipherment.

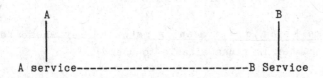

Fig. 1

After receiving a request from A to deliver a key to B the A
service, having discovered the route, sends it to the B service,
suitably enciphered by a KEK. The A service and the B service
must authenticate each other. Their manner of doing this depends
upon a number of factors,including whether a KDC is involved and
whether the KEK is a public or secret key. Methods are
discussed, for example, in refs.4 and 7. For example, ref. 4
describes protocols for sending a DEA1 key, first when it is
protected by DEA1 encryption and secondly when it is protected by
public key encryption. In both cases the protocol is described
in terms of a user A who wishes to send a key to another user B,
with the aid of a KDC (see fig. 2).

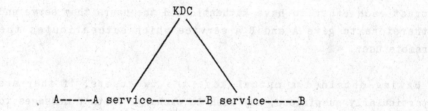

Fig.2

In the first case the protocol has three logical parts viz:

i) A obtains securely from KDC two copies of the key, one
enciphered by A's KEK and the other enciphered by B's KEK.

ii) A sends to B the copy enciphered by B's KEK.

iii) A and B use the key to exchange authentication protocol.

In the second case the protocol has four logical parts viz:

i) A obtains securely from KDC B's public key and the key to
be used.

ii) A sends to B the key enciphered by B's public key.

iii) B obtains securely from KDC A's public key.

iv) A and B exchange authentication protocol.

(For details of the values exchanged to cope with particular
security problems see ref. 4.)

Either of these methods may be hidden from the users at the level
proposed for them here. The appropriate interchanges are
initiated by the function 'mutual key'. A possible improvement
in underlying protocols to remove as yet unknown security flaws
is also hidden from them.

Once the two services have authenticated each other they may trust each other to have authenticated the users they serve and therefore to give A and B a service which authenticates the remote user.

Having obtained a mutual key, the two users, if they are particularly suspicious, may wish to exchange further messages to convince themselves of each other's genuineness. This must depend upon further secret information, which becomes vulnerable if it is sent to the other,as yet untrusted, party, using the newly established connection. They may, for example, exchange passwords using the protection of the connection they do not quite trust. If a correct reply password is not received within the permitted number of attempts the first one is compromised and there is a suspicion that the key distribution service is in error. The users may, on the other hand, have private encipherment keys, previously delivered, which they use only to protect their private authentication protocol. If the protocol reveals a doubt of correct identity no secret user information is compromised but, as before, the trustworthiness of the key distribution service is in doubt. This kind of consideration is inevitable if there is a standard service which distributes keys and attempts to guarantee that the sender and recipient are genuine. An alternative is that the service does not use encipherment to authenticate the users, but leaves it to them. Another is that the identity of the recipient is guaranteed but that he is only sure that the originator is an authorised user of the key distribution service. Neither of these possibilities seems as useful since one or both users must either risk compromising secret information or must hold a key personally. They may well do so but they should not be forced to.

Another point to consider is that a user who wishes to connect to a remote resource may not be directly identifiable by that resource. For example, a database interrogation service may contain no check of its user's authority, assuming that his identity was established as part of the identification procedure when he logged in and that the resources at his disposal, including the interrogation service, were thereby decided. There will then be an entity, at the same location as the user who wishes to connect, which is concerned with resource allocation, which knows which users are allowed to use which resources and which checks permission before allowing the user's connection to

be made. This entity has a privileged position in remote user
authentication in that it is trusted by remote parts of the
service (entities of the same kind as itself) to guarantee that
the users it serves are only given authorised connections. It is
useful to build into the service some mechanism to guarantee to
such privileged entities that they are communicating with their
own kind. The simplest way of doing this is to design the
control software so that all connections to remote processes are
handled by such entities and that they check access permission at
one or both of the sites involved. If we assume that this is not
the case and that there is a need to make connections between
processes which will do their own checking of authorisation then
a possible way of identifying the entities which are to be given
more trust is to allocate exclusively for their use a special
type of key. The encipherment service guarantees to the remote
encipherment service that such a key may only be used
successfully by such an entity. Ref. 2 introduces the idea of
type values which it is useful to bind securely to keys (e.g. DEK
or KEK). A useful type value which is not mentioned there is one
which guarantees that the key may be used only by an entity
authorised to check access rights.

There are applications where it is useful to be able to generate
the same key at two remote sites rather than sending the key from
one to the other and without sending values used to generate it
via the telecommunication link. For example, a customer is
supplied with a plastic card which is used to help identify him.
The card contains a value which is to help generate the key to be
used in sending information to a central installation. In
addition he is required to type in a PIN value which also
contributes. Another contributory value comes from the terminal
into which he inserts his card (the terminal value may be changed
periodically for greater security). The central installation
holds these values. When it is told in clear who the customer and
the terminal claim to be it generates a key using the stored
values, knowing that the genuine terminal can generate the same
on behalf of the genuine user. For this and similar cases the key
generation functions in section 2 contain a seed value, with the
assurance that the same seed will generate the same key. When an
unrepeatable key is wanted the seed is omitted. There is, of
course, a danger in this facility and it may well be that it
should be denied to some users.

In making a request for a transport connection, as described in the Open Systems Interconnection model, it is envisaged that a user may ask that it be secure. The details of what this means are not yet spelled out but it certainly implies encipherment. A connection request message may contain 'security parameters' (see ref. 9) and we may suppose that they will indicate the key to be used, either as the actual key (suitably enciphered) or as a reference to a key already known to both parties. We may then consider the applicability of the functions described here. First if the two parties have an established mutual KEK used to encipher keys they wish to send each other the functions are not applicable. The key to be used for the connection is enciphered by a call on the sender's encipherment service. It may then either be placed in the connection request message or it may be sent beforehand (for example as one of a batch of keys to use that day) and a reference to it may be placed in the connection request message. If the two parties do not have such a mutual KEK and do not have a supply of session keys to choose from then the function 'mutual key' applies. However, it cannot be used to encipher the key which is then placed in the connection request because that is not its function. Its function is to deliver the key. Neither is it reasonable to suppose that a key should be extracted from the connection request as it passes from one KEK domain to another (and there may be such separate domains for security purposes). The use of 'mutual key' in this case is to establish a mutual key for the two end users so that they may use it to encipher the keys to be used subsequently for transport connection protection. It must be done as a separate previous operation and, at least the first time, must be sent over an 'insecure' transport connection. This does not matter as the function handles its own security.

3.2 Data Privacy & Data Authentication

Once keys have been successfully exchanged by the two end users of a telecommunication link or by their local services on their behalf data privacy may be achieved by data encipherment and decipherment. Each local service must therefore provide enciphering and deciphering functions. The user may also wish to encipher and decipher keys using key enciphering keys to produce and make use of key hierarchies. These topics are dealt with for

example in refs.1 and 2, which describe means of protecting keys
such that they never appear in clear outside a trusted
encipherment environment. They are relevant to this paper in
that the user of the key manipulation facility needs the ability
to operate explicitly upon keys of a chosen type, but should not
need to know how the types are indicated or need to be wary of
operations upon keys of a particular type which might prejudice
security. Data authentication and greater assurance of privacy
are obtained by using particular modes of operation of
encipherment (for example cipher block chaining or cipher feed
back when using block ciphers) and by the addition of checking
information (for example enciphered sum checks to reveal illicit
modification and various identifying values to reveal illicit
insertions and replays). These functions are not directly
concerned with key generation and distribution and are not dealt
with in this paper.

3.3 Digital Signatures

A digital signature depends upon a sender using a key that no one
else has and the receiver being able to demonstrate that the key
has been used. To do this the sender may use the secret key of a
public key cipher, such as RSA, and make the public key available
to the receiver (ref.5). Using the functions described here a
type value would be assigned to mean a public key pair. The
effect of a public key cipher may be achieved by adding type
information, meaning "encipher only" or "decipher only" to a
symmetric cipher key in a trusted environment, with the knowledge
that it can only be removed and acted upon in a trusted
environment (ref.2). Another possibility is to use an algorithm
which has an associated public and private key but which
transforms the text to be signed by some means other than
encipherment. Such keys can also be indicated by type
information in the functions described in section 2.

3.4 Stored Secure Files

The key generation function may be used to generate a key which
enciphers a file stored locally or whose medium is to be
physically removed from the computer environment. If a file is
stored for a long time or is transferred to a separate site it
will be necessary to re-encipher. Ref.1 points out that a

hierarchy of keys is needed in such a case. Refs. 1 and 2 discuss how this may be achieved securely. The exact method is hidden at a lower level and visible in the functions described here only in the fact that keys are generated with an explicit type which indicates Key Enciphering Key or Data Enciphering Key.

3.5 Protection of Software Copyright

Ref.2 points out that type information securely attached to a key may be used, given a secure execution environment, to safeguard copyright. Software to be protected would be enciphered by the key and the key would be supplied to the user enciphered by a KEK which was available only inside the secure execution environment. When the software was used it would be deciphered as an implicit part of the loading operation. This idea anticipates the commercial availability of such an execution environment. However, when appropriate, a type value could be assigned in the functions of section 2.

4. Relationship to Detailed Key Manipulation Schemes

This section discusses how the functions described in section 2 can be implemented using a number of techniques described elsewhere. The functions are dealt with in turn.

4.1 Generate key

Let us assume we are using one of the key management schemes described in refs.1, 2, and 3. Each of them, when it generates a key and makes it available outside the trusted encipherment facility protects it by enciphering it. The schemes differ in how they do this and in how they ensure that the keys may not be misused (for example that a DEK may not be deciphered and made available outside the encipherment facility in clear form). They differ in the amount of protection they give the keys. The Key Notarization Scheme guarantees that a key can only be used successfully by the intended users by making the encipherment and decipherment of the key a function of the identities of the users

for whom the key is intended. Since a user must establish his
identity in a way which satisfies security criteria (for example
by supplying a password) he cannot successfully use someone
else's key. The IBM scheme protects the key from exposure and
ensures that some different types of key cannot be confused. To
do this different master keys at an instalation are used to
encipher KEKs, session keys and keys used to encipher files. The
operating system is relied upon to ensure that the keys are used
by the intended users. The ICL scheme enciphers a key, together
with type information indicating how it may be used, by a KEK (in
some cases by an instalation master key). It can, therefore,
potentially restrict keys in ways which may be defined and could
include the equivalent of the Key Notarization scheme. The
functions supplied in terms of key type therefore overlap and
where they coincide they are not implemented in the same way. The
functions described in section 2 may be mapped on to any of the
three, with the proviso that some of the key types envisaged are
not present in some cases.

The local name produced by "generate key" is then in the context
of ref.1 the form enciphered by KMO, KM1 or KM2 according to its
type. In the context of ref.2 it is the key and concatenated type
enciphered by the master key. In the context of ref.3 it is the
form supplied by the Key Notarisation Facility.

If a key is to be associated securely with its users as in ref.3
then extra associated software is needed if the basic
encipherment facility does not provide it. Whether it is always
desirable to tie a generated key immediately to particular users
is a debatable point.

4.2 Give key

Assume that the user to whom the key is to be given is at a site
which uses a similar system in terms of refs.1, 2 and 3. If the
first site has the necessary KEK it can re-encrypt the generated
key and send it directly to the second site. There the service
re-encrypts it for the second user if the key used to protect it
in transit is not the one which protects it when it is stored
there. There may, on the other hand be a series of re-
encipherments en route because of the need to cross different key
domains. The user of the "give key" function may remain unaware

of this.

As in ref.4., a Key Distribution Centre may be used to generate
the key in a form suitable for transmission to another site. This
also may be hidden from the user of the "give key" function.

If the sender and recipient are encipherment services which
differ in the way they encode keys for protection (as in refs. 1,
2, and 3) more manipulation is needed to effect the transfer.
There must be a transformation function, which operates in an
environment as secure as the one used to encipher the data in the
first place, which deciphers and re-enciphers, reformatting as
necessary. This also can be hidden from the user of "give key",
although a standard way of formatting keys and their associated
information is clearly desirable.

4.3 Mutual key

In some cases this may be only a shorthand way of writing
"generate key", followed by "give key". However consider the
following cases.

a) When a KDC is used to generate the key it may be necessary
to tell it the identity of the other partner in the connection so
that it may encipher it appropriately (see, for example, ref.4).

b) The generation of the key may need the involvement of the
encipherment services at both ends of the connection (for
example when using the Diffie/Hellman algorithm (ref. 6).

For such reasons"mutual key" is needed as a primitive function
at this level.

4.4 Take key and Destroy key

If the underlying implementations are those of refs. 1, 2 or 3
these functions are barely necessary. If a generated key is
stored by the encipherment service and a reference to it passed
back to the user then an explicit destruction of keys is needed.
"Take key" may also be used to inform the service that a
particular user is no longer entitled to use a key.

5. Relationship to Communication Standards

We may expect the emerging Open Systems Interconnection standards
to provide secure services. For example, as already mentioned,
an enhancement of the transport service is likely to provide
authentication of users, data privacy and data authentication.
The two entities which communicate to provide this service must
establish jointly agreed keys and initialisation variables and
would make use of functions such as those described in this
paper. The form of the transmitted key and its accompanying
information is an obvious candidate for standardisation and would
avoid the need to transform the key en route, other than to
change its key encryption key. In seeking a standard form we have
to consider:

   i) the length of the key,

   ii) the permitted users (if this is to be declared explicitly),

   iii) information about the type of use permitted.

The methods referred to in this paper do not all allow the same
restrictions of key use to be described. Moreover, in some
cases, the restriction is implied in the manner of enciphering
the key (e.g. the Key Notarization scheme). A standard which
explicitly stated the users could therefore be considered
redundant in this case. However, if the basic key manipulation
method does not involve the user's identity (as in ref.1 and in
ref.2 in its simplest form) the addition gives added security.

The basic encipherment algorithm affects both the length of the
key and the type information which is relevant. For example, an
indication of "encipherment" or "decipherment" is irrelevant to
an RSA key.

Ref. 2 has suggested that the "parity" bits in the DES key could
be used to indicate typing information. This may be unacceptable
as an international standard. The typing information must then
be held separately from the 64 bit key variable.

Bearing these points in mind the following is a tentative
suggestion for a standard form for a key and associated
information. First, the clear form. It has the format:

>   key length, key, key type, users

where "key length" is an integer which gives the length of the
following key;

where "key" is the key as a binary string;

where "key type" is a binary string whose bits have the following
significance:

1st bit	DEK or KEK,
2nd bit	enciphering key or not,
3rd bit	deciphering key or not,
4th bit	software protection key or not,
5th bit	key usable by any process or only by one authorised to check access rights,

>   (meanings for other bits are likely to prove useful);

and where "users" consists of either one or two alphanumeric
strings which identify the permitted user or users.

If such a composite item is to be transmitted over an insecure
telecommunication line it must be enciphered. The form this
takes depends upon the enciphering method. Using a 64 bit block
cipher, for example, one must use some method of ensuring that
the separate blocks which form the item cannot be changed
unnoticed. One might, for example, form an enciphered sum check
of the whole item and send it with it. A method which enciphered
a block as long as the composite item could dispense with this.

6. Conclusions

This paper has discussed a number of issues related to the standardisation of the interface to an enciphering service at a particular level.

Several ways of providing basic key manipulation features have been considered. It would be logically possible to evolve a standard way which made use of the best features of those considered. This would make standardisation of the form of the key and associated information easier.

An enciphering service may or may not make use of a separate Key Distribution Centre, depending on the number of communicating locations and the complexity possible in each. This design option is likely to survive. The functions suggested here deliberately hide this choice, taking the view that it is a part of the service implementation which the user should be able to ignore.

When a key is sent to a remote user it may need to be transformed because a different way of protecting it is needed. It may need to be enciphered by the remote user's location master key. During its journey it may need to be enciphered by a KEK used only for transportation. It may need to be re-enciphered by several such keys in the course of its journey. Such transformations should be hidden from the user at as low a level as possible so that logic can be written irrespective of the context created by the way the network of users is organised.

New methods of enciphering are likely to be developed. We should attempt to protect users from the need to know the underlying changes they bring. This is, of course, an aim which cannot necessarily be fulfilled. At the level chosen for the functions of this paper we reveal the essential difference between symmetric and asymmetric ciphers. New methods may bring their own characteristics which should not be hidden.

New applications of encipherment and related techniques are likely. Two mentioned here are digital signatures which do not use encipherment of a form which can be used for data privacy and a new key type dedicated to controlling resource use.

For' such reasons the subject is one which will continue to develop and the points made in this paper are offered as part of the discussion needed to find functions and techniques which may develop as our knowledge of the subject grows.

References

1. Ehrsam W.F., Matyas S.M., Meyer C.D. and Tuchman W.L. : "A cryptographic key management scheme for implementing the data encryption standard." IBM Systems Journal, vol.17, no.2.

2. Jones R.W. : "Some techniques for handling encipherment keys." ICL Technical Journal, vol.3, no.2.

3. Smid M.E. : "A key notarization system for computer networks. "NBS Special Publication 500-54, US Dept. of Commerce.

4. Price W.L. & Davies D.W. : "Issues in the design of a key distribution centre." NPL Report DNACS 43/81, National Physical Laboratory, Teddington, Middlesex, UK

5. Rivest R.L., Shamir A and Addleman L. "A method of obtaining digital signatures and public key cryptosystems." Communications of the ACM, February 1978.

6. Diffie W and Hellman M.E. "New directions in Cryptography." IEEE Transactions on Information Theory, vol.IT-22, no.6.

7. Needham R.M. & Schroeder M.D. "Using encryption for authentication in large networks of computers." Communications of the ACM, December 1978.

8. International standard ISO/IS 7498. Information processing systems -Open systems interconnection - Basic reference model.

9. Draft International Standard ISO/DIS 8073. Information processing systems -Open systems interconnection - Connection oriented transport protocol specification.

AN OPTIMAL CLASS OF SYMMETRIC KEY
GENERATION SYSTEMS

Rolf Blom

Ericsson Radio Systems AB

S-163 80 Stockholm, Sweden

Abstract.

It is sometimes required that user pairs in a network share secret information to be used for
mutual identification or as a key in a cipher system. If the network is large it becomes
impractical or even impossible to store all keys securely at the users. A natural solution then
is to supply each user with a relatively small amount of secret data from which he can derive
all his keys. A scheme for this purpose will be presented and we call such a scheme a
symmetric key generation system (SKGS). However, as all keys will be generated from a
small amount of data, dependencies between keys will exist. Therefore by cooperation, users
in the system might be able to decrease their uncertainty about keys they should not have
access to.

The objective of this paper is to present a class of SKGS for which the amount of secret
information needed by each user to generate his keys is the least possible while at the same
time a certain minimum number of users have to cooperate to resolve the uncertainty of
unknown keys.

Introduction

We picture an application in which messages in a network are protected by a symmetric cipher. Each user pair should have a unique key which enables them to encipher messages to be exchanged and thereby get protection against information disclosure to other users and possible wiretappers. The keys shared between users are distributed at start up time by what we will call a key generation authority. The keys could be seen as master keys used to generate session keys.

A network with n users implies that each user must have access to n-1 keys. Now, if n is large it becomes impractical or even impossible to store all keys securely. A natural solution would then be to supply each user with a relatively small amount of secret data from which he can derive all his keys. A scheme for this purpose will be called a symmetric key generation system (SKGS). However, if all keys are generated from a small amount of data attention must be payed to the fact that dependencies between keys will exist. These dependencies will be such that a group of cooperating users might be able to decrease their uncertainty about keys they should not know about.

In this paper we will present a class of SKGS for which the amount of secret data, needed by each user, is as small as possible while at the same time a certain minimum number k of users have to cooperate to determine keys which are used by other user pairs. The presentation will be made without proofs. For a more detailed analysis and proofs the interested reader is refered to (1).

Preliminaries.

Let G denote the generator matrix of a (n,k) linear code over GF(q). Here n denotes the length of the codewords and k is the dimension of the code, i.e. G is a kxn matrix with elements in FG(q), q a prime power. The number of codewords is q^k and the set of codewords consists of all linear combinations of the rows of G. If $d \in GF(q)^k$ denotes a vector of k information symbols, they will be encoded into c=dG.

A MDS code is usually defined by the condition that the minimum distance of the code is n-k+1. This condition can be shown to be equivalent with the condition that every k columns in G are linearly independent. For a general introduction to MDS codes see (2). From the property that every set of k columns in the generator matrix of a MDS code is independent it follows that a codeword is uniquely determined by any k elements in the codeword. It also follows that knowledge of less than k elements of a codeword reveals no information about another element.

MDS codes exist when n<q+2. In the application we consider, q should be much larger than n, so suitable codes will always exist.

A class of SKGS based on MDS codes.

Let the users in the system be numbered consequtivly from 1 to n. Also assume that at least k users shall have to cooperate to get any information about a key they should not have access to. We also assume that the keys should be in $GF(q)$.

The construction of the SKGS starts with selecting a (n,k) MDS code over $GF(q)$ with generator matrix G. This G will be known by all users in the network. Then the key generating authority draws a random symmetric matrix D, also with elements in $GF(q)$. The keys to be used by the user pairs are then given by

$$K = (DG)^T G.$$

User pair (i, j) will use $(K)_{i,j}$ i.e. the element in row i and column j in K. Obviously K is symmetric and hence $(K)_{i,j} = (K)_{j,i}$. Then if user i knows row i of K and user j knows row j of K, they have a common key.

The i:th row in K is given by the i:th row in $(DG)^T$ and G. But G is assumed publicly known so the only data that the key generation authority has to distribute to user i is the i:th row of $(DG)^T$.

$(DG)^T$ is a nxk matrix which means that each row consists of k elements in $GF(q)$. Thus the required secret store at each user is $kxlb(q)$ bits. This is really the least possible value for a SKGS with the assumed parameters (see (1)).

At last we will give a simple explanation of why at least k users have to cooperate to get any information about keys they do not have. Assume m < k users cooperate. Then they know m rows of K. But K is symmetric and then they also know m columns. This means that they know m elements in each row of K for all other users. They do not know any other elements in these rows. Now observe that each row in K is a codeword in the code generated by G. Then from what was stated in the Preliminaries, knowledge of less than k elements in a codeword does not reveal any information about any other element in the codeword. So if less than k users cooperate they get no information about an unknown key. However, if k or more users cooperate they know all of K, because knowledge of k elements in a codeword uniquely determines the codeword.

Implementation aspects.

From a theoretical point of view it is a straightforward task to implement a SKGS based on MDS codes. All that is needed is a generator matrix and computational capability for matrix multiplication. However, rather much storage space is required to store a general generator matrix. To decrease this amount of storage space one could use a punctured Reed-Solomon code because the elements in the generator matrix are given by a simple expresseion, viz.

$$(G)_{i,j} = \alpha^{(i-1)(j-1)}$$

where α is a primitive element in $GF(q)$. Then if $c = dG$ the j:th element in c will be given by

$$c_j = \sum_{i=1}^{k} d_i \, \alpha^{(i-1)(j-1)}$$

This technique is easily applied on the class of SKGS described in the previous section and it shows that a simple and practical implementation exists.

References

(1)   R. Blom, "An optimal class of symmetric key generation systems", Report LiTH-ISY-I-0641, Linköping University, 1984.

(2)   F.J. MacWilliams and N.J.A. Sloane, The Theory of error correcting codes, North-Holland, New York, 1977.

ON THE USE OF THE BINARY MULTIPLYING CHANNEL IN

A PRIVATE COMMUNICATION SYSTEM

B.J.M. Smeets

Department of Computer Engineering

University of Lund

P.O. Box 725, S-220 07   Lund/SWEDEN

Abstract. A novel cryptosystem is presented in which the protection of the messages is based on the special properties of the binary multiplying channel. In the system the receiver is mainly responsible for the protection of the messages and not the transmitter. In the paper a small area network realization with a binary multiplying channel is discussed.

The research was supported in part by the National Swedish Board for Technical Development under grants 81-3323 and 83-4364 at the University of Lund.

1. Introduction.

In this paper a novel cryptosystem will be discussed that is based on a special two-way communication channel, i.e. the binary multiplying channel (BMC). New in this system is that the task of protecting the messages is mainly one for the receiver. This in contrast with the classic cryptosystems where the transmitter has this task. The receiver in a classic cryptosystem must know the key used by the transmitter in order to be able to invert the encryption mapping. The fact that keys must be shared causes great practical problems since practical classic cryptosystems require large keys [1],[3],[4]. One of the reasons for using large keys is the fact that the encrypted message is publicly known [1].

When a BMC is used in a communication system it will be possible to realize the protection of the messages in a simpler way. In Section 2 the problem of the construction of communication strategies for the BMC will be discussed without considering the security aspects. Though recently there has been much progress in solving this problem [7],[8], the actual construction of communication strategies for the BMC requires some ad-hoc solutions. In Section 3 the special aspects of security are discussed when the BMC is used in a communication network. Furthermore a communication strategy is presented that provides a good protection of the messages sent via a network. In the last section an application of the new system is discussed.

2. Coding strategies for the BMC.

Consider the communication situation given in Fig. 1a. Two messages m_1 and m_2 are to be transmitted over the binary multiplying channel. The BMC is a deterministic two-way channel with two binary inputs x_1 and x_2 and a binary output $y=x_1 x_2 \in \{0,1\}$, $x_i \in \{0,1\}$, i=1,2. A simple realization of the BMC is given in Fig. 1b.

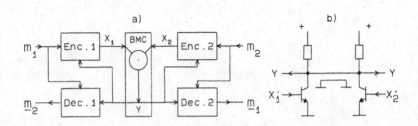

Fig. 1   The BMC in a two user communication network and
a wired-and realization of the BMC.

To meet our later requirements and in order to keep the codes quite simple we assume that

    a)   the messages m_i, i=1,2 are taken from a finite set

of messages $M=\{0,1,...,m-1\}$, and that

b) the encoders and decoders are pairwise identical.

Furthermore we assume that

c) the messages m_1 and m_2 are uniform and independently distributed.

Consider the situation where each terminal has chosen a message; say terminal 1 has chosen m_1 and terminal 2 has chosen m_2. The terminals start to communicate via the BMC in order to determine the messages chosen by their opponents. For that purpose they both use a set of rules. All these rules together make the encoder and the decoder. In the sequel the encoding rules will be called a coding strategy. If the reconstructed message $m_i=m_i$ for all sended messages m_i, then one calls the coding strategy complete. A complete coding strategy satisfying a) and b) is refered to as a symmetric discrete complete coding strategy; a SDC-strategy for short. If a coding strategy also optimizes the average transmission rates R_{12} and R_{21} then the coding strategy is called optimal as well. Here is $R_{12}:=n^{-1}I(M_1;Y|M_2)$ and $R_{21}:=n^{-1}I(M_2;Y|M_1)$, i.e. the normalized average mutual information between m_1 and y when m_2 is known and the normalized average mutual information between m_2 and y when m_1 is known, respectively; n is the average number of transmissions. The general problem of determining the region of rate pairs (R_{12},R_{21}) where reliable communication is possible, i.e. the capacity region, C(BMC), of the BMC has been studied for more then two decades [2]. Recently it has been shown by Schalkwijk [6] that the achievable rate region as discussed in [7] is indeed C(BMC). His coding scheme is however not constructive and therefore some coding strategies will be discussed in this section. Note that in the case of a SDC-strategy one has $R_{12}=R_{21}$.

Based upon ideas given in [5] there exists a convenient method for representing the coding strategies. Let $(m_1,m_2)\in M\times M$, the cartesian product of the message sets, and let us further associate a unit-square with each message pair (m_1,m_2). Then one can imagine regions, clusters of unit-squares, in a mxm square of possible message pairs in which the actual message pair has to lie. The coding strategy is used in successive transmissions to partition these regions into smaller sub-regions until at both sides of the channel the position of the message pair in the mxm square is unambiguously known.

For example, consider the case $M=\{0,1,2,3\}$. The channel input x_i for the first transmission is taken 1 if $m_i=0,1$ or 2 and 0 if $m_i=3$, $i=1,2$, see Fig. 2a. The result of the first transmission will be $y_1=1$ if $x_1=x_2=1$ and $y_1=0$ otherwise, Fig. 2b. Note that one has obtained two regions. One characterized by $y_1=1$ and one characterized by $y_1=0$. Suppose that $y_1=1$ has been received. The fact that both terminals know that $y_1=1$ is used in the second transmission. The channel inputs for the second transmission are taken 1 if $m_i=0,1$ and 0 if $m_i=2$. If $y_2=0$ is received then one knows that $(m_1,m_2)\in\{(2,0),(2,1),(2,2),(1,2),(0,2)\}$. Since the correct message pair cannot be determined at this stage of the transmission session one continues by sending a 1 if $m_i=1,2$ and 0 if $m_i=0$. Suppose one has received $y_3=0$, then one has $(m_1,m_2)\in\{(2,0),(0,2)\}$. Now it is possible for the terminals to remove the remaining ambiguity by taking their own messages into account. Hence the transmission session is finished. Fig. 2c gives a complete coding strategy for the 4x4 square.

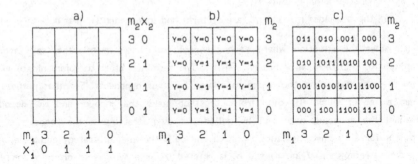

Fig. 2   A coding strategy for the 4x4 square.

The transmission rates R_{12} and R_{21} are easily calculated by exploiting condition c). If $w(m_1=i,m_2=j)$ denotes the number of transmissions required to determine the message pair (i,j) in the mxm square and $\overline{w}$ is the average of w over all message pairs then $R_{12}=R_{21}=H(M_1)/\overline{w}=.593$ bits per transmission. Here is $H(M_1)$ the average binary entropy of the messages m_1. Note that $R_{12}=R_{21}>.5$ bits/tr, hence the rate pair (R_{12},R_{21}) lies outside the time-sharing region !. Larger instances of m have been studied by Post and Ligtenberg [8]. They looked for methods to construct high rate coding strategies.

Some comments should be made concearning the message pairs and the corresponding y-sequence entries in the mxm square, Fig. 2c. Let $S(\underline{y})$ denote the number of message pairs that have $\underline{y}$ as the y-sequence entry in the mxm square. Then the following holds for all SDC-strategies.

Proposition 1 If $\underline{y}$ is a y-sequence entry corresponding with (m_1,m_2),
then $S(\underline{y})=1 <=> m_1=m_2$.

From the above follows instantaneously.

Corollary There are m different message pairs for which $S(\underline{y})=1$.

The proof is given in the appendix.

3. The BMC and private communication.

In this section a communication network is considered that uses a BMC. Recalling the realization in Fig. 1b it is clear that the channel outputs y are public in a communication system in which several terminals are connected; see Fig. 3. In such a system communication is considered to take place between two terminals at the same time while the other terminals cannot interrupt.

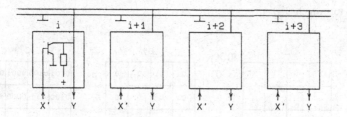

Fig. 3   A communication system with a BMC.

Like in other communication systems is jamming a severe threat to our system. However, here we will only consider a wire tapping attack of an "unfriendly" terminal. Therefore we will look at how much information the wire tapper gets by looking at the channel signals y. The worst that can happen is that during a message transfer one terminal is always a receiver since there is no real difference between the legal receiver and the wire-tapper. Assume for the time being that messages are only sent from one terminal to another. Without loss of generality we may assume that terminal 1 sends to terminal 2. Communication is totally insecure in the system. In order to disturbe the channel signals terminal 2 starts to transmit randomly chosen messages. From Section 2 it is clear that the wire tapper knows immediately the correct (message,noise message) pair if the noise message was equal to the message m_1 at terminal 1. Is however the noise message $m_2 \neq m_1$ then $S(\underline{y}) > 1$, where $\underline{y}$ is the y-sequence produced by (m_1, m_2). These observations are now to be analysed under the conditions a) and b) in Section 2.

Let p_{ij} denote the probability that message j is chosen at terminal i, i=1,2. Assume that $p_{ij} > 0$ for all j=0,1,...,m-1, i=1,2, and let m_1 and m_2 be independently chosen from the message set M. Using proposition 1 of the previous section we obtain the average probability of correct interception, P_{int}, by the wire tapper:

$$P_{int} = \sum_{S(\underline{y})=1} pr(\underline{y}) = \sum_{i=0}^{m-1} pr(m_1 = i, m_2 = i) = \sum_{i=0}^{m-1} p_{1i} p_{2i}.$$

It can be shown that

<u>Proposition 2</u> If the messages are chosen independently from the set M and none of the messages has probability zero, then the receiver can make the probability of interception $P_{int} \leq 1/m$ for all SDC-strategies for the BMC, (see appendix).

At this point one could stop and use the coding strategies of the type discussed in Section 2. However, note that if $S(y) > 1$ then the message pair (m_1, m_2) is not unambiguously determined by $\underline{y}$, hence $H(M_i | \underline{y}) > 0$. Therefore coding strategies that obtain higher values for $S(\underline{y})$ then those of the previous type are of interest. In Fig. 4 such a coding strategy is given for the 4x4 square. The transmission rate of this coding strategy is less (.57 bits/transm.) than of the one shown in Fig. 2c. However, the new coding strategy has a y-sequence for which $S(\underline{y})=4$.

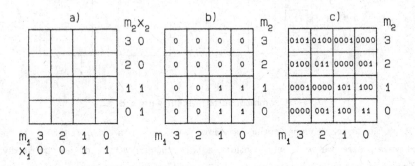

Fig. 4   An alternative coding strategy for the 4x4 square

For both the coding strategies, Fig. 2c and Fig. 4c, the average conditional entropies $H(M_1|y_1,...,y_k)$ have been calculated. Here denotes $y_1,...,y_k$ the first k y-signals obtained by using a given strategy. In Fig. 5 these calculations are summarized. One sees that the coding strategy of Fig. 4c is better from a security point of view.

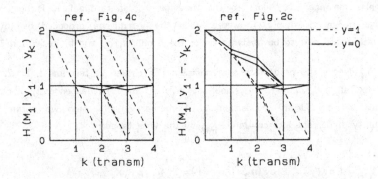

Fig. 5   The average conditional entropies $H(M_1 | y_1,...,y_k)$ of the coding strategies of Fig. 4c and Fig. 2c.

The coding strategy given here can be regarded as a generalization of a code given by Hagelbarger [2]. From the successive squares shown in Fig. 4 it is not difficult to see how one should proceed to construct structural equivalent coding strategies in cases where $m=2^n, n=1,2,3,....$

4. Practical considerations.

In many practical situations the number of correct intercepted messages will be too high. Especially, this will be the case if the source statistics are such that there is a high probability of having $S(\underline{y})=1$. In such a case one should try to obtain a more uniform probability distribution of the message pairs. If condition c) is satisfied one needs only to take a large value of m to lower P_{int}. If this is not satisfactory one could think of using one of the following solutions to the problem. First one could still use some classic cryptosystem to encrypt the messages. This cryptosystem could be quite rudimentary since most of the encrypted messages cannot be correctly intercepted. For the same reason the use of source encoding would be a solution too. A different type of solution would be the use of a randomly determined permutation. Suppose the two communicating terminals will not start with communicating their messages but they will send randomly generated messages first. If at a certain moment enough, say N, noise pairs are generated for which $S(\underline{y})>1$ (or maximal), then these noise pairs determine a permutation of the messages. If the probabilities $pr(m_1=i,m_2=i)$ are the same for all values of $i \in M$, it will be difficult for a wire-tapper to reconstruct this permutation.

Besides the listen-only attack and the problem of jamming, there are some other severe attacks on a network such as the one given in Fig. 3. If an attacker splits the network into two groups he will be able to monitor all communications between the groups. Furthermore if two attackers work closely together they can in principle tap the "wire" by comparing the timing of the signal patterns at different points. Therefore the channel itself must be well protected to provide security.

5. Conclusions.

The binary multiplying channel has interesting properties for use in a private communication system. First, one can send with a total average transmission rate which is larger than 1 bit per channel use. Furthermore, in a communication system that uses a BMC the protection of the messages can be realized by the receiver. Therefore there is no need to use keys when protecting the messages. However, keys might be used to solve the problem of determining the authenticity of the user.
A "wired-and" realisation of the BMC gives the opportunity to construct a small communication network that is well protected against tapping. In general, the security of a communication network that uses a BMC requires saveguarding of the channel itself against attacks.

6. Acknowledgement.

Thanks are due to J.P.M. Schalkwijk, who got me interested in the subject. Furthermore

346

the stimulating conversations with R. Johannesson and T. Herlestam are gratefully acknowledged.

Appendix.

Consider a SDC-strategy for the coding of a mxm square. The condition that the strategy is complete is here reformulated as having $H(M_i ; \underline{y} | m_j)=0$, $i,j=1,2$, $i \neq j$, for all possible y-sequence entries in a completed square.

Let $y^k(m_1,m_2)$ denote the y-sequence $y_1,...,y_k$ produced by the message pair $(m_1,m_2) \in M^2$ up to the k-th transmission. Furthermore denotes $y^c(m_1,m_2)$ the y-sequence obtained by using (m_1,m_2) when the communication is completed. Let $E(m_1,y^k(m_1,m_2))$ denote the encoding of message m_1 after receiving $y^k(m_1,m_2)$.

Lemma 1 Let $m_1,m_2,m_3,m_4 \in M$. Assume that $y^c(m_1,m_2)=y^c(m_3,m_4)$ and $x_{2,1},...,x_{2,c}$ are the inputs produced by encoder 2 using (m_1,m_2) and $\tilde{x}_{2,1},...,\tilde{x}_{2,c}$ those by using (m_3,m_4). If $x_{2,i}=\tilde{x}_{2,i}$ for i=1,...,c, then $y^c(m_1,m_4)= y^c(m_1,m_2)$.

Proof: Let (m_1,m_4) be the transmitted message. Obviously $y^1(m_1,m_4)=y^1(m_1,m_2)$ since the first input letters depend only on the m´s. So let $y^k(m_1,m_4)=y^k(m_1,m_2)$ for all k<N+1<c. First observe that the encoder 1 output equals $x_{1,N+1}=E(m_1,y^N(m_1,m_4))=E(m_1,y^N(m_1,m_2))$. The encoder 2 output can be calculated as $x_{2,N+1}=E(m_4,y^N(m_1,m_4))=E(m_4,y_1,...,y_N)= =E(m_4,y^N(m_3,m_4))=\tilde{x}_{2,N+1}=E(m_2,y^N(m_1,m_2))$. Thus $y^{N+1}(m_1,m_4)=y^{N+1}(m_1,m_2)$.//

Let $(i,j) \in M^2$ and define $Reg^k(i,j):= \{ (m_1,m_2) \in M^2 | y^k(m_1,m_2)=y^k(i,j) \}$ for all $k \in N$ for which $y^k(i,j)$ is defined. $Reg^0(i,j)$ is equal to MxM for all $(i,j) \in M^2$.

Lemma 2 $(m,m) \in Reg^c(m,n)$ with $m \neq n$ is impossible.

Proof: Let $(m,m) \in Reg^c(m,n)$ with $m \neq n$. Then $y^c(m,m) =y^c(n,m)=y^c(m,n)= \underline{y}$. This implies however that $H(M_1 ; \underline{y} | m_2=m)>0$ which contradicts with the completeness of the strategy.//

Lemma 3 $y^c(m_1,m_1)=y^c(m_2,m_2) => m_1=m_2$ for all $m_1,m_2 \in M$.

Proof: Let $y^c(m_1,m_1)=y^c(m_2,m_2)$ and let also $m_1 \neq m_2$. If $y^c(m_1,m_1)=y^c(m_2,m_2)$ then the inputs are the same at both sides of the channel. So by Lemma 1 we now have $y^c(m_1,m_2)=y^c(m_1,m_1) \in Reg^c(m_1,m_1)$ which is impossible by Lemma 2.//

Lemma 4 Let $m,m_1,m_2 \in M$, is $(m,m) \neq (m_1,m_2)$ then $y^c(m_1,m_2) \neq y^c(m,m)$.

Proof: let $y^c(m_1,m_2)=y^c(m,m)$ and $(m,m) \neq (m_1,m_2)$. If $m_1=m_2$ then by Lemma 3 $m_1=m_2=m$. So let $m_1 \neq m_2$ and because of Lemma 2 also $m_i \neq m$, i=1,2. Obviously we have $(m_1,m_2),(m_2,m_1),(m,m_2),(m_2,m) \in Reg^0(m,m)$. Let k be an integer and $(m_1,m_2),(m_2,m_1)$,

$(m,m_2),(m_2,m) \in Reg^k(m,m)$ for all $k<N+1<c$. If $y_{N+1}(m,m)=y_{N+1}(m_1,m_2)=1$ then $E(m,y^N(m,m))=1$ and $E(m_2,y^N(m,m_2))=1$. Thus the y_{N+1}-th channel output using (m,m_2) is $y_{N+1}(m,m_2)=y_{N+1}(m_2,m)=1$. Is $y_{N+1}(m,m)=y_{N+1}(m_1,m_2)=0$ then $E(m,y^N(m,m))=$ $=E(m,y^N(m,m_2))=0$ ∵ $y_{N+1}(m,m_2)=y_{N+1}(m_2,m)=0$. Therefore we have $(m_1,m_2),(m_2,m_1),(m,m_2)$, $(m_2,m) \in Reg^{N+1}(m,m)$. This all ultimately leads to $(m_1,m_2),(m_2,m_1),(m,m_2),(m_2,m) \in Reg^c(m,m)$. In particular we have $(m,m) \in Reg^c(m,m_2)$ which is impossible by lemma 2.//

Proof of proposition 1

(=>) Let $\underline{y}=y^c(m_1,m_2)$ such that $S(\underline{y})=1$. If $m_1 \neq m_2$ then via $y^c(m_1,m_2)=y^c(m_2,m_1)$ we have $(m_1,m_2),(m_1,m_2) \in Reg^c(m_1,m_2)$ ∵ $S(\underline{y})>1$. So $m_1=m_2$.

(<=) Now let $m_1=m_2=m$. Suppose $S(\underline{y})>1$. Then by Lemma 3 there exists a message pair $(k,l)=(m,m)$, $k \neq l$, for which $y^c(k,l)=\underline{y}$. This however contradicts with Lemma 4.//

Define for $n=2,3,4,5,....$ the functions F_n as $F_n(a_0,....,a_{n-1})=a_0^{-1}+...+a_{n-1}^{-1}$ with $a_i \in R^+$.

Lemma 5 F_n is convex over R^{+n}.

Proof: Let $\underline{a}=a_0,...,a_{n-1}$ and $\underline{b}=b_0,...,b_{n-1}$ with $a_i,b_i \in R^+$, then for $x \in (0,1)$ one has $xF_n(\underline{a})+(1-x)F_n(\underline{b})-F_n(x\underline{a}+(1-x)\underline{b})=x(1-x)\Sigma_i [a_i-b_i]^2[a_ib_i(xa_i+(1-x)b_i)]^{-1} \geq 0.//$

Proof of proposition 2

Let the receiver be terminal 2. Assume that the messages have a distribution such that $p_{2j}p_{1j}=$constant(>0). The channel outputs can be used to set the p_{2j}'s such that this is true. By straightforward calculations we get $P_{int}=m(\Sigma_j p_{1j}^{-1})^{-1}$. Now is P_{int} maximal when $\Sigma_j p_{1j}^{-1}$ is minimal. Observe that the latter summation is in fact $F_m(p_{1,0},....,p_{1,m-1})$. Observe also that by Lemma 5 F_m is convex and $\Sigma_j p_{1j}=1$. Maximizing $-F_m+l \Sigma_j p_{1j}$, with l a Lagrange multiplier, gives a minimum for F_m at $p_{1j}=1/m$, $j=0,...,m-1$. Hence $\min_{p_{1j}} F_m(p_{1,0},....,p_{1,m-1})=m^2$ ∵ $\max_{p_{1j}} P_{int}=m^{-1}.//$

REFERENCES:

[1]   Shannon C.E., "Communication Theory of Secrecy Systems," Bell Systems Tech. J., Vol.28, No.4, October 1949, pp. 656-715.

[2]   Shannon C.E., "Two-way communication channels," Proc. 4th. Berkely Symp. Math. Statist. and Prob., vol.1, pp. 611-644, 1961. Reprint in Key Papers in the Development of Information Theory, (D. Slepian, Ed) New York, IEEE Press, 1974, pp. 339-372.

[3]   Rivest R.L., Shamir A. & Adleman L., "A method for obtaining digital signatures and public key cryptosystems," Comm. A.C.M., Vol.21, Feb. 1978, pp. 120-126.

[4]   Odlyzko A.M., "Discrete logarithms in finite fields and their cryptographic
        significance," preliminary report.

[5]   Schalkwijk J.P.M., "The binary multiplying channel- A coding scheme that
        operates beyond Shannon's innerbound region", IEEE Trans. Inform. Theory,
        vol.IT-28, Jan. 1982, pp. 107-110.

[6]   Schalkwijk J.P.M., private communication, Jan. 1984.

[7]   Schalkwijk J.P.M., Rooyackers J.E. & Smeets B.J.M., "Generalized Shannon
        strategies for the binary multiplying channel," Proc. 4-th. Symp. on Inform.
        Theory in the Benelux, 1983, pp. 171-178. Acco Publ. Co., Leuven, Belgium, 1983.

[8]   Post K.A. & Ligtenberg L.G.T.M., "Coding strategies for the binary
        multiplying channel in the discrete case," Proc. 4-th. Symp. on Inform.
        Theory in the Benelux, 1983, pp. 163-170. Acco Publ. Co., Leuven, Belgium, 1983.

SECRECY AND PRIVACY IN A LOCAL AREA
NETWORK ENVIRONMENT

by

Gordon B. Agnew
Department of Electrical Engineering
University of Waterloo
Waterloo, Ontario, Canada, N2L 3G1

Abstract

In recent years, much effort has gone into the development of high
bandwidth communication networks for use over relatively short (local)
distances, e.g. an office, an industrial complex, a research laboratory,
etc.. The high bandwidth of these networks allows many of the services now
requiring separate networks such as facsimile, digitized voice, file
transfer and interactive terminal data, to be integrated into a common
transmission facility. Manufacturers are currently developing products
which conform to the recently established IEEE 802 standard for Local Area
Networks (LANs). This standard is based on the concept of a layered, "peer
entity" communication protocol put forth in the International Standards,
Organization's (ISO) seven layer model for Open Systems Interconnection
(OSI).

In this paper we define the notions of secrecy and privacy as they
relate to a LAN environment and the various services a network is required
to provide such as data integrity, authentication and digital signature
services. We also describe the cost-benefit tradeoff involved in attain-
ing various levels of privacy and secrecy.

1.1 Introduction

This paper will be presented in two parts; the first part is a general description of the secrecy and privacy requirements in a local area network environment. In the second part of the paper we present some observations and proposed methods for integrating secrecy and privacy into established network protocols.

In the past few years, much research and development has been concentrated in the area of local communication networks. In general, local area communication networks (LANs) provide a multiple access environment over a relatively small geographical area such as a room, building or group of buildings with maximum network lengths of a few kilometers. An introduction to local area networks and there applications can be found in [1]. The main characteristics of a LAN can be summarized as follows:

1. Topology - ring, bus or star are the most popular configurations (see Fig. 1)
2. Transmission medium and technology - there are two popular methods
   coaxial cable - baseband or RF modulated
                    transmissions
   fibre optic
3. Media Access Protocol- there are two broad classes of media access protocols - contention (random access) protocols and non-contention protocols
4. Communication protocols and type of services provided by the network (i.e. unacknowledged connectionless services, connection oriented services[1]).

LANs are finding increasing applications in research, industrial and office environments where the trend is towards the integration of many services such as digitized voice, interactive terminal data, facsimile transfer, file transfer and electronic mail into a single common communications facility linking all users. A characteristic which is common to all LANs is the ability to establish a connection between any pair of users (transceivers). This is usually accomplished by broadcast techniques where the message is transmitted on the network along with source and destination information in such a way that all of the transactions on the network can be heard by every network transceiver. In addition to the study of various applications, work is proceeding on the development of communications protocols for LANs.

1.2 The Open System Interconnection Model

The International Organization for Standardization (ISO) has proposed a model for communication protocols in networks called the Open Systems Interconnection (OSI) model and is currently being used as a basis for the IEEE Project 802 standard for LANs [3]. The OSI model, shown in Fig. 2, defines seven layers of complementing protocols where communication is defined as taking place between equivalent or peer entities at each user site. To facilitate this, the upper layers are built on the services of the lower layers (as well as adding value to the services) in such a manner as to isolate the user from the physical operation of the network. The n-layer services of a layer are the capabilities it offers to n-layer users. Thus, at the higher layers, the user is not aware of, or concerned with, the operation of the network as this becomes transparent. A summary of the OSI model can be found in [2].

---

[1] These terms are consistent with Type I and Type II Logical Link Control (LLC) services of IEEE 802.2.

1.3 IEEE Project 802

The IEEE 802 standard is actually a family of standards 802.1 through 802.6 which deal with the physical and data link layers of the OSI model. Fig. 3 shows the relationship between the IEEE Project 802 standard and the ISO model.

Standard 802.1 is used to describe the relationship between these standards and the OSI model. Due to the diversity of media-access methods and transmission technology (as was described previously), a number of standards were required to cover the physical and data link layers. In the 802 standard, the data link layer is split into two sublayers, a common Logical Link Control sublayer (LLC) and a Media Access Control (MAC) sublayer which is contoured to the requirements of the various types of LANs i.e.:

> 802.3 standard for CSMA/CD bus networks
> 802.4 standard for token-passing bus networks
> 802.5 standard for token-passing ring networks
> 802.6 standard for metropolitan area networks (MANs).

This structure allows a common interface at the LLC sublayer and information (Protocol Data Units) passing into and out of the LLC from above (Network Layer) or from below (MAC sublayer), are standardized.

A detailed description of these standards is beyond the scope of this report (see [4]-[6]) but we will describe a few of the basic principles. As mentioned previously, all layers are built on the services they provide or use. The general format of messages to/from the various layers is shown in Fig. 4.

> Messages may be of three generic types:
> i)Request - a primitive for requesting n-layer services from a n-layer user
> ii)Indication - a primitive used to indicate to a n-layer user of an internal n-layer event which may be significant (e.g. a remote service request)
> iii)Confirm - a primitive which conveys to a n-layer user the results of a previous request for n-layer service

All communication and information passing is performed using this type of hierarchical structure.

The LLC layer supplies two types of message exchange services: i)Type I, Unacknowledged Connectionless Service and ii)Type II, Connection Oriented Service. In Unacknowledged Connectionless service, network layer entities exchange Link Service Data Units (LSDUs) without establishing a data link level connection. In Connection Oriented service, LLC provides the means for establishing, using, resetting and terminating data link layer connections along with data link layer sequencing, flow control and error recovery procedures. Thus, the message transfer services can be loosely coupled ("datagram") or tightly coupled ("virtual circuit") type connections.

1.4 The Problem

The increased use of digital communications for business transactions also increases the need for secrecy and privacy. Unfortunately, the two requirements are sometimes contradictory. On one hand, we require access to a wide variety of services yet, we may wish to keep the information exchanged secret. The various types of traffic on the network will have different characteristics and requirements such as delay, buffer space and priority. In addition, different types of traffic will have different security requirements. For instance, in an industrial environment, top level memos may require complete secrecy. In the banking environment, more emphasis is placed on the authentication of a transaction than on its secrecy. In the most basic time-

sharing systems, the operating system must ensure only legitimate users
are allowed access. For digitized voice, most people are content with the
level of privacy provided by an unencoded analog telephone connection;
their only real concern is that a conversation does not allow "party-line"
interception, that is, no casual listener can overhear their conversation, thus, the normal level of privacy for voice is minimal. Data bases
tend to be available to all users but clearly, steps must be taken
to prevent unauthorized additions or deletions. If we consider the concept of an electronic mail service, one would envisage a central mail
server which would act as a temporary depository for messages which could
not be immediately delivered. This type of service presents a difficult
problem in that messages must be authenticated when they are placed in the
service, they must be protected from unauthorized disclosure, addition,
modification and deletion while in the mail server and they must be delivered in a manner which will preserve the privacy of the message (this
tends to be a more complex problem than a secure database system).

Our objective in this paper is to outline some possible methods by
which secrecy, privacy, and authentication techniques can be incorporated
into a hierarchically structured network using already established protocols as a base. An example of the type of network where these methods may
be applied is the Waterloo Experimental Local NETwork (WELNET) which is
classified as a non-contention broadcast network which conforms to the
IEEE 802.2 standard for Logical Link Control (LLC) (see [7]).

In the IEEE 802 standard and OSI model a (N-1) layer may supply
services to more than one N layer entity. The (N-1) layer and N layer
communicate through Service Access Points (SAPs) which are addressable
points in each layer. When a message is generated, the source N layer
entity and destination N layer entity addresses are appended to the message. This is then passed to the (N-1) layer. At this layer, the corresponding source/destination addresses for the (N-1) entities are also
appended. Upon reception, the address information is stripped away as the
message is passed up through the layers to its destination. The addressing is thus structured so that each layer only requires the part of the
address which allows that layer to pass the message to the appropriate
SAP. In Fig. 5, we show the message format adopted for WELNET as it
passes from the Network layer, LLC and the MAC sublayers.

1.5 Classification of Threats in a Network

We now define a few of the terms which will be used throughout this
study: A LAN is classified as an open broadcast network in which we
assume messages may be received by both the intended recipient and unauthorized listeners. This will, in general, be the case unless the
entire network, including the transmission media and all access
points, are made physically secure. In most cases this is impractical.

The points where attacks can be made in the network are shown in
Fig. 6. Here the network consists of the transmission medium, a
network interface (transceiver) and the user equipment (terminal, host,
etc.).

1.5.1 Low Level Threats

The types of threats present in a LAN environment can be broken
down into a number of categories. The simplest form of attack is that
of the passive listener (eavesdropper). In Fig. 6, we show the points
in the network where the wiretapper may position the listening
(recording) device. The position of the tap determines the complexity
of the device, the amount of information available and the security
procedures the wiretapper must overcome to gain the information. If a

tap is placed on the transmission medium, the listener can intercept messages intended for any user on the network since messages contain
source/destination addressing plus virtual circuit and sequencing information (the job is much easier than that of intercepting telephone information since all signals and information required to separate them are
carried on one transmission medium). If the tap is placed at the
terminal connection, only information for a specific user is available,
but, the wiretap device can be relatively simple and this method has
the added advantage of defeating any security procedures installed in the
network itself. The problem also changes with the type of LAN involved.
Consider a LAN which uses a broadcast bus structure, this system has the
property that it is very easy for a passive wiretapper to obtain information from the bus without detection, but it is very difficult for an
active wiretapper to impersonate another transceiver without detection
(assuming the operating system of the transceivers will check to determine
if the header address is correct). This property is not true in a ring
network where one can easily conceive of using two transceivers to
surround a legitimate transceiver and originate, alter or delete messages
(although how one taps into the loop without detection is not clear).
        The transmission medium also plays a role in the difficulty facing
an attacker. Coaxial cable is easy to tap and this can be done without
interruption of service. Passive listening can be performed with a direct
connection or by inductive means. An answer to this problem is the use of
fibre optics but fibre optics do not lend themselves to bus architectures.
        In consideration of fibre optics as the transmission medium, one
also observes that they are not prone to wiretap by inductive pickup or
electromagnetic emission. To tap the fibre, some portion of the signal
must be diverted which, by current techniques results in detectable attenuation factors at the receiving end. To counter this problem, the attacker could introduce an active tap which would repeat the signal compensa-
ting for any attenuation, but this again necessitates interruption of the
fibre which should be detectable.

1.5.2 Higher Level Threats

        In the previous discussion it was assumed that the attacker was
tapping the network itself to gain the information or send the messages he
required. These are basically attacks against the lower layers of the OSI
model. We now look at the case where the attacker has gained entry
(either an authorized user making unauthorized use or someone obtain
ng authorized use by breaking the login procedure). From this point
on the network serves merely as a transport method for accessing the
service under attack. (This is shown in Fig. 7-8). All safeguards
incorporated into the lower protocol levels will be nullified once valid
entry is obtained.
        The threats to the higher levels of the network can be quite
varied. The main objective is to protect user data, data bases, hardware and the host operating system from deletion, modification, disclo
ure and unauthorized use. Each type of data is different and will
require a differ approach to secrecy and privacy.
        In this study, we will only be concerned with the problems of
security in a network environment. At present, there is a strong interaction between the various LAN configurations outlined above and each
will have its own repercussions when the implementation of secrecy and
privacy is considered.
        In the OSI model, security is introduced into level six of the
model. If we look at the system model, there is a division of tasks
between the network and the host computer. This division is shown in
Fig. 8. Below this division, protocols are needed to protect the messages

on the network form the passive of active eavesdropper. Above the division, the network is used purely as a means of access and any attacks are
directed at the host computer (we also consider here, the concept of the
layered protocol is to make the operations of the underlying network transparent to the user). The isolation present in the OSI model also
decouples any "real-time" protection form the upper layers, i.e., since
the upper layers are independent of the lower layers such as the media
access protocol, an authentication and data integrity system based on a
time stamp approach could not be implemented at a high layer in the model.
An example of this would be the wide variance of access times present in a
moderately to heavily loaded CSMA/CD system. These examples tend to
indicate that certain forms of protection must be implemented very close
to the physical layer of the protocol; in addition, some of the services
may be built on top of these services at the low layers, thus we can
conceive of a secrecy and privacy implementation which is, itself a
layered protocol which uses the services of the layers underneath it.

1.6 Network Security

The main objectives of network <u>Security</u> as defined in [8]-[10] are
to:

> i)prevent unauthorized release (disclosure) of information
> ii)prevent unauthorized message addition, deletion or
> modification
> iii)prevent unauthorized denial of resource use.

Network security can be broken down into two subtopics; 1)Secrecy and
Privacy techniques and 2)Authentication and Data Integrity techniques.
Secrecy and Privacy techniques are intended to provide protection against
passive attacks (as per requirement (i)). Authentication deals with the
ability to uniquely (and correctly) identify the originator of a message
while Integrity deals with the uncorrupted transport of user messages
(requirements (ii) and (iii)) in the presence of active attacks.

Many of the current approaches to secrecy and privacy are ad hoc in
nature, many of them evolving as remedies for problems found in
existing systems. A review of the various techniques which have been
applied to networks can be found in references [11]-[15].

Part II - Observations and Implementations

2.1 Cryptanalytic Effort

The primary objectives of a secrecy system can be summarized as
follows:

> i)provide as much protection to the user's messages as possible
> (i.e. maximize the amount of work an attacker must perform in order
> to recover message contents)
> ii) minimize the amount of information which the attacker can gain
> if cryptanalysis is successful (i.e. this can be done by changing
> keys regularly or by using multiple keys in the system)
> iii) minimize the effort required to perform network maintenance
> i.e. to change keys, manage keys and to initiate secure communications, etc.

Observation I

It is generally accepted that, from a secrecy and privacy point of
view, the use of multiple keys in a network increases the protection for
users' messages and decreases the amount of information an attacker can
obtain by successful cryptanalysis. Thus, it is advantageous to maximize

the number of keys in the system (ideally, each user would have its own
key). Unfortunately, this leads us to deal with the problem of key
management and distribution. If the number of keys is large, the problem
of maintaining the security of the keys and distributing new keys requires
serious consideration (this problem has been the object of considerable
study [16]-[17]).

Observation II

Let's consider the effort required by the attacker to recover a key
by cryptanalysis under the following assumptions:

i) a message on the network will belong to a class i , $1 <= i <= n$,
if it is enciphered with key K_i

ii) messages are indistinguishable before cryptanalysis (i.e.
source/destination information is also enciphered as part of the
message)

iii) the attacker must recover at least two messages of the same
class for successful cryptanalysis

iv) the probability of a particular message being of class i is $1/n$
(i.e. messages of the various classes are equally likely)

v) the effort to cryptanalyze one pair of messages is 1 work unit

Under these assumptions, we can calculate the expected number of tries and
thus the expected effort the attacker must make before recovering two
messages of the same class. It is easily shown that the expected effort
is:

$$E(W) = \sum_{i=2}^{n} i \; \{(n-1)/n\}^{\,i-2} (1/n)$$

$$= n$$

Thus, the effort required by the attacker is linear in n, that is,
increasing the number of keys by a factor m simply increases the effort
required by the attacker by approximately the same amount. If we now
consider the effort required to manage and distribute keys and it also
increases at least linearly in n (i.e. it takes twice as much effort to
manage two keys as one, etc.) then nothing is gained by using multiple
keys, that is, under these constraints, it is better use one key and
change it regularly.

An improvement could be made if we increased the _effective_ number
of keys without increasing the actual number of keys. In the next section
we will examine one method by which this could be done.

2.2 Horizontal/Vertical Keying

In part I of this paper we described the protocols of the IEEE 802
standard and the OSI model. In that section we note that the message
structure was such that the address and control information for a
particular level (N) is encapsulated in the frame structure of the layer
below (N-1). If we expand this structure as shown in Fig. 9, we see that,
even though there are n entities at the top level, the address space is
the product of the address spaces at each level (i.e. two messages can
share the same address at layer N but are different at the (N-1) layer.
Thus a unique path through the tree is defined even if addresses at the
upper layers are reused.

At this point we will introduce two terms; horizontal-keying refers
to the process of assigning individual keys to each of the n entities at
the uppermost layer. If we take advantage of the reuse of address space
and define a set of keys the number of which is equal to the address space
of that layer and use multiple encryption i.e., the message is first

encrypted with the key of the peer destination entity[2], then passed to
the next lower layer where it is encapsulated and encrypted using the key
of the peer destination entity of that layer (Note: by default, each half
of a transaction is separately encrypted thus presenting an even more
difficult task for the attacker). Assuming a block type encryption method
that does not expand the message (for example DES [18]) and the multiple
encryption process cannot easily be factored, then the effective number of
keys is the product of the number of keys at each level while the actual
number of keys is the sum of the number of keys at each level. If we look
at the implementation shown in Fig. 5, where there are two layers (LLC and
MAC), the maximum number of entities is:

$$n = 2^{16} \ast 2^6 = 2^{22}$$

while the number of keys required in the system is

$$k = 2^{16} + 2^6 = 0(2^{16})$$

if all of the address space is used for just these two layers.

As we noted in our discussion of the addressing format, when messages (Protocol Data Units) are passed from layer N to layer (N+1), the N
layer only needs to know the address of the appropriate Service Access
Point (SAP) for that layer (i.e., upon delivery, address and control information is "peeled" away from the message). Thus, to implement the structured enciphering method, we must ensure that the address information is
easily recoverable at each level. This could be done by i)enciphering
only the message portion of the PDU leaving the address information to be
enciphered at the next lower layer or, ii)enciphering the entire PDU
including the addresses before passing it to the next lower layer. Upon
delivery, method (i) allows the N layer to directly determine which N-SAP
to pass the message to while method (ii) requires a test of all the keys
at that layer (which will add overhead to the system). The advantage of
method (ii) is that, even if an N-layer key is recovered, it does not
reveal the grouping of messages for the (N+1) layer (i.e. which of the
(N+1) layer keys the message is enciphered under).

2.3 Secrecy, Privacy, Authentication and Data Integrity

In the previous part, we noted that the IEEE 802.2 LLC standard
supports two types of services; loosely coupled unacknowledged connection
less service and a tightly coupled (by sequencing, flow control and error
detection procedures) connection-oriented service. The requirements for
secrecy and privacy in our definitions are met by the first type of
service, that is, the multiple encryption scheme prevents the attacker
from easily recovering information by passive techniques. If authentication and data integrity is required, a connection oriented service
should be used. The sequencing and error detection techniques integral i
the service will prevent most active attacks.

Summary

We have shown that by using the hierarchical protocol structure
proposed for local area networks, we can improve the difficulty presented
to the passive attacker by using multiple encryption techniques. In most
networks, a trade-off exists between the number of keys (which should be
maximized) and the difficulty of distributing and managing the keys. By

---

[2] We assume here that the keys for a particular layer are known by all
entities of that layer. In addition, since destination keying is performed, there is a different key used for each direction of a conversation
thus providing additional difficulty for the attacker.

using the address structure used in the protocol models, we can reduce the actual number of keys by a significant factor while still presenting a high level of difficulty to the attacker.

The use of the two types of services supplied by the IEEE 802.2 standard, we can choose between a service which supports private and secret communication or one which tightly couples the communication in such a way as to allow authentication (i.e. prevention of active attacks on the network).

We also note that these features are transparent to the network users and further services can be built upon these services (e.g. a Public Key System for extra secrecy or digital signature, etc.). This area will continue to be an area of interest as more manufacturers begin to supply equipment conforming to the new standards.

Bibliography

1. D. Clark, K.T. Pogran, D.P. Reed, 'An introduction to local area networks', Proc. of IEEE, Vol. 66, No.11, Nov. 1978.
2. H. Zimmermann, 'OSI reference model - The ISO model of architecture for Open Systems Interconnection', IEEE Trans. on Comm., Vol. COM-28, Apr. 1980, pp. 425-432.
3. IEEE Project 802.1 Local Area Network Standard - Technical Report
4. IEEE Project 802 Local Area Network Standard, P802.2 Logical Link Control, Draft E, Sept 1983.
5. IEEE Project 802 Local Area Network Standard, P802.4, Draft IEEE Standard 802.4, Token Bus, Draft D, Dec. 1982.
6. IEEE Project 802 Local Area Network Standard, P802.5, Draft IEEE Standard 802.5, Token Ring, Dec. 1983.
7. J. Mark, J. Field, J. Wong, T. Todd, J. McMullan, G. Agnew, 'WELNET A High Performance Local Area Communications Network', CCNG report series, Dept. of Elec. Eng., Univ. of Waterloo, May 1983.
8. W. Diffie, M. Hellman, 'Privacy and authentication : An introduction to cryptography', Proc. of the IEEE, Vol. 67, March 1979, pp. 397-427.
9. S.T. Kent, 'Security requirements and protocols for a broadcast scenario', IEEE Trans. on Comm., Vol. COM-29, June 1981, pp. 778-786.
10. V. Voydock, S. Kent, 'Security Mechanisms in High-Level Network Protocols', Computing Surveys, Vol 15, June 1983.
11. D. Parker, 'Computer abuse perpetrators and vulnerabilities of computer systems', NCC'76, June 1976, New York, pp. 65-73.
12. N. Nielson, B. Ruder, D. Brandin, 'Effective safeguards for computer system integrity', NCC'76, June 1976, New York, pp. 75-84.
13. E. Gudes, H. Koch, 'The application of cryptography for data base security', NCC'76, June 1976, New York, pp. 97-107.
14. G. Purdy, 'A high security log-in procedure', Comm. of ACM, Vol. 17, Aug. 1974, pp. 442-445.
15. B. Walker, I. Blake, 'Computer Security and Protection Structures' Dowden,Hutchinson, Ross, Stroudsburg, Penn., 1977.
16. I. Ingemarsson, D.T. Tang, C.K. Wong, 'A conference key distribution system', IEEE Trans. on Info. Theory, Vol. IT-28, Sept. 1982, pp. 714-720.
17. W. Chou, A. Nilsson, 'Key distribution and authentication procedures in internetworking environment', Computer Networking Symposium, National Bureau of Standards, Maryland, Dec 1982, pp. 50-54.
18. 'Data Encryption Standard', National Bureau of Standards, Federal Information Processing Standard (FIPS), Pub. No. 46, Jan. 1977.

358

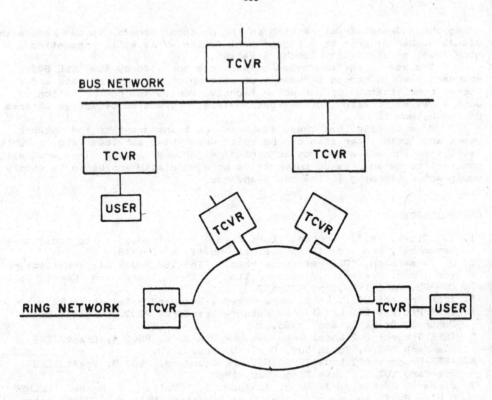

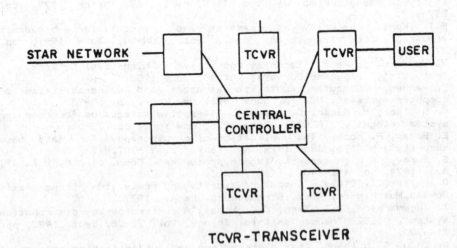

Fig. 1 Typical LAN Configurations

359

PEER ENTITIES

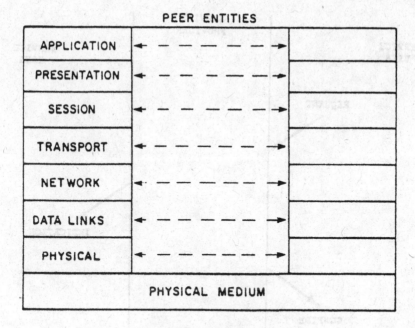

Fig. 2 <u>Open Systems Interconnection</u>
<u>Model</u>

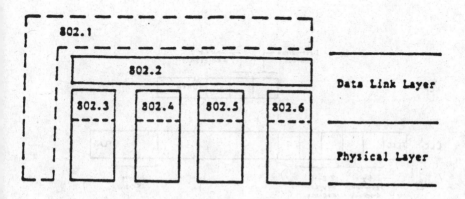

Fig. 3 <u>IEEE Project 802 Format</u>

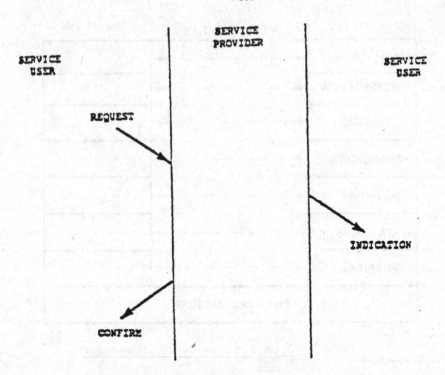

Fig. 4 Format for Service Primitives

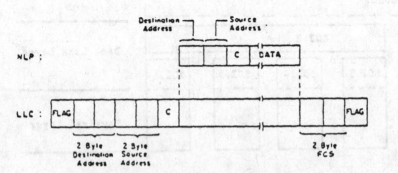

Fig. 5 Address and Data Format for Network Layer and LLC

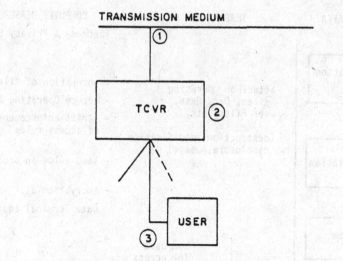

Fig. 6   Points of Attack in a LAN

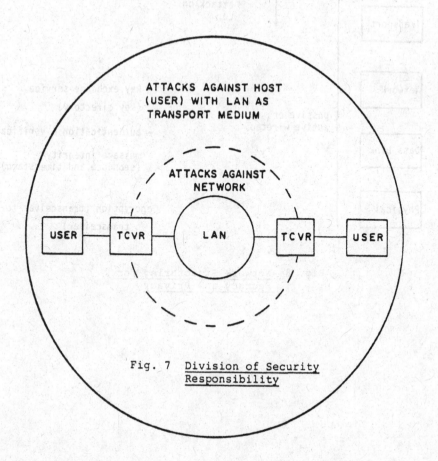

Fig. 7   Division of Security
Responsibility

362

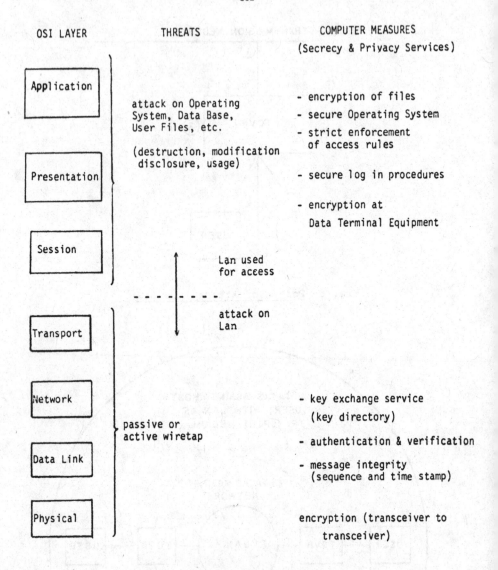

| OSI LAYER | THREATS | COMPUTER MEASURES (Secrecy & Privacy Services) |

Fig. 8   Network Structuring for
          Secrecy and Privacy

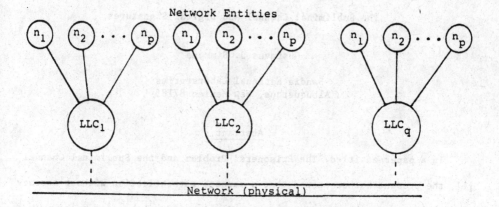

Fig. 9 Structuring of Network
Entities and Addresses

The Subliminal Channel and Digital Signatures

Gustavus J. Simmons

Sandia National Laboratories
Albuquerque, New Mexico 87185

Abstract

In a paper entitled "The Prisoners' Problem and the Subliminal Channel" [1], the present author showed that a message authentication without secrecy channel providing m bits of overt communication and r bits of message authentication could be perverted to allow an $\ell < r$ bit covert channel between the transmitter and a designated receiver at the expense of reducing the message authentication capability to $r-\ell$ bits, without affecting the overt channel. It was also shown that under quite reasonable conditions the detection of even the existence of this covert channel could be made as difficult as the underlying cryptoalgorithm was difficult to "break." In view of this open -- but indetectable -- existence, the covert channel was called the "subliminal" channel. The examples constructed in [1], although adequate to prove the existence of such channels, did not appear to be feasible to extend to interesting communications systems. Fortunately, two digital signature schemes have been proposed since Crypto 83 -- one by Ong-Schnorr-Shamir [2] based on the difficulty of factoring sufficiently large composite numbers and one by Gamal [3] based on the difficulty of taking discrete logarithms with respect to a primitive element in a finite field -- that provide ideal bases for implementing practical subliminal channels. This paper reviews briefly the essential features of the subliminal channel and then discusses implementations in both the Ong-Schnorr-Shamir and Gamal digital signature channels.

---

* This work was performed at Sandia National Labortories supported by the U.S. Department of Energy under contract No. DE-AC04-76DP00789.

Introduction

The subliminal channel was first conceived of as a way of "cheating" in an authentication without secrecy channel of the type considered for various treaty compliance verification schemes [4,5]. More recently, it has been recognized that several digital signature schemes lend themselves equally well to subliminal communictions. Since there are some (significant?) differences between the two, we briefly review the first formulation -- based on perverting a message authentication without secrecy channel -- and then discuss how such channels can also be concealed in digital signatures.

In order to communicate m bits of information and to provide for r bits of authentication, at least m+r bits must be exchanged. The r bits are in a strict sense redundant information since they are only used by the receiver to partition the set of all possible messages into disjoint subsets of acceptable (i.e., authentic) and unacceptable messages. In complete generality, authentication, with or without secrecy of the information from an opponent depends on the message containing- information already known (in some sense) to the receiver. The receiver equates the presence of this prearranged information with the authenticity of the message. Conversely, the absence of this information is interpreted to mean that the communication is not genuine. For example, authentic messages may be required to include a "one time" suffix known in secret to the transmitter and authorized receiver but not to an opponent, as is the common practice in military authentication systems. Since the opponent must be prevented from simply "stripping off" the authenticating information from a genuine message and appending it to a fraudulent or altered message, the information -- both message and authenticating -- is generally secured from outsiders by encryption. In order to make each symbol or collection of symbols in the cipher -- which the opponent may alter -- be a function of all of the symbols in both the message itself and in the authenticator, the encryption is commonly done as a block cipher (if m+r is small enough) or else as a block chain or feedback cipher, so as to produce the desired "spreading" of symbol dependence. In any event, if the cryptoalgorithm is adequately secure, the probability of the opponent being able to deceive the receiver into accepting a fraudulent or altered message as authentic is bounded by:

$$P_A > 2^{-r} \ .$$

In a message authentication without secrecy channel, a third party, commonly called the "host" to the communication channel from the origins of this problem in systems to verify compliance with a comprehensive nuclear weapons test ban treaty, is given the means to decrypt the cipher and thus verify that nothing other than the agreed upon message is contained in the cipher. If a single key cryptoalgorithm is used, this is done by giving him the encryption/decryption session key used to encrypt the immediate past message as soon as the exchange has taken place. If a two-key cryptoalgorithm is used, he is given the decryption key in advance of the exchange. For single key cryptographic systems, the host must "trust" the transmitter/receiver until he receives the decryption key corresponding to the last cipher exchange -- which if the message is very long may involve an unacceptable level of risk (to him) of covert communication. There is no way of avoiding this problem for single key systems though, since if the host has the key in advance so that he can decrypt the cipher, he could also encrypt and hence create an undetectable forgery. The essential -- and vital -- difference for two key cryptosystems is the absence of this need for even a temporary "trust" by either party of the other since the host can have the decryption key in his possession prior to any exchange of messages, and hence have the ability to verify the message content prior to forwarding the cipher. On the other hand, since the host cannot infer the unknown encryption key, the transmitter/receiver are confident that he cannot better his guessing odds of choosing an acceptable cipher. Actual authentication without secrecy channels are frequently much more complex than this simplified description suggests. The chapter entitled "Message Authentication Without Secrecy" in Secure Communications and Asymmetric Cryptosystems [4] is recommended for a more complete discussion of this concept.

The essential points to an authentication without secrecy channel are that;

a)   the receiver authenticates a message through the presence of r bits of redundant, i.e., expected, information in the decrypted cipher,

b)   the host to the communication channel verifies that nothing has been concealed by decrypting the ciphers and verifying that the resulting message is precisely what he expected based on an a priori knowledge of the message.

As mentioned before, the channel is operationally different for the host depending on whether it is based on a single or two key cryptoalgorithm since this determines whether he can check for concealed information before or after the exchange occurs. However, this does not alter the way in which he satisfies himself that nothing is concealed -- namely, that the cipher decrypts to the expected message.

The essential idea involved in setting up a subliminal channel as an indetectable part of a message authentication without secrecy channel is simple. We assume that the authentication channel has been implemented using

368

a two key cryptoalgorithm. In this case the host and/or opponent are given
the decryption key, d, in advance to enable them to verify that the overt
channel is not being misused -- which it isn't. The public (decryption) key
cryptoalgorithm, though, isn't quite what it appears to be. For the moment,
assume that there are two ciphers corresponding to each message, either of
which will decrypt, using the public decryption key, into the same (correct)
message. The host, given either one of a pair of such ciphers, would decrypt
it using his decryption key and be convinced that nothing was hidden in the
message which, technically speaking, is true. The receiver however, could in
addition to decrypting the cipher to authenticate the message and to recover
the overt communication, also be able to learn as much as one additional bit
of information from the identity of the particular cipher used to communicate
the message. It is this "side" channel that is called the subliminal channel.

Figure 1 shows schematically what the host has agreed to and believes
is taking place, i.e., the classical two key message authentication without

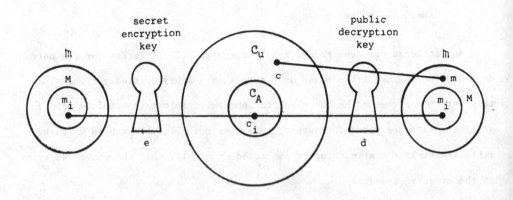

Figure 1. Two Key Message Authentication Without Secrecy Channel

secrecy channel. $\mathbb{m}$ is the set of all possible messages while M is the subset of messages that have the prearranged redundant information and hence will be accepted as authentic by the receiver. For example, if the information is a 48-bit binary number and the authenticating information is a suffix consisting of a 16-bit string of zeroes, $\mathbb{m}$ is the set of 2^{64} 64-bit binary numbers while M is the subset containing only the 2^{48} 64-bit numbers that end in 16 zeroes. It is assumed that the encryption function is a good randomizer, i.e., that the ciphers, C_A, produced by encrypting the messages in M "spread" over the total of 2^{64} ciphers in C in such a way that the opponent -- even if he knows the encryption function (but not the encryption key e of course) and arbitrarily many message/cipher pairs cannot do better at choosing a cipher in C_A than random guessing. The existence of $\mathbb{m}$ as opposed to M is unimportant to the transmitter since he only encrypts messages from the subset M, i.e., messages that will be accceptable to the receiver. The existence of $\mathbb{m}$ is vital, however, to both the opponent and receiver, since it provides the means by which the receiver detects and avoids deception. Using the decryption key, d, the receiver and the host/opponent can decrypt any message in C_A into the proper $m \in M$. C_A is of course unknown (to the opponent) and as difficult to determine as the cryptoalgorithm is cryptosecure. If the opponent chooses a cipher at random, it will with a probability like $\dfrac{|C_u|}{|C_A \cup C_u|}$ be a cipher in C_u and hence be rejected by the receiver as not being an authentic communication. This is what the host believes is happening, and indeed is all that is verifiable by him.

Figure 2 shows what is actually taking place though (in our simple one-bit example). Instead of there being a single encryption key, e, as claimed by the transmitter/receiver and as believed by the host, there are actually two encryption keys, e_1 and e_2, each of which encrypts the set of acceptable

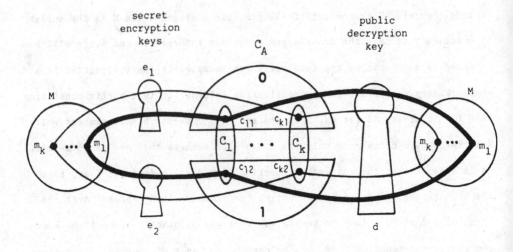

Figure 2.   One Bit Subliminal Channel

messages into a corresponding set of acceptable ciphers disjoint from the
set of acceptable ciphers produced by the other key. The special feature
of the cryptoalgorithm is that either of the ciphers produced by encrypting a
message m_i with e_1 or e_2 decrypts under the key d to m_i. As indicated by the
bold lines in Figure 2 for the specific choice $m_i = m_1$:

$$E(m_i,e_1) = c_{i1} \neq c_{i2} = E(m_i,e_2)$$

while

$$D(c_{i1},d) = m_i = D(c_{i2},d) .$$

Our convention will be that the transmitter will use e_1 to encrypt if he
wishes to send a 0 to the receiver and e_2 to send a 1. The receiver, knowing d, e_1 and e_2 can easily detect the subliminal bit sent by the transmitter.
He first decrypts the cipher c using d to recover an m ε $\bar{M}$. If the message
is authentic, i.e., m = m_i ε M then the received c was actually one of a pair
of ciphers, c_{i1} or c_{i2}. If m ∉ M, then of course the communication would be

rejected by the receiver as inauthentic. If m_i is authentic, he then encrypts it with both e_1 and e_2 to calculate c_{i1} and c_{i2} and hence to determine which cipher was used by the transmitter, i.e., to determine which encryption key was used and thereby to detect the subliminal bit. It should be obvious from this example how the technique can be extended to allow for an arbitrary amount of information to be passed through the subliminal channel. In [1] we discussed one cryptosecure subliminal channel based on the difficulty of factoring sufficiently large products of three distinct primes -- which unfortunately couldn't be extended to practical, large capacity, subliminal channels. In the next section we show how to hide a large capacity subliminal channel in digital signatures.

The Subliminal Channel

Ong, Schnorr and Shamir recently proposed a computationally efficient digital signature channel based on the difficulty of factoring large composite numbers [2]. In the interest of both completeness and brevity we summarize the essential points in their scheme for the three steps: key generation, signature generation and signature verification.

Key Generation

1. Tx chooses a composite n which is computationally infeasible to factor. The factorization of n is kept secret (if known).

2. Tx chooses a random u, $(u,n) = 1$, and calculates $k \ast -u^{-2}$ (mod n). u is kept secret.

3. Tx publishes n and k as his authentication key.

Signature Generation

Given a message m, (m,n) = 1, to be "signed""

1. Tx chooses a random r, (r,n) = 1. r is kept secret.

2. Tx calculates

$$s_1 = \frac{1}{2}\left(\frac{m}{r} + r\right) \pmod{n}$$

$$s_2 = \frac{u}{2}\left(\frac{m}{r} - r\right) \pmod{n}$$

3. The triple (m, s_1, s_2) is transmitted as the "signed" message.

Authentication of Signature

1. Rx receives (m, s_1, s_2)

2. Rx calculates

$$a \equiv s_1^2 + k \cdot s_2^2 \pmod{n}$$

3. The message m is accepted as authentic if and only if

$$a = m .$$

It is important to note that in the digital signature scheme just described, that if we let $\ell = \lceil \log_2 n \rceil$, 3ℓ bits (on average) are transmitted in a signed message (m, s_1, s_2). This communicates ℓ bits of information overtly, and since there are approximately 2^ℓ signatures for any given message, provides approximately ℓ bits of authentication in the signature. The remaining ℓ bits are "wasted" in the digital signature scheme. We propose to use these "free" bits for the subliminal channel. In this respect, using the digital signature channel to implement a subliminal channel differs from what was proposed in [1] where the subliminal bits were obtained by giving up an equal number of bits from the authentication channel. This difference will also be true for the other digital signature scheme discussed later.

To set up the subliminal channel, in addition to the steps taken by the transmitter in the key generation procedure for the digital signature scheme, the transmitter secretly communicates u to the designated receiver, Rx[†], for the subliminal channel. Now, when the transmitter wishes to send a signed message m through the overt channel and a covert message m[*] through the subliminal channel, where it is still desired that both the Rx[†] and third parties be able to verify the authenticity of the signature to m, the transmitter generates the signature as follows.

Signature Generation for the Subliminal/Signature Channel

Given a message m, (m,n) = 1, to be "signed" and a message m*,

(m*,n) = 1, to be communicated subliminally:

1. Tx calculates

$$s_1 = \frac{1}{2}\left(\frac{m}{m*} + m*\right) \ (\text{mod } n)$$

$$s_2 = \frac{u}{2}\left(\frac{m}{m*} - m*\right) \ (\text{mod } n)$$

2. The triple (m, s_1, s_2) is transmitted as the "signed" message.

Authentication of the signature by either the designated receiver, Rx[†], or by third parties is unaffected by the presence of the subliminal communication. The designated receiver, however, knowing u can solve for the subliminal message as follows:

Decoding the Subliminal Message

The subliminal Rx[†], given (m, s_1, s_2) and knowing u, calculates

$$m^* = \frac{m}{s_1 + s_2 u^{-1}} \ (\text{mod } n)$$

to recover the covert message m* "hidden" by the Tx in the signature

of m.

The 3ℓ bits (on average) contained in the signed message (m, s_1, s_2) have now been fully used to provide for an ℓ bit overt channel, an ℓ bit covert channel and ℓ bits of authentication. An opponent or outsider is faced with an equally difficult (computational) task in detecting either that the subliminal channel exists or is being employed and in breaking the digital signature scheme.

Gamal has proposed a digital signature scheme [3] based on the difficulty of taking discrete logarithms with respect to a primitive element in a finite field GF(p). Following the same procedure adopted in presenting the Ong-Schnorr-Shamir digital signature scheme, the Gamal scheme also involves the same three steps: key generation, signature generation and signature verification.

Key Generation

1. Tx chooses a finite field GF(p), p a prime, and a primitive element $\omega \ \epsilon$ GF(p). This is public information and need not even be unique to the transmitter.
2. Tx chooses a random u, u < p, and calculates $k = \omega^u$. u is kept secret.
3. Tx publishes k -- and if need be p and ω -- as his authentication key.

Signature Generation

Given a message m, m < p, to be "signed":

1. Tx chooses a random r, (r, p-1) = 1. r is kept secret.

2. Tx calculates

$$x = \omega^r$$

and solves for y in

$$m \equiv ux + ry \pmod{p-1}$$

using the Euclidean algorithm.

3. The triple (m,x,y) is transmitted as the signed message.

Authentication of Signature

1. Rx receives (m,x,y).

2. Rx calculates

$$a = k^x x^y .$$

3. The message m is accepted as authentic if and only if

$$\omega^m = a .$$

In the Gamal digital signature scheme, where $\ell = \lceil \log_2 p \rceil$, just as in the Ong-Schnorr-Shamir digital signature scheme, 3ℓ bits are transmitted to provide an ℓ bit overt channel and ℓ bits of authentication capability. We can use the ℓ bits left over to achieve another subliminal channel.

To set up the subliminal channel, in addition to the steps taken by the transmitter in the key generation procedure, the transmitter secretly communicates u to the designated receiver, Rx[†], for the subliminal channel. Now, when the transmitter wishes to send a signed message m through the overt channel and a covert m* through the subliminal channel -- where it is still desired that both the Rx† and third parties be able to verify the authenticity of the signature to m, the transmitter generates the signature as follows:

Signature Generation for the Subliminal/Signature Channel

Given a message m, m < p, to be "signed," and a message m*, m* < p, to be communicated subliminally:

1. Tx calculates

$$x = \omega^{m^*}$$

and solves for y in

$$m = ux + m^*y \pmod{p-1}$$

using the Euclidean algorithm.

2. The triple (m,x,y) is transmitted as the signed message.

Authentication of the signature by either the designated receiver, Rx†, or by third parties is unaffected by the presence of the subliminal communication. The designated receiver, however, knowing u can solve for the subliminal message as follows:

Decoding the Subliminal Message

The subliminal Rx†, given (m,x,y) and knowing u, calculates

$$m^* = y^{-1}(m-ux) \pmod{p-1}$$

to recover the covert message m* "hidden" by the Tx in the signature of m.

The general principles underlying the implementation of a subliminal channel in a digital signature scheme, as illustrated in the preceding two examples, are probably applicable to digital signature schemes in general. One of the author's colleagues, John DeLaurentis, has shown how to realize a subliminal channel in the earlier Ong-Schnorr digital signature scheme [6] and the author has more recently shown how to use the cubic OSS-signature scheme [7] in a similar manner. Both of these cases are more complex to use than the two discussed here -- but are fundamentally the same. The bottom line is that (several) digital signature schemes can be adapted to provide high capacity subliminal channels -- in which equally much information flows through the covert channel as through the overt channel.

Postscript

In the week following Eurocrypt 84 at which this paper was presented, J. M. Pollard successfully cryptanalyzed the Ong-Schnorr-Shamir digital signature scheme [8]. This development doesn't affect the validity of the concept of the subliminal channel, but it does eliminate from consideration what was the most attractive and practical implementation.

378

References

1. G. J. Simmons, "The Prisoners' Problem and the Subliminal Channel," Proceedings of Crypto 83, Santa Barbara, CA, August 21-24, 1983, to be published by Plenum Press.

2. H. Ong, C. P. Schnorr and A. Shamir, "An Efficient Signature Scheme Based on Quadratic Equations," to appear Proceedings of 16th Symposium on Theory of Computing, Washington D.C., April 1984.

3. T. El Gamal, "A New Public Key Cryptosystem and Signature Scheme Based on Discrete Logarithms," to appear IEEE Transactions on Information Theory.

4. G. J. Simmons, "Message Authentication Without Secrecy," in Secure Communications and Asymmetric Cryptosystems, ed. by G. J. Simmons, AAAS Selected Symposia Series, Westview Press, Boulder, CO (1982), pp. 105-139.

5. G. J. Simmons, "Verification of Treaty Compliance -- Revisited," Proceedings of the 1982 Symposium on Security and Privacy, Oakland, CA, April 25-27, 1983, pp. 61-66.

6. H. Ong and C. P. Schnorr, "Signatures through Approximate Representations by Quadratic Forms," Proceedings of Crypto 83, Santa Barbara, CA, August 21-24, 1983, to be published by Plenum Press.

7. C. P. Schnorr, "A Cubic OSS-Signature Scheme," private communication, May 1984.

8. J. Pollard, "Solution of $x^2 + ky^2 = m \pmod{n}$," private communication, April 1984.

A Provably Secure Oblivious Transfer Protocol

Richard Berger (1)

René Peralta (2)

Tom Tedrick (2)

Computer Science Division

University of California

Berkeley, California.

ABSTRACT

The idea of the Oblivious Transfer, developed by Rabin, has been shown to have important applications in cryptography. M. Fischer pointed out that Rabin's original implementation of the Oblivious Transfer was not shown to be secure. Since then it has been an open problem to find a provably secure implementation. We present an implementation which we believe will simplify the development of secure cryptographic protocols. Our protocol is provably secure under the assumptions that factoring is hard and that the message is chosen at random from a large message space.

(1) Research sponsored in part by DARPA grant N00039-C-0235-9-83 and GTE fellowship
(2) Research sponsored in part by NSF grant MCS-82-04506

1. Introduction

An Oblivious Transfer protocol (O.T.) is defined as a transfer of information from one party (Alice) to another (Bob) with the following properties:

1. Bob has a chance of $\frac{1}{2}$ of obtaining a message M.

2. The probability that Alice correctly guesses whether or not Bob obtained M is $\frac{1}{2}$.

The following implementation of O.T., based on the assumption that factoring is hard, was proposed by Rabin.[1] The message M is composed of two large primes p and q.

Rabin's Oblivious Transfer Protocol

    step 1: Alice sends Bob $N = pq$.

    step 2: Bob chooses a random number $z \in Z_N$ and sends $z^2 \bmod N$ to Alice.

    step 3: Alice sends u to Bob where u is a square root of $z^2 \bmod N$.

A quadratic residue $z^2 \bmod N$ has exactly four square roots. Distinct roots x, y such that $x \not\equiv -y \pmod N$ are called *twin roots* of z^2. Given twin roots of z^2, it is possible to efficiently factor N (since $GCD(x + y, N) \neq 1$). If Bob and Alice follow the protocol, Bob has a chance of $\frac{1}{2}$ of obtaining twin roots of z^2, thus factoring N (obtaining p and q).

The following problem with Rabin's protocol has not been solved:[2]

> It is conceivable that Bob has a routine P which
> chooses a quadratic residue r mod N such
> that given any root of r Bob can factor N.

If Bob has P then he will always be able to factor N.

We present an O.T. protocol which is provably secure. In addition, our protocol can be used to send many messages under the same modulus N without compromising N's factorization. In applications of the O.T. it is important for Alice and Bob to obtain receipts so that a third party (i.e. a judge) can tell from these receipts whether or not Bob obtained M. The following problem arises:

> Once Bob has obtained the message, how can we
> prevent him from lying about the information that
> he originally sent to Alice? For example, if Bob
> obtains the factorization of N, he can lie about
> which root of $z^2 mod N$ he originally had.

The only solution we know of for this problem in Rabin's protocol is as follows:

At step 2 Bob sends $z^2 = f(d)^2 \bmod N$, where f is a one-way function and d is randomly chosen from the domain of f. Then, after the protocol, Bob can prove to a judge that he knew $z = f(d)$ by displaying $d = f^{-1}(x)$.

Using one-way functions is clearly undesirable since the protocol cannot then be proven secure. In our protocol, the factorization of the modulus is never revealed. This makes it possible to solve the problem above without using one-way functions.

2. Terminology and Axioms.

Definition: A number $N = pq$, where $p \equiv q \equiv 3 \bmod 4$ are distinct primes and $|log(\frac{p}{q})| < 2$ is called a *Blum integer*.

Assumption 1 (about the model of computation) We assume Alice and Bob have computational power equivalent to a poly-time probabilistic Turing Machine (PTM).

Assumption 2 (Factoring Blum integers is hard): Let M be a poly-time PTM. Let ρ_n be the probability that M factors a random n-bit Blum integer. Then $\rho_n \to 0$ *as* $n \to \infty$.

Assumption 3 (about the message space): Every positive integer $< N$ is a valid message. However, Bob knows that the message M is drawn with a uniform probability distribution from a space of possible messages, MS, of size $\geq \alpha N$ for a fixed constant $0 < \alpha < 1$. MS is the set of integers in Z_N which have a non-zero probability of being chosen by Alice.

Definition: The *length* of a protocol is the total number of bits transferred between the parties in the protocol.

Definition: Whenever the set of possible messages is finite, it is very hard to guarantee that Bob will obtain the message with probability exactly $\frac{1}{2}$. This is true even if we assume that both parties follow the protocol, since Bob has a positive probability of simply guessing the message. Instead, we achieve probabilities which deviate by an arbitrarily small ϵ from $\frac{1}{2}$. We call this ϵ the *bias* of the implementation.

Definition: (In an O.T. implementation with bias ϵ) *Alice cheats Bob* if, when Bob follows the protocol, Alice, by deviating from the protocol, is able to:

   i) determine with probability $> \frac{1}{2} + \epsilon$ whether or not Bob obtained M; or
   ii) diminish Bob's chances of obtaining M to less than $\frac{1}{2} - \epsilon$.

Definition: (In an O.T. implementation with bias ϵ) *Bob cheats Alice* if, when Alice follows the protocol, Bob, by deviating from the protocol, is able to obtain M with probability $> \frac{1}{2} + \epsilon$.

Definition: An implementation of O.T. in which it is not possible for either Bob or Alice to cheat is called *secure*.
Given this terminology our goal is to describe an implementation of the O.T. with arbitrarily small bias.

3. A Provably Secure Oblivious Transfer Protocol.

Step 1: Alice sends a random n-bit Blum integer, N, to Bob.
Alice knows the factorization of N, but Bob does not.

Step 2: Alice convinces Bob that N is a Blum integer except for the
fact that p and q might be raised to odd powers.
(See proof of theorem 4)

Step 3: Bob chooses a random integer $z \in Z_N$ and
sends $z^2 \ mod \ N$ to Alice.

Step 4: Alice sends $M^2 \ mod \ N$, where M is her private message;
$b = $ Jacobi symbol $\left[\dfrac{M}{N}\right]$; and a random root w of $M^2 z^2 \ mod \ N$ to Bob.

{At this point the message is defined to be the unique root of $M^2 \ mod \ N$
less than $\dfrac{N}{2}$ and with Jacobi symbol b.}

Step 5: To insure that w is not junk, Bob verifies that $\dfrac{w^2}{z^2} \equiv M^2 \ (\text{mod N})$.

Then, if Jacobi symbol $\left[\dfrac{w/z}{N}\right] = b$, Bob has the message.

Using well known number theoretical algorithms all computations required by the protocol can be done in polynomial time in n.

4. The protocol works when both parties follow the protocol.

First we show that, after step 4, Bob cannot factor N. For simplicity we ignore the Jacobi symbol $\left[\dfrac{M}{N}\right]$ since it is clear that it does not help Bob factor N.

We think of Bob as a poly-time PTM B with oracle A (Alice). Oracle A takes as input a pair (N, z^2) where N is an n-bit Blum integer and z^2 is a quadratic residue in Z_N and returns a random root of $M^2 z^2$ where M is a random element in MS. The input to B is an n-bit Blum integer N. B contains a routine P(N) which returns a pair (z, z^2) where $z \in Z_N$. B is allowed to make *one* call $A(N, z^2)$ to A *provided* z^2 was generated by P, i.e. provided Bob knows a root of z^2.

Theorem 1:

Let ψ_n be the probability that B factors N given that N is a random n-bit Blum integer. Then $\psi_n \to 0$ as $n \to \infty$.

Proof: Construct a PTM B^{smart} as follows:

INPUT: an n-bit Blum integer N.

B^{smart}: simulate B on input N until B makes the call $A(N, z^2)$;
generate a random element M in Z_N;
assume $A(N, z^2)$ returns Mx;
continue simulating B.

By assumption 3, the probability that M is in MS is α. Given that M is in MS the probability that $\pm$ Mx gets chosen as a root of $M^2 z^2$ is $\dfrac{1}{2}$. Thus the probability ρ_n that B^{smart} factors N is $\geq \dfrac{1}{2} \alpha \psi_n$. But B^{smart} is a poly-time PTM and so, by assumption 2, $\rho_n \to 0$. This implies $\psi_n \to 0$ ▽

Theorem 2:

Assume both parties follow the protocol. Let ρ_n be the probability that Bob obtains M. Then $\rho_n \rightarrow \frac{1}{2}$ as $n \rightarrow \infty$.

Proof: The roots of $z^2 M^2 \bmod N$ are $\pm$ xM, and $\pm$ xL where L, M are twin roots of $M^2 \bmod N$. The probability that Alice sends $\pm$ xM is $\frac{1}{2}$. Thus $\rho_n \geq \frac{1}{2}$.

Let E_1 be the event that Bob factors N. Let $prob(E_1) = \psi_n$. Assume for simplicity that, given twin roots of $M^2 \bmod N$, Bob can factor N in 0 steps. Let E_2 be the event that Bob obtains M. Then

$$
\begin{aligned}
\rho_n &= prob(E_2) \\
&= prob(E_2 \,|\, E_1) * prob(E_1) + prob(E_2 \,|\, \neg E_1) * prob(\neg E_1) \\
&\leq prob(E_1) + prob(E_2 \,|\, \neg E_1) \\
&\leq \psi_n + prob(E_2 \,|\, \neg E_1).
\end{aligned}
$$

Now, given $\neg E_1$, Bob can obtain at most one root of M^2 less than $\frac{N}{2}$. Thus he will obtain M if and only if Alice sends $\pm$ xM. The probability of this event is $\frac{1}{2}$. Thus $prob(E_2 \,|\, \neg E_1) = \frac{1}{2}$, which implies $\rho_n = prob(E_2) \leq \frac{1}{2} + \psi_n \rightarrow \frac{1}{2}$ by theorem 1 .▽

Theorem 3:

Assume both parties follow the protocol. Let N be an n-bit Blum integer. Let ρ_n be the probability that Alice correctly guesses whether or not Bob obtained M. Then $\rho_n \rightarrow \frac{1}{2}$ as $n \rightarrow \infty$.

Proof: Let ψ_n be the probability that Bob factors N. If Alice guesses that Bob obtained M, then she is right if either Bob was able to factor N or Bob received $\pm$ xM (probability $= \frac{1}{2}$). Thus she is right with probability p, where $\frac{1}{2} \leq p \leq \frac{1}{2} + \psi_n$. If Alice guesses that Bob did not obtain M, then she is right with probability $1 - p$, where $\frac{1}{2} - \psi_n \leq 1 - p \leq \frac{1}{2}$. Thus $\rho_n \in [\frac{1}{2} - \psi_n, \frac{1}{2} + \psi_n]$. By theorem 1, $\rho_n \rightarrow \frac{1}{2}$ as $n \rightarrow \infty$.▽

Result

Theorems 1,2 and 3 prove that our protocol works for honest parties. Now we must show it is secure.

5. The protocol is secure

We will first assume Bob knows a root of $z^2 \bmod N$. Later we will drop this assumption.

Theorem 4:

Assume that at step 3 Bob knows a root of z^2. Then Alice can not cheat Bob, nor can Bob cheat Alice.

Proof: We look at possible deviations from the protocol and show that they are not useful or cannot be hidden.
Assume Alice follows the protocol. At step 2 Bob must send a quadratic residue because Alice has the factorization of N and can decide quadratic residuosity. Theorem 1 shows Bob obtains at most one root of M^2 independently of how he chose z. Thus not choosing x at random does not constitute cheating. This exhausts the possibilities of

Bob cheating.

Now assume Bob follows the protocol. We do not know of an efficient protocol by which Alice can prove to Bob that N is a Blum integer. However, the remainder of the proof relies only on the fact that N is the product of two distinct primes congruent to 3 mod 4, each raised to an odd power.

N is the product of two distinct primes congruent to 3 mod 4, each raised to an odd power if and only if the following 3 conditions are met:

a) The Jacobi symbol $\left(\frac{-1}{N}\right) = 1$.
b) N has exactly 2 distinct prime factors.
c) quadratic residues have roots with distinct Jacobi symbols.

The first condition is efficiently verifiable by Bob. Goldwasser and Micali [3] have shown that Alice can convince Bob (efficiently, securely and with exponentially small probability of error) that (b) holds. Blum[4] has shown Alice can convince Bob (efficiently, securely and with exponentially small probability of error) that (c) holds.

Now Bob knows that $M^2 \bmod N$ has exactly 2 roots less than $\frac{N}{2}$ and that these roots have opposite Jacobi symbols. At step 4 Alice defines the message to be the (unique) square root of $M^2 \bmod N$ which has Jacobi symbol b and is less than $\frac{N}{2}$. She cannot avoid sending a root of $M^2 \bmod N$, and she has no way of knowing which root she is actually sending.

Theorem 4 assumes that Bob knows a root of $z^2 \bmod N$. The next theorem says Bob cannot cheat Alice at step 3 by sending a quadratic residue without knowing one of its roots.

Theorem 5:

Assume Alice follows the protocol. If, at step 3, Bob does not know a square root of z^2, yet he has probability $\geq \frac{1}{2}$ of obtaining M, then there exists an efficient probabilistic procedure to compute a root of $z^2 \bmod N$ with exponentially small probability of failure.

Proof: We think of Bob as a dishonest PTM $B^{dishonest}$ with oracle A. Recall that oracle A takes as input a pair (N,z^2) where N is an n-bit Blum integer and z^2 is a quadratic residue in Z_N and returns a random root of $M^2 z^2$ where M is a random element in MS.

The input to $B^{dishonest}$ is an n-bit integer N. Since Bob is dishonest we must drop the requirement that the routine P(N) returns a root of the quadratic residue z^2. Thus P(N) will return only the quadratic residue z^2. $B^{dishonest}$ is allowed to make one call A(N,P(N)) to A.

Let ρ_n be the probability that $B^{dishonest}$ gets the message. We will use $B^{dishonest}$ to construct a parallel PTM B^{smart} which computes a root of $z^2 \bmod N$. The sequential version of B^{smart} runs in polynomial time and computes a root of $z^2 \bmod N$ with probability of failure $\left(1 - \frac{\alpha}{4}\right)^r$ for an arbitrarily large constant r. The construction follows:

INPUT: an n-bit integer N.

B^{smart}:

simulate $B^{dishonest}$ until call A(N,P(N)) is made;
{Let $z^2 = P(N)$}
For each of r processors do
begin

generate a random number $y \in Z_n$; { $\sqrt{\dfrac{y^2}{z^2}}$ is called the "fake message" }

Assume $A(N,z^2)$ returns y ;

continue simulating $B^{dishonest}$

if $B^{dishonest}$ gets the fake message all processors stop;
end.

Lemma 1: If any of the r processors gets the fake message then B^{smart} knows a root of z^2.

Proof: The processor that gets the fake message can compute $\sqrt{z^2} = y(\sqrt{\dfrac{y^2}{z^2}})^{-1}$.▽

Lemma 2: The probability that a particular processor gets the fake message is $\geq \dfrac{\alpha}{4}$.

Proof: The probability that $z = \dfrac{y}{z}$ lies in MS is α. Given that z lies in MS, the probability that $\pm y$ gets chosen as a root of $z^2 z^2$ is $\dfrac{1}{2}$. Given this event the probability that $B^{dishonest}$ obtains the fake message is (by assumption) $\geq \dfrac{1}{2}$. Thus the total probability that a particular processor gets the fake message $\geq \dfrac{\alpha}{4}$.▽

Thus the probability that no processor gets the fake message $\leq \left(1 - \dfrac{\alpha}{4}\right)^r$. Therefore, by Lemma 1, B^{smart} obtains a root of $z^2 \bmod N$ with probability $1 - \left(1 - \dfrac{\alpha}{4}\right)^r$.▽

Theorems 4 and 5 establish that our protocol is secure.

6. Generalizations

We state without proof that the following generalizations do not compromise the security of the O.T. protocol:

i) we may replace α by $\dfrac{1}{p(n)}$ for a fixed polynomial p.

ii) If the protocol is implemented "with receipts", i.e. Bob and Alice
send a receipt for each message received, then Bob
can prove to a third party whether or not he received M.

iii) Goldreich has proposed a version of the Oblivious Transfer
in which Alice transfers to Bob exactly one out of two
recognizable messages M_1, M_2. Our protocol can be easily
adapted to perform Goldreich's OT as follows :
Let XOR be the bitwise exclusive-or operator for bit vectors.
Let L be the twin root of M_1. Let $Y = L$ XOR M_2.
(Notice that $M_2 = L$ XOR Y)
At step 4 Alice sends Y along with b and $\sqrt{M_1^2 z^2}$.

386

iv) if we wish to send many independently distributed messages, say
q messages for a fixed integer q, we may replace steps 3, 4, 5
of the protocol by the loop:

for i:= 1 to q do
begin
    Step 3: Bob chooses a random integer $z_i \in Z_N$ and
        sends $z_i^2 \bmod N$ to Alice.

    Step 4: Alice sends $M_i^2 \bmod N$, where M_i is her private message;
        $b = $ Jacobi symbol $\left[\dfrac{M_i}{N}\right]$; and a random root w of $M_i^2 z_i^2 \bmod N$ to Bob.
        {At this point the message is defined to be the unique root of $M_i^2 \bmod N$
        less than $\dfrac{N}{2}$ and with Jacobi symbol b.}

    Step 5: To insure that w is not junk, Bob verifies that $\dfrac{w^2}{z_i^2} = M_i^2$.
        Then, if Jacobi symbol $\left[\dfrac{w/z_i}{N}\right] = b$, Bob has the message.
end

7. Conclusions and Suggestions for Further Research

Thus we have developed a provably secure implementation of the Oblivious Transfer protocol. In our implementation it is essentially impossible for either Bob or Alice to successfully cheat. We have also shown that our implementation has certain properties which will make it an important building block for designing secure protocols. Essential to this research is the creation of a formal model of a protocol. Once this has been accomplished, one could prove theorems about the ways that various protocols can be combined so that the security of the implementation is not compromised.

Acknowledgements:

We are indebted to Manuel Blum for his insight and encouragement, and for providing a wonderful environment for research. We are also indebted to Umesh Vazirani for several enlightening discussions.

References

1.   M. Rabin, *Private Communication*.

2.   M. Fischer, *Private Communication through M. Blum*.

3.   S. Goldwasser and S. Micali, *Proofs with Untrusted Oracles*, Department of Computer Science MIT and Department of Computer Science University of Toronto, 1983.

4.   M. Blum, "Coin Flipping by Telephone," *Proc. IEEE COMPCON*, pp. 133-137, 1982.

On Concurrent Identification Protocols
(Extended Abstract)

Oded Goldreich
Laboratory for Computer Science
MIT,room NE43-836,Cambridge,Ma 02139

Abstract

We consider communication networks in which it is not possible to identify the source of a message which is broadcasted through the network. A natural question is whether it is possible for two users to identify each other concurrently, through a secure two-party protocol. We show that more than the existence of a secure Public Key Cryptosystem should be assumed in order to present a secure protocol for concurrent identification. We present two concurrent identification protocols: The first one relies on the existence of a center who has distributed "identification tags" to the users; while the second protocol relies on the distribution of "experimental sequences" by instances of a pre-protocol which have taken place between every two users.

This research was carried out at the Computer Science Department
Technion - Israel Institute of Technology

1. Introduction

Let N be a set of users in a communication network in which it is not possible to identify the source of a message broadcasted on the network . Thus, identification of the source of a message can only rely on the content of the message. Clearly, this would require some sort of a secure authentication scheme as well as a secure protocol which makes use of it.

The task of reaching concurrent identification is somewhat more involved. It requires not only that identification takes place but also that it takes place concurrently; i.e that through this process there would be no situation in which one party had a "substantial" advantage in guessing and/or computing his counterpart's identity. Methods for reaching concurrent identification may be of value in certain business environments in which transactions are carried out in two stages: first reaching an anonymous agreement and only then yielding the identities of the parties to the agreement, as quickly as possible.(An example of such an environment is a future stock exchange without brokers[dealers] or even a present stock exchange controlled by an agency that wishes to prevent biased deals.)

Clearly, if one allows the participation of trusted third parties in the concurrent identification process, trivial solutions exist. However,we are interested in the existence of two-party protocols through which concurrent identification takes place (hereafter referred to as *Concurrent Identification Protocols* or as *cips*).

In Sec. 2 we show that the mere existence of a PKCS (Public Key Cryptosystem [DH]) and a public file of all public keys does not suffice for the existence of a secure cip in the net (i.e. there exists no secure cip in such a net).

In Sec.3 we present a cip which relies on a trusted center which has prepared and distributed "identification tags" to the users at the time the net has been established. **(This center does not participate in the cip!)** The number of transmissions needed to distribute these tags is linear in the number of users; thus the complexity of establishing a net in which this cip can be used securely is still linear in the number of its users. This fact combined with the simplicity of the cip itself makes its implementation reasonably practical.

In Sec. 4 we present a secure cip which does not rely on the honesty of some center nor even on its mere existence. Instead this cip relies on information which has been passed between every pair of users , via instances of a pre-protocol which have taken place at the time the net was established. The fact that the pre-protocol is fairly complicated combined with the fact that $O(|N|^2)$ instances must take place, cause this concurrent identification scheme to be impractical, especially for large networks. However it demonstrates that concurrent identification can take place even if no center exist (at the time the net has been established as well as later).

In both Sec. 3 and 4 we assume the existence of secure cryptosystems, in particular the existence of a secure public key cryptosystem (PKCS)[DH].

A natural problem which arises when designing identification protocols is the *replay problem*, which is hereafter described. User A may try to impersonate user B by using information B has revealed to him in previous instances of the identification protocol. Note that this information has been used to authenticate B and can be used by A to cheat C, unless the protocol has features which prevent such an attempt to cheat. In case of simple identification it is enough to ask for a signature to some time dependent message. (Note that this can not be done trivially in a cip since a signature to any message will immediately reveal the identity of the signer.)

To solve the replay problem in the concurrent identification protocols presented in this paper we use an *Oblivious Transfer* (OT) subprotocol. The notion of OT was first introduced and implemented by Rabin [R]. Another definition of OT, which we believe to be more natural, was suggested by Even, Goldreich and Lempel [EGL] (and implemented using any PKCS). By their definition an OT of a recognizable message $,M$, is a protocol by which a *sender* $,S$, transfers to a *receiver* $,R$, the message M so that R gets M with probability one half while for S the a-posteriori probability that R got M remains one half. In this work, we use a modification of the above definition; for details see the Appendix.

2. Necessary Conditions for the Existence of a CIP

It was already mentioned that no cip (as well as no identification protocol) can exist in a net if it is not assumed that the users are provided with some secure cryptographic identification scheme. We will assume the existence of both a secure conventional cryptosystem (e.g. the DES[NBS]) and a secure PKCS. However, we shall show that this assumption does not suffice to allow the existence of a secure cip, namely:

Theorem 1: A cip, which relies only on the existence of secure cryptosystems (the instances of which are free of any relation other than the cancellation of encryption by the corresponding decryption and vice versa) and a public file of all public keys, can not be secure.

The proof appears in the full version of this paper.

To conclude this section we point out that the "replay problem" is trivially solvable only under irreasonable assumptions, namely:

(i) Each user eavesdrops on all the instances of the cip and records the information he reads.

or

(ii) Each user notifies all the other users about every instance of the cip he participates in.

3. A CIP which Relies on Preparations by a Trusted Center

In this section we show how identification tags distributed, to the users, by a trusted center can grant the existence of a cip. The center can distribute these tags at the time the network is established. The center must be trusted not to collaborate with any user, in the process of distributing the tags as well as during the time the cip is run. It is preferred that the center would seize to exist after distributing the tags. The tags will bear the center's signature and thus be unforgable. Every user can protect himself against the replay of his tags (by other users), by using a tag only once. Thus, the center should provide each user with enough tags.

We assume the existence of a secure PKCS (e.g. the RSA[RSA]) and of a conventional cryptosystem (e.g. the DES[NBS]). We also assume that all users have equel computing power.

3.1. The Identification Tag

Before describing the structure of the identification tag let us introduce some notation:

(i) F denotes a conventional cryptosystem and $F_K(M)[F_K^{-1}(M)]$ denotes the encryption[decryption] of M by F using the key K.

(ii) E_X , D_X will denote the encryption and decryption algorithms of user X (i.e. the PKCS's instance generated by X). Note that $D_X(M)$ can serve as X's signature to M.

(iii) C denotes the center.

(iv) N_X denotes the binary representation of X's name.

An *Identification Tag* (IT) of user X consists of three parts:

(1) The *header* , which contains an (unforgeable) encryption of X's name : $D_C(z, F_y(S), F_y(N_X))$,where y is a randomly chosen key (of length k) to F and z is a random "serial" number.

(2) The *anti-replay* part , which consist of n pairs of recognizable (and unforgeable) messages. The i-th pair denoted AR_i is $(D_C(z, L_i), D_C(z, R_i))$.

(3) The *certified key-bits* part , which consists of the bits of the key , which was used for the encryption of X's name, certified by the center: the certification of y_i (the i-th bit of y) is $D_C(z, i, y_i)$.

Note that all parts of a IT bear the same serial number and that they are signed by the center. User X is called the *legitimate holder* (or just the holder) of the above identification tag. (Note the although other users can have parts of X's tag only X can have all of it if he follows the cip described below properly.)

Remark: S , the L_i's and the R_i's are arbitrary , fixed messages (i.e. invariant of X ,y and z).

We remind the reader that these IT's will be distributed to the users by C at the time the network is established. Note that at that time only X has X's ITs. In the next subsection we will present a cip in which X uses one of his ITs to identify himself without yielding the entire IT. It will be shown that this prevents the replay of this IT by another user.

3.2. The Protocol

The cip described below uses an OT subprotocol which allows a user to send two recognizable messages such that : (1) his counterpart receives exactly one of them; (2) with probability one half the receiver receives the first message; (3) for the sender the a-posteriori probability that the first message was received remains one half; (4) if the sender tries to cheat the receiver will detect it with probability at least one half.

(An implementation of this OT is described in the Appendix and is based on ideas which first appeared in Even,Goldreich and Lempel [EGL].)

The cip proceeds as follows:

(The parties to the protocol are denoted A and B)
step 1: (linking identity with a secret serial number)
A chooses one of his unused ITs (hereafter denoted t_A)
marks t_A as "used"
and transmits t_A's header to B.
B acts symmetrically transmitting t_B's header to A.
(Each checks whether the center's signature
to the header is authentic.)
step 2: (protection against replay attempts.)
$\underline{for}$ $i = 1$ to n $\underline{do}$ $\underline{begin}$
A sends to B one element out of t_A's AR_i , via OT.
B acts symmetrically w.r.t. t_B .
(Each uses the cheat detection mechanism of the OT.)
$\underline{end}$
step 3: (decreasing the time of computing the identity.)
$\underline{for}$ $i = 1$ to k $\underline{do}$ $\underline{begin}$
A transmits to B the i-th certified key-bit of t_A .
B acts symmetrically w.r.t. t_B .
(Each checks the signature certifying the bit received)
$\underline{end}$

3.3. Analysis of the Protocol and the Structure of the IT

Remarks (for $X \in \{A, B\}$)

(R1) The header of t_X establishes a linkage among X's name (although encrypted) the key y (which is used for the encryption of both N_X and the standard message S) and z (which is used as a serial number). It also provides information for the computation of y although this computation becomes feasible only during step(3).

(R2) The anti-replay of t_X allows X to protect himself against the replay of t_X. Note that if X uses t_X only in one instance of the protocol and execute this instance properly then he is (still) the only user in the net who knows both elements of each AR_i in t_X. (Note that his counterpart to the cip instance only got one element out of each AR_i.) User Y , $Y \neq X$, will succeed in replaying t_X only if he is asked in the OT of each AR_i (which occurs in step (2) of the protocol) to disclose the element of AR_i which is known to him. Note that for Y, both the element he is asked to disclose and the element known to him are randomly chosen out of an AR_i of t_X (this is due to the use of the OT in step(2)). Thus, the probability that Y will succeed in replaying t_X is bounded from above by 2^{-n}. Thus, a proper execution of step (2) of the protocol (only) assures the parties that the identification tags are in the hands of their legitimate holders.

(R3) The third part of t_X (which is exchanged in step (3) of the protocol) allows the gradual decrease in the time of computation which is required to extract N_X from the header of t_X. N_X is extracted by first finding the key y which transforms the message S into the cryptogram $F_y(S)$. Note that this computation becomes feasible (during step(3) of the protocol) only after the tag holder has proven himself to be the legitimate one (by succeeding in an unfaulty execution of step(2) of the protocol).

(R4) If the rate ,in which the time which is required to compute N_X given the header of t_X decreases, is considered to be too fast one may slow it down by using simple "exchange of half bit" schemes (e.g. Tedricks' schemes[T]).

(R5) The interleaving in step(2) of the protocol is not material.

(R6) One can use the "conventional OT" instead of the "one-out-of-two OT" for an oblivious tranfer of each element of the anti-replay. However, the analysis of such a protocol will be more involved.

(R7) There is some similarity between the ideas used in the above anti-replay, and the ideas of Bennett et al. ([BBBW]). However, Bennett et al. consider a specific physical device which stores 2 messages such that only one of them can be read; while we consider a protocol through which one out of two messages is randomly transferred.

We claim that this cip is secure provided the following assumptions hold:

(A1) A trusted center has distributed the identification tags described in sec. 3.1 to the legitimate holders.(The center is trusted not to convey any information about the tags he has provided user X to any other user.He is also trusted not to yield his signature algorithm.)

(A2) All parties have equal computing power.

(A3) Both the conventional cryptosystem and the PKCS used by the protocol are secure. (No one can forge C's signature. Extracting M from $F_K(M)$ given $S, F_K(S)$ and some of K's bits requires exhaustive search on all keys which match the known bits of K ; when no bit of K is known this computation is infeasible.)

Theorem 2: If the above assumptions hold and a user ,U, plays the protocol properly then the following hold:

(1) In any phase during the execution of the protocol, if U's counterpart
can find out U's identity using expected time t then U can
find out what is claimed to be his counterpart's identity in about
the same expected time.

(2) If U's counterparts is honest U will find out his identity.

(3) If U's counterpart is impersonating then with high probability
$(1 - 2^{-n})$ U will find this out before reaching a stage
in which the computation of his identity is feasible.

The proof appears in the full version of this paper.

4. A CIP which Relies on Preparations by Instances of a Pre-Protocol

In this section we (only) assume the existence of a secure PKCS. We show how a pre-protocol, played between every pair of users, can grant the existence of a cip in the net. Note that we do not assume that there exists some (trusted) center and that we do not assume that all parties have equal computing power. (It should be stressed that we do not refer to the public file of the users' encryption keys as a center.) Since instances of the pre-protocol must take place between every pair of users, the result of this section, although being of theoretical interest, is practical only for "small" networks. The purpose of the pre-protocol is to distribute *secure experimental sequences* which will be used in the identification process. These sequences will be unforgeable and will yield the identity of their legitimate holder[1] if some parts of them are read completely. However it will be possible to give away only small (still unforgeable) fragments of the sequence yielding only a "small amount of information" about their legitimate holder.

The idea behind the implementation of these experimental sequences (hereafter referred to as SES's) is to allow a user to conduct experiments on the bits of another user's name. The experiment is gauranteed to give a result equal to the tested bit with some fixed probability greater than one half. Thus conducting enough experiments on a bit gives certainty of knowing its right value ; whereas on the other hand a single experiment does not give much information about the corresponding bit. The cip consist of letting each user experiment on each of his counterpart's name bits by just sending one entry in the experimental sequence. The implementation of a process which constructs secure experimental sequences is discussed in the full version of this paper ([G]). (Its essence is that the SES will be built anonymously by the user who will later experiment on it. The sequence will be built by flipping a biased coin so that its builder will only know the expected value of an entry in it and not the concrete value. This will be achieved by using an OT.)

Remark: The idea of using a biased coin as a tool for exchanging a bit of information was suggested, independently, by Lubi,Micali and Rackoff in their MiRackoLus paper [LMR]. It should be stressed that the problem they were facing was much more difficult

[1]As in Sec.3 it will happen that other users know part of the sequence but only one user (its holder) knows all of it, provided he follows the cip which reveals parts of it properly.

and their solution (a coin the bias of which is determined by the secrets of both parties and without yielding these secrets) much more inspirating. However , the author does not know of any reduction between the biased coin used here and the symmetric biased coin suggested in [LMR]; there are too many differences in the setting, conception and implementation!

4.1. Sketch of the Concurrent Identification Protocol

(The parties to the cip will be denoted A and B)

(0) A notifies B which of B's SESs he would like to examine.
B acts symmetrically w.r.t A's SESs.

(1) A checks whether he is communicating with the legitimate holder of the SES (i.e. B).
B acts symmetrically.
(This is done by testing the anti-replay part of the SES similarly to the way it was done in the cip of Sec. 3.)

(2) _for_ $i = 1$ to q (the number of entries in a SES) _do begin_
    A transmits the i-th entry of his SES to B.
    B acts symmetrically.
end

4.2. Analysis of the Protocol

Under the assumption that there exist SESs in the network it is straightforward to prove that the cip presented above is secure,namely:

Theorem 3: If a user ,U plays the above cip properly then the following hold:

(1) In any phase during the execution of the protocol,if for
U's counterpart the entropy of U's name is e then for U
the entropy of what is claimed to be his counterparts name
is very close to e.

(2) If U's counterparts is honest U will find out his identity.

(3) If U's counterpart is impersonating then with high probability
$(1 - 2^{-n})$ U will find this out before reaching a stage
in which he has revealed any information about his identity .

The proof appears in the full version of this paper.

5. Acknowledgements

I would like to thank Prof. Shimon Even for suggesting the problem to me, for many helpful discussions and especially for a briliant insight that was of much help in the analysis of the cip presented in Sec. 4.

I would also like to thank Prof. Adi Shamir for the discussion which led to the cip presented in Sec. 3.

I am very grateful to Tom Tedrick for carefully reading the manuscript, finding many errors and giving me feedback.

6. References

[A] Abramson,N., *Information Theory and Coding*, M.Graw-Hill,1963, pp. 100-105.

[BBBW] Bennett,C.H., Brassard,G., Breidbart,S., and Wiesner,S., "Quantum Cryptography, or Unforgeable Subway Tokens", in *Advances in Cryptology:Proceedings of Crypto82*, (Chaum,D. et al. editors), Plenum Press, 1983, pp. 267-275.

[DH] Diffie,W., and Hellman,M.E., "New Directions in Cryptography", *IEEE Trans. on Inform. Theory*,Vol. IT-22,No. 6,November 1976, pp. 644-654

[EGL] Even,S., Goldreich,O., and Lempel,A., "A Randomized Protocol for Signing Contracts", in *Advances in Cryptology:Proceedings of Crypto82*, (Chaum,D. et al. editors), Plenum Press, 1983, pp. 205-210

[EGL'] Even,S., Goldreich,O., and Lempel,A., "A Randomized Protocol for Signing Contracts", TR No. 233, Computer Science Dept., Technion, Haifa, Israel, February 1982

[G] Goldreich,O., "On Concurrent Identification Protocols", MIT/LCS/TM-250, December 1983

[LMR] Lubi,M., Micali,S., and Rackoff,C., "How to Simultaneously Exchange a Secret Bit by Flipping a Symmetrically-Biased Coin", *proceedings of the 24th IEEE Symp. on Foundation Of Computer Science*, 1983, pp. 11-21

[NBS] National Bureau of Standards, Data Encryption Standard, *Federal Information Processing Standards*, Publ. 46, 1977

[R] Rabin,M.O., "How to Exchange Secrets by Oblivious Transfer", Technical memo TR-81, Harvard Center for Research in Computing, (1981).

[RSA] Rivest,R.L., Shamir,A., and Adleman,L., "A Method for Obtaining Digital Signature and Public Key Cryptosystems", *Comm. of the ACM* ,Vol.21, February 1978, pp. 120-126

[S] Shannon,C.E., "Communication Theory of Secrecy Systems",*Bell Syst. Jour. 28*, October 1949, pp. 656-715

[T] Tedrick,T., "How to Exchange Half a Bit", to appear in the proceedings of *Crypto83*

7. Appendix: An Implementation of OT

Assume S wants to transfer to R exactly one of the messages M_1 and M_2, such that:

(1) R can recognize both M_1 and M_2
   (e.g. they are signatures to known messages).
(2) If S is honest then R gets M_1 with probability one half.
   For S the a-posteriori probability that R got M_1 remains one half.
(3) If S tries to cheat, R will detect it with probability at least one half.

An implementation of this transfer proceeds as follows:

(0) S chooses ,randomly, two pairs (E_1, D_1) and (E_2, D_2) of
   encryption-decryption algorithms of the PKCS.
   R chooses ,randomly, a key K
   for the conventional cryptosystem F.
(1) S transmits E_1 and E_2 to R.
(2) R chooses ,randomly, $r \in \{1, 2\}$
   and transmits $E_r(K)$ to S.
(3) S computes $K'_i = D_i(E_r(K))$,for $i \in \{1, 2\}$.
   S chooses ,randomly, $s \in \{1, 2\}$ and transmits
   $(F_{K'_1}(M'_1), F_{K'_2}(M'_2), s)$
   to R, where $M'_s = M_1$ and $M'_{3-s} = M_2$.

Remarks:

(1) Assuming that K looks like random noise and that E_1, E_2 have the same range, S can not guess with probability of success greater than one half which of the K'_i's, computed by him is the K choosen by R.

(2) Assume that the instances of the PKCS are free of any relation other than the cancellation of encryption by the corresponding decryption and that K'_i must be known in order to read M'_i.

(3) By (1) and (2) if S is not cheating then R can read M'_i iff $i = r$. Thus, he can detect cheating by S with probability one half.

(4) In the RSA[RSA] scheme, distinct E_i's may have different ranges. However, this difficulty can be overcome (see [EGL']).

(5) One can use a one-time pad instead of the conventional cryptosystem F.

SECTION V

APPLICATIONS

TIME-DIVISION MULTIPLEXING SCRAMBLERS: SELECTING

PERMUTATIONS AND TESTING THE SYSTEM

A. Ecker
Hahn-Meitner-Institut für Kernforschung Berlin GmbH
Glienicker Str. 100, D-1000 Berlin 39, Germany

Abstract

Selecting permutations for speech scrambling with t.d.m.
means to define a suitable weight-function or metric on
S_n (the full symmetric group). This can be done in a lot
of different ways. We study some of that weight-functions
and point out which one should be preferred. An algorithm
is given to generate permutations with a prescribed weight.
Some hints are given how to compute approximately the distribution function of some weight-functions. Finally rank
correlation methods are recommended for testing a t.d.m.-
system.

1. Introduction

We are mainly concerned with some open questions from [2]
(see also Chap. 9 of the book [1]). Selecting permutations
for speech scrambling with t.d.m. means to define a suitable
weight-function or metric on S_n (the full symmetric group).
This can be done in a lot of different ways (see [12] p.84).
In speech scrambling Houghtons shift factor

$$m_1(\delta) = \sum_{i=1}^{n} |\delta(i) - i| \qquad (\delta \in S_n, \; n \geq 1)$$

may be taken as a weight function. We tried to use the generalized weight-functions m_2, m_3,... etc.

$$m_k(\delta) = \sum_{i=1}^{n} |\delta(i) - i|^k \qquad (k \geq 1)$$

They are of independent interest from a combinatorial, number-
theoretical and probabilistic   point of view (see [5, 6],
[10]). A thorough study reveals that m_2 should be preferred.
An algorithm is given to generate permutations with a prescribed
weight. The distribution functions of m_k approach a normal distribution (mean and variance for k = 1,2 are known) for large n.
This approximation is good, even if n is small (n $\geq$5). To compute the distribution function by combinatorial methods seems
to be extremely difficult, only a small number of values are
known exactly. m_2 is related to the problem of representing
an integer number as a sum of squares.

Compared with other crypto-systems speech scramblers have the
capability for testing. The approach taken in [2] for testing
a t.d.m.-system is unsatisfactory because no statistical methods
are used. We recommend rank correlation methods (see [10]) and

that means for example to use Spearman's ρ based on m_2.

It should be noticed that we used the book [2] in its original form as a report (Arbeitsberichte des Instituts f. Mathematische Maschinen u. Datenverarbeitung (Informatik). Bd. 14,9; Erlangen, März 1982). All citations, page numbers etc. are given with respect to that original version of [2].

2. Weights on groups

Let G denote a (multiplicative written) finite group with unit element id and N the natural numbers (zero included).

A mapping

$$p:\quad G \to N$$

will be called a weight-function on G, if

(1) $p(a) = 0 \iff a = id \ (a \in G)$.

(2) $p(a) = p(a^{-1})$ for all $a \in G$.

(3) $p(a \cdot b) \quad p(a) + p(b)$ for all $a,b \in G$.

By means of $d_p(a,b) = p(a \cdot b^{-1})$ we can associate a metric on G to each weight-function on G. This metric has the property: $d_p(a,b) = d_p(a \cdot c, b \cdot c)$ for any $c \in G$; such a metric is called right-invariant. Conversely if there is a right-invariant metric d on G, a weight-function $p_d(a) = d(a, id)$ on G is associated to d. We are only interested in $G = S_n$, where S_n is to be understood as the full symmetric group on $\{1,2,\ldots, n\}$. There are many ways to define a metric on S_n (see for example [4]). Five common examples are given below, where $\|a\|_p$ is written instead of $p(a)$ to emphasize the relationship to some well-known norm-functions.

Examples $\quad \delta, \pi \in S_n \ (n \geq 1)$

a.
$$\|\delta\|_k = \sum_{i=1}^{n} |\delta(i) - i|^k \qquad\qquad (k = 1,2,\ldots)$$
$$d_k(\delta, \pi) = \sum_{i=1}^{n} |\delta(i) - \pi(i)|^k$$

b. $\|\sigma\|_I$ = number of inversions in σ (if $k < l$ and $\sigma(k) > \sigma(l)$ we call this an inversion of σ).

$d_I(\sigma, \pi)$ = the minimum number of pairwise adjacent transpositions needed to bring $\{\sigma^{-1}(1), \ldots, \sigma^{-1}(n)\}$ into the order $\{\pi^{-1}(1), \ldots, \{\pi^{-1}(n)\}$. Here σ^{-1} and π^{-1} are the permutations inverse to σ and π .

c.

$\|\sigma\|_T$ = the minimum number of transpositions required to bring $\{\sigma(1), \ldots, \sigma(n)\}$ into the order $\{1,2,\ldots,n\}$.

$d_T(\sigma, \pi)$ = the minimum number of transpositions required to bring $\{\sigma(1), \ldots, \sigma(n)\}$ into the order $\{\pi(1), \ldots, \pi(n)\}$.

d. $\|\sigma\|_\infty = \text{Max} \ |\sigma(i) - i|$
$$i = 1, \ldots, n$$

$d_\infty(\sigma, \pi) = \text{Max} \ |\sigma(i) - \pi(i)|$
$$i = 1, \ldots, n$$

e. $\|\sigma\|_H = |\{i \mid \sigma(i) \neq i\}|$.   (Hamming-Norm)

$d_H(\sigma, \pi) = |\{i \mid \sigma(i) \neq \pi(i)\}|$ (Hamming metric)

We have the following inequalities

$$\|\sigma\|_\infty \le \|\sigma\|_1 \le \|\sigma\|_2 \le \cdots \le \|\sigma\|_k$$

for all $\sigma \in S_n$.

For a general review of metrics on discrete groups and semi-groups see [3].

3. Combinatorics

We start our investigations on weight-functions on the S_n by a combinatorial approach. We are especially interested in $\|\cdot\|_1$ and $\|\cdot\|_2$ and use the notation $m_k(\sigma) = \|\sigma\|_k$ ($\sigma \in S_n$) given by J.L. Davison [5,6]. Let $\varsigma \in S_n$ be the reverse permutation $\varsigma(i) = n+1-i$ ($1 \le i \le n$). Throughout the paper we will write $\varsigma = (n, n-1, \ldots, 1)$ and more general if $\sigma = \begin{pmatrix} 1 & 2 & \cdots & n \\ \sigma(1) & \sigma(2) & \sigma(n) \end{pmatrix}$

is any permutation, then we will write $\delta = (\delta(1), \delta(2),\ldots,\delta(n))$.
Multiplication $\delta \cdot \bar{\pi}$ (δ , $\bar{\pi}$ ϵS_n) of permutations goes from right
to left, e.g. if $\delta = (2,3,4,1)$, $\bar{\pi} = (4,1,3,2)$ then $\delta \cdot \bar{\pi} = (1,2,4,3)$.

Lemma 3.1 If $\delta \epsilon S_n$, then $m_k(\delta) \leq m_k(\gamma)$ and $m_k(\delta)$ is an even
integer for any $k \geq 1$.

Lemma 3.2 The maximal values attained by m_1 and m_2 are

$$M_{1,n} = m_1(\gamma) = \begin{cases} \dfrac{n^2}{2}, & \text{if } n \text{ is an even number} \\[2mm] \dfrac{n^2-1}{2}, & \text{if } n \text{ is an odd number} \end{cases} = [\dfrac{n^2}{2}]$$

$$M_{2,n} = m_2(\gamma) = \dfrac{1}{3} n(n^2-1)$$

(We use the shorthand notations M_1, M_2).

In table 3.1 we have listed the maximal values for the different
weight-functions considered in section 2. Instead of $\| \cdot \|_T$,
$\| \cdot \|_I$ ... etc., we use the shorthand notations T, I... and
so on. As can be seen from table 3.1 the domain of the functions
H, ∞, T is very small related to the number n! of permutations.
That means it is impossible to make strong distinctions between
different permutations.

weight-function	maximal value
m_2	$\frac{1}{3}n(n^2-1)$
m_1	$[\frac{1}{2}n^2]$
I	$\frac{1}{2} n(n-1)$
H	n
∞	$n-1$
T	$n-1$

Tab. 3.1

A useful result due to Cayley states that $T(\delta) = n - C(\delta)$,
where $C(\delta)$ is the number of cycles in δ . If a permutation
has an inversion at (k,l), $1 \leq k < l \leq n$, that means $\delta(k) > \delta(l)$
then $\delta(k)-\delta(l)$ is called the weight of that inversion.

<u>Lemma 3.3</u> Let $V(\delta)$ denote the sum of weights taken over all inversions that δ has, then

$$m_2(\delta) = 2V(\delta).$$

<u>Lemma 3.4</u> If $\tilde{\delta} \in S_{n-2}$ $(n\geq 3)$ we can construct a $\delta \in S_n$ with
$$m_k(\delta) = 2(n-1)^k + m_k(\tilde{\delta}).$$

<u>Theorem 3.1</u> For $k = 1,2$; $m_k(S_n) \subseteq [0, M_k] = I_k$ and if $n\geq 4$, let w be an even integer, $w \in I_k$. Then, there exists a $\delta \in S_n$ with $m_k(\delta) = w$.

<u>Remarks</u> The proof of theorem 3.1 goes through even if $k\geq 3$, see Davison [6], Theorem 1. p. 72. It should be noted that Davisons proof together with some corollaries are only true if $k\geq 3$. As can be seen from the proof of theorem 3.1 the value M_2 is attained by m_2 only if $\delta = \varsigma$ and this remains true for $k\geq 3$ and M_k. What concerns m_1 it can be seen by examples that it is possible to have $m_1(\delta) = M_1$ and $\delta \neq \varsigma$. In the case $k\geq 3$ we have $M_k-4 \notin m_k(S_n)$ for $n\geq 3$ and that means not all even values in $[0, M_k]$ will be attained by m_k. Let $k=3$ and $n\geq 10$ then all even numbers in $[0, M_3-112]$ are in the range of m_3. There exists indeed always numbers α_k, n_k for all $k\geq 1$ that have the properties: m_k attains on S_n all even numbers in $[0, M-\alpha_k]$ for $n\geq n_k$. An optimal selection for $k=1,2$ will be $n_1=2$, $\alpha_1=0$ and $n_2=4$, $\alpha_2=0$. In case $k>3$ there are no nontrivial values of n_k,α_k known (see Davison [6] 3.p.74).

<u>Definition 3.1</u> Let r be a real number, $r\geq 0$.

$S(\|\cdot\|_a, n,r) = \{\delta \mid \delta \in S_n, \|\delta\|_a = r\}$ $(a=1,2,\ldots,I,T,\infty,H)$

$B(\|\cdot\|_a, n,r) = \{\delta \mid \delta \in S_n, \|\delta\|_a \leq r\}$

$|S(\cdot,\cdot,\cdot)|$ or $|B(\cdot,\cdot,\cdot)|$ denotes the number of elements in that sets.

<u>Theorem 3.2</u> We have

$$|S(m_1,n,M_1)| = \begin{cases} (\frac{n}{2}!)^2 & \text{if n is an even number.} \\ n \cdot (\frac{n-1}{2}!)^2 & \text{if n is an odd number.} \end{cases}$$

Theorem 3.3 We have for $\delta \in S_n$ $(n \geq 2)$,

$$m_2(\delta) + m_2(\delta \cdot \varsigma) = M_{2,n}$$

and $\qquad m_2(\varsigma \cdot \delta) = m_2(\delta \cdot \varsigma)$.

Corollary 3.3.1 Let $n \geq 4$, and let w be an even integer, $w \in [0, \frac{1}{3}n(n^2-1)]$. Then, there exists a $\delta \in S_n$ with $m_2(\delta) = w$.

Lemma 3.5 Let $n \geq 5$, then $n(n^2-1)/6 \leq (n-1)((n-1)^2-1)/3$ and equality holds if and only if n=5.

Lemma 3.6 Let $n \geq 5$ and w an integer number $w \in [\frac{1}{6}n(n^2-1), \frac{1}{3}n(n^2-1))$. Then, either $\bar{w} = \frac{1}{3}n(n^2-1)-w \leq \frac{1}{3} \cdot 4 \cdot (4^2-1)$ or there exists a least integer number $\bar{n}$, $5 \leq \bar{n} < n$ and $\bar{w} \in (\frac{1}{6}\bar{n}(\bar{n}^2-1), \frac{1}{3}\bar{n}(\bar{n}^2-1))$.

Lemma 3.7 Let $n \geq 5$ and w an even integer with $\frac{1}{6}n(n^2-1) \leq w < \frac{1}{3}n(n^2-1)$. Then exists a permutation $\bar{\delta} \in S_{\bar{n}}$ with $\bar{n}<n$ and $\| \tilde{\delta} \cdot \varsigma \|_2 = w$, where $\tilde{\delta}$ is an extension of $\bar{\delta}$ from $S_{\bar{n}}$ to S_n.
$\tilde{\delta}$ is defined by $\tilde{\delta}(i)=i$ for $i = \bar{n}+1, \ldots, n$.

This gives us a constructive method for finding for any given even number w, $0 \leq w \leq \frac{1}{3}n(n^2-1)$ a permutation $\delta \in S_n$ with $\| \delta \|_2 = w$. We have thus proved any given integer w may be (constructive!) represented as a sum of squares (see Davison [5] Th.1.).

Example $\delta \in S_8$, $\| \delta \|_2 = 128$ we are looking for such a permutation.

(1) $w = 128$, $\frac{1}{6} \cdot 8 \cdot 3 = 84 < 128 < 168 = \frac{1}{3} \cdot 8 \cdot 35$, $n = 8$

(2) $\bar{w} = 40$, $\frac{1}{6} \cdot 6 \cdot 35 = 35 < 40 < 70 = \frac{1}{3} \cdot 6 \cdot 35$, $\bar{n} = 6$

(3) $\bar{\bar{w}} = 30$, $\frac{1}{6} \cdot 5 \cdot 24 = 20 < 30 < 40 = \frac{1}{3} \cdot 5 \cdot 24$, $\bar{\bar{n}} = 5$

(4) $\bar{\bar{\delta}} = (3,5,2,4,1) \in S_5$, $\| \bar{\bar{\delta}} \|_2 = 30$

(5) $\tilde{\bar{\delta}} = (3,5,2,4,1,6) \in S_6$, $\| \tilde{\bar{\delta}} \|_2 = 30$

$\bar{\delta} = (3,5,2,4,1,6) \cdot \underbrace{(6,5,4,3,2,1)}_{\varsigma} = (6,1,4,2,5,3)$

$\| \bar{\delta} \|_2 = 40$

(6) $\tilde{\delta} = (6,1,4,2,5,3,7,8) \in S_8$, $\| \tilde{\delta} \|_2 = 40$

$\delta = (8,7,3,5,2,4,1,6) = \tilde{\delta} \cdot \varsigma$

$\| \delta \|_2 = 128 = 7^2+5^2+0^2+1^2+3^2+2^2+6^2+2^2$

It is possible to generate immediately a second permutation of m_2-weight 128. We note that by theorem 3.3 it is admissible to multiply by ϱ from the left side in steps (5) and (6) above. This gives:

$$\varrho_2 = (5,7,4,6,3,8,2,1)$$
$$128 = 4^2+5^2+1^2+2^2+2^2+2^2+5^2+7^2$$

Taking into consideration all possible combinations of left and right multiplication by ϱ gives four permutations at all.

$$\varrho_3 = (8,7,1,6,3,5,2,4)$$
$$128 = 7^2+5^2+2^2+2^2+2^2+1^2+5^2+4^2$$
$$\varrho_4 = (3,8,5,7,4,6,2,1)$$
$$128 = 2^2+6^2+2^2+3^2+1^2+0^2+5^2+7^2$$

In Figure 3.1 another approach for generating permutations of m_2-weight 128 is seen. We will not go into the details of an algorithm that generates a lot of different permutations. Our description is only an informal one a more formal treatment will be given elsewhere.

There are important relations between the various weight-functions which generally take the form of inequalities.

Theorem 3.4 Let $\varrho \in S_n$, then

(U1) $2I(\varrho) \le m_2(\varrho) \le 2(n-1) \cdot I(\varrho)$

(U2) $m_2(\varrho)/n-1 \le m_1(\varrho) \le \text{Min} \{m_2(\varrho), (n \cdot m_2(\varrho))^{\frac{1}{2}}\}$

(U3) $m_2(\varrho) \ge \text{Max} \{4/3I(\varrho) \cdot (1+I(\varrho)/n), 2I(\varrho)\}$
        (Durbin-Stuart inequality)

(U4) $I(\varrho) + T(\varrho) \le m_1(\varrho) \le 2I(\varrho)$
        (Diaconis-Graham inequality)

The Diaconis-Graham inequality suggests that the difference between I and m_1 is not very great. The results in Table 3.1 suggest that H, ∞ and T are unsuitable for use, having a very small range. There remains only m_2 that has the largest range and indeed as Lemma 3.3 shows is of a kind essentially different from I and m_1.

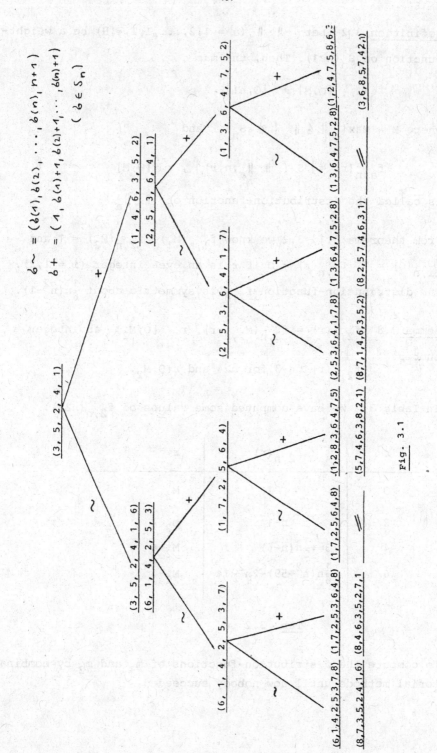

$$\delta \sim = (\delta(1), \delta(2), \ldots, \delta(n), n+1)$$

$$\delta + = (1, \delta(1)+1, \delta(2)+1, \ldots, \delta(n)+1)$$

$$(\delta \in S_n)$$

Fig. 3.1

<u>Definition</u> 3.2 Let $\|\cdot\|_a (a = 1,2,\ldots,I,T,\infty,H)$ be a weight-function on $S_n (n\geq 1)$. Then, the map

$$f_{a,n} : [O,M] \rightarrow [O,n!]$$

where $M = \text{Max}\{ \|\phi\|_a \mid \phi \in S_n \}$ and

$$f_{a,n}(r) = | S (\|\cdot\|_a,n,r) | , \quad r \in [O,M]$$

is called the distribution-function of $\|\cdot\|_a$.

From theorems 3.1, 3.2 we know $f_{1,n}(M_1)$, $f_{2,n}(M_2) = 1$ and $f_{i,n}(O) = 1$, $f_{i,n}(r) = O$ if r is an even integer $(i = 1,2)$. The distribution-function $f_{2,n}$ is symmetric about $\frac{1}{6}n(n^2-1)$.

<u>Lemma</u> 3.8 $f_{2,n}(r) = f_{2,n}(M_{2,n}-r)$, $r \in [O,M_2]$ an integer number.
$$f_{2,n}(r) \geq n-3 \text{ for } n\geq 4 \text{ and } r\neq O,M_2.$$

In Table 3.2 we have computed some values of $f_{2,n}(n\geq 4)$.

r	$f_{2,n}(r)$	r
O	1	M_2
2	$n-1$	M_2-2
4	$3 +\frac{1}{2}n(n-5)$	M_2-4
6	$\frac{1}{6}n(n^2+59)-2n^2-14$	M_2-6

<u>Tab</u>. 3.2

To compute the distribution-functions of m_1 and m_2 by combinatorial methods until now nobody succeeded.

4. Statistics

An example from Kendall [10] p.3 will clarify the discussion.
Consider a number of boys (or girls) ranked according to their
ability in mathematics and in musics:

Boy	A	B	C	D	E	F	G	H	I	J
Mathematics (6)	7	4	3	10	6	2	9	8	1	5
Music (π)	5	7	3	10	1	9	6	2	8	4

We are interested in whether there is any relationship between
ability in mathematics and music. In statistics widely used
non-parametric measures of associations such as Kendall's τ
and Spearman's ϱ lead to natural metrics or weight-functions
on S_n. Statisticians most often normalize metrics so that they
have the properties of a correlation coefficient. The translation is the following one: if d is a metric on S_n and its maximal value is M, define a rank correlation coefficient by:

$$K(\pi,6) = 1 - \frac{2\,d(\pi,6)}{M}$$

Most of the metrics that we mentioned in section 2. were known
for a long time in statistics as measures of disarray.

$$\tau(\pi,6) = 1 - \frac{2 \cdot I(\pi \cdot 6^{-1})}{\frac{1}{2}n(n-1)} \qquad \text{(Kendall, 1938)}$$

$$\varsigma(\pi,6) = 1 - \frac{6 \cdot m_2(\pi \cdot 6^{-1})}{n^3 - n} \qquad \text{(Spearman, 1904)}$$

$$R(\pi,6) = 1 - \frac{2 \cdot m_1(\pi \cdot 6^{-1})}{\left[\frac{1}{2}n^2\right]} \qquad \text{(Spearman's footrule, 1906)}$$

Most of the combinatorial results given in section 3. are therefore known in statistics, e.g. nearly all results of Davison
[5,6].

We look at weight-functions now from the point of view of
probability theory. Then S_n is the sample space and a weight-
function is a random variable on that sample space. We assign
the probability 1/n! to each event (permutation) in S_n. As can
be seen from a graphical representation the distribution of the
weight-functions corresponds with the normal curve. A limit
theorem for $\|\cdot\|_I$ and $\|\cdot\|_T$ was given by Feller [8], p. 256,
what concerns $\|\cdot\|_1$, $\|\cdot\|_2$ the limiting normality was proved by
Kendall [10] Chap. 5.8, p. 72 by computation of higher moments
or one can use Hoeffding's [9] Th. 3, p.560 combinatorial central limit theorem. In Table 4.1 mean and variance of m_1, m_2, I
and T are given. Its now very easy to calculate approximately
the number of permutations $\delta \in S_n$ with $r_1 \le \|\delta\|_a \le r_2$ $(a=I,T,m_1,m_2)$.
Let

$$x_1 = \frac{r_1 - (E(\|\cdot\|_a)+1)}{(Var(\|\cdot\|_a))^{1/2}} \quad , \quad x_2 = \frac{r_2 - (E(\|\cdot\|_a)-1)}{(Var(\|\cdot\|_a))^{1/2}}$$

then we have approximatively

$$n! \cdot \frac{1}{(2\pi)^{1/2}} \int_{x_1}^{x_2} e^{-\frac{1}{2}x^2} dx \qquad (1)$$

permutations $\delta \in S_n$ with $r_1 \le \|\delta\|_a \le r_2$.

weight-function	mean	variance
m_1	$\frac{1}{3}(n^2-1)$	$\frac{2}{45}n^3 + O(n^2)$
m_2	$\frac{1}{6}n(n^2-1)$	$(\frac{n^3-n}{6})^2 \cdot \frac{1}{n-1}$
T	$n-\log n$	$\log n$
I	$\frac{1}{4}n^2$	$\frac{1}{36}n^3$

Tab. 4.1

In Table 4.1 for T, I only the leading terms of the mean and
variance are indicated. The results in Table 4.1 suggest again
that m_2 should be preferred. Of the four metrics m_2 has the
greatest variability.

From the report of Beth et al. [2] we have taken the distribution of m_1 on S_8 and listed in Table 4.2. In Table 4.3 we have calculated that distribution by formula (1) by means of a HP25 pocket-caluclator. In comparison with Table 4.2 it becomes quite clear that for all practical purposes such an approximation is good enough.

m_1-weight	score	m_1-weight	score
0	1	20	5708
2	7	22	5892
4	33	24	5452
6	115	26	4212
8	327	28	2844
10	765	30	1764
12	1523	32	576
14	2553		
16	3696		
18	4852		

Tab. 4.2 Distribution of m_1 on S_8

m_1-weight	approximate score	true score	error in %
22	6551	5892	+ 11
22 - 24	12006	11344	+ 6
22 - 26	15957	15556	+ 2,5
22 - 28	18274	18400	- 0,7
22 - 30	19433	20164	- 3,6
22 - 32	19920	20740	- 4
32	487	576	- 15

Tab. 4.3 Normal approximation to the distribution
of m_1 on S_8.

The distribution of m_2 on S_n is known for $n = 4-13$ from tables given by Kendall [10] (Appendix Table 2, pp. 174-177), if $n \geq 14$ then the normal approximation is good enough.

5. Testing a t.d.m.-system.

We look at an example given by Beth et al. [2], pp. 136, 140. Six different texts together with their intelligibility and the permutation used for scrambling are listed in Table 5.1 This gives the following ranking.

$$
\begin{array}{ccccccc}
 & & & & & \overbrace{\text{ties}} & \\
1 & 2 & 3 & 4 & 5\ 1/2 & 5\ 1/2 \\
1 & 3 & 4 & 5 & 2 & 6
\end{array}
$$

where equal weights of the last two permutations give rise to ties. We then have

$$\rho = 1 - \frac{16}{35} = 0.56$$

where the rank correlation coefficient ρ is modified because of the tied ranks (see Kendall [10] Chap. 3). The standard error of ρ is $\frac{1}{\sqrt{5}} = 0.45$. Thus the observed value is $0.56/0.45 = 1.24$ times the standard error. This is barely significant.

text no.	permutation	intelligibility	m_1-weight
1	(1,2,3,4,8,6,5,7)	1	6
2	(7,1,3,4,5,2,6,8)	3	12
3	(7,2,6,3,4,5,8,1)	4	20
4	(6,4,8,1,2,7,3,5)	5	26
5	(5,6,7,8,1,2,3,4)	2	32
6	(6,5,8,7,2,1,4,3)	6	32

Tab. 5.1

413

Rank order statistics are thus well-suited for use in testing a t.d.m.-system. What concerns refinements and further possibilities we refer to Kendall [10]. We emphasize that a thorough testing of a t.d.m.-system should improve its security.

References

[1] H. Beker and F. Piper: Ciper Systems.
                                Northwood Books, London(1982).

[2] Th. Beth, P. Heß, K. Wirl: Kryptographie.
                                Teubner, Stuttgart (1983).

[3] G. Cohen and M. Deza: Distances invariantes et L-
                                cliques sur certains demi-
                                groupes finis.
                                Math.Sci.Humaines 67,(1979),
                                49-69.

[4] G. Cohen and M. Deza: Some metrical problems on S_n.
                                Annuals of discrete math. 8,
                                (1980), 211-216.

[5] J.L. Davison: A result on sums of squares.
                                Cand. Math. Bull. 18(3),(1975),
                                425-426.

[6] J.L. Davison: Some mappings associated with
                                permutation groups.
                                Canad. Math. Bull. 20(1),(1977)
                                71-75.

[7] P. Diaconis and R.L. Graham: Spearman's footrule as a
                                measure of disarray.
                                J. Roy. Statist. Soc. Ser.B39-2
                                (1977), 262-268.

[8] W. Feller: An Introduction to Probability
                                Theory and Its Applications,
                                Vol. 1, Wiley, New York (1968),
                                3rd edn..

[9]   W. Hoeffding: A combinatorial central limit
                                       theorem.
                                       Ann. Math. Statist. 22, (1951),
                                       558-566.

[10] M.G. Kendall: Rank Correlation Methods.
                                       Griffin, London (1970),
                                       4th edn..

[11] M.R. Lagrange: Quelques résultats dans la mé-
                                       trique des permutations.
                                       Ann. Sci. Ecole Norm. Sup. 79
                                       (1962a), 199-241.

[12] N.J.A. Sloane: Encryption by Random Rotations.
                                       Lecture Notes in Computer Science
                                       Vol. 149, Springer Verlag (1983),
                                       pp. 71, Cryptography (Proc.,
                                       Burg Feuerstein 1982, Ed. Th. Beth).

SECURITY OF TRANSPORTABLE COMPUTERIZED FILES

A. Bouckaert, M.D., Ph.D.
School of Public Health
Catholic University of Louvain
B-1200 Brussels, Belgium

1. SCAMPI (Starting on conception automatic medical profile of indi-
          vidual)

The SCAMPI system is a generalization of the personal medical file.
It includes features like transportability, continuous update, protection of confidentiality, unerasability. As a distinctive charac-
ter, it includes a summary of pregnancy and birth as its first subset.
Other points of interest, together with the main specificities of the
system are described below.

A) The file is stored on a floppy disk belonging to the patient (ID).
    Since the data were coded using a binary conversion, they are dif-
    ficult to understand without a specific program. This specific
    program is not the patient's property. It includes a double key
    requiring for each access the simultaneous agreement of the pa-
    tient and of the "master of the data". The meaning of "master of
    the data" and "owner of the program" will be made explicit later
    on.

B) ID is entirely made of records made by persons who are generally
    medical doctors, or medical personnel. Those data producers will
    be considered as "masters" of the data they have produced (and
    recorded), i.e. of a sub-ID.
    For example, the gynecologist is the master of the data he fed
    into the file during pregnancy. To be master is to be responsible
    and co-owner.
    Consequently, any ID can be broken down into sub-IDs with diffe-
    rent masters, each one being co-owned by its master and by the
    ID owner. For example, in the sub-ID dealing with birth, data
    were produced by the gynecologist but also by the anesthesist and

by the pediatrician. These three persons share the medial secret
of the sub-ID together with their collective co-ownership of the
sub-ID according to the traditional rules of shared medical secrets.

C) An integral copy of the ID is produced together with the ID itself. While it seems to be wise to ask to the family doctor to
keep the copy, a more complicated system will actually be described in the next section.
The family doctor has no right to access the whole ID but only a
subset defined by the validity extent of the double key patient-
master.

D) The only program allowing to read the whole ID is the property
of the designers of the SCAMPI Software. However, even that person is not likely to be able to read the ID completely very often
since this would require prior communication of the key of the
patient and of all the keys of the masters.

E) Data entry, display and update require the use of a PASCAL code.
The PASCAL source is never communicated to data producers or
owners. Hence; no paper or other visual memo will allow to break
the rules of double keys by additional programming. Each sub-ID
is accessed by a different program. Programs belong to three main
classes :

1° data entry, cheking, copy (for medical practitioners)
2° administrative forms production (for public services and hospital administrators)
3° statistics (for epidemiologsts and public health managers).

Classes 1° and 2° are subjected to the traditional rules of medical ethics. Class 3° falls under the jurisdiction of the statistical secret. The latter is no less exacting than the medical secret since it requires for example a programmed deletion of all
identifications, as well as special measures of protection
against indirect identification that will be discussed below.

F) Since January 1st, 1984, the first program of class 1° with ID
production is run in the obsetrics department of the St. Luke
Hospital in Brussels. By the end of 1984, that program will be

complemented by others belonging to classes 2° and 3°. A postneonatal pediatric follow-up will then become mandatory (immunization timetable, growth charts). It seems that SCAMPI can be expected to result into significant consequences in at least three fields :

1) From a medical point of view, a pediatric follow-up and a feed-back between obstetrics and pediatrics can be obtained without any additional clerical work.
2) For administrators, the system could mean considerable improve-ment since the six to eight forms that are routinely produced now by hand for each birth will now be produced automatically with no limit on the number of copies. Important also for public health, the compulsory linkage between birth premium and a mini-mum number of prenatal visits can now be more easily and reaslis-tically enforced.
3) As a social consequence, the ownership of the data about her own pregnancy is a modest but real increase of the mother's responsa-bility and autonomy.

2. DATA ENTRY

The SCAMPI development was initiated by a PASCAL program used on the micro-computer Apple II for the obstetrics department of the St. Luke Hospital. The program runs interactively for data entry, storage, re-trieval, corrections.
Two kinds of data are fed into the micro-computer during birth :

a) A pregnancy record (about 300 pieces of information) extrac-ted from the hand record just before it leaves the department to be included in the Central Archives of the hospital.
b) A birth record (about 100 pieces of information) whose data are entered in real-time, and including an anesthiological sub-record.

While the child stays in the neonatal department, the past part of the data is entered. Neonatal data entry cannot proceed later than the departure of mother and child from the hospital. Informations communicated by neonatal metabolic screening (PKU, hypothyroidism) will usually not be available at the time and will have to be ente-red later on.
Interactivity means e.g.

a) That logical mismatches or impossibilities are diagnosed and their entry into the file is prevented.

b) No missing data should be tolerated. Partial filling of a file for one birth precludes data entry for the next one (but for special procedures unknown to common operators).

c) Data are stored on floppy disks. They can be retrieved, displayed, altered.

d) The same program uses the same data in text-processing mode to print a letter to the family doctor.

This program (PETERPAN) was produced by a general PASCAL program (GENFORM) used to generate interactive questionnaires defined parametrically GENFORM (except some minor improvements) was written in 1982. It requires comments, controls and some other parameters to be able to produce any computer questionnaire. GENFORM was used for a variety of medical problems (leprosy, school medicine, dental health). Data stored on floppy disk are first grouped into the PASCAL "record" structure. The record includes all data stored in a "packed array of CHAR" except anesthesiological data (REAL) and identifications (STRING). About 100 records can be stored on a signle-density Apple II diskette. Replacement of STRINGS by numeric codes for identification allows the content of the floppy disk to reach 200 records. A floppy disk with PASCAL formatting and one single record is given to the mother when she leaves (ID of child).

3. FOLLOW-UP

The ID follows the child for all its life, growing at the same pace as it grows. It conforms the first day of its production to the two rules of patient ownership and shared use by programming.
Shared use means :

1) To read the ID, one needs as many programs as there are sub-IDs.

2) As a rule, any data producer owns the program that allows him to visualize the data he entered by himself.

3) Moreover he is entitled to read the data entered by other producers so far as this does not require another program in addition to his.

Traditionnally, and leaving aside any technical consideration, it is accepted that the medical secret is shared if this can be of any usefulness to the patient. The pediatrician is entitled to know what happened during pregnancy to the child he treats. This is no more a break of confidentiality than the usual rule of medical practice demanding that all data that could possibly be of interest to the physician in charge should be communicated to him. The same reasoning leads to other evidences : the proper treatment of the child does not require a full knowledge of the gynecological past of the mother. Since this is no more in the utmost interest of the patient, it is actually forbidden and should be made technically unfeasible by appropriate software or hardware protections.

The same rules hold true for the information flow through pediatrics and school medicine.

4. INFORMATION SHARING

Some data deserve special consideration, like the neonatal metabolic screening results and the immunization timetable. The diagnosis of an inborn error of metabolism should be considered as a medical emergency and the relevant information should be communicated by phone or by fast mail to the family practitioner. Changing house or changing of family doctor at the moment of communication can be very hazardous and threaten to reduce the benefits of screening to nil. It is suggested that some device should be used to signal the temporary ignorance of the screening results. Since these results are usually not yet available in the hospital, and since communication between screening labs and hospital are likely to be faster than between lab and family, the ID copy of the hospital will signal by a "red flag" that the screening produced pathological results requiring immediate care. As soon as the hospital doctors are confident that a proper treatment has been started, the "red flag" is replaced by the identification of the family doctor, the screening results and the opening of a special subfile for subsequent biochemical controles.

A similar system can be used with the patient's ID in order to avoid interfering with the immunization timetable.

4.1. Ownership and use

Use and ownership are kept separate. The child (and up to the adult age, his legal representationes i.e. his parents) is the owner of the ID. But he receives no program that would enable him to read it. He is also supposed to maintain the physical integrity of the ID. Copies will be supplied to compensate for loss or destruction but this will be charged to the owner in order to discourage carelessness.

The user can read all the data he produced himself as well as the data shared by other producers, and with the taking into account the programmed compliance with medical confidentiality regulations. Any copy to a central file (as would occur for scientific processing for example) requires that identifications should first be cleared.
Some users are completely outside of the medical secrecy. Hence their share of the data is narrowly limited.
For example, hospital administration, insurances, the Ministry of Health and the town administrations can be allowed to a specific subset of the data without any medical connotation, related to accounting and certifications.
One of the long-term objectives of SCAMPI is to ban hand copies from the processing of medical informations.

4.2. Advantages and inconveniences

a) Increased productivity of the hospital manpower.
   Clericals tasks and, prominently, hand copies, were consuming a disproportionate share of their time availability.
b) Information persistence : In the present situation, a large percentage of medical information can be considered as lost within a few years. To support this opinion, it is well known that the praediatrician has to trust the mother's memories at the first visit in school medicine in order to learn the borth weight of a child. Later on, those information losses will grow worse and more expensive (E.g. some cases of PKU went three times through the diagnostic procedure and the parents are still not aware of the specific risk at the time of the next pregnancy).
   As a rule, the multiplication of diagnostic procedures in patients whose previous results were lost contributes for a certain degree to the costs of our expensive medical system.
c) Scientific use of information : Most retrospective epidemiologi-

cal studies are plagued by the inacurracy of collected data.

d) Threats : Floppy disks cannot be seriously contemplated as long-
    term information supports. Hence, they should be dropped from the
    SCAMPI system as soon as possible. A satisfactory support should
    fulfill at least the following requirements :

    1° not erasable (READ ONLY)
    2° not alterable
    3° cheap
    4° transportable
    5° inexpensive retrieval
    6° obsolescence-protected by being readily transferred on a new
        storage medium

    (N.B. : The "smart card" could probably meet those requirements)

e) Threats : The impression of confidentiality for non-computerized
    medical records reflects principally their heterogeneity and
    systematic loss. Abuses are uncommon because information synthe-
    sis is as difficult for abusers as it is for legitimate users.
    As soon as the ID can be accessed, the potential profit of abuse
    increases dramatically.
    Summarizing, the medical secrecy of non-computerized records is
    usually the secrecy surrounding information already lost.
    Problems of security are likely to be met as soon as the informa-
    tion is available. Potential abusers include business, insurance
    companies, security agencies.

f) Conclusion : In order to earn acceptability, SCAMPI needs effi-
    ----------   cient coding procedures. These procedures should be
                  allowed to evolue at the same pace as the cryptolo-
                  gical art since no absolute protection is known.

BIBLIOGRAPHY

K. Boehm in "Medical Informatics Europe 78" Ed. by DAB Lindberg and
PL Reichertz, Springer, Berlin, 1978.
B.R. Beier et V.M. Brannigan in "Medinfo 83" Ed. by JH Van Bemmel,
MJ Ball et OW Gertz, North Holland, Amsterdam, 1983.
L. Horbach in "Cryptography" Ed. by G Goos et J Hartmanis, Springer,
Berlin, 1983.

4.3. Medical Secrecy

The very old concept of medical secret is a particular by sensitive
aspect of professional secret.
The interests of patient and society are best served if information
collected in the course of medical activities is kept secret, and
this has been acknowledged for centuries. The medical secret is not
only binding for the doctor but also for all persons that happen to
be drawn into it (family, colleagues, medical personnel). Secret
sharing by medical practioners is a natural complement of the medical secret since there is no other way to allow the patient to benefit from the diverse experience of the medical community. Its limits
are consequent to the well-understood benefit of the patient : RX data,
are obviously to be shared with the surgeon while psychiatric data
are not to be communicated to the dermatologist.

Moreover, the patient has no right to allow disclosure of the medical
secret whose provisions can only be lifted by a higher imperative
justified by patient and society benefits. To accept the patient's
right to lift the secret would obviously make him vulnerable to
blackmail.

Since the principles are clear enough and received detailed legal and
jurisprudential treatment, their translation into software should
still be realized. Such a translation will make sure that no confusion arises between normal secret sharing between colleagues and
criminal secret violation.

4.4. Notary

In the present situation, the medical secret is kept by the doctor
and follows him in the grave. This is clearly information spillage
and does not agree with our general concept of ownership of the data.
A computerized protocol of data communication can be implemented that
is activated not only by the patient's decision of going to another
practioner or by the loss of ID copy but also by the death of the
practitioner.
Generalizing, it amounts to using a medical notary rather than the
family doctor as the respository of the integral ID.
Such a move involves more than just a change of denomination. The
functions of keeper and user of medical information are more clearly

dissociated in the person of a medical notary than they could be in a medical practitioner.

Moreover, the medical notary does not need to be one physical person. It seems specially attractive to consider the case where two physical halfnotaries must cooperate. Each halfnotary owns a half ID and the addresses that allow the merging of the two halves and each halfnotary is aware of the identity of his counterpart.
No program allows to read the complete ID. The halfnotaries can only use programs that allow to merge specific parts of the ID as a preliminary step towards data communication on authenticated request of both patient and doctor.

4.5. The dictator

A dictator is useful to access some data of the ID without preliminary agreement of patient or doctor. The dictator's usefulness is obvious in cases of unconsciousness, emergency, etc. ... Many deaths or severe injuries result from the difficulty of communicating with unconscious persons. Most frequently, this occurs with brain damage, uraemia, metabolic shock ... and these emergencies are routinely neglected because they are misclassified as acute alcoholic intoxication. In large towns of the West, problems like drug, AV block, diabetes, are likely to be met with increasing frequency as a result of medical progress and social involution.
The dictator is able to read some informations (related to drug allergies, blood groups, previous diagnoses of shock). Any dictator's access should be authenticated and identified; the dictator will be held responsible of his actions before the appropriate jurisdictional court.

4.6. Transfers

A specific physically unique localization is unnecessary for the ID. It is sufficient to be able to assemble its halves, possibly by telecommunication from the halfnotaries.

4.7. Benefits and inconveniencies

The legal concepts that call for data encryption can also be invoked for new definitions like the medical notary and dictator. The theo-

retical legal basis of these concepts should be carefully investigated at the same time as the relevant software is developed.

ENCRYPTION AND KEY MANAGEMENT FOR THE ECS SATELLITE SERVICE

Serpell, S.C., and Brookson, C.B.

British Telecom Research Laboratories, Martlesham Heath,
Ipswich, Suffolk. IP5 7RE.

ABSTRACT

This contribution describes the encryption and key management
techniques realised with prototype hardware by British Telecom
Research for use on the SatStream service offered on the
European Communication Satellite. The security objectives,
channel unit functions and operation, encryption methods and key
management systems are described.

INTRODUCTION

British Telecom International's European SatStream service (1) will offer business telecommunications by satellite. This service will include digital single-channel-per-carrier and continuous mode frequency division multiple access links via the European Communication Satellite (ECS). The broadcast capability of SatStream allows customers' transmissions to anywhere in Europe with relatively small and cheap earth stations. This is a significant advantage over the terrestrial network, but at the same time it makes the links more vulnerable to eavesdropping.

The unauthorised reception of SatStream traffic would require considerable expertise and financial investment; nevertheless it was decided to develop an optional encryption facility to provide for the total security of sensitive customer data when this is required. This facility renders the data on the SatStream link entirely unintelligible to all except the intended recipient stations. Similar encryption facilities have been defined for the United States Satellite Business Systems (2) and French Telecom 1 (3) business satellites.

SECURITY OBJECTIVES

The SatStream encryption scheme is designed to meet the following security objectives:
- To render customer data transmissions unintelligible to unauthorised   receivers,
- To prevent inadvertent transmission of unencrypted data even under equipment failure conditions,
- To prevent theft, unauthorised use, or unauthorised modification of cryptographic equipment while installed,
- To prevent unauthorised disclosure or modification of sensitive data (plaintext, unencrypted key-variables....) while in cryptographic equipment,
- To support secure key-variable generation and key-variable management.

These principles were kept constantly in view during the design of the earth station baseband channel units which incorporate the encryption facility.

CHANNEL UNIT BASEBAND FUNCTIONS

The British Telecom baseband channel unit for the SatStream service consists of transmit and receive half units. Each half unit may be used independently of the other, and this is of importance since one of the SatStream service options requires the ability for one transmitter to broadcast to a number of receive-only stations.

The transmit half unit performs the following functions:
- Synchronisation to the incoming user data, which may be in CCITT G703 format (64 kilobits per second codirectional) , X21 format (nx64 kilobits per second, where n = 2 to 30), or G732 format (2.048 Megabits per second),
- Conversion of the incoming data to a G732-like framed structure if it is not already in that format,
- Calculation of the encryption parameters and insertion into the G732-like format at multiframe level,

-Encryption of the user data,
-Transmission of the encrypted data in the G732-like
multiframe format.

The receive half of the unit performs a complementary set of
functions to those of the transmit unit, namely:
-Synchronisation to the incoming data with the G732-like
multiframe format,
-Recovery of the encryption parameters from the multiframe
structure,
-Decryption of the data,
-Output of the recovered data in its original G703, X21 or
G732 format.

A block diagram of these functions is set out in figure 1. Some
further baseband processing is also performed on the data before
it is passed to the earth station modulator or received from the
demodulator, in particular half- rate error protection using the
Viterbi Forward Error Correction algorithm is applied to all
data. Data is also scrambled to remove long strings of binary
'1's or '0's, or short cyclic periodic structures embedded in
data, since data with these characteristics would cause problems
over the satellite link.

FRAME AND MULTIFRAME STRUCTURE

All data flowing over SatStream links is structured into a
format similar in conception to the CCITT G732 specification as
used in the 30 channel Pulse Code Modulation (PCM) systems in
the terrestrial network, but with certain important
modifications. This structure is used to advantage to the ensure
reliable operation of the encryption system.

The structure is shown in figure 2. Each data frame comprises 64
time slots (or bytes) of 8 bits each, thus each frame is
effectively a 'double' G732 frame (one 'odd' plus one 'even'
frame in G732 terminology). All the time slots within the frame
contain customer data apart from four time slots reserved for
special purposes. These are time slot (TS) 0, which contains the
frame unique work, TS16 with TS48, which may be used for
signalling information, and TS32, which contains message fields.

The 512-bit frame thus contains (64-4)x8=480 bits of customer
data. Customer data presented in G703 or X21 format is therefore
subject to   an expansion of 32/30 over the satellite path,
while data already in G732 format remains unexpanded. The frame
unique word contains a fixed 7 bit code, the presence of which
denotes the first time slot of a new frame.

A multiframe is defined as 64 frames, and a fixed multiframe
unique word is carried in time slot TS32 during the course of the
multiframe. Other TS32 bits are used to convey Initialisation
Vectors (IVs) for encryption synchronisation, the identification
of the encryption key-variable in use, and the identification of
the transmitting station (16 bits) and station channel unit (
8 bits).

ENCRYPTION FACILITY

Design

The encryption facility on the channel unit is designed for very high security against attack by an adversary. This security derives from the digital encipherment of the customer data using a complex algorithm in stream cipher mode under the control of long, random key-variables.

Encryption method

The method of encryption is shown in figure 3. The customer data (or "plaintext") is "Exclusive ORed" with a randomising pattern (or "key-stream") from the cryptographic engine to produce an unintelligible output ("ciphertext"). Synchronised 'Exclusive ORing' of an identical key-stream at the receive end of the link will then regenerate the plaintext. This process is termed "stream ciphering" and is well-suited to SatStream because the resulting encryption is transparent to customer data and it has no error extension property. Each error on the enciphered satellite path causes only one error in the deciphered plaintext. This is essential in a satellite application when high error rates are the rule in fading conditions. The stream cipher mode is not self-synchronising and an overhead is incurred as a result.

The equipment on the transmit side thus structures the data and forms the ciphertext using keystream output from the cryptographic engine, while the receive unit disassembles the frame and applies the converse operation to recover the plaintext. The keystream pattern is controlled by the cryptographic algorithm, the contents of the cryptographic engine input register, and by the secret key-variable. These are discussed in turn below.

Algorithm

The security of the encryption facility is made to depend only on the key-variable in use by selecting a sufficiently strong cryptographic algorithm. Following normal cryptographic philosophy the SatStream facility has moreover been designed so that it is impracticable for an adversary to deduce a key-variable even given full knowledge of all the hardware and quantities of matched plaintext and ciphertext ("Known plaintext attack"). In particular, the number of possible key-variables is so large that it is computationally infeasible for an adversary to discover the key-variable in use by exhaustive search.

The United States' Data Encryption Standard (DES) was considered for this application but would have caused difficulties in supply and uncertainty regarding intellectual property. An alternative, unencumbered, algorithm was made available by British Telecom Cryptographic Products, which was internationally adopted for exclusive use on the SatStream service. This algorithm has been called TACA (Telecommunications Administrations Cryptographic Algorithm) and uses a 96 bit key-variable.

Encryption synchronisation

Correct decryption of an encrypted transmission in the stream
cipher mode requires the synchronised addition of identical
keystreams at both ends of a link. In particular this implies
the maintenance of identical entries in the cryptographic engine
input registers at transmit and receive ends of a link. In
traditional point-to-point duplex links, this may be
accomplished by bidirectional set-up protocols. However,
SatStream services must also support unidirectional and
broadcast (point to multipoint) links, and new receiving
stations must be able to join a network without disturbing other
network stations. This problem is overcome by controlling the
encryption synchronisation entirely from the transmit end of the
link, through the generation and transmission of an
Initialisation Vector (IV) on each path every multiframe. The
IV is used to force into a new synchronisation the state of
every receiving cryptographic engine at the start of each
multiframe. Thus any receiving station joining into an existing
network for the first time, or rejoining the network after a
service break, is assured of rapid synchronisation with the
transmitting station. This technique may also be used to allow
multi-destinational links.

If for any reason the transmit and receive ends of a link use
different IVs, a different keystream is then applied to the
customer data and a 50% error rate results. It is consequently
essential that IVs are strongly error protected in transmission
since each incorrect IV reception will cause the loss of one
complete multiframe of customer data. Further complications
arise from the presence of the Viterbi convolutional coding
units on the satellite side of the encryption units. The Viterbi
units generally improve the error rate greatly by correcting
most of the Gaussian-type errors occuring on the space path, but
occasionally produce lengthy error bursts. The IVs are therefore
protected by:
    -The Viterbi units,
    -The addition of a (12,8) shortened Hamming block code
    capable of correcting single errors within any sequence of
    8 IV data bits,
    -The spacing of the Hamming code protected IV bits so that
    a typical Viterbi-type error burst cannot affect more than
    one bit of any 12 bit block.

These combined measures render the probability of erroneous IV
reception negligible.

Key-variable synchronisation

The same keystream is only produced so long as the same key-
variable as well as the same IV is in use at both the transmit
and receive station. The key-variables are changed on a regular
basis to prevent too much customer data being committed to any
one key-variable. Synchronised changeover of key-variables is
therefore required and this is achieved by associating an
identification number with each key-variable. This number is
continuously signalled by the transmit station. The key-variable

changeover is automatic and initiated by the transmission of a new key-variable identifier. The encryption facility retains a store of key-variables in semiconductor memory. This allows long periods of secure and continuous operation before a new batch of randomly generated key-variables need be loaded into the encryption unit. The system is further designed so that during this period of dynamic key-variable change there are no service interruptions or corruptions of the customer's data.

The key-variable identifiers not only benefit from all the protection afforded to the IVs, but in addition the the receiver unit will only change to a new key-variable on the receipt of a two identical key-variable identifiers which differ from that of the key-variable presently loaded into the encryption engine. As each key-variable is exhausted it is overwritten and no trace remains within the encryption unit, preventing any possible retrospective reading of the key-variables.

KEY MANAGEMENT

A key-variable management scheme has been designed and built to allow for the secure generation of encryption key-variables from a truly random source and their secure handling and distribution, and to ensure that the correct key-variables are loaded into the correct equipment in a timely manner.

International

The European offering of SatStream using the European Communication Satellite will allow the encryption of international as well as national satellite links. International key-variable distribution will be achieved in a secure manner, with key-variables being protected in transit by a one-time pad. International key-variable distribution may also use the more automated system described below, which was designed to simplify UK national key management.

UK National

The key-variables are distributed to the earth station encryption units by key guns or key transfer devices. The key guns are small hand-held devices capable of holding up to 16 batches of key-variables with a self contained liquid crystal display displaying the station and channel identification for each batch. The key guns themselves are previously filled with key-variables either at a secure key management centre or at a remote location connected to a key management centre by secure and encrypted links. Key-variables are generated at key management centres using a true random process and are checked against known undesirable key-variables to eliminate any unfortunate values. Figure 4 shows the key management scheme. A small computer system is used as the principal key management unit.

The key-variables are loaded into the encryption units from the key guns via a short physical wire link when a manually initiated request is received from the encryption unit, subject to certain physical controls to prevent unauthorised operation.

SECURITY FEATURES

The security of the earth station encryption unit and the key
management system are important considerations in a system such
as that developed for SatStream. The encryption unit is
incorporated into the channel unit from the initial design
phase, and it is protected by being encased within a tamper
resistant module securely embedded within the surrounding
equipment.

Key-variable security

Key-variables may not be read out of the tamper resistant
module. This module will, on the detection of any tampering or
attempted removal from the surrounding units, completely erase
all key-variables contained within itself, while simultaneously
raising system alarms. Similar considerations have also been
applied to the key gun, and in this case a facility is also
provided for complete erasure of all sensitive data by manual
operator action.

Bypass

The encryption unit has been so designed that it contains no
physical or logical internal bypass paths, since these could
potentially allow transmission of unencrypted data. Under
certain failure conditions transmission equipments transmit AIS
or 'All-Ones' in place of customer data, and this failure signal
must appear to pass transparently through the entire system
including the encryption unit. Since the unit has no internal
bypass circuits an AIS generator is incorporated which takes
over the encryption unit output if AIS is detected at the input.
The exclusion of any bypass capablity ensures that under no
conditions can any unencrypted customer data be transmitted.

Transmission in depth

The security of the data is compromised if the same
cryptographic engine input register state occurs more than once
within the lifetime of any given key-variable ('Transmission in
depth'). Special methods are used in the generation of IVs to
overcome this problem.

TESTS

The design and operation of the channel unit equipment and
associated key management principles have been thoroughly tested
in both laboratory tests and using satellite links over the
Orbital Test Satellite (OTS). The encryption methods employed
have proved to be highly robust and able to accomodate the
severe carrier-to-noise characteristics encountered on space
paths, with the synchronisation and error correction facilities
performing exactly as those which were predicted. The encryption
facility has been proven not to affect the overall channel error
rate.

CONCLUSIONS

The optional encryption facility developed for the European
SatStream service offers a very high level of security on the

satellite path, backed up by good equipment physical security, sound key-variable generation, distribution and management. It uses redundancies within the SatStream G732-like data structure and so does not require expansion of the existing frame structure. It is completely transparent to customer data and has no effect on channel performance. It permits unidirectional and multidirectional (point-to-point and -multipoint) encrypted links without the need for reconfiguration if the number of participating stations changes, and represents a considerable service enhancement for users concerned about the sensitivity of their data.

ACKNOWLEDGEMENTS

Acknowledgement is made to the Director of Research, British Telecom, for permission to publish this paper.

This paper was presented at the IEE International Conference on 'Secure Communication Systems', London, 22nd-23rd February 1984. Copyright of this paper is held by the IEE and acknowledgement is made to the IEE for permission to publish this paper.

REFERENCES

1.   McGovern,D., and Kernot, R.J.,"A Second-Generation SCPC System for Business Satellite Communication", September 1983, 6th International Conference on Digital Satellite Communications, Phoenix, Arizona, USA, III-12 to III-17.

2.   Stein, F.L., "An Integrated Multiple Transponder TDMA Bulk Encryption Satellite Communications System", September 1983, 6th International Conference on Digital Satellite Communications, IX-16 to IX-20.

3.   Bic,J.C., Bousquet,J.C., and Oberle,M., "Privacy over Satellite Links", 23-26 March 1981, Proc. 5th International Conference on Digital Satellite Communications, Genoa, Italy, 243-249.

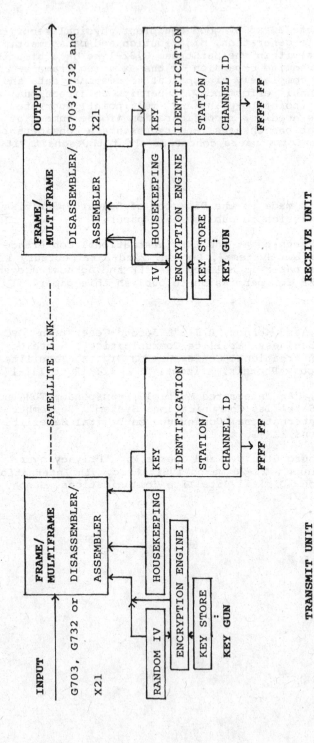

Figure 1. Channel unit schematic diagram

435

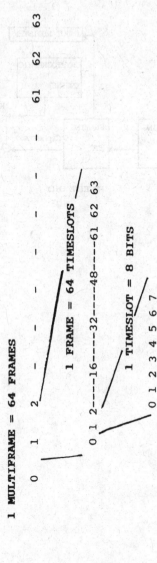

1 MULTIFRAME = 64 FRAMES

0 1 2 - - - - - 61 62 63

1 FRAME = 64 TIMESLOTS

0 1 2 ----16----32----48----61 62 63

1 TIMESLOT = 8 BITS

0 1 2 3 4 5 6 7

TS0 : FRAME UNIQUE WORD   - 0 0 1 1 0 1 1
TS16: SIGNALLING FIELD   R 1 R R R R R R *
TS32: MESSAGE FIELD
TS48: SIGNALLING FIELD

* R- Reserved bits for the multiframe unique word, channel
  and station identifiers and encryption parameters.

Figure 2 Data format

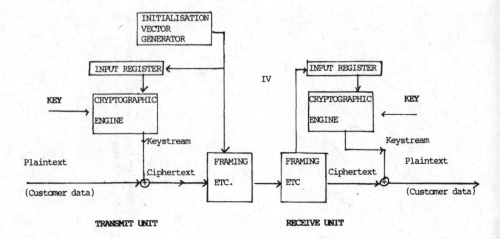

Figure 3 Encryption functions of the channel unit

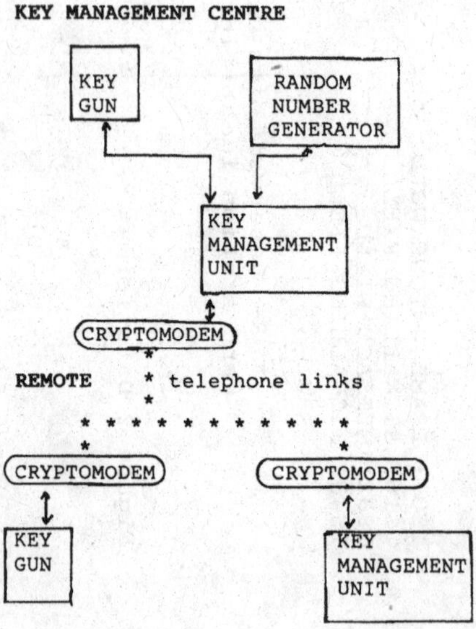

KEY MANAGEMENT CENTRE

Figure 4 Key management scheme

AN ENCRYPTION AND AUTHENTIFICATION PROCEDURE
FOR TELESURVEILLANCE SYSTEMS

*Odoardo Brugia** - *Salvatore Improta*** - *William Wolfowicz**

* Fondazione Ugo Bordoni - Sede Legale -
   v. le Trastevere 108 - 00153 Roma
** FATME SpA

Work carried out at the Fondazione Ugo Bordoni under the agreement
between the Istituto Superiore P.T. and the Fondazione Ugo Bordoni.

ABSTRACT - To perform message authentication in a telesurveillance system, the paper proposes a non linear time varying encryption algorithm, based on key layering in three levels (system key, intermediate key, running key) and on encryption organization into two or more sets of three operations (running key rotation, message digit substitution and transposition). The algorithm was designed to be implemented on an 8-bit microprocessor.

1 - INTRODUCTION

The telesurveillance system we are concerned with includes a control center (CC) and a certain number of environment detection devices (DD) located in the places to be kept under surveillance. The CC asks the remote DD's ciclically about the parameters they are detecting and each DD sends the appropriate answer back taking it from a finite set. The CC and DD's can be linked either by a private network or by leased channels.

To prevent modifications or imitations of the messages interchanged between the CC and the DD's, an effective authentication procedure is needed. Encryption is one of the most effective methods to perform authentication; for this purpose, the encryption algorithm must meet two fundamental requirements: non linearity of the relation between plaintext and cyphertext; time variability of the algorithm parameters. If the former requirement is met, any intruder attempting message modifications without

ATA

knowing the secret key would be unable to make the appropriate changes in the encrypted signature required for his modification to escape disclosure. The latter requirement is necessary to avoid that an intruder can record properly encrypted messages and sabotage the system playing them back later.

The encryption algorithm proposed in this paper meets these requirements and can be implemented on an 8-bit microprocessor. It is based on the layering of the key in three levels: system key, intermediate key and running key (sec.2), and on encryption organization into two or more sets of three operation: running key rotation, message digit substitution and transposition (sec.4). The running key consists of segments of the binary sequence generated by a non linear pseudorandom generator whose parameters are functions of both the intermediate and the system key (sec.2). The binary message to be encrypted consists of three fields containing telesurveillance, key changing and authentication information respectively (sec.3). Authentication and telesurveillance procedures are described in sec.5.

2 - KEY GENERATOR

Whenever an encryption or decryption operation has to be performed in the system, a running key request signal starts the key generator shown in fig.1, where M denotes a buffer memory and $G_1, G_2, G_3, G_1', G_2', G_3'$ are linear feedback shift registers (LFSR). The first three LFSR's have primitive characteristic polynomials of degree N_1, N_2, N_3 respectively and form a Geffe generator [1], whose output sequence has [2]: equally likely 1's and 0's; a period equal to lcm $(2^{N_1}-1, 2^{N_2}-1, 2^{N_3}-1)$ and a complexity equal

to $N_1N_2+(N_2+1)N_3$. After each running key request, 8 digits of this sequen-

ce are generated and written into M to update its content.

The second three LFSR's, together with the 8-digit delayer D,

form a modified Geffe generator; the characteristic polynomial of G_2' is

primitive, while the feedback connections of G_1' and G_3' and the initial sta-

tes of G_1', G_2', G_3' are determined as functions of the content of M under

the constraints that: the three characteristic polynomials have an odd num-

ber of terms and fixed degrees N_1', N_2', N_3' the initial state of each LFSR

has at least one digit set to 1. If the polynomial coefficients of G_1' and

G_3' and the initial states of G_1', G_2', G_3' were constant (so as the polyno-

mial coefficients of G_2' are), the modified Geffe generator would generate

a binary sequence having a period P and a complexity C such that:

$3(2^{N_2'}-1)\le P \le$ lcm$(2^{N_1'}-1, 2^{N_2'}-1, 2^{N_3'}-1)$ and $2+N_2' \le C \le N_1'N_2'+(N_2'+1)N_3'+N_2'$; the

lowest and highest values of P and C are taken respectively with probabili-

ties $2^{8-N_1'-N_3'}$ and $\varphi(2^{N_2'}-1)\,\varphi(2^{N_3'}-1)/N_2'N_3'\,2^{N_2'+N_3'-4}$, where φ indicates the

Euler totient function. After each running key request, 64 digits of this

sequence are generated.

The time varying parameters of the modified Geffe generator are

changed according to the content of M whenever a given number of digits ran-

domly generated in the CC coincides with the content of an equal number of

fixed memory cells.

The system key, which provides the coefficients of the characte-

ristic polynomial of G_1, G_2, G_3, G_2' and the initial states of G_1, G_2, G_3, is

generated by a program fulfilling the requirements that the aforesaid poly-

nomials are primitive and each initial state vector contains at least a 1.
The intermediate key, which provides the coefficients of the characteristic
polynomials of G'_1, G'_3 and the initial states of G'_1, G'_2, G'_3, is taken from
M. The running key consists of the 64 digits generated by the modified
Geffe generator.

Since the intermediate key is changed at random, the sequence ge
nerated by the modified Geffe generator is usually aperiodic and it is
meaningless to define its complexity.

3 - MESSAGE STRUCTURE

Every message consists of 64 binary digits subdivided in three
fields: a 40-digit information field, reserved to the telesurveillance information; an 8-digit signalling field, devoted to the transmission of
key-changing information; a 16-digit authentication field, for transmission of authentication information. The information field is subdivided
in two sectors, devoted respectively to the transmission of CC's interroga
tions and DD's answers; the CC uses the second sector too, to transmit a
replica of the interrogation; the DD's use the first sector too, to transmit a replica of the received interrogation. In the signalling field the
CC inserts the key-changing signal   and the DD inserts a replica of the
received key-changing signal. The sequence to be inserted in the authenti
cation field can be get either by taking the remainder of the modulo 2 division of the d-transform [3] of the information and signalling field contents by a 16 degree polynomial, or as the result of 16 parity checks. The

probability that intentional or unintentional message modifications can elu
de the controls is greatly reduced owing to the high message redundancy
and check number.

4 - ENCRYPTION

Encryption consists of two or more iterations of three operations:
running key rotation; plaintext digit substitution; transposition of the di
gits resulting from the preceding operation. Substitution is performed by
adding modulo 2 each plaintext digit to the corresponding digit of the running key (without rotation in the first iteration, and after suitable running key shifts in the following iterations); the substituted sequence is
segmented in eight 8-digit blocks which are arranged in an 8x8 matrix, whi
le the running key is segmented in sixteen 3-digit blocks. Transposition
is performed by shifting each row and then each column of the matrix ciclically
by a number of positions given by the decimal value of the appropriate key
block.

5 - TELESURVEILLANCE PROCEDURE

The CC shares individual system keys with the DD's: the key gene
rators sharing the same system key evolve synchronously at 64-digit steps ,
generate the same running key and change the intermediate key on the initia
tive of the CC.

To interrogate each DD about its state, the CC sends a message
encrypted with the specific running key.

The DD decrypts the message and either verifies that the 16 authentication digits coincide with the remainder of the modulo 2 division of the
d-transform of the information and signalling field contents by the prefixed 16 degree polynomial or performs #6 parity checks according to the authentication approach used in transmission.

If the message authenticity is recognized, the DD reads the information and signalling field contents. If a key-changing signal is present
in the signalling field, the DD gets ready to change the intermediate key at
the next running key request. Moreover, the DD prepares a message con -
taining: the replica of the received interrogation and the corresponding answer, in the information field; the replica of the received key-changing signal, in the signalling field; and the authentication sequence, in the authentication field. This message is encrypted with a new running key.

Failure of authentication check can be due, or not, to the reception of a cleartext by which the CC communicates it did not recognize the
authenticity of the message previously sent by the same DD. In the former
case the DD changes the intermediate key and encrypts the preceding message with the new running key. In the latter case, the DD sends a non authentication message in clear, keeps its key generator up with the corresponding CC's one by letting it run by 64 digits, and gets it ready to change
the intermediate key. Both non authentication messages consist of 64 digits obtained by repeating the DD address a certain number of times.

An alarm is given in the CC whenever one of the following events
occurs: lack of DD answer within a prefixed time interval; non authentication of three consecutive messages coming from a same DD; alarm indication
and consective alarm confirmation from the part of a same DD; a combination
of non authentication and alarm messages.

REFERENCES

[1]   P.R. GEFFE: "How to protect data with ciphers that are really hard
        to break" Electronics, jan.4, 1973, p.99-101.

[2]   E.L. KEY: "An analysis of the structure and complexity of non li-
        near binary sequence generators" IEEE Trans. on Inf.Th., v.IT-22,
        n.6, nov.1976, p.732-6.

[3]   A. GILL: "Linear sequential circuits" Mc.Graw Hill, 1967.

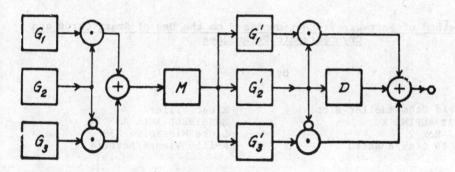

$\odot$ = *Modulo 2 multiplier*

$\oplus$ = *Modulo 2 adder*

$G_1, G_2, G_3, G_1', G_2', G_3'$ = *Linear feedback shift registers*

M = *Buffer memory*

D = *Delayer*

Fig. 1_ *Key generator*

A Method of Software Protection Based on the Use of Smart Cards and Cryptographic Techniques

by

Ingrid Schaumueller-Bichl
VOEST ALPINE AG
P.O. Box 2
A-4010 Linz/Austria

Ernst Piller
HONEYWELL BULL AG
Linke Wienzeile 236
A-1150 Vienna/Austria

Abstract

The paper presents a software protection system that prevents
"software piracy" reliably while allowing to produce an unlimited
number of program copies.

Based on a combination of smart card technology and cryptographic
techniques the system provides not only a high level of security, but
also enhanced ease-of-use for the software manufacturer as well as for
the user.

I) Introduction

According to estimates made in 1983 software manufacturers loose at
least 50% of their turnover due to "illegal copying" or - to be more
accurate - to "unauthorized execution" of programs. The problem is
especially serious in the field of mini- and microcomputers and is
growing steadily.

Presently the way to compensate the losses caused by software piracy
is to raise software prices accordingly. Thus there is an urgent
need for software protection systems from the manufacturers as well
as the users point of view.

In particular there are two up-to-date methods that seem specially
suited to solve problems like these - smart card technology and
cryptographic techniques.

Smart cards, plastic cards equipped with a microprocessor to execute
special security algorithms and a protected memory to store even
highly confidential data, present a mean to realize security systems
of various kinds, that are not only highly secure, but also provide
a plain and clear user interface. So it is possible for the first
time to make high level security systems available in everyday life,
thus meeting the strongly rising security demands the new
technologies bring with them.

The software protection system described below is based on CP8-cards
- smart cards developed by BULL France - and card readers.

The cards are used in their standard form and linked with the system
via special software, the card reader is connected to the computer
via a V.24-interface (RS 232).

The cryptographic techniques used for protection comprise standard
methods provided by CP8-cards as well as specially developed
algorithms. Encipherment and decipherment of data is accomplished by
the algorithm "C80".

II) Design Criteria / Requirements

The central goal of a software protection system is to protect
software against "piracy".

A detailed analysis of the problem shows that this does not
necessarily mean to prevent the production of program copies, but
rather their illegal use.

So the first and central goal of a software protection system has
to be:

to prevent unauthorized execution of programs.

Copying is allowed unlimitedly.

In addition to the security demands, an up-to-date software
protection system has to fulfill strong requirements with regard
to its ease-of-use, applicability and flexibility.

The software manufacturer needs a system that is

- of reasonably low cost, relative to the losses caused by
  software piracy

- independent of storage media

- applicable independently of the computer manufacturer

For the software user the most attractive feature of the system
is that protected software can be sold at a greatly reduced price.

In order to raise acceptance levels, two additional criteria have
been demanded for the software protection system presented below:

- greater ease-of-use of the protected software

- additional protection of user software and data against
  unauthorized access

III) The Method of Protection

Basic Idea

The software to be protected is connected with a proper,
specially issued smart card, so that the execution of programs is
possible if and only if the card is inserted in the card reader.

As it is impossible to copy smart cards, the software can only be
executed by users who legally bought a licence and got a card then.

Copying of programs can be performed unrestrictedly.

If wanted, several different programs can be associated with a
single smart card.

Protection Mechanisms

The connection between the software to be protected and the proper smart card is established in three different ways:

1) Repeated inquiries if the card is inserted in the card reader:

   At certain stages the protected software calls the "TELEPASS function" that is inherently integrated in every CP8-card. Certain data, in our case pseudo random numbers, are transmitted to the card, where they are enciphered by a certain algorithm under a secret key that is stored in the card, and retransmitted.

   The calling program enciphers the PRN too and compares the results. If they are equal the authenticity of the card can be taken for granted.

   The use of a new PRN whenever the TELEPASS function is called ensures that the transfer of data between smart card and card reader is unpredictable and irreproducable.

   So an "active" wiretaper can not break the system by intercepting data, storing them and recording them later.

2) Storing selected enciphered program data on the card.

   The following rules are to be observed:

   - Only those data may be stored that will certainly never be changed in subsequent program releases. Else for every new program version new cards would have to be distributed.

   - Among others, initial values of variables and data, that are needed at highly important program stages, are well suited for storage in the card.

   - The data are stored and transmitted in enciphered form. Transmission of data between card and program is again protected by the use of encryption and pseudo random numbers. Deciphering is done either immediately or a while before the data are needed.

3) Enciphering highly valuable programs, storing them on the card and executing them in the card reader / card:

   Parts of the software to be protected, that are of particularly high value or central importance, are enciphered and stored in the card.
   Together with that card the card reader forms an external computer that in the present version executes the programs.

   As soon as freely programmable smart cards are available, the execution can be performed by the card.

   The communication between the calling program and the external computer is again protected by cryptographic methods and the use of pseudo random numbers.

The Cryptographic Background

At the heart of the cryptographic algorithms applied in the software
protection system is the cipher algorithm C80.

It is used

- to encipher and decipher the program data stored in the card

- to protect the communication between the card, the card reader
  and the calling programs against passive and active wiretapping

- to encipher and decipher the programs stored in the card

- to produce pseudo random numbers

C80 is a block cipher algorithm that is similar to the DES in its basic
structure. The left and the right halves of a text are interchanged
repeatedly and one half is XOR-ed with a binary vector depending on the
text and the key. A sketch of the algorithm is given in the
following:

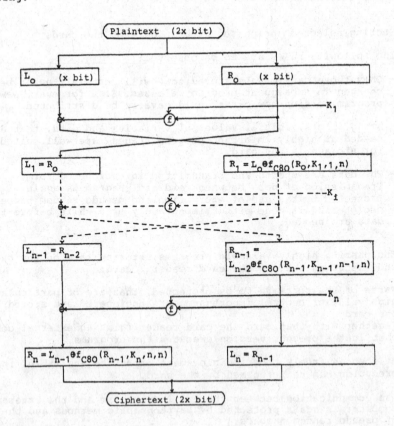

In contrast to the DES C80 does not use S-boxes, permutations or any other tables of fixed sizes.
For this reason it is highly flexible - it employes variable numbers of rounds, variable block- and key-lengths - and can be well adapted to the special problems.

A detailed description of C80 and a security analysis are given in "Zur Analyse des DES und Synthese verwandter Chiffriersysteme", Thesis, I. Schaumueller-Bichl, Linz/Austria, May 1981.

For the software protection system the freely selectable parameters for the C80 were chosen to decrease computation time and still provide a degree of security that is essentially higher than that of the DES.

As the C80 has approximately the same good error propagation and statistical properties as the DES, it can be used also for the generation of pseudo random numbers.

In a very complex way it generates the 48-bit-numbers needed by the TELEPASS-function.

IV) System Properties

The software protection system we described above meets the requirements and design criteria stated in chapter 2:

- It prevents the unauthorized execution of software:
  Like all practical solutions our system does not provide absolute and unconditional security. But the degree of security was chosen so high that it is considerably easier and cheaper to buy a licence or even to write an equivalent program than to copy protected software.

- It can be applied by software manufacturers without support of hardware manufacturers:
  The method is realized in software, the hardware components required (cards and card readers) can be easily connected with the computer.

- It is independent of specific CPU's:
  The system does not make use of special CPU numbers or similar. Thus protected software can be executed on each suitable computer. This is of special importance in the case of hardware troubles, when a computer is to be replaced.

- It is independent of storage media:
  As the system does not physically prevent copying but execution of programs the software can be protected no matter where and how it is stored.

- Copies can be produced without restrictions:
  The user of a protected program can make as many copies as he wants and use any of them for further work without having to perform additional procedures.

The protection system also provides special advantages for the user as side effects of the methods applied:

- As for the execution of a protected program the smart card is absolutely needed, the system provides additionally some protection of software against unauthorized access. This is of special importance in the case of multiuser systems and computer networks.
It is possible to additionally provide the system with a Personal Identification Number (PIN) known only by the user and thus making it a real access control system.

- Enhanced ease-of-use:
A part of the memory implemented in the smart card can be used to store several commands that usually have to be typed by the user. By releasing the user from these routine functions the ease-of-use and consequently the rate of acceptance of a program can be raised considerably.

V) Fields of Application

The software protection system can be used in a variety of cases:

- Protection against multiple use of a single licence:

  Guarantees the observance of software licence contracts

- Protection of software during and after testinstallations:

  If programs are protected in the way described above, the proper card can be returned to the software manufacturer or be destroyed automatically after the end of the testinstallation. From that point on the software cannot be executed by the user.

- Protection of software during transport:

  As the software cannot be executed as long as the proper card is unavailable programs can be sent to a customer e.g. by ordinary mail without any further protection. This is especially valuable for the distribution of new program releases.

Prospects of Application

As stated above the presented software protection system shows
several strong points compared to other systems concerning

- security
- universal applicability
- flexibility
- ease of use

Undoubtedly it also shares the weak points inherent to every
software protection system, caused by the additionally necessary
hard- and software.

For the software manufacturer these disadvantages - having to
implement and maintain additional components - are fully compensated
by the protection the system provides for his software and consequently
by the increase of his turnovers.

For some software user protected software might be unattractive at
the first glance as there is no more chance to produce resp. execute
unauthorized copies for himself or others. But on the other hand
protected software can be sold at a considerably reduced price, a
feature that is for the benefit of all users.
The possibilities to enhance the ease-of-use as well as the security
against unauthorized access are another crucial reason for a user to
buy software protected by the described system.

There is one point left for discussion: the price of the protection
system and its relation to the software prices.

The application of the method presupposes the availability of a card
reader at every PC resp. terminal.
As smart card technology is very new and card readers are scarcely
spread, the card readers usually have to be an integrated component of
the protection system.

The full costs of this system - including protection software, card and
card reader - have to be taken over by the software manufacturer, the
free card reader being another motivation for the software purchaser.

For this reason the system should presently be applied mainly for
high-value software.
The threshold for profitableness is in the average at a price of 3000
to 5.000 US$ for the software to be protected, depending on the
expected rate of unauthorized to authorized copies.

454

For the future it is to be expected that card readers - as external
devices or integrated in terminals - will be a common device of mini-
and microcomputers as floppy disk drives or printers are today.
In this case the hardware costs comprise merely the costs for smart
cards (estimated less than 5 US$ for mass production), so the
protection system can well be applied also for the protection of
cheap standard software like textprocessing systems.

In order to be able to apply the system already now for low cost,
widely sold software, two ways of proceeding can be conceived:

- construction of card readers dedicated to the specific problem and
  thus available at a lower price
- an agreement between software companies to share the costs for a
  card reader, that can be used for different programs of different
  companies

Summary

The protection system presented secures that software can only be
executed in combination with a specially issued, uncopyable smart card.
It is realized by software and standard hardware (CP8-cards
and card readers).

Its high level of security, flexibility and ease-of-use makes it
interesting for manufactures of software as well as for users.

SECTION VI

SMART CARDS

SESSION ON SMART CARDS

TUESDAY APRIL 10

INTRODUCTORY REMARKS

by Alain TURBAT
DGT - Délégation Carte à Mémoire

Since a few years, smart card has began to appear in the field of cryptography. Today it is possible to hold a special session of Eurocrypt 84 on this subject because, after a period of experiments, the smart card is now becoming a commercial product, especially in France.

You all know what a smart card is : this standard dimensioned plastic card contains a micro electronics package including a memory and a microprocessor controlling read and write access to this memory.

This new card differs from magnetic stripes cards, not so much by its memory capacity, as by its internal computing power, hence its name : the smart card.

Cryptographic computation using personal secrete keys, is possible inside the card itself, allowing the smart card to carry out complex dialogues with the external environment. This permit a high degree of security in a large field of applications through processes of autenthication of the card, identification of the user, confidentiality of transmitted information, certification of a transaction by all the parties involved.

The card internal processing capacity, and its ability to store a non erasable record of each transaction provide an unrivaled degree of security and performances such that it will, during the coming decade, become one of the key elements in the expansion of electronic funds transfert, as well as an extremely reliable mean of identification for access to buildings, data banks, videotex services, pay TV channels and so on.

It would also be very helpful as a personal electronic file in applications that require portability and self contained security, for instance in the medical services field.

Therefore, by making information storage and processing possible anywhere, the smart card opens up new horizons in the design of networks, in regard to security and cost.

In France, the first project coming just now to mass production is the smart card payphone project. The French Telecommunications Administration have already ordered more than 10 000 payphones and one million cards including 200 000 with the microprocessor monochip designed by BULL, which are capable of both payphone and banking functions including point of sale, home banking and telepayment. Such a multifunction card will be used this year for all these applications in BLOIS, in the area of castles on the Loire.

All the French Banks and Financial Instutions have also decided to adopt a mixed smart/magnetic stripe card to be generalized in the whole country before the end of the eighties.

But the subject today is the link between smart card and cryptography which will be explained in many details by the different experts.

I suggest just to listen them.

SMART CARD APPLICATIONS IN SECURITY AND DATA PROTECTION

by Jean GOUTAY   Président de la Société INFOSCRIPT

INTRODUCTION

The several security elements of the smart card are based on
phisical and logical barriers.

- Materially, the smart card is a monolithic component including
  a microprocessor and a memory of 8 K bits, this memory being
  indelible.

  .In addition entry test points have been destroyed before acti-
  vating the smart card.

  .In practice it is impossible to read, modify or duplicate the
  contents of the smart card.

- Logically, the chip is able to memorize the different wrong
  access attempts and invalidate the electronic circuit after
  three repeated attempts for example or N attempts on the
  whole.

  Let's see in addition that the dialogues between the chip
  and the exterior depend on a random value, which is a known
  element of security and a protection against the passive
  intrusion and possibilities of simulation.

- What are the uses of the smart card, specially in matter of
  protection of information and more generally in security ?

  They concerned : Identification
                     Authentication
                     Enciphering and key management

  They allow the security of :
                  - The access to premises or to a network
                  - the payment at P.O.S. or at distance
                  - the transmission in networks, electronic
                    messeging for instance
                  - access to services such as: broadcoast
                    videotex or toll TV, interactive videotex,
                    database.

First let's look at the different uses of the smart card.

1. Portable Protected Data

- The smart card contains a memory not very big (from eight to
  sixteen K) but protected against the exterior by a microprocessor (or a firmware) and it is possible to store in it clear
  confidential data. These data will be accessible only on
  production of a secret code.
  The applications are : protected portative file such asmedicine,
  student portable file, ...

- However the smart card is able probably to encipher
  short messages, store and transmit them.
  In particular this system can be used for sending enciphered
  keys at distance.

2. Identification

Thanks to the content of the secret and inviolable area in the
smart card, thanks to computation which remains with in the card,
it is possible to verify a personal code with a very good security
and so to identify the card's bearer.

But a better identification can be obtained by a more secure
storage of patterns bounded with physical characteristics of the
person, such as :
- the finger prints
- the speech
- or the dynamic signature.

3. Data Authentication

After data compression by an algorithm (hash code, ...).
it is possible to compute and to store in the smart card an
"electronic signature", function of this compression and of the
transmitter identity. In another connection this signature is
added to the original text, a fact wich permits the verification.

This process can apply for the certification of accountant,
original documents, banking orders and transfers, files and
software, at different levels of development for instance.

4. Software protection

In matter of software protection, several systems can be envisaged,
wether at the transport level with the encipherment of the software and the deciphering key stored in the smart card
     or at the level of running with computation elements in the
program requiring the presence of the smart card
     or with holes in the program which can be restored with
the smart card only.

It is easy to see the applications in the domestic computers
area or in the area of video cassettes.

We can see in this case that decoding must be put at the monitor
level.

Now let's see other applications.

5. Reciprocal recognition and access control

A simple algorithm computed in the card permits verification, with a random value E , that the two cards are well matched, e.g. $R_a = R_b$.

Whether in the case of the access control to premises, or a network or a data base.

In the network case, every passive intrusion on the line does not allow either listening or simulation or re-use of the dialogue, the informations being completely random.

In the case of access control, the combination changes at every access because the key R is fugitive.

6. Card authentication by general system

Another application can be the recognition of the smart card by the system, that is to say it's authenticity, based in theory on public key use.

Using a random message M , the system computes
$C = f(M)$, f being the public key.

C is transmitted to the card which contains the secret part of the function.

The big advantage is that the system, which can be a general public terminal, doesn't require any secret function.

So in the case of electronic payment at point of sale, the system verifies : - the authenticity of the smart card and of the bearer
- the guarantee limit
- possibly the black list.

Let's see in this case that the card allows the management of several access codes : banker code for the valorization, bearer's code, service providers codes ...

But the possibilities of the smart card are even more interesting in the networks, in matter of security.

In addition to the previously described functions, they allow the automatic logging the management of preloaded credit fields and if they can't encipher at this moment they provide solutions to the delicate problems of key management.

7. Exchange ol enciphered data

With a generator of enciphered bits and a random number E , messages can be enciphered thanks to the smart card along a network, with keys R which can be changed at a desire frequency.

In particular the enciphering algorithm A can be very simple.

This system can be set up on any encipherment equipment in networks and provides a solution to delicate problems of key transportation.

One application is given in electronic mail where the cards are used for reciprocal identification of interlocutors and encipherment of informations by fugitives keys.

Let's see now very present applications.

8. The telepayment

The first wordwide experiment of telepayment has been in Velizy, near Paris, "TELETEL" and allows a suscriber to make from a vidéotex terminal, the minitel :
- the bank statement display
- the remote cash transfer
- the telepayment of goods providers
      as retraiters La Redoute .

The smart card (with it's reader) consequently permits :
- the sure identification of the suscriber
- the encipherment of messages on line and generation of "certificates" ensuring it's integrity ang giving the proof that the information is well registered in the card.

All is in an environment at distance non controlled.
The security of the system is based on the exchange of fugitive random keys.

Another system of telepayment wouldbe possible.

With the use of public keys and the signature of the messages by a secret key of the user, whose the public part, signed by the key of the bank, would be transmitted previously by the user. This system does'nt require any black box at the central processor.

9. Protected electronic messaging.

General systems can be envisaged to protect in addition informations during the storage in the mailbox of the service computer.

It is possible for example to encipher on line the data, and to decipher them immediatly with synchronous mode, finally to encipher again with another key for the storage.

It would be possible also to envisage another scheme with the use of public key for authentication of the transmitter, but also for transportation of the random key the message being enciphered it self with this key changing at every message.

10. Broadcast interactive vidéotex

In the case of access to toll services, whether broadcasted
programs or videotex services or data base, we have two possible
systems :

- one using the preliminary enciphering and decoding informations thanks to the smart card for those who have paid?

- the other one (pre-payment) permitting the access to the
  services after having destroyed bits area in the card,
  previously credited.

In conclusion, by its vast possibilities not yet explored,
the smart card open new vistas in matter of security, networks
and data protection.

Thank you for your attention.

BULL CP8 SMART CARD USES IN CRYPTOLOGY

Yves GIRARDOT

BULL CP8

rue Jean Jaurès

78340 LES CLAYES SOUS BOIS

FRANCE

ABSTRACT

The CP8 smart card has memory and intelligence.
These two characteristics joined to its technology, make of it an unfraudable
and unduplicable portable strong box.
Thus CP8 is a very secure and convenient device to transport, generate or transmit cryptologic keys or data.

THE CP8 CIRCUIT

The CP8 circuit designed in FRANCE by BULL, is a monolithic silicon chip, con-

taining an eight bit microprocessor, three kinds of memories, and alimentation

and dialog interfaces.

- The 36 bytes RAM memory is a scratch one, whose content is lost when the cir-

  cuit is not powered.

- The 1,6 K bytes ROM memory is an unerasable one. This memory is loaded during

  the fabrication of the chip itself, and contains a software corresponding to

  the intelligence given to the circuit.

  Each kind of software called "mask" corresponds to a specific array of appli-

  cations such as payment, toll television, software protection, etc...

- The 1 K byte PROM memory is the application unerasable storage memory. This memory is empty at the fabrication of the chip, and is loaded later during the different steps of the life of the circuit.

A very important and specific characteristic of the CP8 circuit concerning security is the fact that writing in the PROM memory is totally controled by the microprocessor. Thus the CP8 circuit is a "self-programmable" one.

- Communications with the CP8 circuit are insured by only six points.

Powering needs three connexions (ground, logical tension, writing tension for the PROM).

Operating the chip needs two signals coming from the outside (initialization and clock).

The dialog itself is done by only one connection is an asynchroneous bidirectionnal way.

THE CP8 SMART CARD

The CP8 SMART CARD is a plastic ISO card in which a CP8 circuit is embedded. Connections with the circuit are insured through a round printed goldered patch divided into 8 zones (6 only are used). Yet for special applications it is possible to insert the CP8 circuit on various different supports such as ticket, jock, pen, key...

PROM MEMORY

The PROM memory contains 256 words of 32 bits, and is divided into several zones corresponding to different uses and accesses modes from the outside of the card. The lengths of these zones are parametrable.

- The SECRET ZONE is impossible to read from outside the chip, either by logical or physical way.

The logical protection is insured by the microprocessor and its associated software located in the ROM memory.

The physical protection is due to the technology chosen to built the circuit.

This zone is loaded by several keys (fabrication, issuer, user's key) and by a secret which is a pattern of about one hundred bits (3 words of 32 bits).

- The ACCESS ZONE is a service one, in which are memorized accesses using the issuer's or the user's keys.

This memory allows to count good or wrong submitted keys, and to lock the circuit in case of several wrong tentatives (usually three).

- The CONFIDENTIAL ZONE can be read if the good issuer's or user's key is given. It contains generally personal or sensitive data.

- The TRANSACTION ZONE is used during the current life of the card. This zone can be read or written, with or without a key, according the application.

- The FREE ZONE can be read without any key and contains non sensitive data.

- The FABRICATION ZONE is a service one. It contains data related to the nature of the card and to the organization of its PROM memory.

ROM MEMORY

The ROM MEMORY contains three kind of programs :

- Service programs dealing with all what is necessary to initialize and currently use the card.

- Security programs insuring a very high level of security by checking flags and data, in order to detect abnormal or fraduleous operations.

- A program corresponding to the implementation of an algorithmic function, to
   be executed in the card itself

One of these algorithms is the TELEPASS one-way function.

A result R (64 bits) is obtained given three inputs. Two of them are taken in
the card. The secret S (96 bits) and an Identifier I (32 bits) located at an
address i to be chosen.

The third parameter E (64 bits) is given to the card.

$$R = f(Ei, I, S)$$

CP8 AND SECURITY

CP8 is a very high security card

This is due to its architecture, its technology and its unerasable unduplicable
memories (resistant to magnetic fields, UV and X rays).

CP8 allows to treat with a very smart and secure manner classical security problems such as identication, authentication, message certification, integrity
checks...

Dialogs are randomised using random numbers as input parameters in the TELEPASS
ALGORITHM, executed simultaneously in the user's card, and in the reference
card connected to the host system.

CP8 AND CRYPTOLOGY

The main problem in cryptology is key management.

All the security given by cryptologic equipments depends on the protection of
keys during their preparation, their transport or transmission, their storage
and their use.

- Transport and storage problems can be solved with CP8, considering that it is
a true portable strong box to be opened or closed by electronic codes.
The issuer's code allows to load a set of keys corresponding for instance to a
week, a month, a year, according to the application.

The capacity of the card represents for instance 50 keys of 150 bits, to be
loaded in one or several operations.
The loaded CP8 container card can be transported or mailed without problems.
It is an infraudable, induplicable, very convenient, and very secure key
vector.
The user's code allows to read the key in the card and to load the cryptologic
equipment.

For more security during storage before usage, the user has the ability to
choose a new user's code only known by him.
For more security during loading and reading operations, it is recommanded to
use "habilitation cards" given only to security responsibles.
These CP8 habilitation cards are able to generate issuer's or user's codes
from the data contained in the habilitation card itself and in the key vector
cards. These codes TELEPASS generated are longer and so more secure than manual ones.

- With CP8, key loading and reading operations are automatised, hence operators
need not read, or write, or punch them. The values of the keys remain secret.

- Another manner to prevent problems during keys transportation is to suppress
this operation. Two accorded CP8 cards (same secret and same Telepass
Algorithm) are able to generate two equal secret numbers, given a common unse-
cret one transmitted on the line.

These two equal numbers can attack at both sides directly the cryptologic equipments,or a pseudo ramdom numbers generator connected to it.

This procedure is limited to symetric key systems.

- Transmission of keys can be done by ciphered ways, using CP8 as ciphering and deciphering systems at the both sides.

In this case the CP8 card contains simultaneously the ciphering or deciphering key (the secret pattern in the secret zone of its PROM) and a reversible algorithm (written in its ROM).

Operating the cryptologic cards can be under the control of habilitation cards.

CONCLUSION
_____

The CP8 smart cards security characteristics have been recognized and are now currently used in many applications such as points of sale, home banking, logical access control, portable file, physical access control, toll services...

Their use in cryptology begins now first at key management level, but will increase in the future by dealing with data requiring more processing power in order to execute quicker more sophiticated algorithms.

<u>ESTIMATION OF SOME ENCRYPTION FUNCTIONS</u>

<u>IMPLEMENTED INTO SMART CARDS</u>

H. Groscot

76, rue A. Briand, 93220, Gagny, France .

<u>Abstract</u> .

We study a family of encryption functions , wich is particularly adapted for the situations that arise in smart cards .

Probabilistic arguments show us that "big key" is not synonymous of "good security" for these functions .

We think that the security of such functions has to rely on other criteria .

I. GENERALITIES

1. About protocols using smart cards .

The interest of smart cards not only lies in their intelligence but their security performances concern us as well . These allow the implementation of encryption functions , in order to perform authentication procedures, as those needed in long-distances payments or in checking acces control to buildings .

In this paper, we first show on a small example that smart cards allow us to design cryptographic protocols . In this example, it is assumed that the cards are issued by an organisation on business purpose and may accomplish long-distances operations .

They contain an encryption function γ depending on a secret key S, wich is the same in all the cards .

Before each transaction with a customer at a sail's point, one has to be sure that the customer's card is a valid one, therefore contains γ and S. So one connects the sail's point to a central by means of a telecommunication network. This central has a valid card and a pseudo random generator at his disposal.

After the insertion of the card in the terminal of the sail's point it is proceed as follows:

a. The card sends any message to the center .

b. The center sends a random message E back to the card .

c. The card computes $\gamma_S(E)$ and gives the result back .

d. The center computes $\gamma_S(E)$ by means of its card and compares it with the customer's result .

e. The communication is refused if the results are both different .

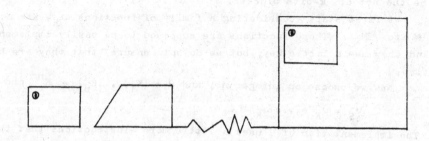

figure 1.

This is just a simple example; but it is possible to design a similar protocol where each card has a different secret key, i.e. depending on a P.I.N., N . Here, the card has to send N in the phase a of the protocol . It is also possible to add a password for the user , so that one can authenticate a valid card and its legal user .

Let's remark that all these protocols don't use the inverse function of γ, if it exists .

2. Introduction to the functions studied in this paper .

We have just seen that it is important to device one-way encryption functions for smart cards . The problem with these new objects is that their ROM, wich contains the software (i.e. the code of the encryption function γ), is relatively small . We have to design "simple" functions that are "complicated" enough to be secure ! On the other side, the RAM is exceedingly small. We are interested in algorithms that, at any step of the computations, load the smallest part of the data as possible in this RAM .

Here, we describe a family of functions that satisfy these requirements. We shall see that these functions can accept very big keys. Therefore we shall study the security of these functions in term of the length of these keys .

II. THE FUNCTION

1. Description .

The set $\mathbb{M}$ of messages that we consider includes the plaintext and enciphered messages . Let k be a small number (i.e. k = 8) and let $\mathbb{K}$ be the set of k-bits blocks .

We first start considering a family of functions ω_K, $K \in \mathbb{K}$, from $\mathbb{M}$ to $\mathbb{M}$. These functions are supposed to be easily implemented and they use a little key, but we do not ensure that they are bijective.

Now we choose an integer n , and $S = (K_1,\ldots,K_n) \in \mathbb{K}^n$ and we set

$$\gamma_S = \omega_{K_n} \circ \ldots \circ \omega_{K_1} .$$

The implementation of γ uses a little more instructions that the ω 's one and its key can be as large as desired . Moreover, each step of the computation of $\gamma(E)$, $E \in \mathbb{M}$, consists of a calculation of ω and so, uses only a small part of the key S .

463

2. The problem .

We have to keep in mind that the user of a card will eventually compute as many encrypted messages $\gamma_S(E)$, $E \in \mathbb{M}$, as he wishes . So a first question is :

"Is it possible to guess the secret key S from a big amount of couples $(E, \gamma_S(E))$ where $E \in \mathbb{M}$?" .

However, it is easy to request that the cards compute $\gamma_S(E)$ if and only if E has a definite standard form (i.e. the last byte of E represents the current year modulo 2^8). Then, the opponent user will have to choose the messages E in a subset $\mathbb{M}'$ of standard messages of $\mathbb{M}$. In fact, it will be seen that, if the functions ω are not bijective and satisfy some reasonable hypotheses, the following question has an affirmative answer :

"Is it possible to guess the secret key S by means of a big amount of encrypted messages $\gamma_S(E)$ where $E \in \mathbb{M}'$?" .

3. Notations and hypotheses .

The notations concerning $\mathbb{M}$, $\mathbb{M}'$, $\mathbb{K}$, ω_K and γ_S are kept on .

As ω is a "little" cipher function, its program uses a "small" flow chart. It is therefore possible to go backward on it so that we have a relatively fast algorithm, with a mean running time of T, wich gives for each $(F,K) \in \mathbb{M} \times \mathbb{K}$ the list of all the E in $\mathbb{M}$ such that $\omega_K(E) = F$. By means of a spanning tree algorithm, we determine and define the following numbers and sets :

$$A_K(F) = \left\{ E \in \mathbb{M}, \omega_K(E) = F \right\} \quad ,$$
$$A_{K_m, \ldots, K_1}(F) = \left\{ E \in \mathbb{M}, \omega_{K_m} \circ \ldots \circ \omega_{K_1}(E) = F \right\} \quad ,$$
$$X_K(E) = \text{Card } A_K(E) \quad ,$$
$$X_{K_m, \ldots, K_1}(E) = \text{Card } A_{K_m, \ldots, K_1}(E) \quad .$$

The functions X_K and $X_{K_m, \ldots, K_1}$ have to be considered as random variables on the set $\mathbb{M}$. The hypotheses that are given below give a reasonable model for γ .

(H1) The random variables X_K, $K \in \mathbb{K}$, are pairwise independent and have the same law as an integer random variable Y .

We set, for every $n \in \mathbb{N}$, $p_n = \text{Prob}(Y = n)$.

(H2) The number p_0 is not null .

(H3)   Let K, L be in $\mathbb{K}$. Let's suppose that F and G are randomly and independently chosen in $\mathbb{M}$ so that $\omega_K(F) = \omega_K(G) = E$. On the one hand, there are no a priori correlations between $X_L(F)$

and $X_L(G)$; on the other hand there is no correlation between $X_L(F)$ and $X_K(E)$.

(H4)   Let $K_1,\ldots,K_m,L$ be elements of $\mathbb{K}$. If E is chosen randomly in $\mathbb{M}$ and if F is selected at random in $A_{K_m,\ldots,K_1}(E)$, there is no correlation between $X_L(F)$ and $X_{K_m,\ldots,K_1}(E)$.

(H5)   It is recalled here that the smart card accepts to perform the computation of $\gamma_S(E)$ if and only if $E \in \mathbb{M}'$. Moreover it is assumed that the law of X_K, $K \in \mathbb{K}$, is the same on $\mathbb{M}'$ as on $\mathbb{M}$.

(H5)   This is a technical hypothese that says that p_1 is not null .

Some remarks .

a. The hypotheses H2, which is obviously satisfied when ω is not bijective, gives the start point of the search of the key S . Let F , in $\gamma_S(\mathbb{M})$, be such that $X_L(F) = 0$, where $L \in \mathbb{K}$; then one clearly has $L \neq K_n$. That gives a way to through little blocks of keys away .
b. The hypotheses H1, H3, H4 are sound because ω is presumed to mix up the bits contained in E and K . Moreover, an unsuspected dependence , which could invalidate one of these hypotheses, could as well result in a new way of attack against the secrecy of S .
c. The hypothese H6 is not fundamental but the search of S is faster with it .
d. The main task of H5 is to prevent the kind of attack where one chooses many E in $\mathbb{M}$ and then analyses the so obtained couples $(E, \gamma_S(E))$. It is possible to show that, if H5 is false, such a search of S is very easy for the owner of a card .

4. Study of the random variables $X_{K_m,\ldots,K_1}$.

It is deduced from the hypotheses H1, H3, H4 that for every $m \in \mathbb{N}^*$ and $(K_1,\ldots,K_m) \in \mathbb{K}^m$, the random variables $X_{K_m,\ldots,K_1}$ have the same law as a variable that will be noted Y_m, from now on . The law of Y_m is deduced from Y_{m-1} as follows :
"Y_m is the sum of Y_{m-1} independent variables with the same law as Y_1" .

Let f be the generating function of Y_1 and f_m be the one of Y_m . The end of the paragraph III.15 of "Calcul des probabilités" of Renyi (Dunod) gives :
Proposition 1.   The functions f_m satisfy $f_{m+1} = f_m \circ f$, for every $m \in \mathbb{N}^*$.

Let σ be the standard variation of Y and, for every r.v. Z, let $E(Z)$ and $\sigma(Z)$ stand respectively for the mean value and the standard variation of Z . The proposition 1 allows us to study Y_m and we obtain the following assertions :

Proposition 2.

a. For every $m \in \mathbb{N}^*$, one has $E(Y_m) = 1$ and $\sigma(Y_m) = \sqrt{m}\,\sigma$.

b. The series Prob $(Y_m = 0)$ has 1 as limit when $m \to \infty$ and

$$1 - \text{Prob}\ (Y_m = 0) \sim 2/\sigma^2 m \ .$$

c. For every $\varepsilon > 0$, there is a constant $C > 0$ such that, for every $m \in \mathbb{N}^*$ one has :

$$\text{Prob}\ (Y_m = 1) > C/m^{2+\varepsilon} \ .$$

Demonstration .

First we compute $E(Y_1)$. To do this, one has to compute $E(X_K)$ where K is any element of $\mathbb{K}$. The numbering of $\mathbb{M}$ gives

$$\text{Card } \mathbb{M} = \sum_k k.(\text{Prob}(X_K = k) \ . \ \text{Card } \mathbb{M}) \ ,$$

and $\sum k.p_k = 1$. Therefore we have $E(Y_1) = 1$. Then, it is easy to see that

$$E(Y_m) = E(Y_1)^m = 1 \ .$$

The calculation of $\sigma(Y_m)$ is done recursively on m . We use the following formulas :

$$\sigma^2(Y_1) = f''(1) + f'(1) - f'(1)^2 = f''(1) \ ,$$
$$f'_m(1) = 1 \ ,$$
$$f''_m(z) = f''(z).f'_{m-1}(f(z)) + f'(z).f''_{m-1}(f(z)) \ ,$$

we obtain :

$$f''_m(1) = \sigma^2 + f''_{m-1}(1) \ ,$$

and one has the part a of the proposition .

Now the series $(f_m(0))$ is strictly increasing and has 1 as limit . In order to obtain b, one shows the following fact:

For every $\varepsilon > 0$, there exists an $M \in \mathbb{N}$ such that, for every $m > M$, one has

$$\frac{\sigma^2}{2+\varepsilon}\ m < \frac{1}{1-f_m(0)} < \frac{\sigma^2}{2-\varepsilon}\ m \ .$$

Let m be an integer and set $a = 1 - f_m(0)$. From the Taylor formula, there is a real $\theta \in\ ]0,1[$ such that

$$f(1 - a) = 1 - a + \frac{a^2}{2}\ f''(1 - \theta a) \ .$$

Therefore :

$$\frac{1}{1-f_{m+1}(0)} - \frac{1}{1-f_m(0)} = \frac{1}{2} \frac{f''(1-\theta a)}{1-\frac{a}{2} f''(1-\theta a)}$$

The right hand side is a continuous function of (θ, a) that takes the value $\sigma^2/2$ at $(0, 0)$; therefore there exists an integer m_0 such that the left hand side lies in the interval $]\sigma^2/(2+\varepsilon/2)$, $\sigma^2/(2-\varepsilon/2)[$ for every $m > m_0$. That gives b to us .

The demonstration of c starts from the following formula ;

$$f'_m(0) = f'(f_{m-1}(0))\ldots f'(f_1(0)).f'(0) \quad ,$$

which is a consequence of the proposition 1 . Because of the hypothese H6, this term is not null . One uses the estimation of $f_k(0)$ just given to apply the Taylor formula at $f'(f_k(0))$. One has then to find a lower bound for the following product

$$\prod_{k=b}^{n} (1 - a/k)$$

where $a = 2+\varepsilon$ and $b > 0$. This last product is equivalent to

$$\frac{\Gamma(b+1)}{\Gamma(b-a+1)} n^a$$

(use the Stirling formula) , and one can conclude .

We end this section with the study of the random variables $X_{K_n, \ldots, K_{n-m+1}} \circ \gamma_S$, where $m \leqslant n$. Let $\Upsilon_m \circ \gamma$ be that variable . It is met when one takes $E \in M'$ at random and then computes $F = \gamma_S(E)$ by means of the card to observe $A_{K_n, \ldots, K_{n-m+1}} (F)$.

Proposition 3. For every r $\mathbb{N}$, one has

Prob $(\Upsilon_m \circ \gamma = r) = r.$Prob $(\Upsilon_m = r)$.
The generating function of the r.v. $\Upsilon_m \circ \gamma$ is $z \longmapsto z.f'_m(z)$.

The second assertion is directly deduced from the first one and gives with the proposition 2 :

Corollary .
a. For every $\varepsilon > 0$, there is a constant $c > 0$ such that, for every m , one has

Prob $(\Upsilon_m \circ \gamma = 1) > c/ m^{2+\varepsilon}$.

b. $E(\Upsilon_m \circ \gamma) = 1 + m \sigma^2$.

In order to show the proposition 3, we have to give an estimation of Prob $(\Upsilon_m \circ \gamma = r)$. First we start numbering the elements $x \in M$ such that $\Upsilon_m(\gamma(x)) = r$, which is the same as to sum the $\Upsilon_n(y)$ where $y \in \mathbb{M}$ and $\Upsilon_m(y) = r$. Therefore

$$\text{Prob } (Y_m\text{o} = r) = \frac{1}{\text{Card } M} \sum_{l \in \mathbb{N}} 1 \sum_{y \quad M, Y_m(y)=r, Y_n(y)=1} 1$$

$$= \sum_{l \in \mathbb{N}} 1 . \text{Prob } (Y_m = r \text{ and } Y_n = 1)$$

$$= \sum_{l} 1 . \text{Prob}(Y_n = 1 \quad Y_m = r) . \text{Prob } (Y_m = r) \quad .$$

Let's keep in mind that Y_n and Y_m represent respectively $X_{K_n,\ldots,K_1}$ and $X_{K_n,\ldots,K_{n-m+1}}$. Therefore Y_n is the sum of r independent r.v. with the same law as Y_{n-m} when it is known that $Y_m = r$. The conditional mean value if Y_n is then equal to r when $Y_m = r$. Therefore , we obtain the proposition 3 .

5. The search of the key .

It is shown here how some elements of $\omega_L (M')$ can be used to find L ; wich directly applies to search K_n . Let $(F_i)_i$ be a random series of elements of M and, for every $L \in \mathbb{K}$, let $J(L)$ be the smallest index i such that $X_L(F_i) = 0$. The mean value of $J(L)$ is $1/p_0$.

Let h be an integer and $L_1,\ldots,L_h$ be elements of $\mathbb{K}$. We suppose that we have chosen the F_j in $\omega_{L_0} (M')$, for some unknown $L_0 \in \mathbb{K}$, where $L_0 \neq L_i$ ($1 \leqslant i \leqslant h$) . We want to guess that $L_0 \neq L_i$, using the minimum number of F_j . Let J be the maximum of the values $J(L_1),\ldots,J(L_h)$. We know now that, for every L_i, if we compute $X_{L_i}(F_1),\ldots,X_{L_i}(F_k),\ldots$, there will be some j such that $X_{L_i}(F_j) = 0$, with $j \leqslant J$. So we can eliminate L_i with less than J tries (cf. the remark after the hypothese H2) . If we compute, for every F_i, the vector $(X_K(F_i))_{K \in \mathbb{K}}$, (remember that $\mathbb{K}$ is a relatively small set) , J vectors are enough for the elimination of all the L_i ($1 \leqslant i \leqslant h$) . An easy computation shows that the mean value of J is $O(\text{Log } h)$.

Now, the search of the key S is done step by step .

To find K_n, as we have $\gamma_S(M') \subset \omega_{K_n} (M)$, we pick at random messages $F \in \gamma_S(M')$ and, for every such F, we compute the vector $(X_K(F))_K$. We through each K such that $X_K(F) = 0$ away . This elimination process is complete after $O(\text{Log Card } \mathbb{K}) = O (k)$ vector computations .

Now let $m \neq n$; the main difficulty here is to find random messages $F \in \omega_{K_{n-m}} (M)$. We proceed recursively and we suppose that $K_n,\ldots,K_{n-m+1}$ are known . First of all, we look for messages $E \in M'$ such that the set $A_{K_n,\ldots,K_{n-m+1}} (\gamma_S(E))$ has exactly one element F . The corollary of the proposition 3 says that we must perform a mean value of $O(m^{2+\varepsilon})$ tries to find such a message . We then apply the above mentioned method at about $O(k)$ messages F to find K_{n-m} .

Figure 2.

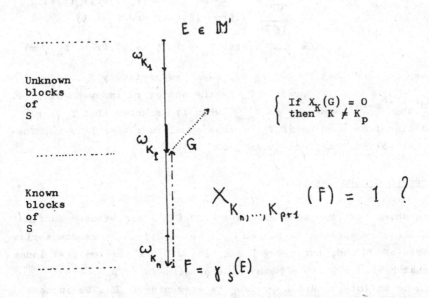

$E \in \mathbb{M}'$

Unknown
blocks
of
S

ω_{K_1}

$\begin{cases} \text{If } X_K(G) = 0 \\ \text{then } K \neq K_p \end{cases}$

ω_{K_ℓ} G

Known
blocks
of
S

$X_{K_n, \ldots, K_{p+1}}(F) = 1$?

ω_{K_n} $F = \gamma_S(E)$

Before giving the result of this paragraph, we have to perform the estimation of the mean number of operations needed to compute $Y_m \circ \gamma_S$ at any $E \in \mathbb{M}$. Let G be the mean number of operations needed to compute ω ; $\gamma_S(E)$ needs about nG operations when computed at any (E, S) in $\mathbb{M} \times \mathbb{K}^n$. Let's remember that the mean number of operations needed for the calculation of Y_1 is T. To obtain $X_{K_n, \ldots, K_{n-m+1}}(F)$, one has to develope a tree whose depth is m. The root, of depth 0, is F; the sons of every node of depth p are its antecedents by $\omega_{K_{n-p}}$. Every node F' of depth p induces the calculation of an $A_K(F)$, which means about T operations. The mean number of these nodes is $\sum_{p=1}^{m-1} E(X_p \circ \gamma) = 0(m^2)$. Therefore $0(m^2 T + nG)$ operations are approximately needed to compute $Y_m \circ \gamma$.

Figure 3.

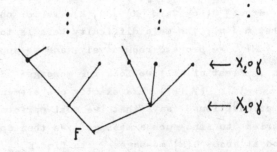

$\leftarrow X_\ell \circ \gamma$

$\leftarrow X_1 \circ \gamma$

F

Now, we apply these results and the corollary of the proposition 3 with $\varepsilon = 0.1$ to conclude this paper with the following proposition :

Proposition 4.   With the above mentionned hypotheses, there exists an algorithm that allows the owner of a smart card using γ , who is allowed to compute enciphered messages of IM' at will, to find the secret key of γ with a mean number of

$$O \left(kTn^{5.1} + Gn^{4.1} + k2^k Tn \right)$$

operations .

SMART CARDS AND CONDITIONAL ACCESS

Louis C GUILLOU

Chef du département "Accès aux Services et Protocoles"

Centre Commun d'Etudes de Télédiffusion et de Télécommunications
BP 59   -F35510 CESSON SEVIGNE
FRANCE

Synopsis : Smart cards are introduced through chip design, card
interface, and card security. Applications are divided in three
classes : log books, certified records, key carriers.
Conditional acces is analyzed with a clear distinction between
entitlement checking and entitlement management. The key carrier CP8
card is then described. Smart card cryptology is examined, and also
the probable evolution towards digital signatures.

I - INTRODUCTION TO SMART CARDS

According to ISO (International Organization for Standardization), an IC (Integrated Circuit) card is an ID (Identification) card including in its thickness (.76 mm) one or more integrated circuits.

An IC card is "smart" when the integrated circuit is a microprocessor, with processing power combined with permanent storage capacity. The operating system in the microprocessor controls and manages all the accesses to the electrically programmable memory.

I.1 - Chip design

The first step in the design of a dedicated chip for smart cards is to choose some central processor unit and some EPROM technology (such as UV-erasable REPROM, and soon, single voltage EEPROM). The CPU must be redrawn in the EPROM technology.

The design of the buses must allow EPROM self-programming under control of the operating system in masked ROM. Various traps and mechanisms must be introduced to increase physical security and to facilitate tests during the manufacturing process.

The CP8 chip, till now the only one in the world, is manufactured by MOTOROLA Inc. in GLASGOW (SCOTLAND) under licence by BULL CP8 established in LES CLAYES SOUS BOIS (FRANCE). This chip is described here as an illustration : a 6805 CPU, 1.6 kbyte masked ROM, 1 kbyte EPROM, 36 bytes RAM, 18 mm^2.

The operating system is masked programmed, so that the same production line provides chip for various applications, and that new applications are easy to develop.

In the future, new chips will appear in order to reduce prices and to increase performances ; but due to interface standardization, remote controlled terminals will not become obsolete.
And moreover, chip evolution can keep the security features one or two steps ahead the efforts of them trying to defeat them.

I.2 - Card interface

Smart cards are intended for transactions negotiated between the outside and the microprocessor through the interface.

Only six electrical contacts are required in the French proposal presented by AFNOR (Association Française de Normalisation) to ISO. While suitable signals are provided by the outside on five contacts : GND (Ground), VCC (power supply), VPP (programming voltage), CLK (clock), and RST (reset), information may be exchanged in half-duplex asynchronous mode on the sixth contact : I/O (input / output). In its answer to reset, the card instructs the outside in its performances, its conventions and its nature.

A transaction with the card consists of the successive operations : activation of the contacts, reset of the card, processing of one or more instructions, deactivation of the contacts. As a result of a transaction, the card modifies its content (data storage, event memorization,...) and/or delivers information (stored data, computation results,...).

An instruction (always initiated by the outside through I/O) tells the card what to do in a 5-byte header (APP-INS-A1-A2-L) and allows the transfer of one block of data (D1-D2... DL) in one direction under control of procedure bytes from the card. The header consists of the application name (APP), the instruction code (INS) completed by a reference (A1-A2), and the length (L) of the block of data. Procedure bytes allow the card to manage the programming voltage and to control the data transfer.

I.3 - Security

Smart cards have security features that only a computing device could provide. The transactions are negotiated between the outside and the internal microprocessor. The passive cards with magnetic stripes and digital optical records do not have such properties, like complex choices.

The physical security relies upon the impossibility to modify the operating system in the masked ROM, and upon the difficulty to read secrets in the protected memory : a clever chip design increases significantly the physical security of the cards.

The logical security relies upon the processing power of the chip and upon the cryptographic algorithms used in the application : the operating system must be written very carefully. An improved processing power may increase significantly the logical security of the cards.

Absolute security does not exist, for smart cards no more than for other computing devices. So in a new application, the designer must consider the consequences of successful violations. The secrets in a user card must be individualized, tied to the card identity ; a card violation results then in an attack against one user not endangering the whole system.

2 - SMART CARD APPLICATIONS

Smart cards are portable information carriers with three fundamental aims :

- Secure memorisation in the card - destruction of the corresponding writing mechanisms prevents further alteration of recorded data.

- Personalized memorisation in the card - confidential codes recorded in the EPROM memory and checked by the card itself allow operator recognition by the card.

- Cryptographic computation in the card - cryptographic algorithms described in the operating system are executed under control of secret keys recorded in the EPROM memory.

Depending on the leading aim, smart card applications can thus be divided into three classes : log books, certified records, key carriers.

2.1 - Log books

First aid efficiency should be considerably improved by reliable and convenient personal medical files. A user code is not recommended in case of emergency.

Student cards are being experimented at PARIS University.

Such cards can be used as repairment and maintenance note books for vehicles : cars, planes, trucks, ships...

2.2 - Certified records

Confidential codes control the life of such cards : manufacturer code, issuer code, user code. When an incorrect code has been entered three times in a row, even on different terminals, the card locks itself preventing any further operation.

The card tests its availability and its purchasing power before recording a new operation (date and amount). The banker will consider a readable card as a begin of proof in a settlement of dispute between a user and a retailer.

2.3 - Key carriers

Assuming chip inviolability and cryptographic algorithm security, the holder cannot get a copy of the keys recorded in his card. A highly secure identification of the bearer is achieved through use of cryptography to defeat fraud, and through use of confidential codes to defeat theft. Key carriers are particularly suitable in conditional access to services, to resources, to selected areas...

3 - CONDITIONAL ACCESS

In conditional access, a key carrier card materializes authorizations : the holder can use the card, but the card itself remains under issuer ownership.

Each authorization is an entitlement. A remote controller, through an insecure transmission line and an insecure domestic terminal, can securely negotiate a transaction with the card :

- VERIFY the validity of an entitlement,

- DEVALORIZE an entitlement either on a substractive basis by consuming a credit, or on an additive basis by storing a debit,

- VALORIZE an entitlement, either by delivering credits, or by clearing debits,

- ENTITLE, by delivering a new entitlement.

The transaction negotiated through the card interface includes an instruction requesting a cryptographic computation by the card. An important distinction is made between transactions to check entitlements (VERIFY, DEVALORIZE), and transactions to manage entitlements (VALORIZE, ENTITLE). This description of conditional access is influenced by the work of EBU (European Broadcasting Union) on Direct Broadcasting Satellite.

3.1 - Entitlement checking

An entitlement checking transaction is used to verify or to devalorize an entitlement. The aim of such a transaction is to deliver control words. The cryptographic computation during such a transaction is executed with an authorization key.

An authorization key is common to a group of customers for a limited time. The usage of such a key may be restricted by additional parameters to be compared with the authorization status in the card.

Authorization keys encipher control words. The corresponding cryptograms are known as the verification signal.

Depending on the application, control words may be sent back to the remote controller for verification, or used in the terminal as cryptographic keys.

3.2 - Entitlement management

An entitlement management transaction is used to valorize or to entitle. The aim of such a transaction is to increase the value of a card. The cryptographic computation during such a transaction is executed with a distribution key.

A distribution key is unique to each card, or a very small group of cards. The distribution keys belong to the card issuer ; they allow the management of distributed authorizations owned by the card holder.

A distribution key enciphers individual customer messages and/or authorization keys. The corresponding cryptograms are known as the validation signal.

3.3 - Implementations

In access control through interactive networks to services or resources (videotex, public telephone, data networks, teletex, files and computers...), the control word can be sent back on the line to prove user's right to access, or used by the terminal to decipher subsequent data.

In conditional access to broadcast services, the control word must be used in the decoder, according to synchronisations, in order to descramble the service components (video and sound, teletext pages, various data...).

The entitlement management can be done over-the-air by addressing through a broadcast signal, as well as on-line through switched networks. The management can also involve other networks like mail or banks.

4 - A CP8 CARD FOR CONDITIONAL ACCESS

Conditional access key carrier cards are now manufactured by BULL CP8 : the specifications were elaborated for application to ANTIOPE teletext ; but these cards are now proposed for pay-TV, for taxation of videotex databases, and for identification purposes in so various fields as public telephone, computers, and selected areas.

The card may carry up to thirty two authorizations consisting of an authorization key (127 bits), an identifier (24 bits), and a status (variable in size and structure).

486

4.1 - Mode of operation

In the instruction requesting a cryptographic computation, the block of data given to the card consists of an identifier (24 bits), a parameter (24 bits) and a cryptogram (127 bits).

The identifier names the authorization concerned by the transaction. The status of this authorization must be compatible with the parameter. For example, when the authorization is a subscription, the date indicated in the parameter must lie in the interval (validity date and period) indicated in the status.

When the conditions are verified, the card performs the computation : a result (61 bits) is obtained from the cryptogram (127 bits), the parameter (24 bits), and the secret key (127 bits).

During an entitlement checking transaction, on an instruction requesting the result, the outside gets the control word as a 8-byte block. The authorization status is modified or not depending on the operation : a devalorization or a verification.

During an entitlement management transaction, the card must apply the distribution key (varying from one card to another). The card checks the result (the four first bytes must be equal to the four last bytes), and modifies the status of the designated authorization.

4.2 - Card elaboration

Chips still on the wafer are tested by a dedicated machine writing a serial number and a manufacturer secret code in each valid chip. Testing points are then destroyed, thus definitely disabling invalid chips. This operation is known as chip creation.

Thereafter chips are cut and inserted in ID cards. The card issuer then writes in each card a distribution key computed from the chip serial number. The issuing secret function may be materialized by another card. This distribution key must be correctly used to write any other secret in the card, and to manage authorizations in the card. Assuming the secrecy of the issuing function, only the card issuer can do these operations : he will really control the card life.

The card is now ready to receive authorizations. A wide variety of card life scenarios can be prepared during the card configuration.

After these three successive operations (chip creation, card issue, card configuration), the cards are distributed to the public.

5 - SMART CARDS AND CRYPTOLOGY

Cryptographic algorithms are essential in conditional access. But widely known algorithms does not fit the CP8 chip :

- a 36 byte RAM is sufficient for the DES, but the microcode size is about 1.6 kbyte which is the size of the masked ROM.

- with a 36 byte RAM, one can compute exponentials modulo a composite number up to ninety bits. So a 128 byte RAM is a minimum to implement a medium security RSA scheme, with 320 bit composite numbers. And a 192 byte RAM is hoped for a good security.

5.1 - Actual algorithms

- A first algorithm (one-way, 200-byte microcode) is known as TELEPASS. A result R (64bits) is computed from secret key S (96 bits), data I_n (32 bits) stored at address n, and input E (64 bits).

$$R = P (S, I_n, E)$$

This first algorithm is used to remotely verify rights and identity claimed by a card, and to remotely verify the writing of some information at the right address in the card.

- A second algorithm (inverting another algorithm; 300-byte microcode) is known as the double-field algorithm. A result K (61 bits) is computed from a cryptogram M (127 bits) and a secret key C (127 bits) modified by a parameter P (24 bits).

$$K = g (C + P , M)$$

Inversibility is essential : in a broadcast system, the same control word is described by as many entitlement checking messages as there are audiences authorized to access the information. For example, the same movie may be accessible by impulse-pay-per-view as well as by subscription, or by a prepaid ticket.

Inversibility is essential also to ensure entitlement management : enciphered personalized directives may be addressed to an identified card.

- A third algorithm (invertible, 200-byte microcode), also named TELEPASS, has been prepared for the new bank card specifications. This algorithm allows the introduction of key carrier philosophy in the bank cards.

The evolution will strengthen these algorithms. But a question is opened : what is the most complex algorithm on a 6805 CPU with the performances : 200-byte microcode, 30-byte RAM, a half second execution time ?

5.2 - Identity certificates

Improved card personalization is obtained by recording identity certificates in the card.

Such a certificate (a 320-bit RSA scheme in IPSO bankcards used on public telephone) is computed by applying a signature function (take the cubic root modulo) to the concatenation of chip serial number (50 bits), subscriber identifier (50 bits), various codes (60 bits), date and period of validity (40 bits), completed by some easily checked redundancy (120 bits).

Any remote or local controller can verify the genuineness of identity certificates by applying the verification function (raise to the cube modulo). Forgery being computationally infeasible, black lists on serial numbers and user identifiers are then very efficient.

5.3 - Some reflexions

The actual key carriers allow only pseudo off-line systems, well fitting hierarchical situations with a central authority, such as a computer and time-sharing terminals.

In IPSO payment experiments, the main proof remains inside the card. Computation results may be stored by the retailer in order to certify records in the card, but only the authority can check the genuineness of such results. There is an important parallel with arbitrated signature schemes.

6 - TOWARDS DIGITAL SIGNATURES

Secret functions of a public key cryptosystem can play two parts in an electronic mail environment :

- regenerate the control word deciphering the subsequent message.
- sign an authentication code added to the message.

But in both cases, the security of the secret function is essential ; if this function is materialized by a key carrier card with a good level of physical security, the legitimate holder himself has the greatest difficulty to get a copy.

Depending on the main part played by the secret function, such a key carrier can be seen :

- as a paper-knife, opening the protection envelope,
- or as a signature stamper, certifying the letter.

Such smart cards are now under investigation ; and this evolution will lead to off-line systems and digital signatures.

6.1 - Scenario for electronic payment

- 1 - The user controls the parameter generation on some domestic device producing random primes under additional conditions so as to construct a composite number. In the example, the composite number has the special form $N = 2^{4X} + K$, with $2K \quad 2^{3X} \quad K$. So the 240-bit K describes the 321-bit N.

The prime factors are recorded as secret parameters in a stamper : a key carrier card dedicated to signatures (take the cubic root modulo N). And the value K is recorded as a public parameter describing the verification (raise to the cube modulo N).

- 2 - The banker tests the stamper produced by the user. He computes a stamper registration by applying his own signature (take the cubic root modulo a 512-bit number) to the concatenation of the public value K (240 bits) given by the stamper, the user identifier (50 bits), the bankcard serial number (50 bits), date and period of validity (40 bits), various codes (60 bits), and an easily checked redundancy (72 bits).

The banker issues the bank-card by recording in it the stamper registration.

- 3 - The retailer checks the stamper registration by applying the bank verification (raise to the cube modulo the 512-bit number published by the bank), thus regenerating the user's public value K. The retailer consults the black lists on card serial numbers and on user identifiers. The user stamps the financial operation (date and amount), thus producing a signature easy to check by raising to the cube modulo $2^{320} + K$.

The electronic check thus consists of two informations : the stamper registration (issued by the banker), and the operation signature (issued by the user). Such a check can be efficiently checked at each step in the clearing circuit between banks.

7 - CONCLUSION

The current needs concerning new services, dedicated to business as well as opened to the general public, are secrecy, discretion, identification, authentification, certification, signature, attestation, confirmation, acknowledgement of receipt... GARANTIR is the French word that best describes all these concepts. It requires only a step further to create a new word : "garantics" to say "implementation of security in new services".

Cryptographic algorithms, security protocols, smart cards are the basic tools of garantics.

Let us keep in mind : the more our countries are computerized, the more bank frauds, economic sabotages, and industrial spying are prejudicial !

AUTHOR INDEX